KILL ME ♥ Kiss Me

Volume 2
by Lee Young You

HAMBURG // LONDON // LOS ANGELES // TOKYO

ALSO AVAILABLE FROM TOKYOPOP®

MANGA

.HACK//LEGEND OF THE TWILIGHT
@LARGE
ABENOBASHI: MAGICAL SHOPPING ARCADE
A.I. LOVE YOU
AI YORI AOSHI
ANGELIC LAYER
ARM OF KANNON
BABY BIRTH
BATTLE ROYALE
BATTLE VIXENS
BRAIN POWERED
BRIGADOON
B'TX
CANDIDATE FOR GODDESS, THE
CARDCAPTOR SAKURA
CARDCAPTOR SAKURA - MASTER OF THE CLOW
CHOBITS
CHRONICLES OF THE CURSED SWORD
CLAMP SCHOOL DETECTIVES
CLOVER
COMIC PARTY
CONFIDENTIAL CONFESSIONS
CORRECTOR YUI
COWBOY BEBOP
COWBOY BEBOP: SHOOTING STAR
CRAZY LOVE STORY
CRESCENT MOON
CULDCEPT
CYBORG 009
D•N•ANGEL
DEMON DIARY
DEMON ORORON, THE
DEUS VITAE
DIGIMON
DIGIMON TAMERS
DIGIMON ZERO TWO
DOLL
DRAGON HUNTER
DRAGON KNIGHTS
DRAGON VOICE
DREAM SAGA
DUKLYON: CLAMP SCHOOL DEFENDERS
EERIE QUEERIE!
END, THE
ERICA SAKURAZAWA: COLLECTED WORKS
ET CETERA
ETERNITY
EVIL'S RETURN
FAERIES' LANDING
FAKE
FLCL
FORBIDDEN DANCE
FRUITS BASKET
G GUNDAM
GATEKEEPERS

GETBACKERS
GIRL GOT GAME
GRAVITATION
GTO
GUNDAM BLUE DESTINY
GUNDAM SEED ASTRAY
GUNDAM WING
GUNDAM WING: BATTLEFIELD OF PACIFISTS
GUNDAM WING: ENDLESS WALTZ
GUNDAM WING: THE LAST OUTPOST (G-UNIT)
GUYS' GUIDE TO GIRLS
HANDS OFF!
HAPPY MANIA
HARLEM BEAT
I.N.V.U.
IMMORTAL RAIN
INITIAL D
INSTANT TEEN: JUST ADD NUTS
ISLAND
JING: KING OF BANDITS
JING: KING OF BANDITS - TWILIGHT TALES
JULINE
KARE KANO
KILL ME, KISS ME
KINDAICHI CASE FILES, THE
KING OF HELL
KODOCHA: SANA'S STAGE
LAMENT OF THE LAMB
LEGAL DRUG
LEGEND OF CHUN HYANG, THE
LES BIJOUX
LOVE HINA
LUPIN III
LUPIN III: WORLD'S MOST WANTED
MAGIC KNIGHT RAYEARTH I
MAGIC KNIGHT RAYEARTH II
MAHOROMATIC: AUTOMATIC MAIDEN
MAN OF MANY FACES
MARMALADE BOY
MARS
MARS: HORSE WITH NO NAME
METROID
MINK
MIRACLE GIRLS
MIYUKI-CHAN IN WONDERLAND
MODEL
ONE
ONE I LOVE, THE
PARADISE KISS
PARASYTE
PASSION FRUIT
PEACH GIRL
PEACH GIRL: CHANGE OF HEART
PET SHOP OF HORRORS
PITA-TEN
PLANET LADDER

03.03.04T

ALSO AVAILABLE FROM 🐾 TOKYOPOP®

PLANETES
PRIEST
PRINCESS AI
PSYCHIC ACADEMY
RAGNAROK
RAVE MASTER
REALITY CHECK
REBIRTH
REBOUND
REMOTE
RISING STARS OF MANGA
SABER MARIONETTE J
SAILOR MOON
SAINT TAIL
SAIYUKI
SAMURAI DEEPER KYO
SAMURAI GIRL REAL BOUT HIGH SCHOOL
SCRYED
SEIKAI TRILOGY, THE
SGT. FROG
SHAOLIN SISTERS
SHIRAHIME-SYO: SNOW GODDESS TALES
SHUTTERBOX
SKULL MAN, THE
SMUGGLER
SNOW DROP
SORCERER HUNTERS
STONE
SUIKODEN III
SUKI
THREADS OF TIME
TOKYO BABYLON
TOKYO MEW MEW
TOKYO TRIBES
TRAMPS LIKE US
UNDER THE GLASS MOON
VAMPIRE GAME
VISION OF ESCAFLOWNE, THE
WARRIORS OF TAO
WILD ACT
WISH
WORLD OF HARTZ
X-DAY
ZODIAC P.I.

MANGA NOVELS

CLAMP SCHOOL PARANORMAL INVESTIGATORS
KARMA CLUB
SAILOR MOON
SLAYERS

ART BOOKS

ART OF CARDCAPTOR SAKURA
ART OF MAGIC KNIGHT RAYEARTH, THE
PEACH: MIWA UEDA ILLUSTRATIONS

ANIME GUIDES

COWBOY BEBOP
GUNDAM TECHNICAL MANUALS
SAILOR MOON SCOUT GUIDES

TOKYOPOP KIDS

STRAY SHEEP

CINE-MANGA™

ALADDIN
ASTRO BOY
CARDCAPTORS
CONFESSIONS OF A TEENAGE DRAMA QUEEN
DUEL MASTERS
FAIRLY ODDPARENTS, THE
FAMILY GUY
FINDING NEMO
G.I. JOE SPY TROOPS
JACKIE CHAN ADVENTURES
JIMMY NEUTRON: BOY GENIUS, THE ADVENTURES OF
KIM POSSIBLE
LILO & STITCH
LIZZIE MCGUIRE
LIZZIE MCGUIRE MOVIE, THE
MALCOLM IN THE MIDDLE
POWER RANGERS: NINJA STORM
SHREK 2
SPONGEBOB SQUAREPANTS
SPY KIDS 2
SPY KIDS 3-D: GAME OVER
TEENAGE MUTANT NINJA TURTLES
THAT'S SO RAVEN
TRANSFORMERS: ARMADA
TRANSFORMERS: ENERGON

**For more
information visit
www.TOKYOPOP.com**

03.03.04T

Translator - Jihae Hong
English Adaptation - Paul Morrissey
Copy Editor - Alexis Kirsch
Retouch and Lettering - William Suh
Cover Layout - Anna Kernbaum
Graphic Designer - Yoohae Yang

Editor - Bryce P. Coleman
Digital Imaging Manager - Chris Buford
Pre-Press Manager - Antonio DePietro
Production Managers - Jennifer Miller, Mutsumi Miyazaki
Art Director - Matt Alford
Managing Editor - Jill Freshney
VP of Production - Ron Klamert
President & C.O.O. - John Parker
Publisher & C.E.O. - Stuart Levy

Email: info@TOKYOPOP.com
Come visit us online at www.TOKYOPOP.com

A  Manga

TOKYOPOP Inc.
5900 Wilshire Blvd. Suite 2000
Los Angeles, CA 90036

Kill Me Kiss Me Vol. 2

ISBN: 1-59182-594-6

First TOKYOPOP printing: May 2004

10 9 8 7 6 5 4 3 2

Printed in the USA

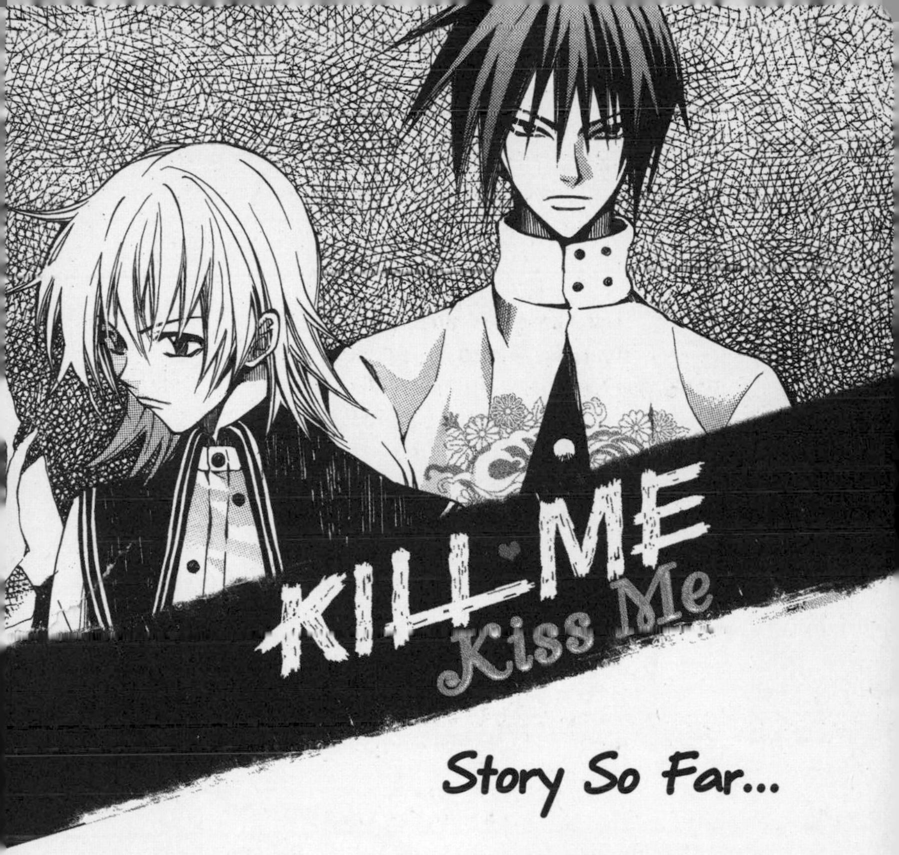
KILL ME
Kiss Me

Story So Far...

When Tae Yeon Im finds out that the male-supermodel she's adored for ages is currently attending the same school as her identical cousin, Jung-Woo Im, she convinces her kin to exploit their similitude and pull a little cross-dressing switcheroo. She will dress like Jung-Woo, attend his school and get close to her lover boy, the hunky Kun Kang—while Jung-Woo slips into Tae's skirt and wallows in the sea of babes at her school. But the already shaky plan quickly begins to fall apart when their innocent subterfuge leads to sexual confusion, scandalous behavior and some serious butt-kicking.

Kun Kang

A male model who has reached idol status. His celebrity and busy schedule result in his missing a lot of school. But does he really have a mind to develop in the first place?

Tae Yeon Im

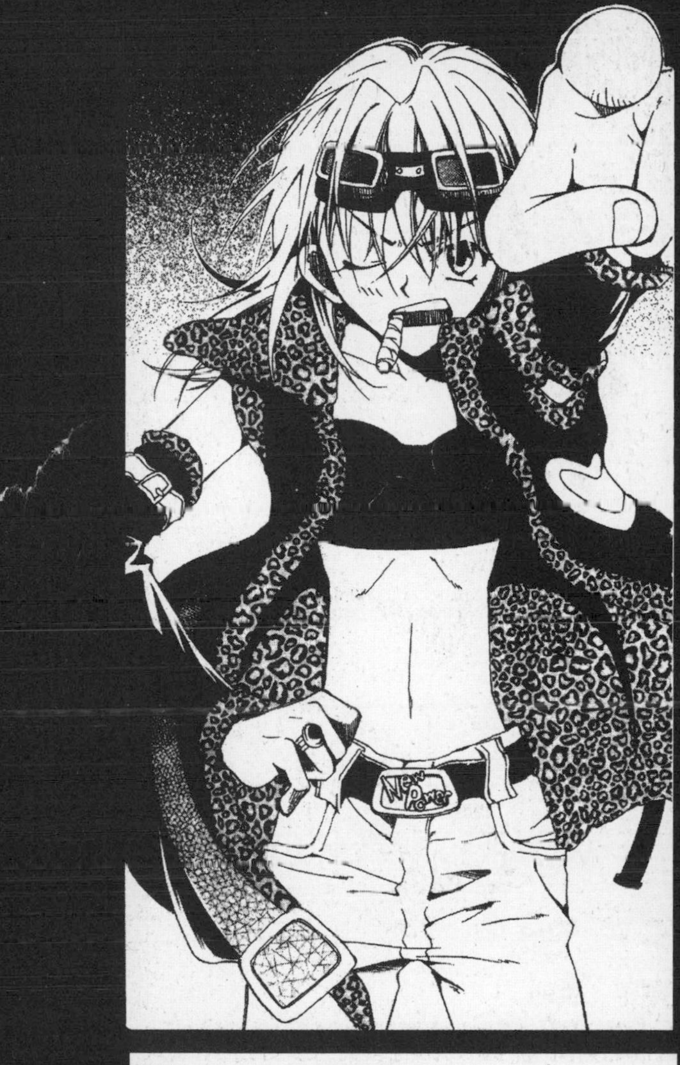
New Power

A high school student in love with a famous teen idol named Kun. Once she finds out that Kun goes to her identical cousin's school, she arranges to switch places with him, forcing her cousin Jung-Woo to attend her all-girls school in drag.

Ga-Woon Kim

A school bully with a penchant for targeting Jung-Woo. However, lately he's been having some inexplicable attraction for his prey.

Jung-Woo Im

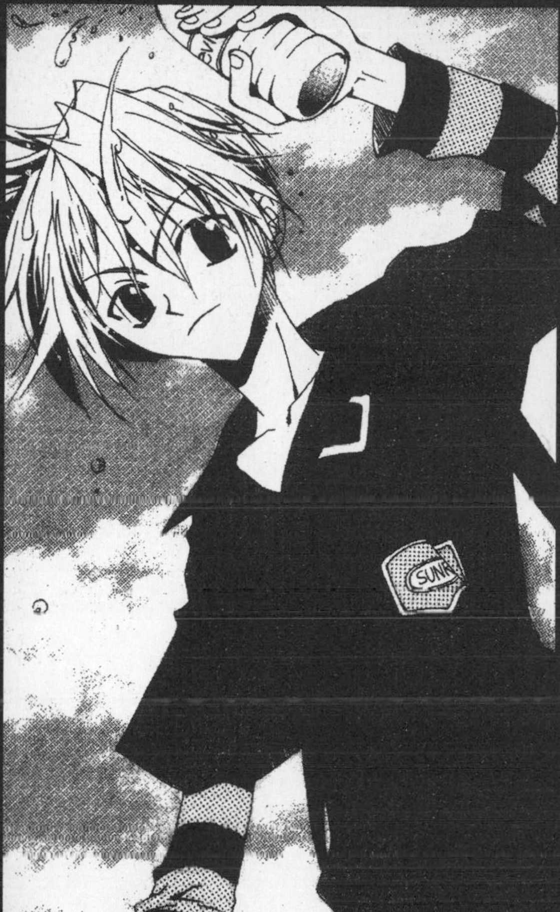

SUNF

Switches places with his female cousin. He dresses in drag and attends an all-girls school...something that doesn't seem to really upset him that much. Either he likes to be around girls, or he's very comfortable wearing a skirt!

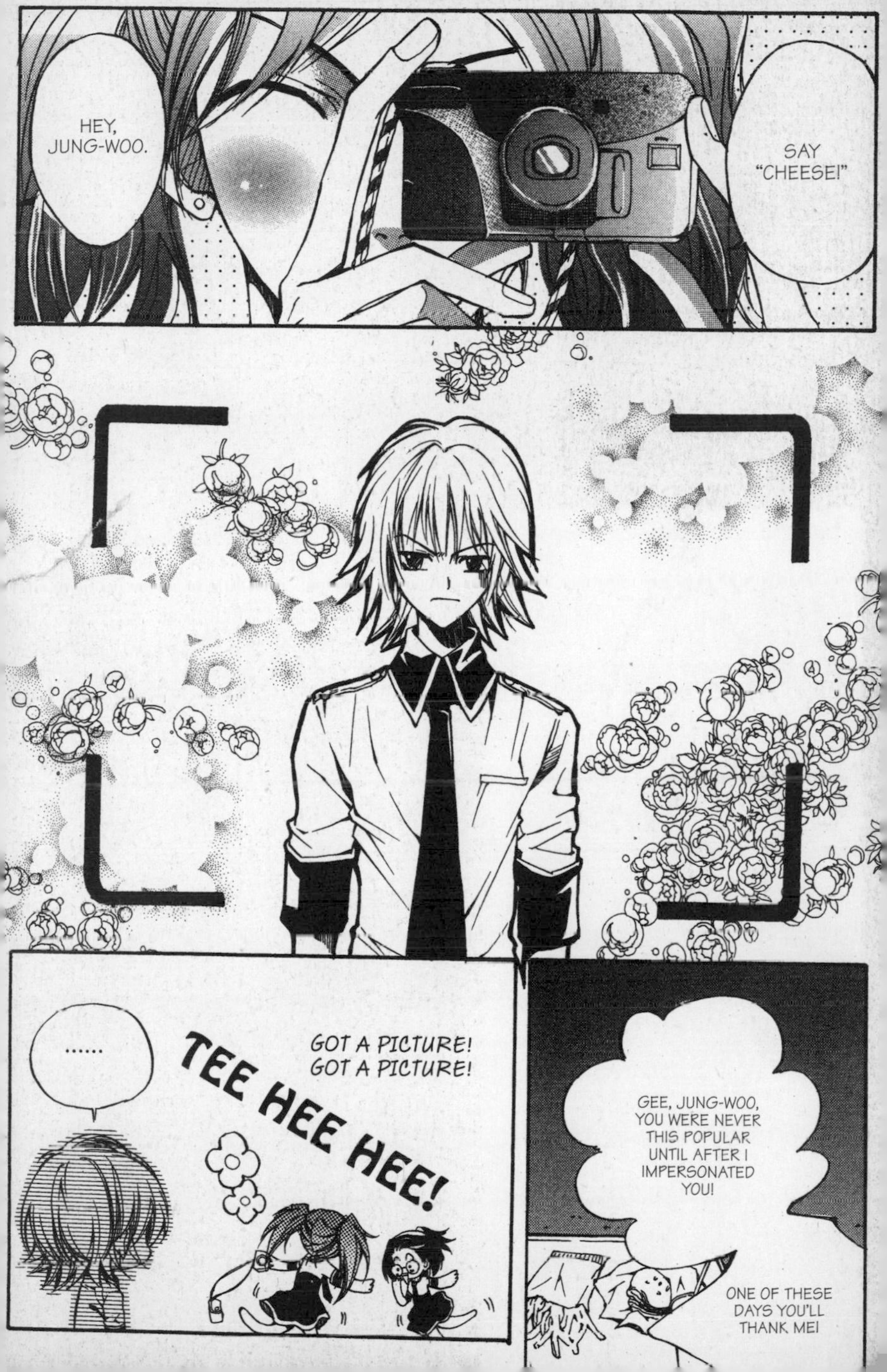
HEY, JUNG-WOO.
SAY "CHEESE!"
......
TEE HEE HEE!
GOT A PICTURE! GOT A PICTURE!
GEE, JUNG-WOO, YOU WERE NEVER THIS POPULAR UNTIL AFTER I IMPERSONATED YOU!
ONE OF THESE DAYS YOU'LL THANK ME!

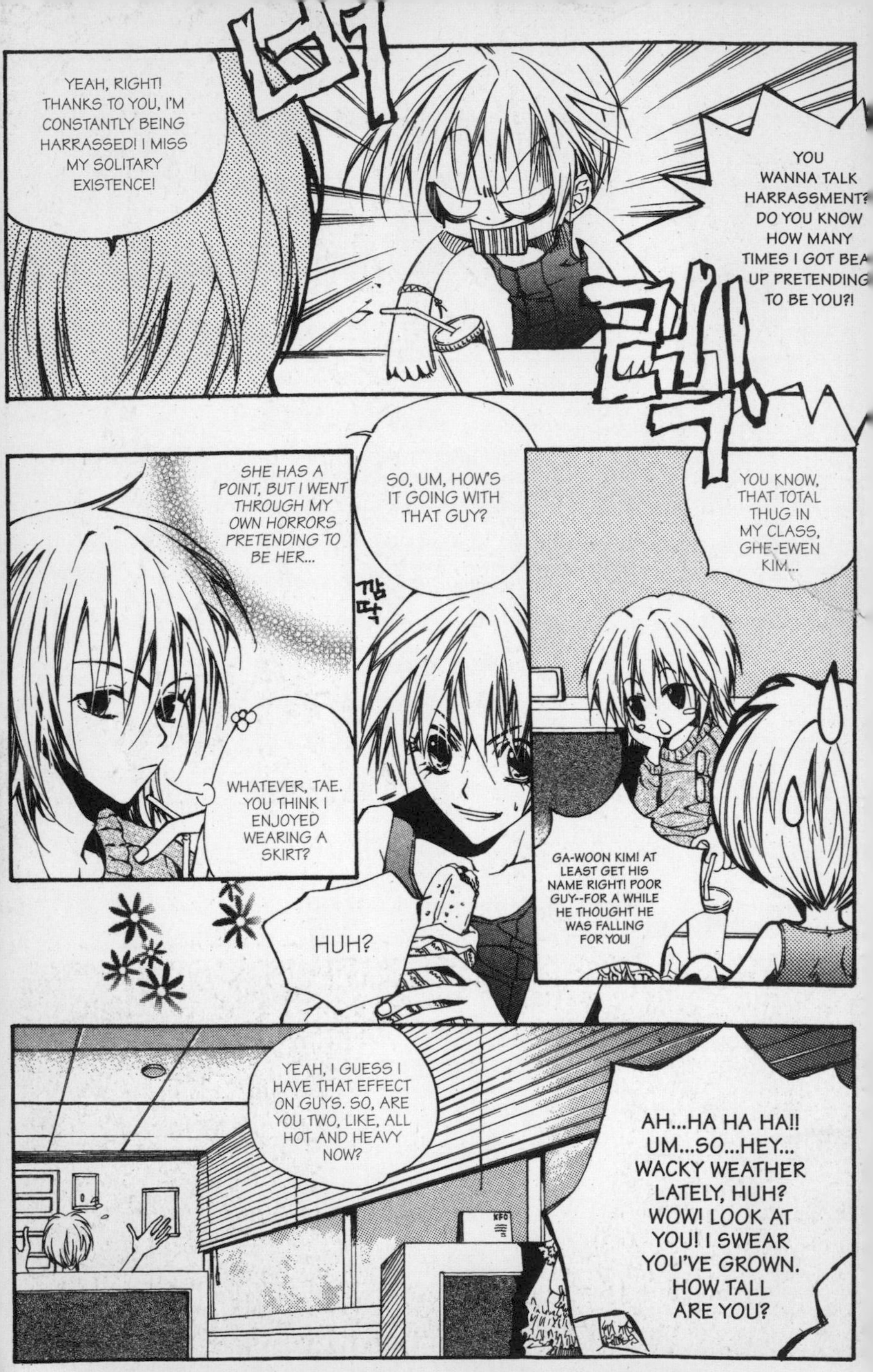
YEAH, RIGHT! THANKS TO YOU, I'M CONSTANTLY BEING HARRASSED! I MISS MY SOLITARY EXISTENCE!
YOU WANNA TALK HARRASSMENT? DO YOU KNOW HOW MANY TIMES I GOT BEA UP PRETENDING TO BE YOU?!
SHE HAS A POINT, BUT I WENT THROUGH MY OWN HORRORS PRETENDING TO BE HER...
WHATEVER, TAE. YOU THINK I ENJOYED WEARING A SKIRT?
SO, UM, HOW'S IT GOING WITH THAT GUY?
HUH?
YOU KNOW, THAT TOTAL THUG IN MY CLASS, GHE-EWEN KIM...
GA-WOON KIM! AT LEAST GET HIS NAME RIGHT! POOR GUY--FOR A WHILE HE THOUGHT HE WAS FALLING FOR YOU!
YEAH, I GUESS I HAVE THAT EFFECT ON GUYS. SO, ARE YOU TWO, LIKE, ALL HOT AND HEAVY NOW?
AH...HA HA HA!! UM...SO...HEY... WACKY WEATHER LATELY, HUH? WOW! LOOK AT YOU! I SWEAR YOU'VE GROWN. HOW TALL ARE YOU?

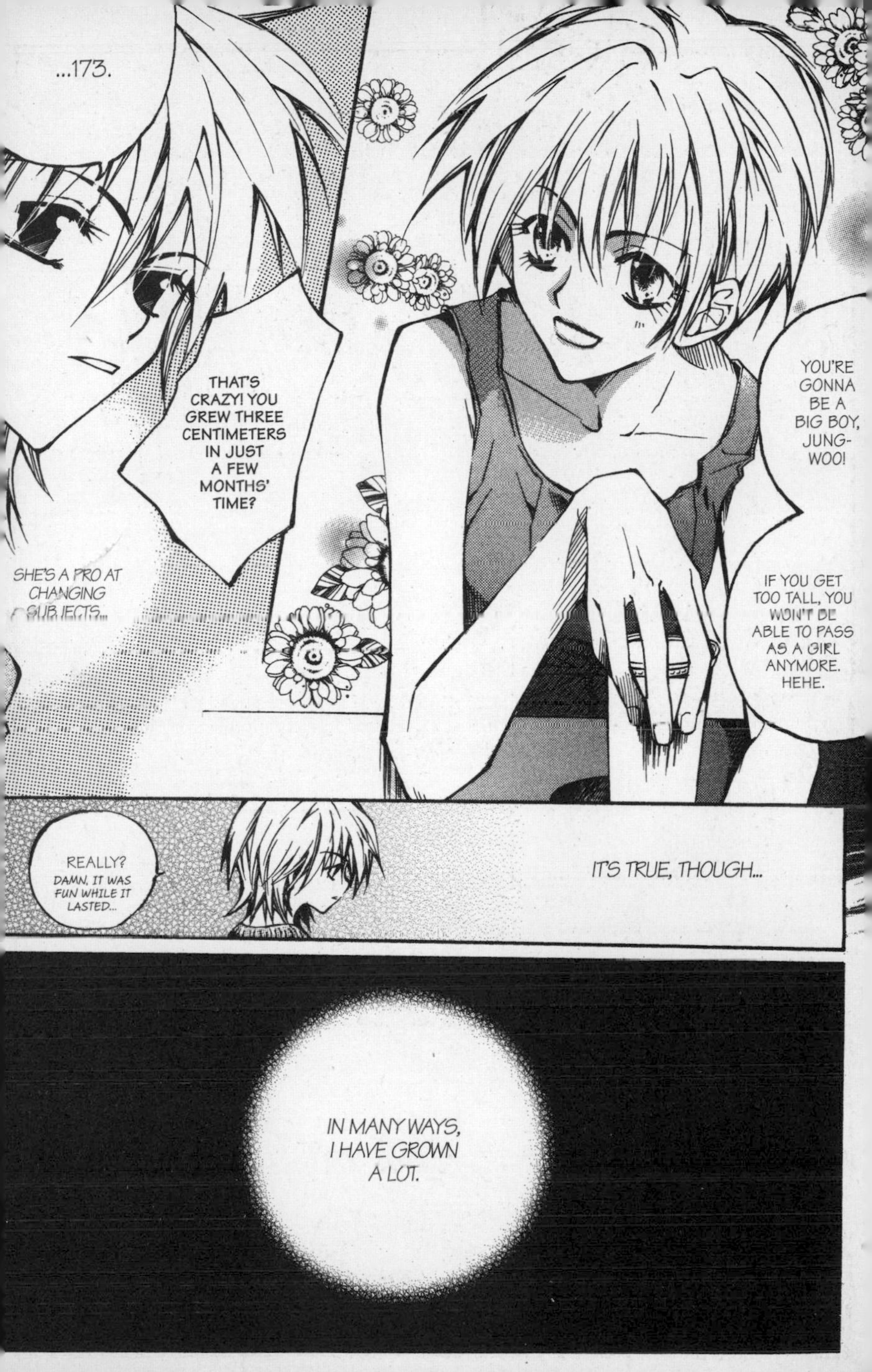
...173.
THAT'S CRAZY! YOU GREW THREE CENTIMETERS IN JUST A FEW MONTHS' TIME?
SHE'S A PRO AT CHANGING SUBJECTS...
YOU'RE GONNA BE A BIG BOY, JUNG-WOO!
IF YOU GET TOO TALL, YOU WON'T BE ABLE TO PASS AS A GIRL ANYMORE. HEHE.
REALLY?
DAMN, IT WAS FUN WHILE IT LASTED...
IT'S TRUE, THOUGH...
IN MANY WAYS, I HAVE GROWN A LOT.

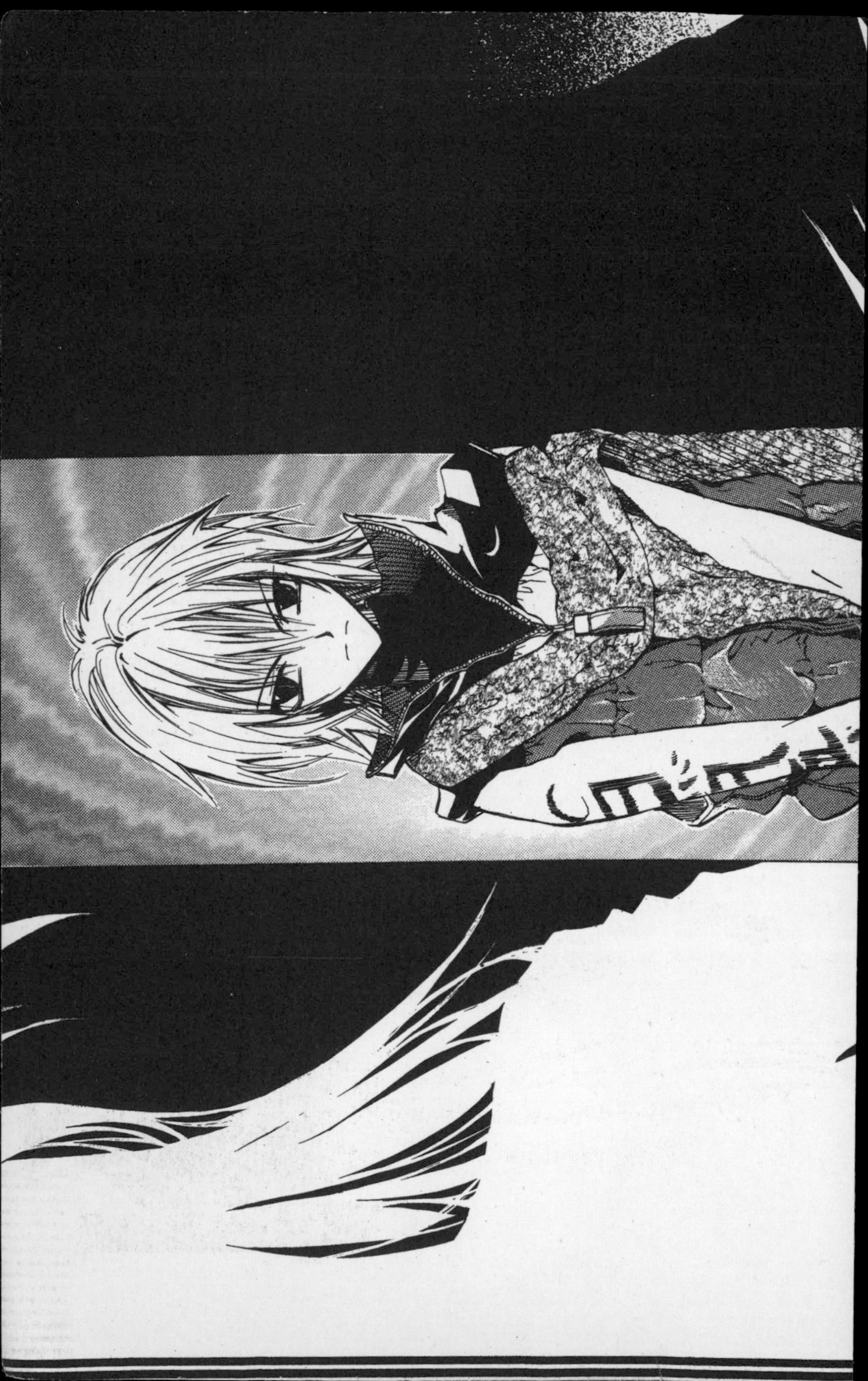

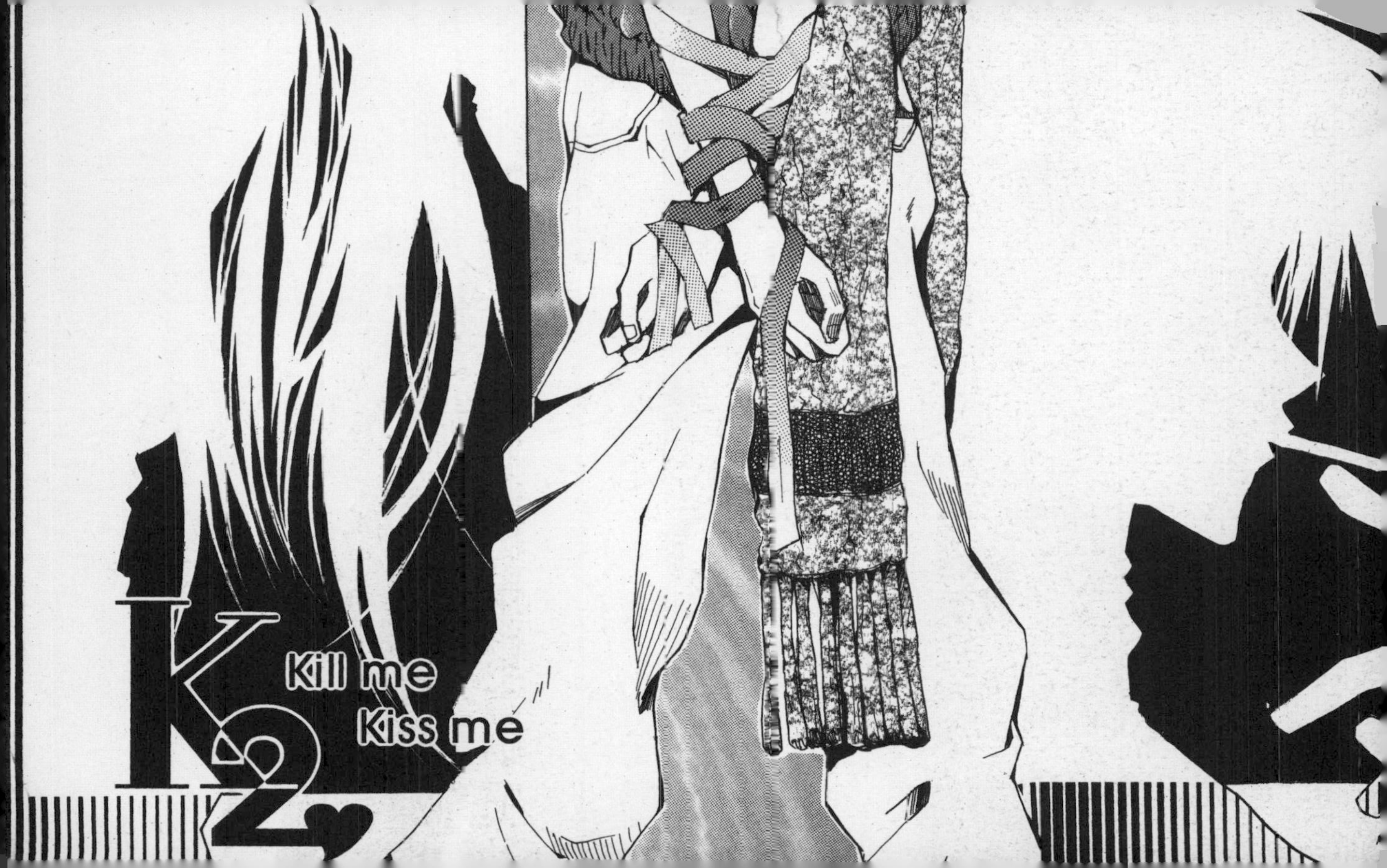
K2
Kill me
Kiss me

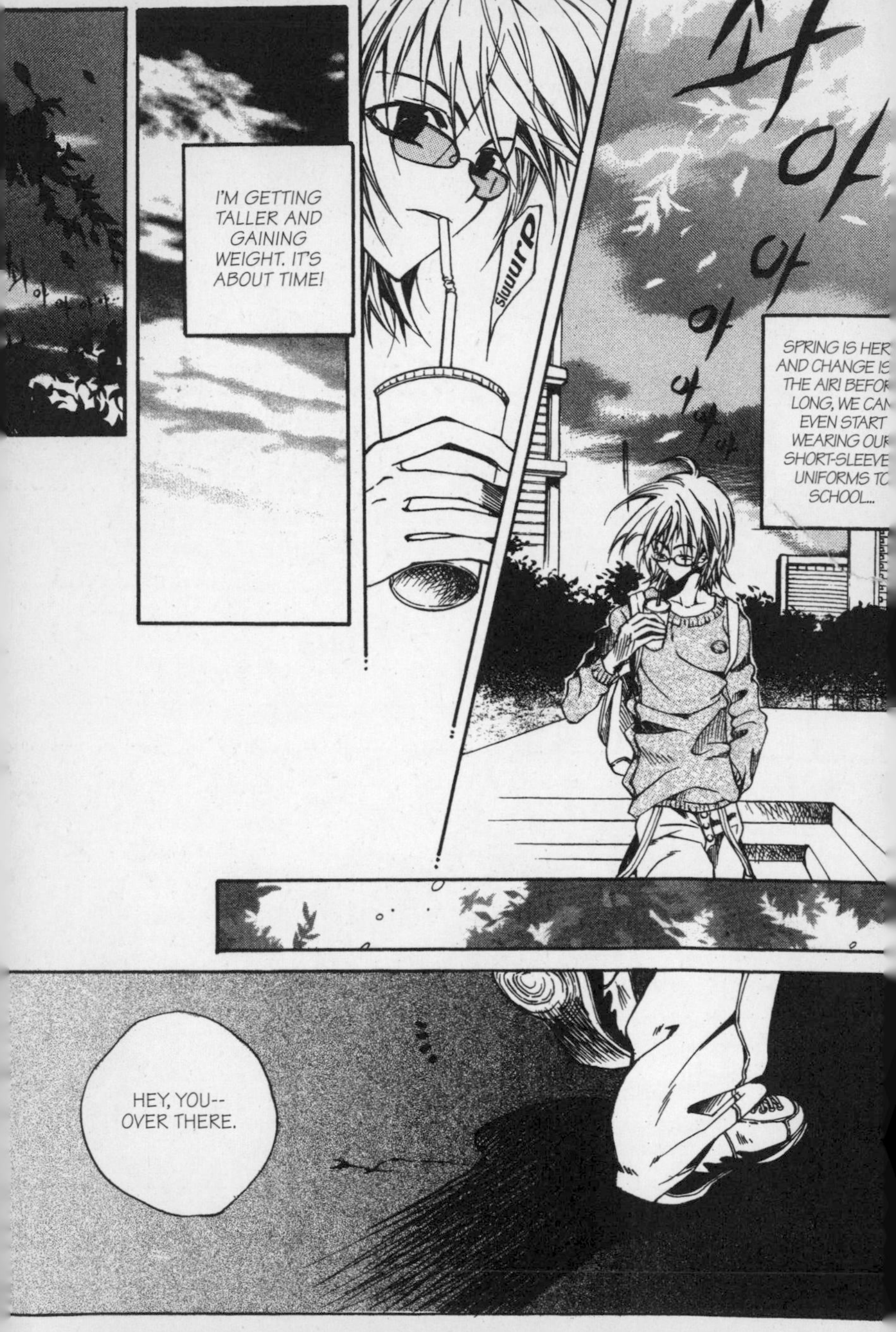
I'M GETTING TALLER AND GAINING WEIGHT. IT'S ABOUT TIME!
sluuurp
SPRING IS HER AND CHANGE IS THE AIR! BEFOR LONG, WE CAN EVEN START WEARING OUR SHORT-SLEEVE UNIFORMS TO SCHOOL...
HEY, YOU-- OVER THERE.

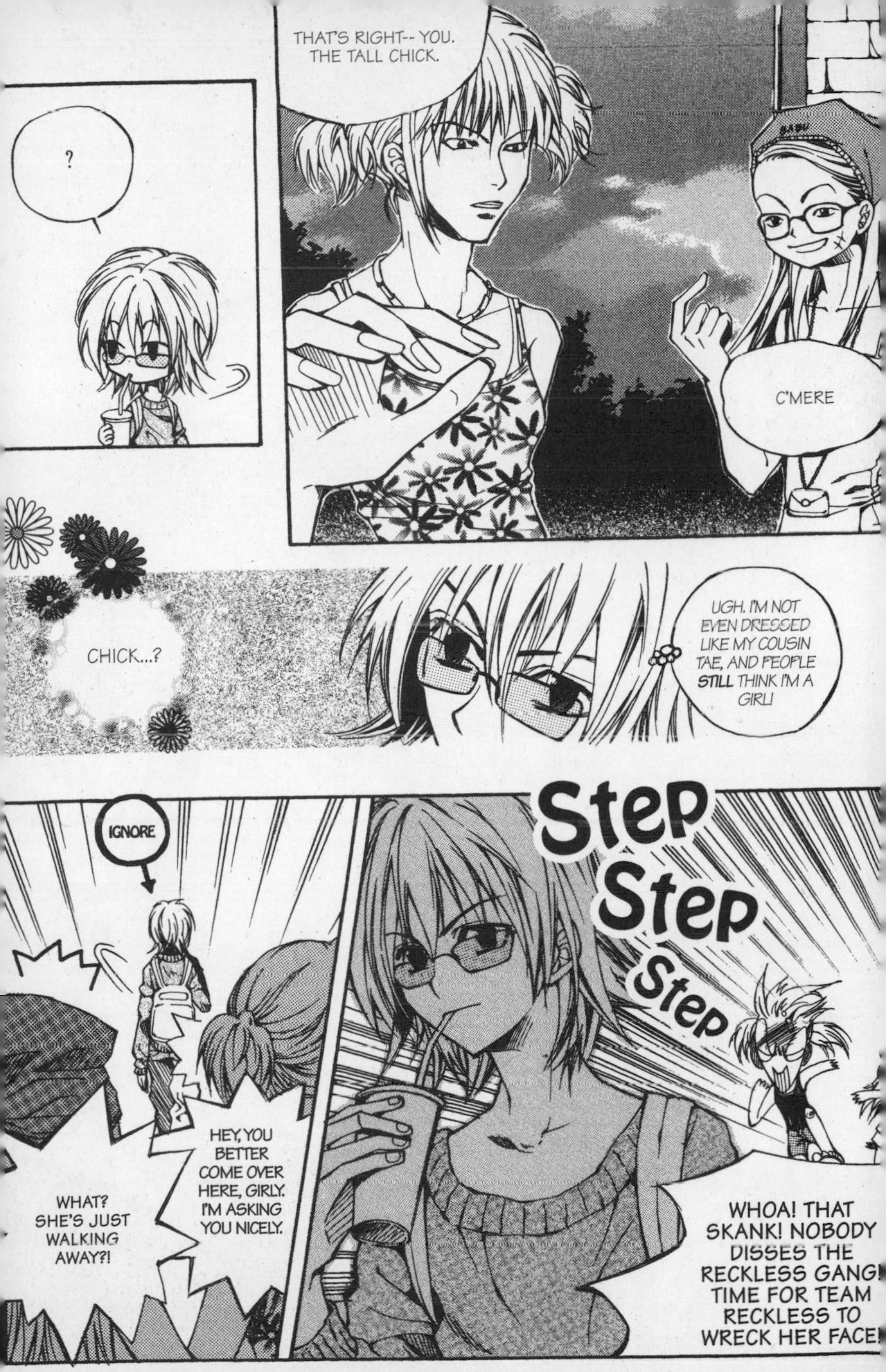
?
THAT'S RIGHT-- YOU. THE TALL CHICK.
C'MERE
CHICK...?
UGH. I'M NOT EVEN DRESSED LIKE MY COUSIN TAE, AND PEOPLE STILL THINK I'M A GIRL!
IGNORE
WHAT? SHE'S JUST WALKING AWAY?!
HEY, YOU BETTER COME OVER HERE, GIRLY. I'M ASKING YOU NICELY.
Step Step Step Step
WHOA! THAT SKANK! NOBODY DISSES THE RECKLESS GANG! TIME FOR TEAM RECKLESS TO WRECK HER FACE!

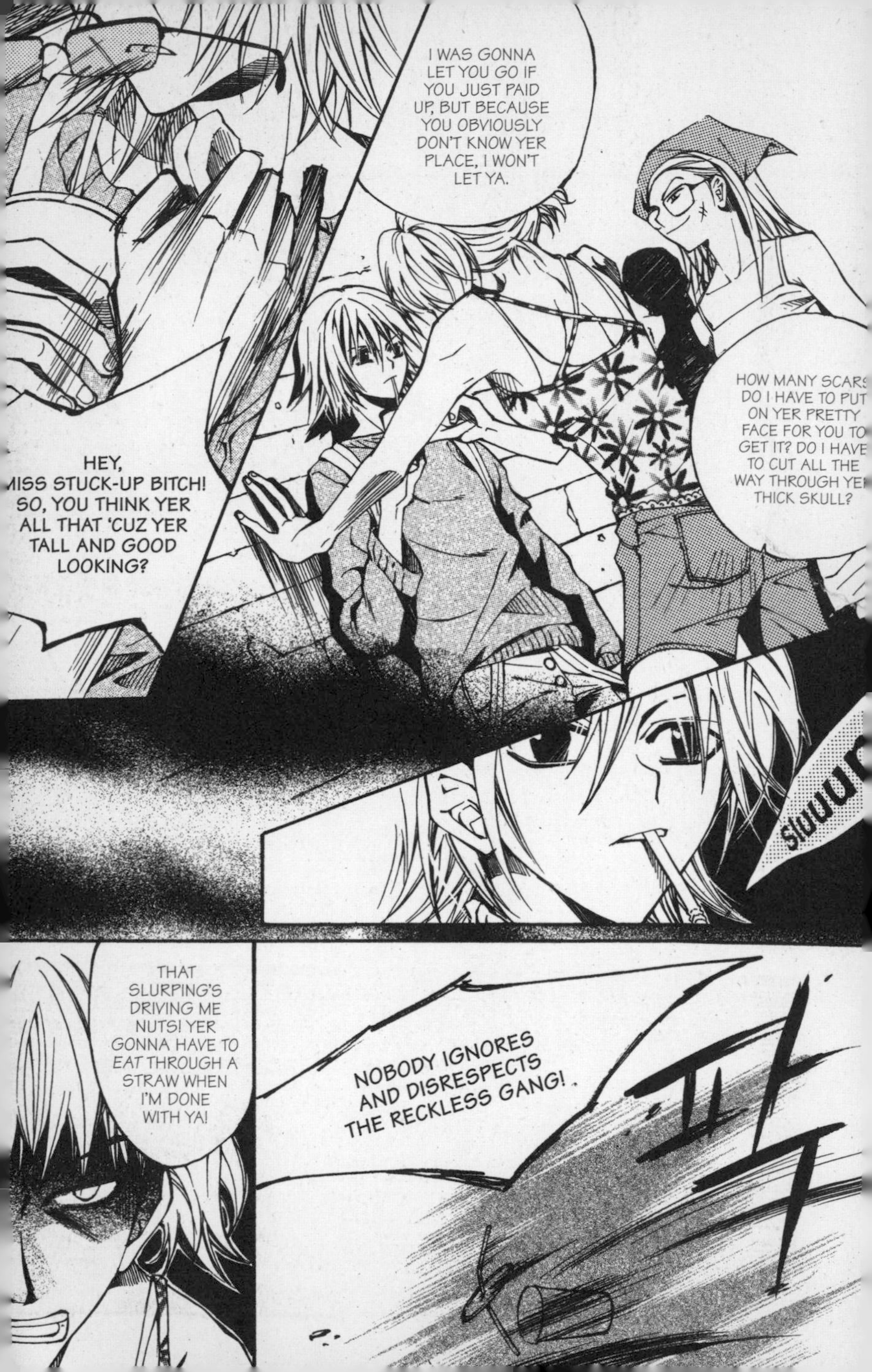
I WAS GONNA LET YOU GO IF YOU JUST PAID UP, BUT BECAUSE YOU OBVIOUSLY DON'T KNOW YER PLACE, I WON'T LET YA.
HEY, MISS STUCK-UP BITCH! SO, YOU THINK YER ALL THAT 'CUZ YER TALL AND GOOD LOOKING?
HOW MANY SCARS DO I HAVE TO PUT ON YER PRETTY FACE FOR YOU TO GET IT? DO I HAVE TO CUT ALL THE WAY THROUGH YER THICK SKULL?
THAT SLURPING'S DRIVING ME NUTS! YER GONNA HAVE TO EAT THROUGH A STRAW WHEN I'M DONE WITH YA!
NOBODY IGNORES AND DISRESPECTS THE RECKLESS GANG!

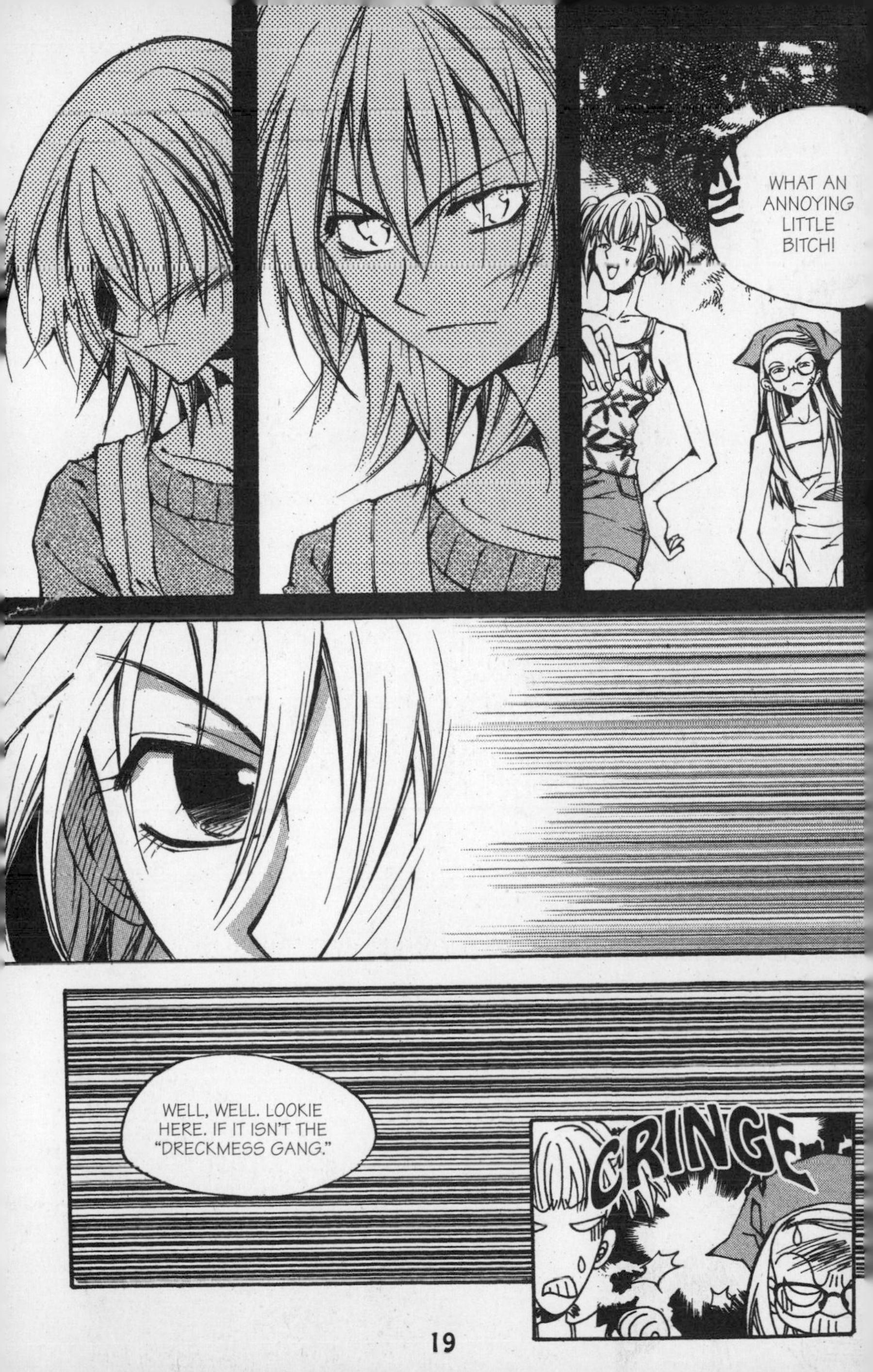
WHAT AN ANNOYING LITTLE BITCH!
WELL, WELL. LOOKIE HERE. IF IT ISN'T THE "DRECKMESS GANG."
CRINGE

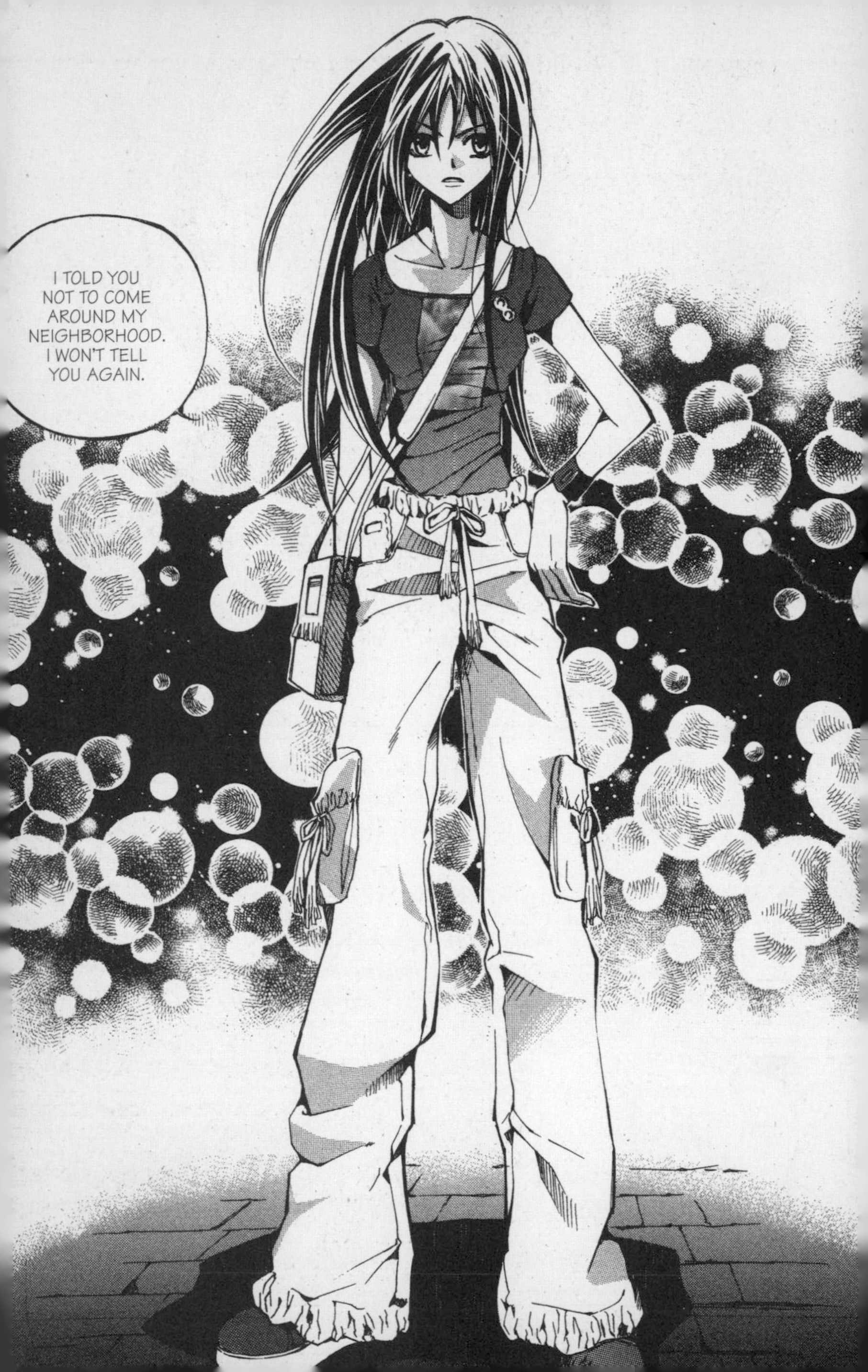
I TOLD YOU NOT TO COME AROUND MY NEIGHBORHOOD. I WON'T TELL YOU AGAIN.

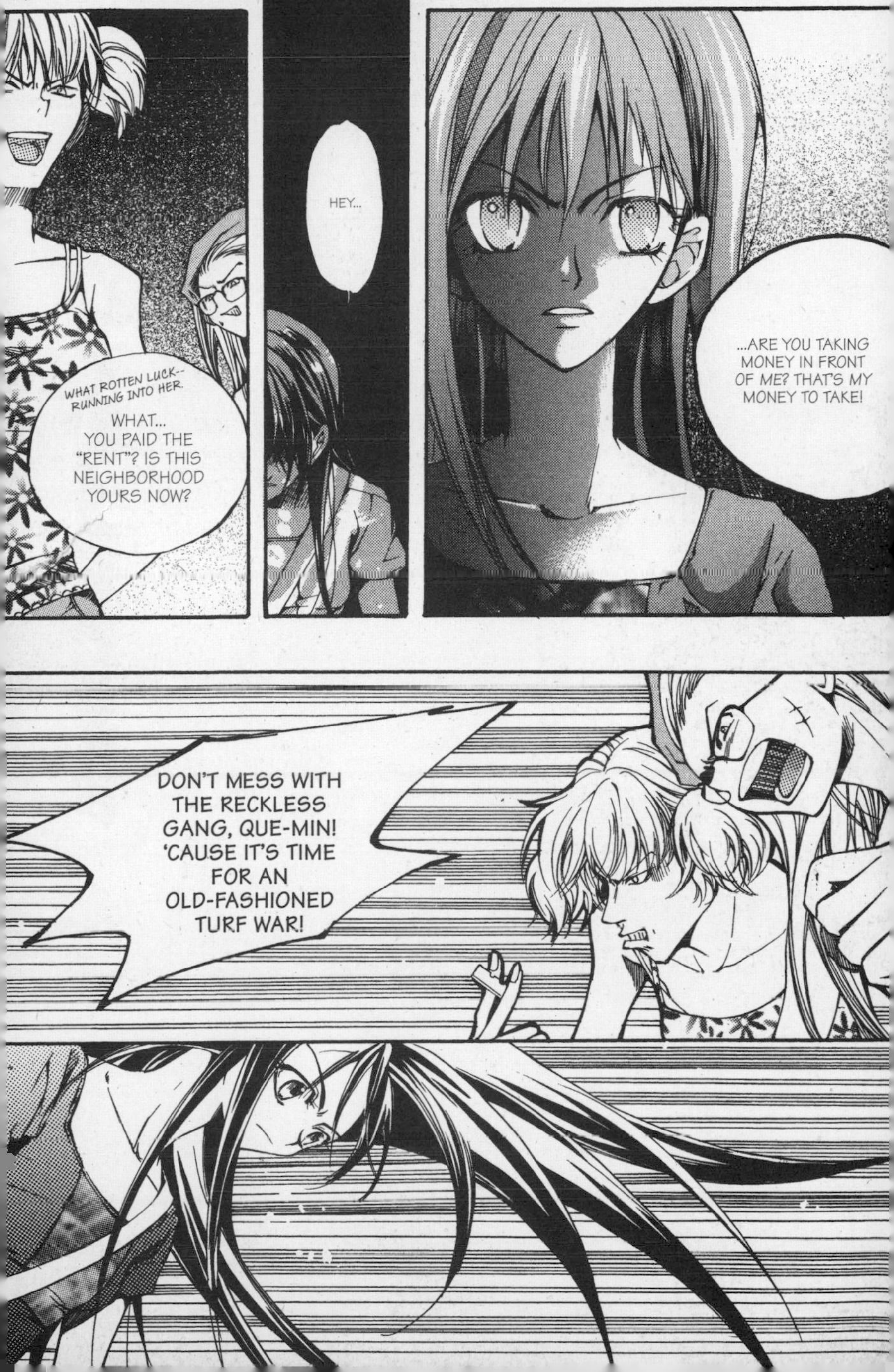
WHAT ROTTEN LUCK--RUNNING INTO HER.
WHAT... YOU PAID THE "RENT"? IS THIS NEIGHBORHOOD YOURS NOW?
HEY...
...ARE YOU TAKING MONEY IN FRONT OF ME? THAT'S MY MONEY TO TAKE!
DON'T MESS WITH THE RECKLESS GANG, QUE-MIN! 'CAUSE IT'S TIME FOR AN OLD-FASHIONED TURF WAR!

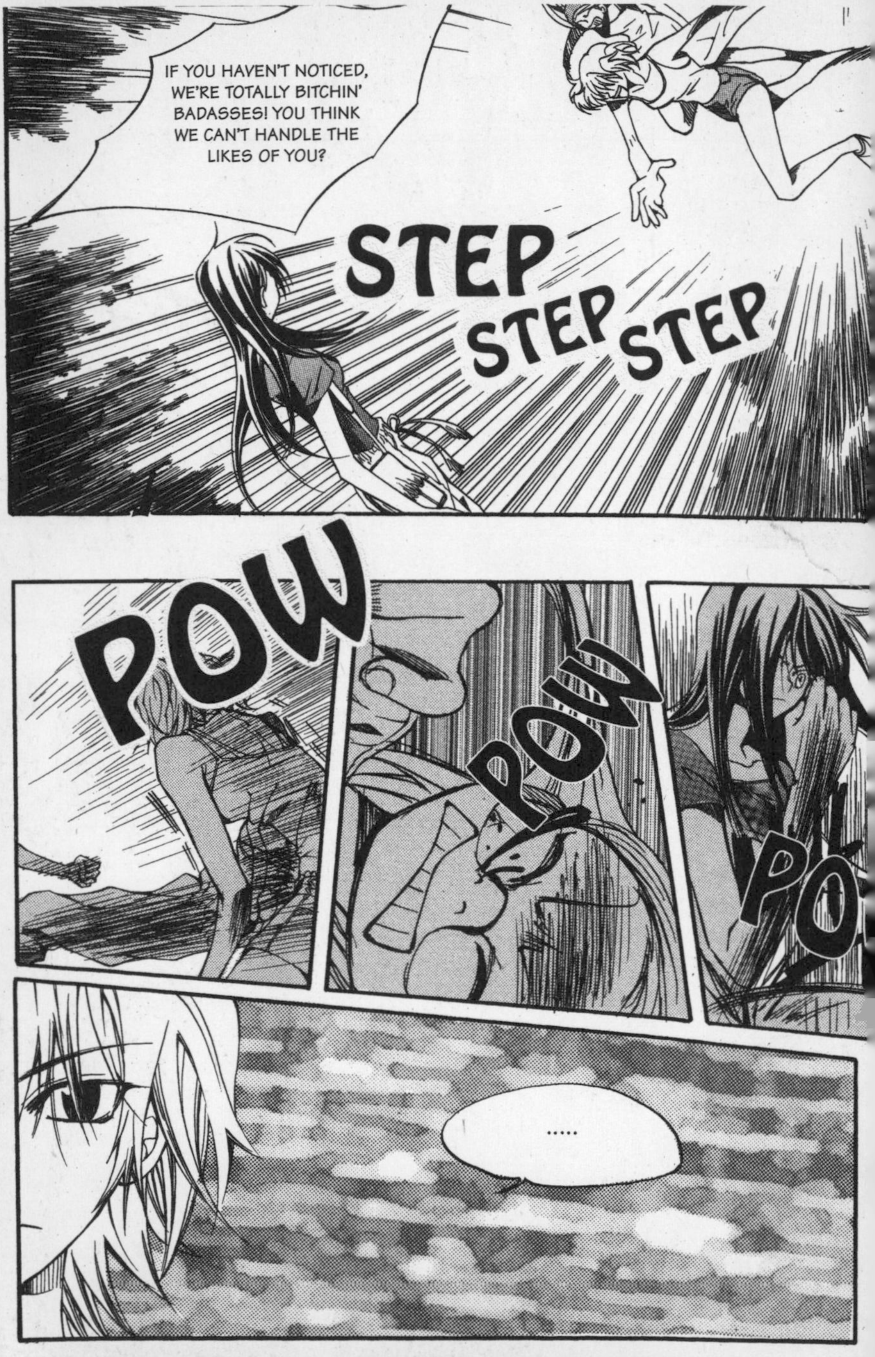
IF YOU HAVEN'T NOTICED, WE'RE TOTALLY BITCHIN' BADASSES! YOU THINK WE CAN'T HANDLE THE LIKES OF YOU?
STEP
STEP
STEP
POW
POW
PO
.....

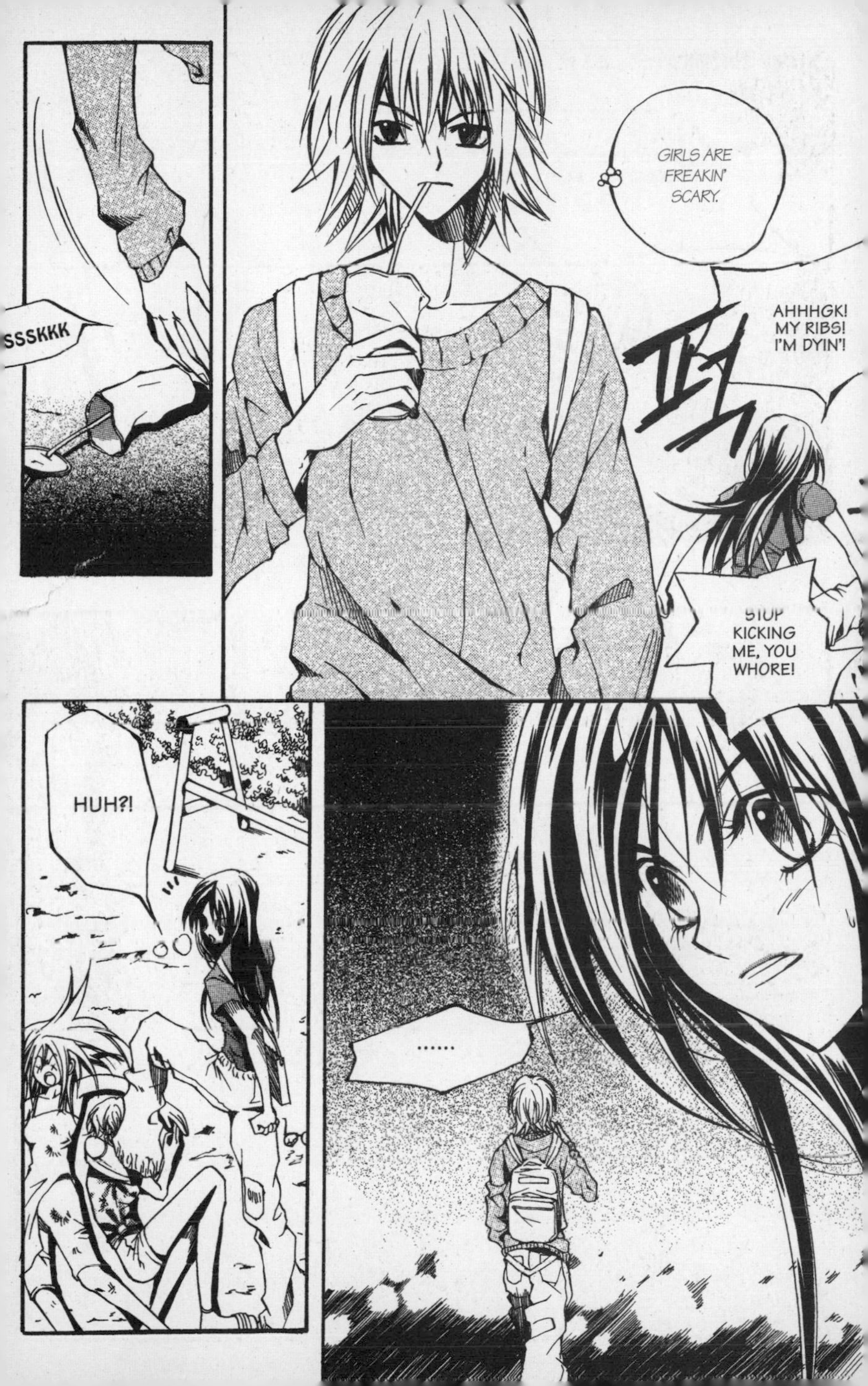

SSSKKK
GIRLS ARE FREAKIN' SCARY.
AHHHGK! MY RIBS! I'M DYIN'!
STOP KICKING ME, YOU WHORE!
HUH?!
......

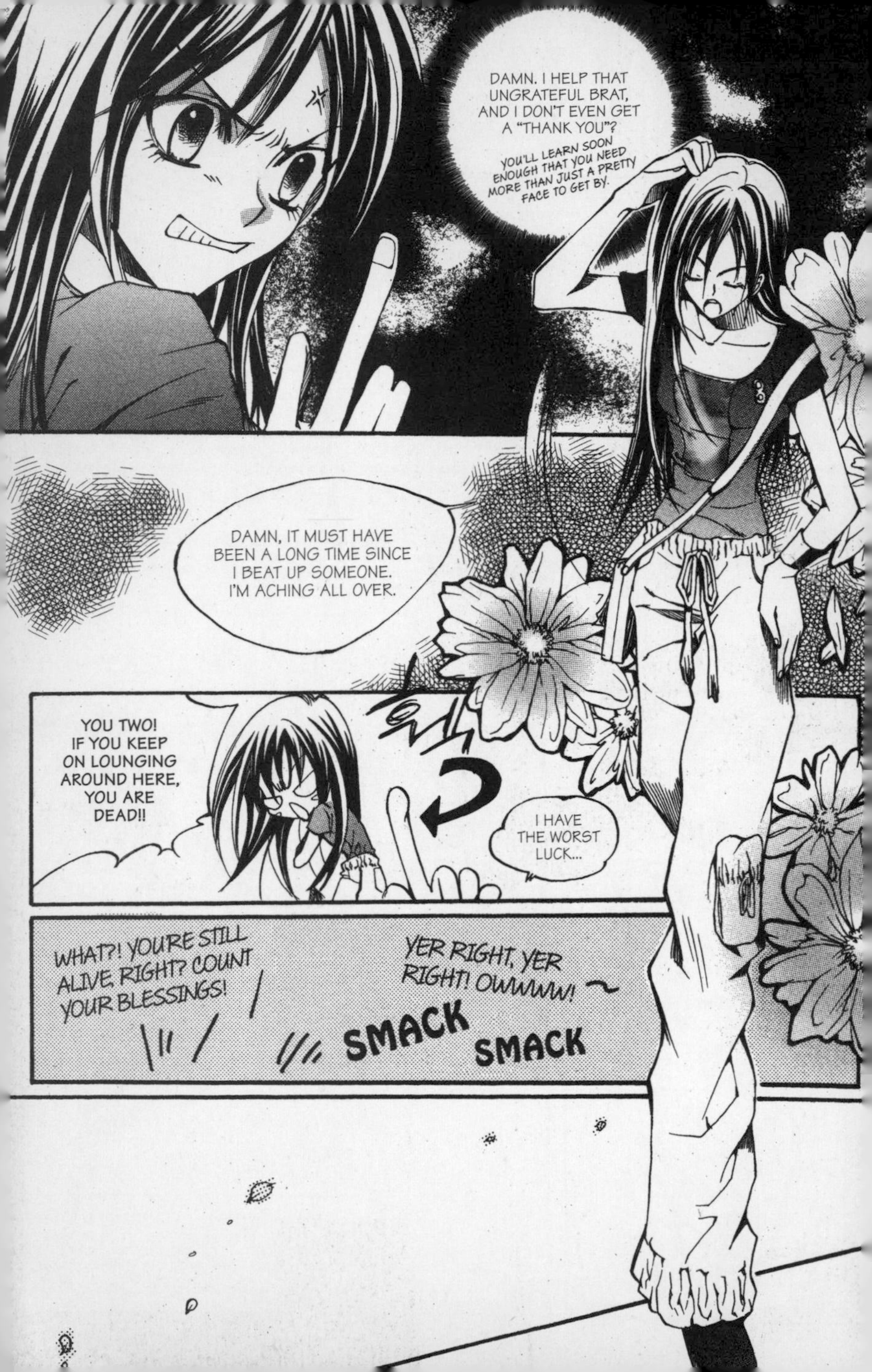
DAMN. I HELP THAT UNGRATEFUL BRAT, AND I DON'T EVEN GET A "THANK YOU"?
YOU'LL LEARN SOON ENOUGH THAT YOU NEED MORE THAN JUST A PRETTY FACE TO GET BY.
DAMN, IT MUST HAVE BEEN A LONG TIME SINCE I BEAT UP SOMEONE. I'M ACHING ALL OVER.
YOU TWO! IF YOU KEEP ON LOUNGING AROUND HERE, YOU ARE DEAD!!
I HAVE THE WORST LUCK...
WHAT?! YOU'RE STILL ALIVE, RIGHT? COUNT YOUR BLESSINGS!
YER RIGHT, YER RIGHT! OWWWW!
SMACK
SMACK

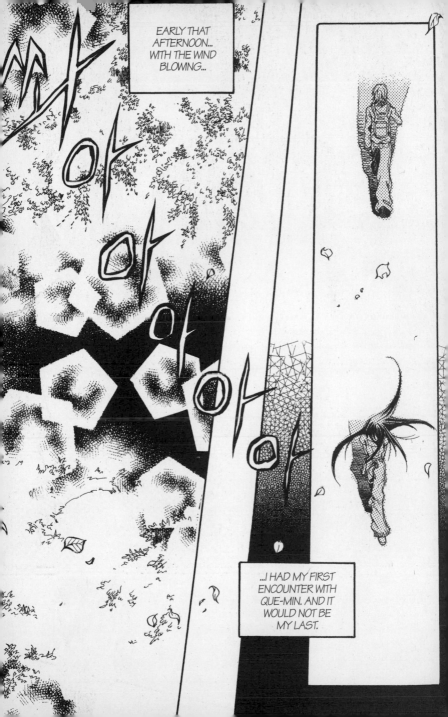

EARLY THAT
AFTERNOON...
WITH THE WIND
BLOWING...

...I HAD MY FIRST
ENCOUNTER WITH
QUE-MIN. AND IT
WOULD NOT BE
MY LAST.

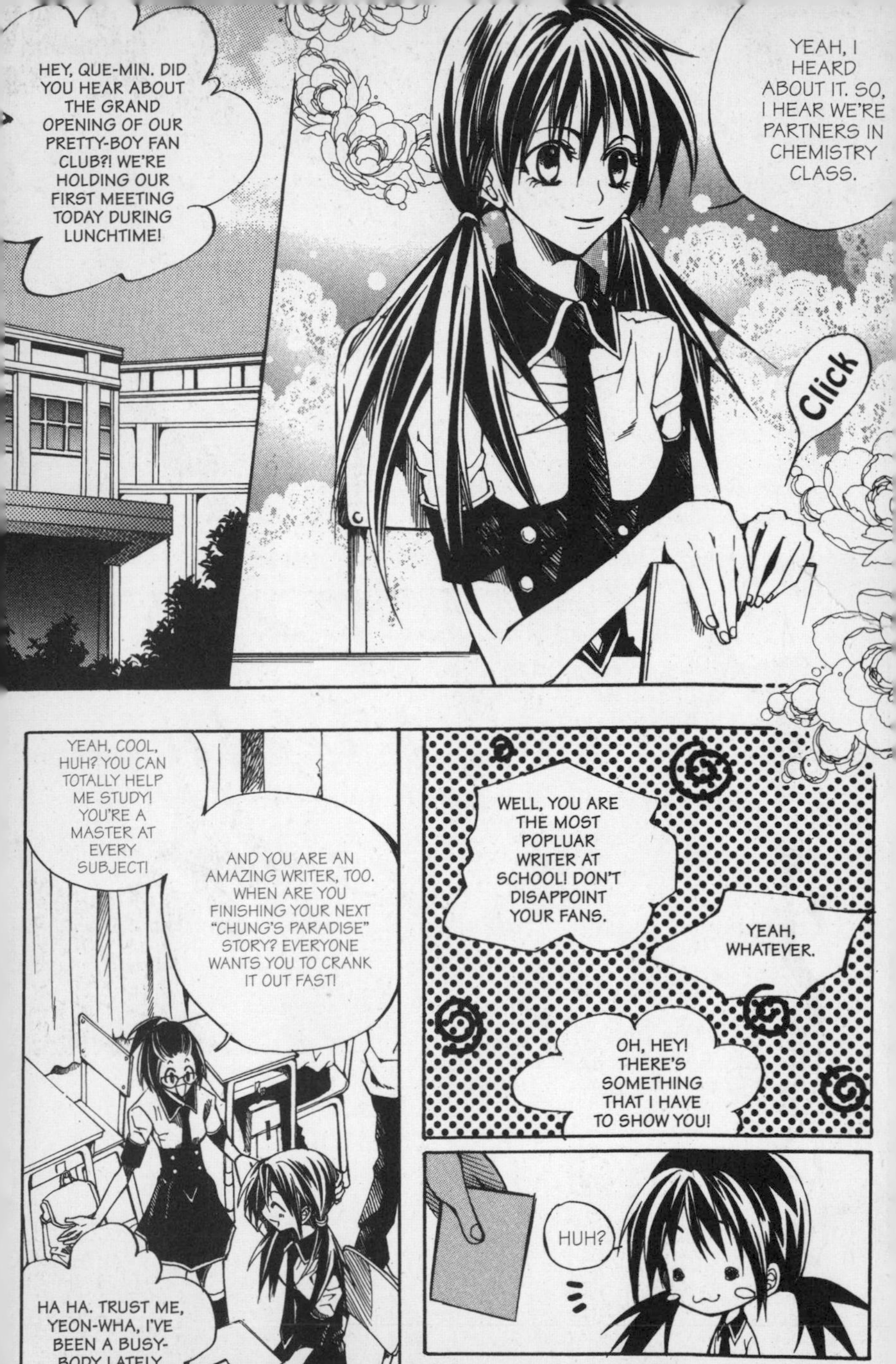
HEY, QUE-MIN. DID YOU HEAR ABOUT THE GRAND OPENING OF OUR PRETTY-BOY FAN CLUB?! WE'RE HOLDING OUR FIRST MEETING TODAY DURING LUNCHTIME!
YEAH, I HEARD ABOUT IT. SO, I HEAR WE'RE PARTNERS IN CHEMISTRY CLASS.
Click
YEAH, COOL, HUH? YOU CAN TOTALLY HELP ME STUDY! YOU'RE A MASTER AT EVERY SUBJECT!
AND YOU ARE AN AMAZING WRITER, TOO. WHEN ARE YOU FINISHING YOUR NEXT "CHUNG'S PARADISE" STORY? EVERYONE WANTS YOU TO CRANK IT OUT FAST!
HA HA. TRUST ME, YEON-WHA, I'VE BEEN A BUSY-BODY LATELY.
WELL, YOU ARE THE MOST POPLUAR WRITER AT SCHOOL! DON'T DISAPPOINT YOUR FANS.
YEAH, WHATEVER.
OH, HEY! THERE'S SOMETHING THAT I HAVE TO SHOW YOU!
HUH?

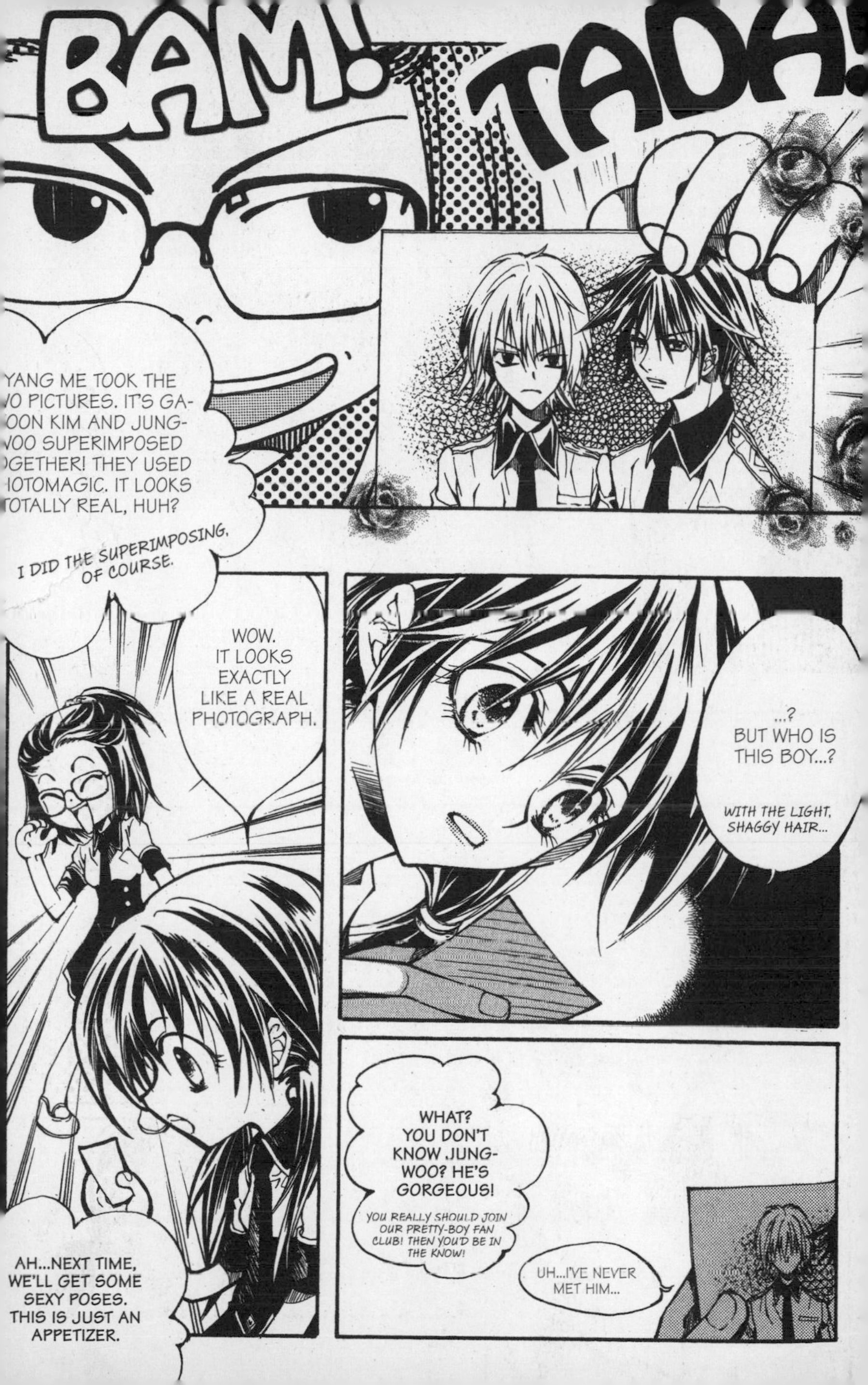
BAM!
TADA!
YANG ME TOOK THE
/O PICTURES. IT'S GA-
OON KIM AND JUNG-
/OO SUPERIMPOSED
GETHER! THEY USED
IOTOMAGIC. IT LOOKS
TOTALLY REAL, HUH?
I DID THE SUPERIMPOSING, OF COURSE.
WOW. IT LOOKS EXACTLY LIKE A REAL PHOTOGRAPH.
...? BUT WHO IS THIS BOY...?
WITH THE LIGHT, SHAGGY HAIR...
AH...NEXT TIME, WE'LL GET SOME SEXY POSES. THIS IS JUST AN APPETIZER.
WHAT? YOU DON'T KNOW JUNG-WOO? HE'S GORGEOUS!
YOU REALLY SHOULD JOIN OUR PRETTY-BOY FAN CLUB! THEN YOU'D BE IN THE KNOW!
UH...I'VE NEVER MET HIM...

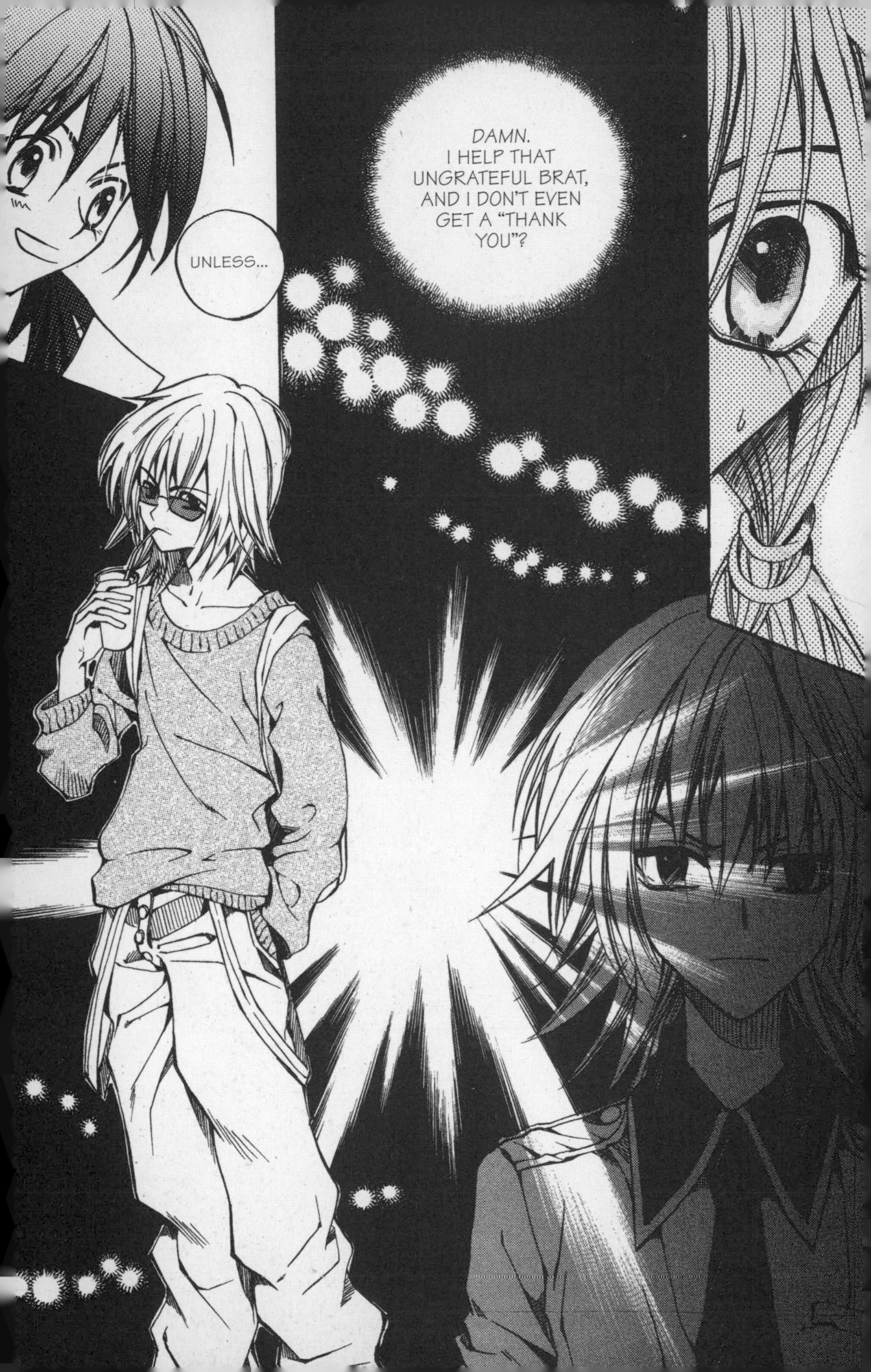
UNLESS...
DAMN. I HELP THAT UNGRATEFUL BRAT, AND I DON'T EVEN GET A "THANK YOU"?

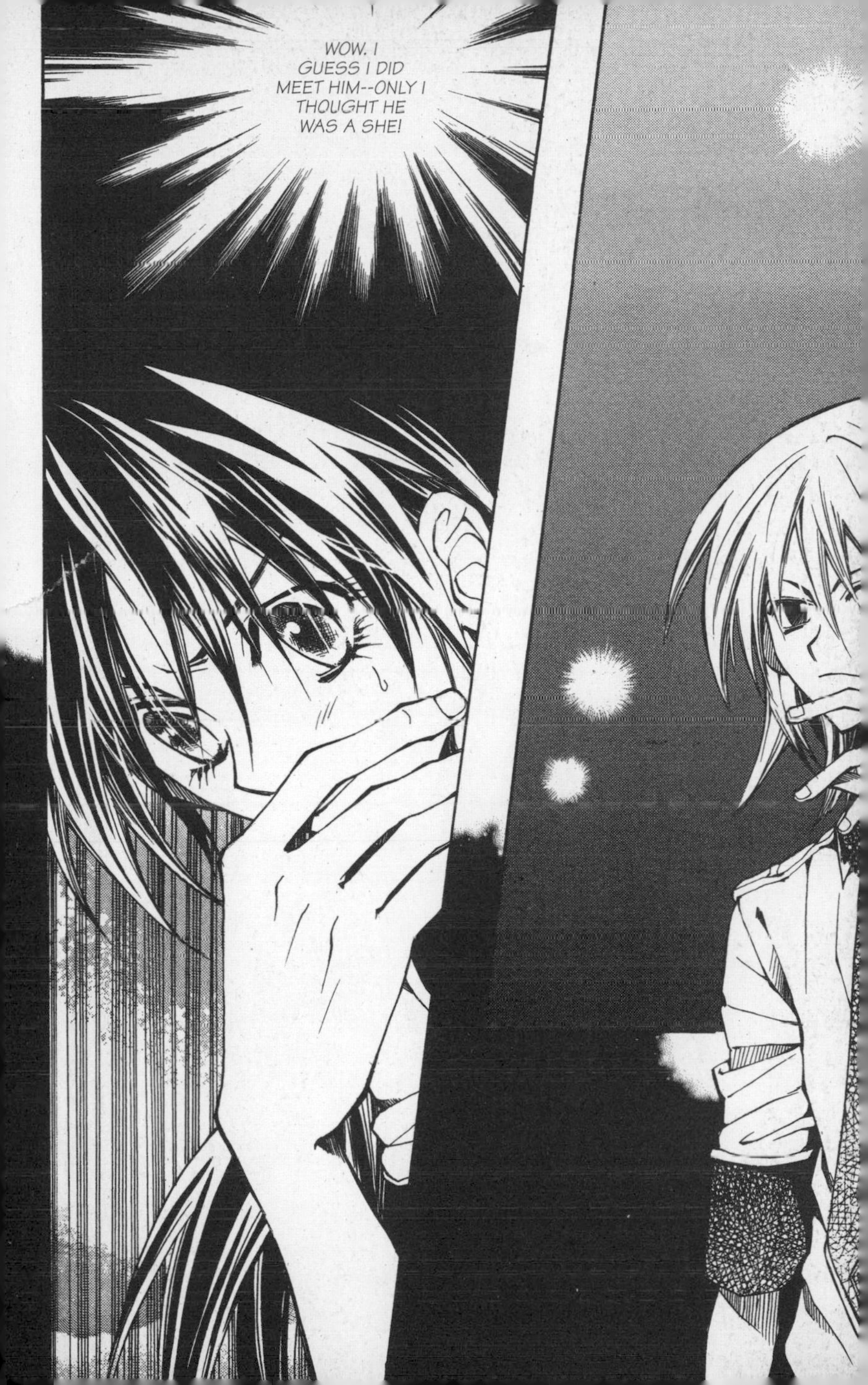
WOW. I GUESS I DID MEET HIM--ONLY I THOUGHT HE WAS A SHE!

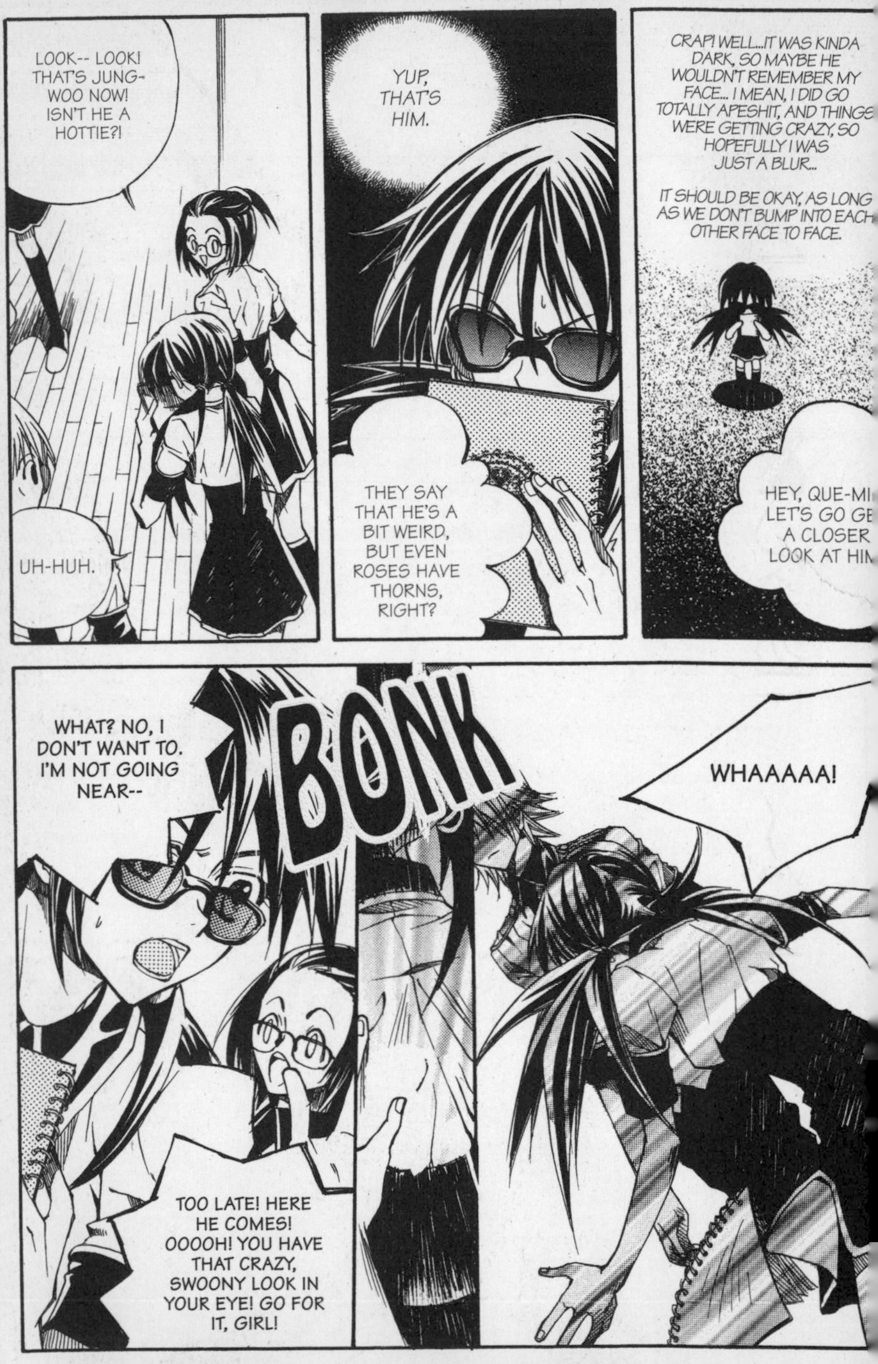

LOOK-- LOOK! THAT'S JUNG-WOO NOW! ISN'T HE A HOTTIE?!
UH-HUH.
YUP, THAT'S HIM.
THEY SAY THAT HE'S A BIT WEIRD, BUT EVEN ROSES HAVE THORNS, RIGHT?
CRAP! WELL...IT WAS KINDA DARK, SO MAYBE HE WOULDN'T REMEMBER MY FACE... I MEAN, I DID GO TOTALLY APESHIT, AND THINGS WERE GETTING CRAZY, SO HOPEFULLY I WAS JUST A BLUR...
IT SHOULD BE OKAY, AS LONG AS WE DON'T BUMP INTO EACH OTHER FACE TO FACE.
WHAT? NO, I DON'T WANT TO. I'M NOT GOING NEAR--
BONK
TOO LATE! HERE HE COMES! OOOOH! YOU HAVE THAT CRAZY, SWOONY LOOK IN YOUR EYE! GO FOR IT, GIRL!
WHAAAAA!

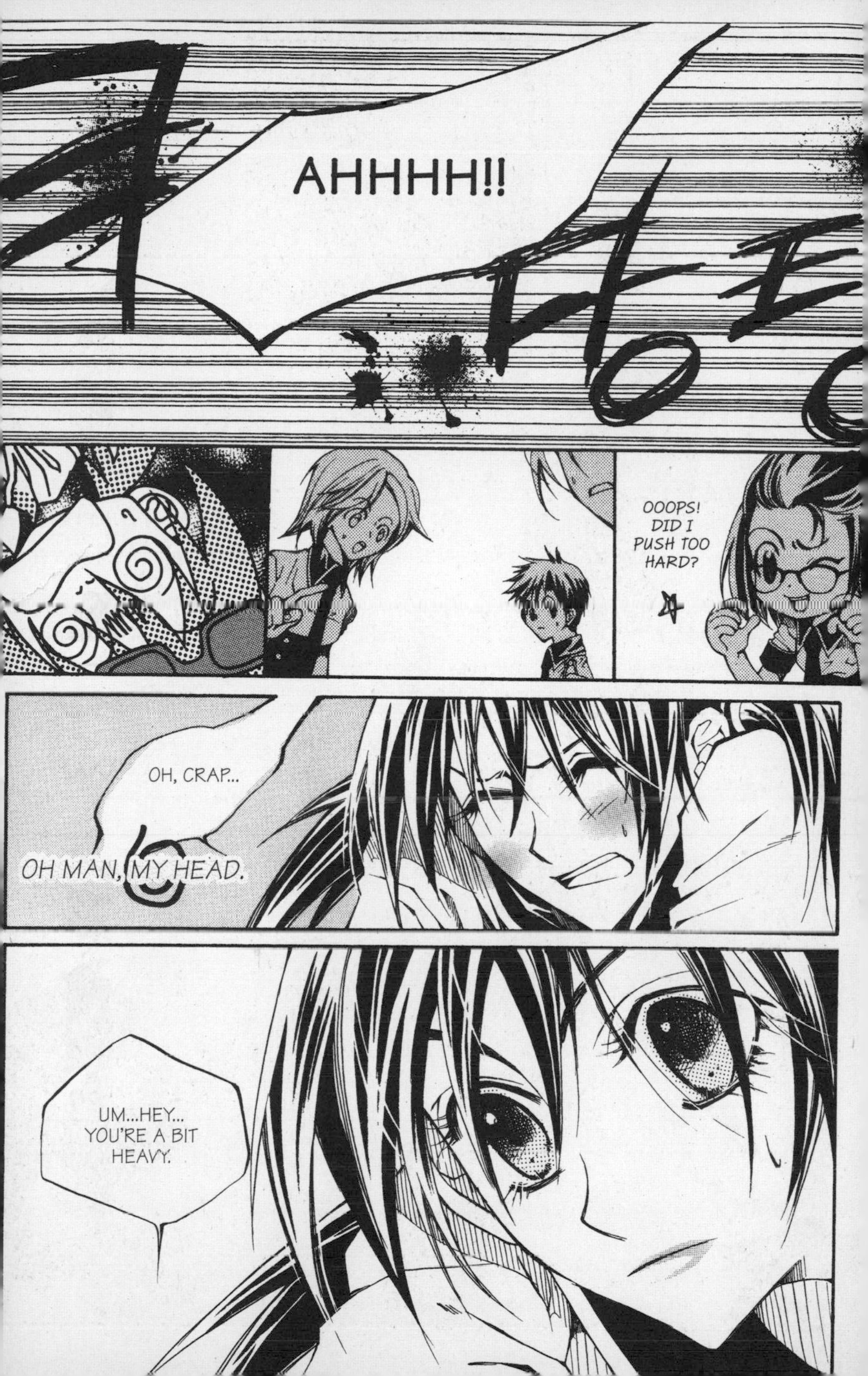
AHHHH!!
OOOPS! DID I PUSH TOO HARD?
OH, CRAP...
OH MAN, MY HEAD.
UM...HEY... YOU'RE A BIT HEAVY.

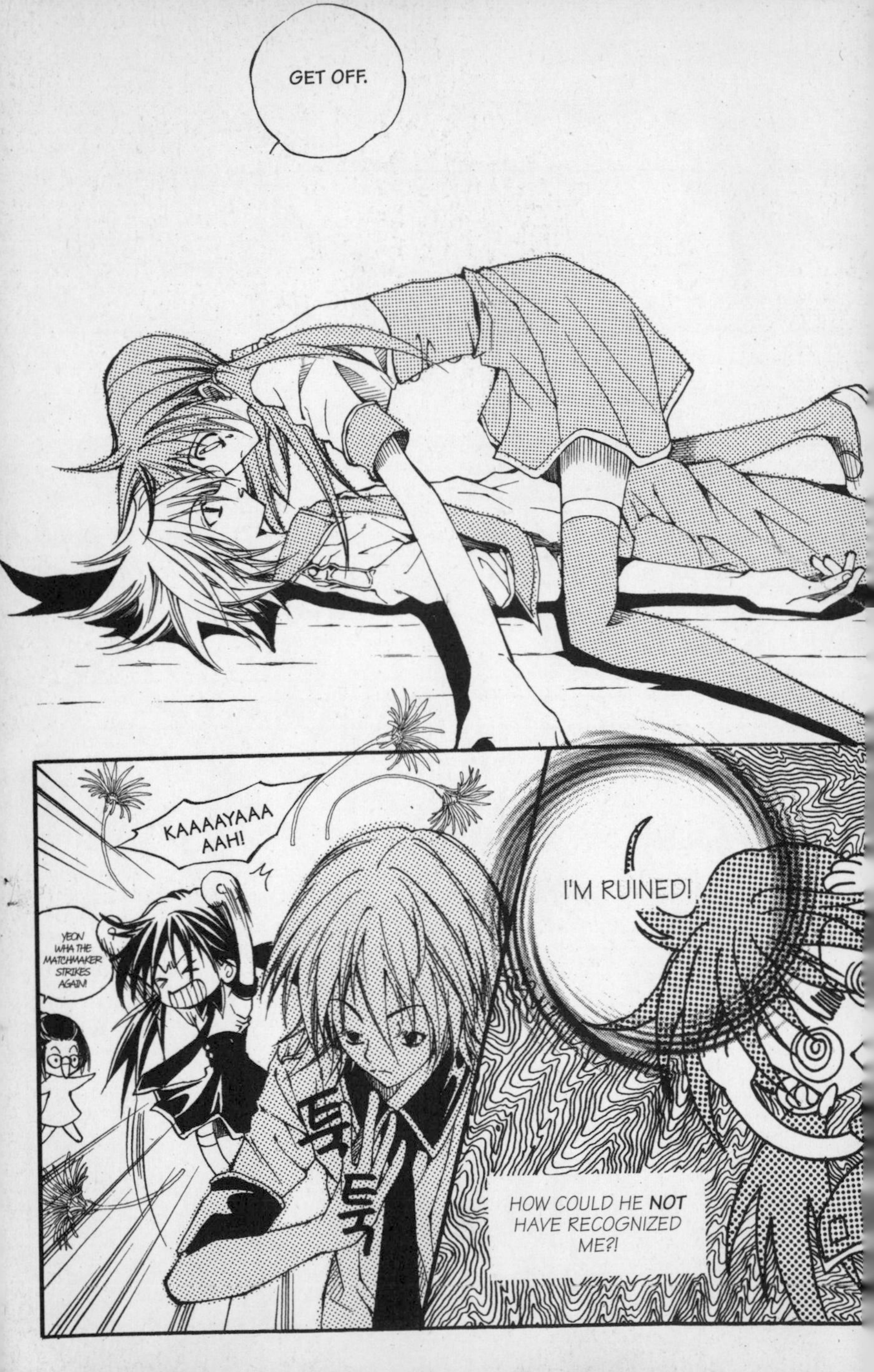
GET OFF.
KAAAAYAAA AAH!
YEON WHA THE MATCHMAKER STRIKES AGAIN!
툭 툭
I'M RUINED!
HOW COULD HE **NOT** HAVE RECOGNIZED ME?!

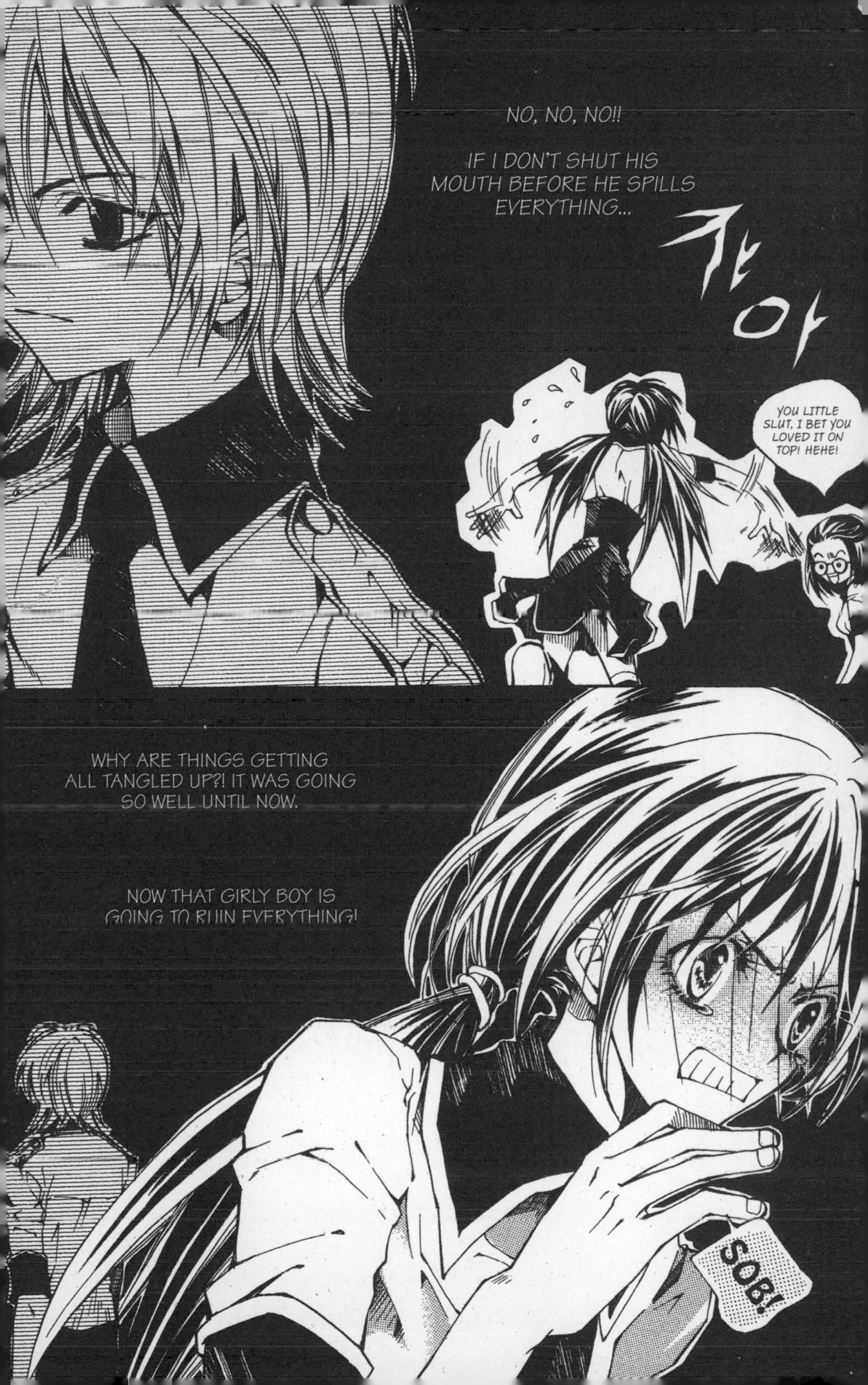

NO, NO, NO!!
IF I DON'T SHUT HIS MOUTH BEFORE HE SPILLS EVERYTHING...
카아
YOU LITTLE SLUT, I BET YOU LOVED IT ON TOP! HEHE!
WHY ARE THINGS GETTING ALL TANGLED UP?! IT WAS GOING SO WELL UNTIL NOW.
NOW THAT GIRLY BOY IS GOING TO RUIN EVERYTHING!
SOB!

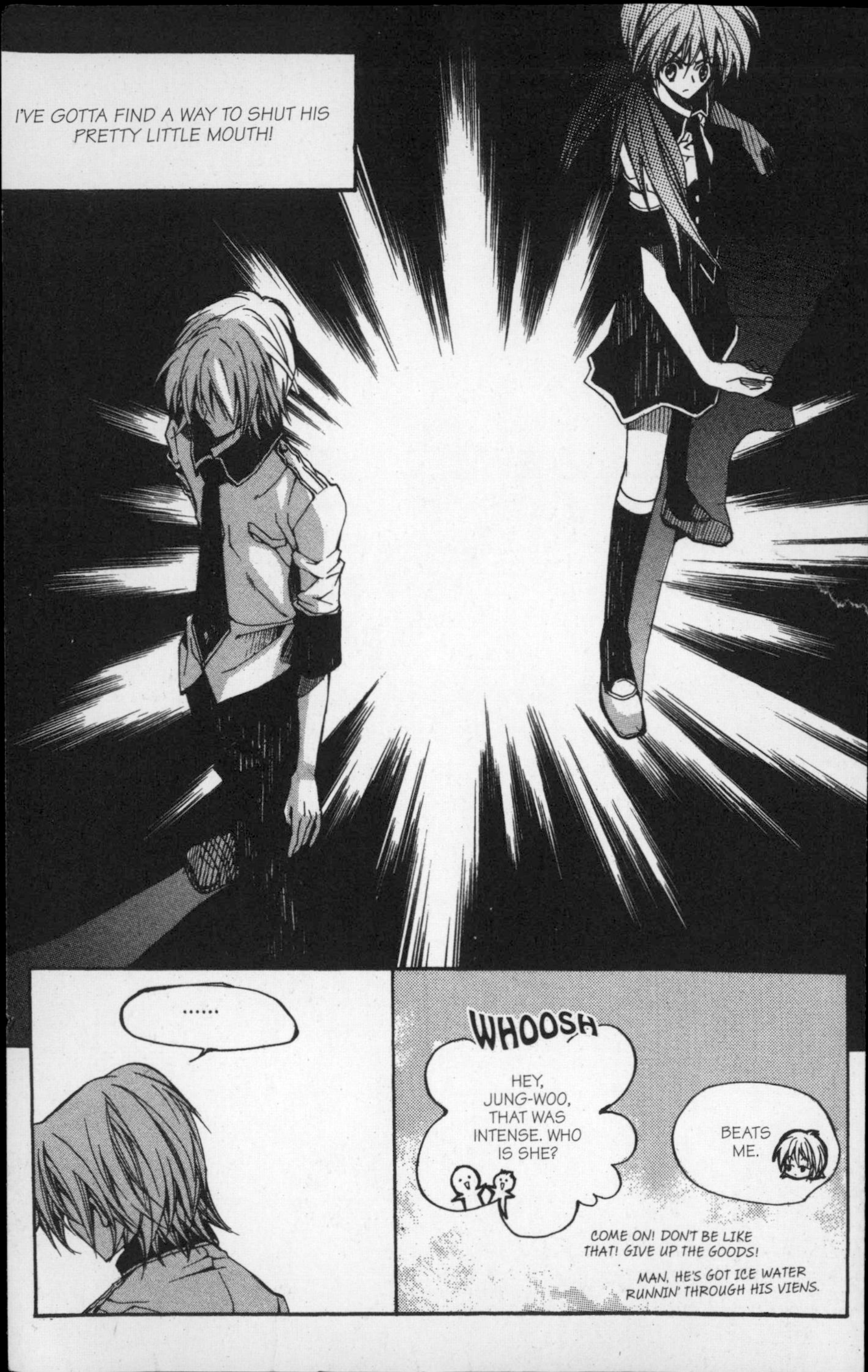
I'VE GOTTA FIND A WAY TO SHUT HIS PRETTY LITTLE MOUTH!
......
WHOOSH
HEY, JUNG-WOO, THAT WAS INTENSE. WHO IS SHE?
BEATS ME.
COME ON! DON'T BE LIKE THAT! GIVE UP THE GOODS!
MAN, HE'S GOT ICE WATER RUNNIN' THROUGH HIS VIENS.

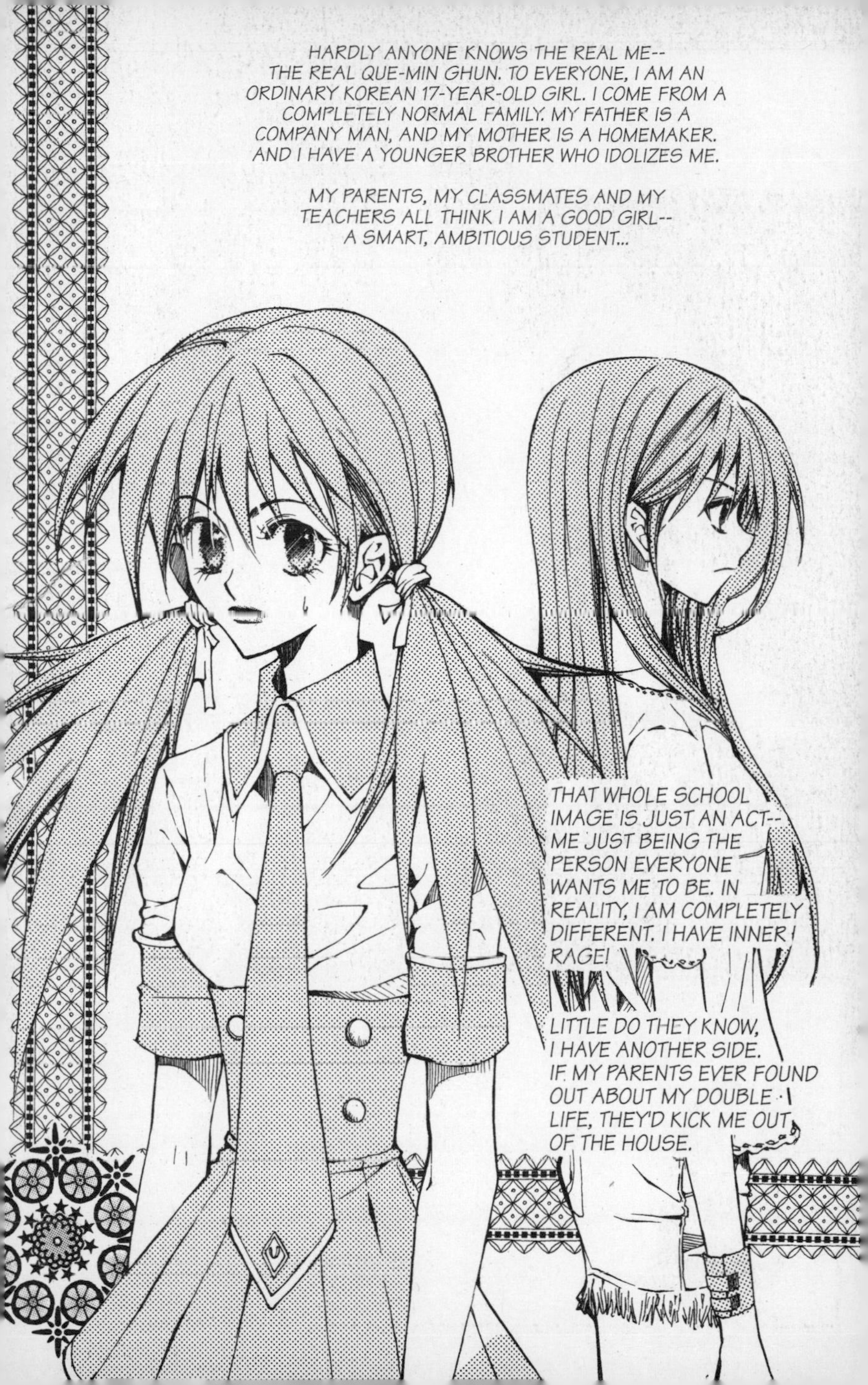
HARDLY ANYONE KNOWS THE REAL ME-- THE REAL QUE-MIN GHUN. TO EVERYONE, I AM AN ORDINARY KOREAN 17-YEAR-OLD GIRL. I COME FROM A COMPLETELY NORMAL FAMILY. MY FATHER IS A COMPANY MAN, AND MY MOTHER IS A HOMEMAKER. AND I HAVE A YOUNGER BROTHER WHO IDOLIZES ME.
MY PARENTS, MY CLASSMATES AND MY TEACHERS ALL THINK I AM A GOOD GIRL-- A SMART, AMBITIOUS STUDENT...
THAT WHOLE SCHOOL IMAGE IS JUST AN ACT-- ME JUST BEING THE PERSON EVERYONE WANTS ME TO BE. IN REALITY, I AM COMPLETELY DIFFERENT. I HAVE INNER RAGE!
LITTLE DO THEY KNOW, I HAVE ANOTHER SIDE. IF MY PARENTS EVER FOUND OUT ABOUT MY DOUBLE LIFE, THEY'D KICK ME OUT OF THE HOUSE.

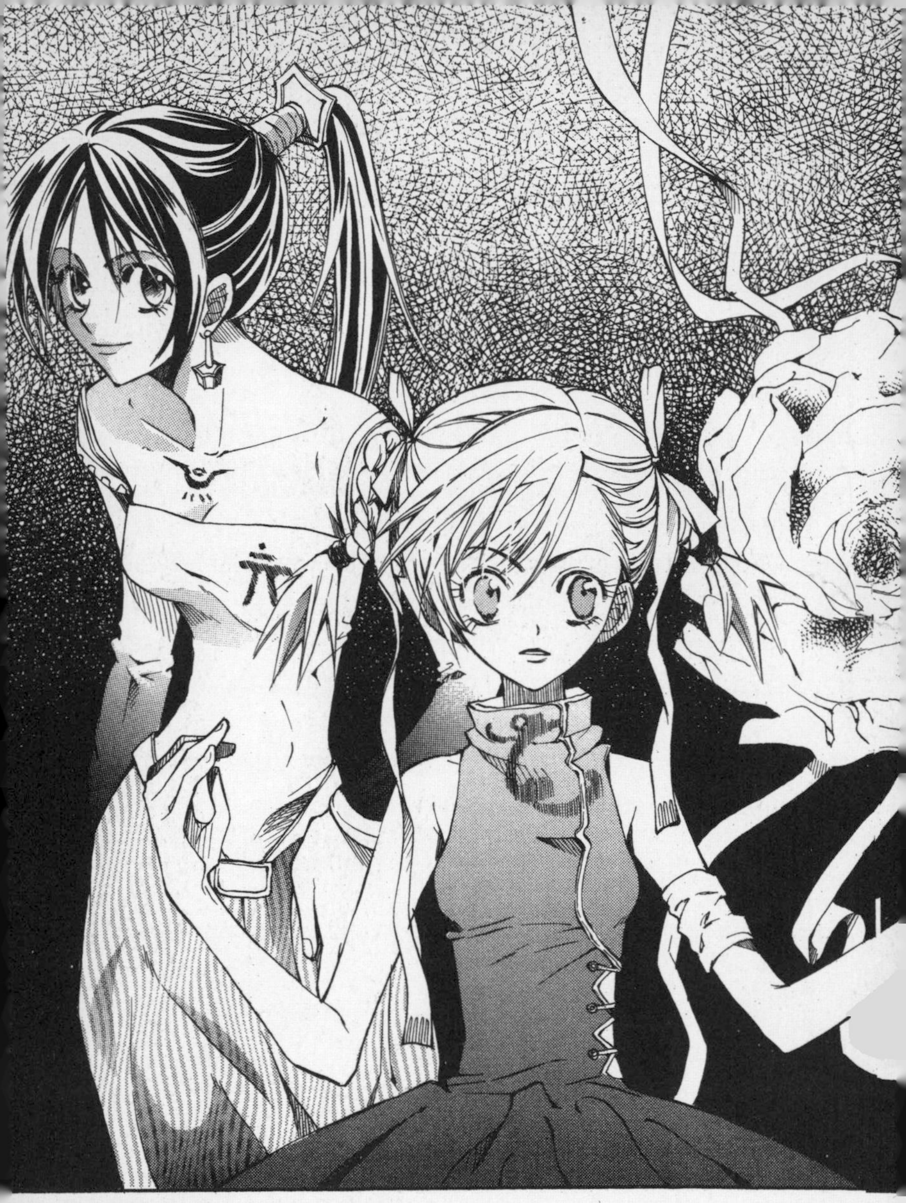

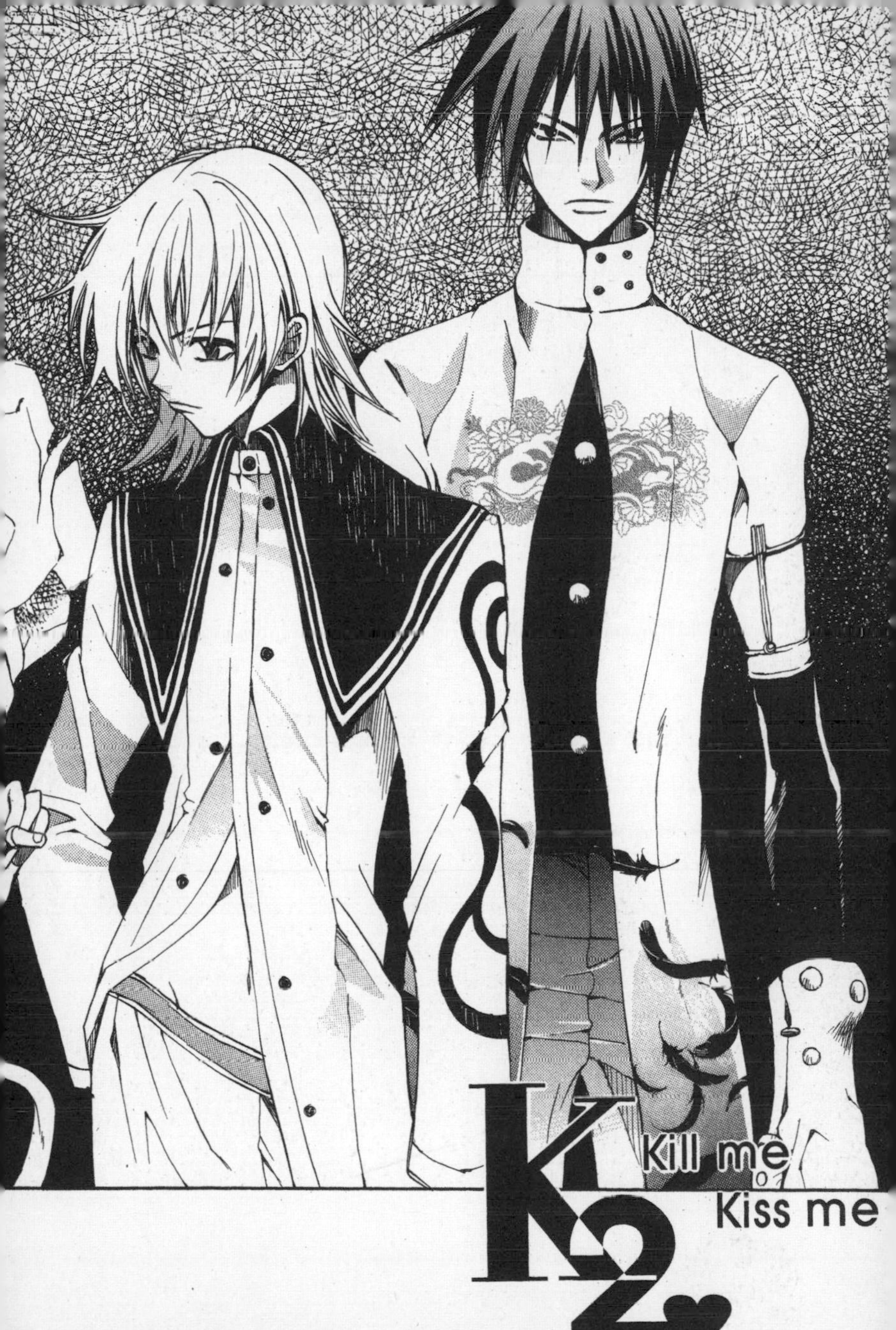
K2
Kill me
Kiss me

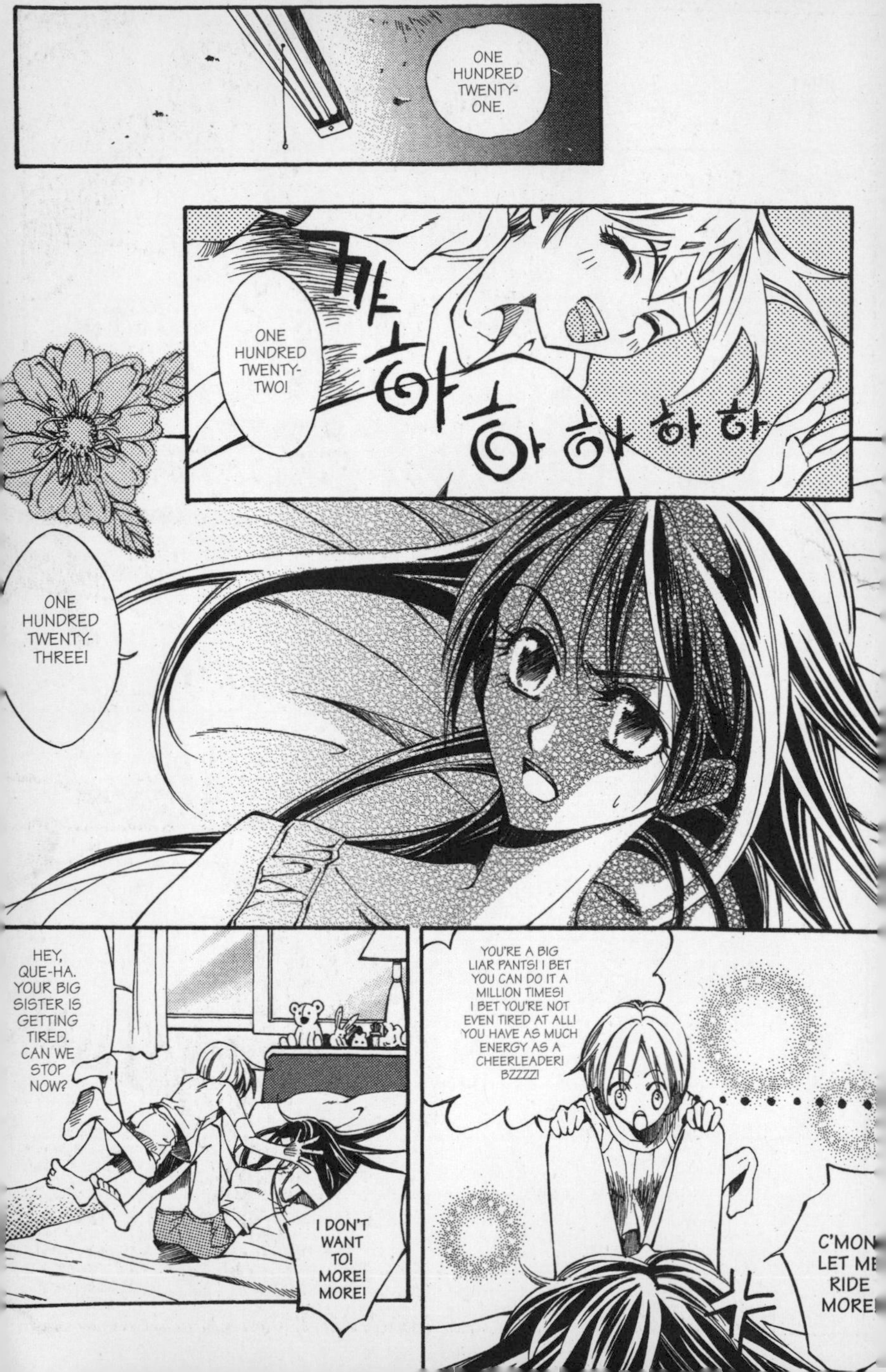
ONE HUNDRED TWENTY-ONE.
ONE HUNDRED TWENTY-TWO!
꺄하하하하하
ONE HUNDRED TWENTY-THREE!
HEY, QUE-HA. YOUR BIG SISTER IS GETTING TIRED. CAN WE STOP NOW?
I DON'T WANT TO! MORE! MORE!
YOU'RE A BIG LIAR PANTS! I BET YOU CAN DO IT A MILLION TIMES! I BET YOU'RE NOT EVEN TIRED AT ALL! YOU HAVE AS MUCH ENERGY AS A CHEERLEADER! BZZZZ!
C'MON LET ME RIDE MORE!

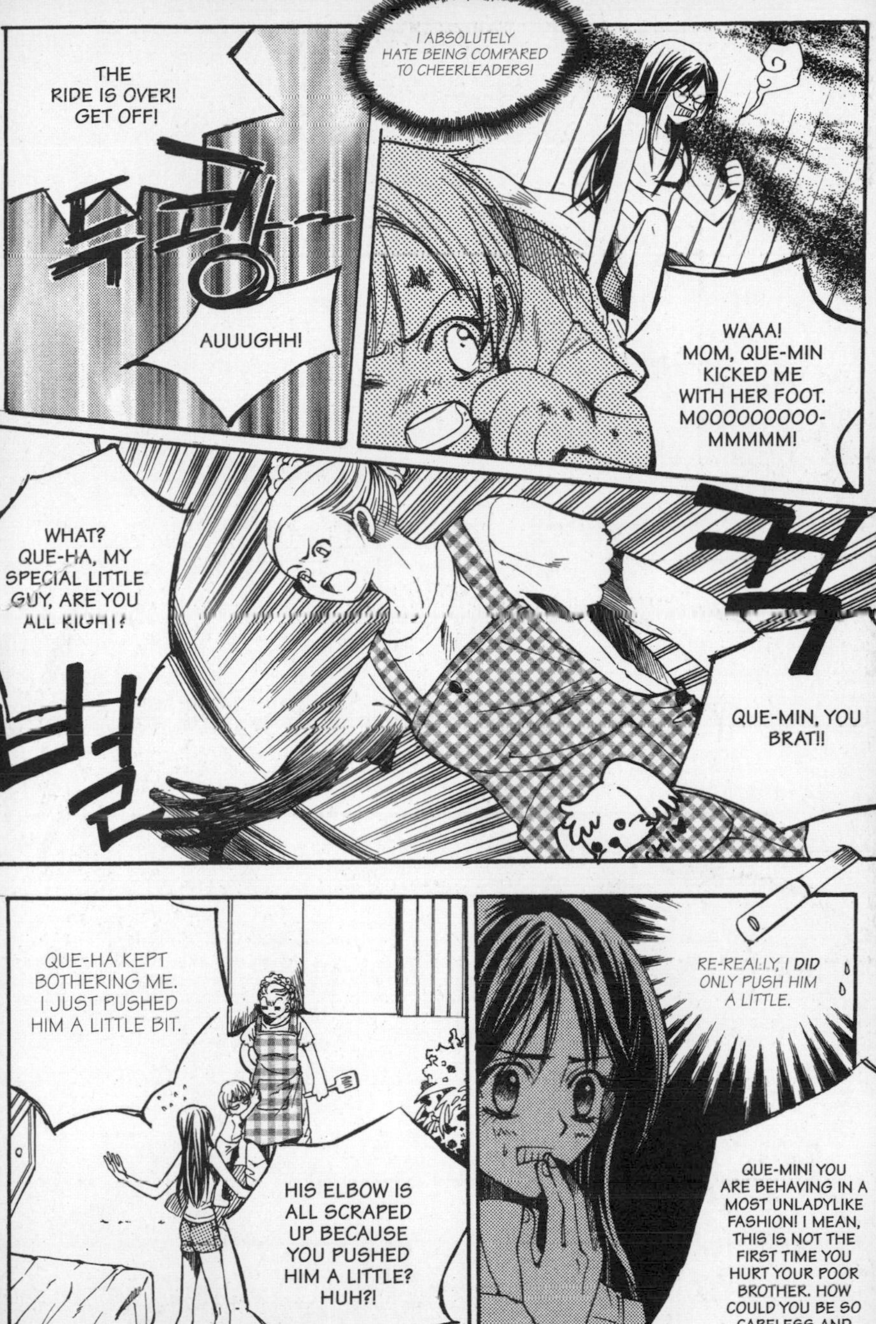
THE RIDE IS OVER! GET OFF!
AUUUGHH!
I ABSOLUTELY HATE BEING COMPARED TO CHEERLEADERS!
WAAA! MOM, QUE-MIN KICKED ME WITH HER FOOT. MOOOOOOOOO-MMMMM!
WHAT? QUE-HA, MY SPECIAL LITTLE GUY, ARE YOU ALL RIGHT?
QUE-MIN, YOU BRAT!!
QUE-HA KEPT BOTHERING ME. I JUST PUSHED HIM A LITTLE BIT.
HIS ELBOW IS ALL SCRAPED UP BECAUSE YOU PUSHED HIM A LITTLE? HUH?!
RE-REALLY, I **DID** ONLY PUSH HIM A LITTLE.
QUE-MIN! YOU ARE BEHAVING IN A MOST UNLADYLIKE FASHION! I MEAN, THIS IS NOT THE FIRST TIME YOU HURT YOUR POOR BROTHER. HOW COULD YOU BE SO CARELESS AND BRUTISH?

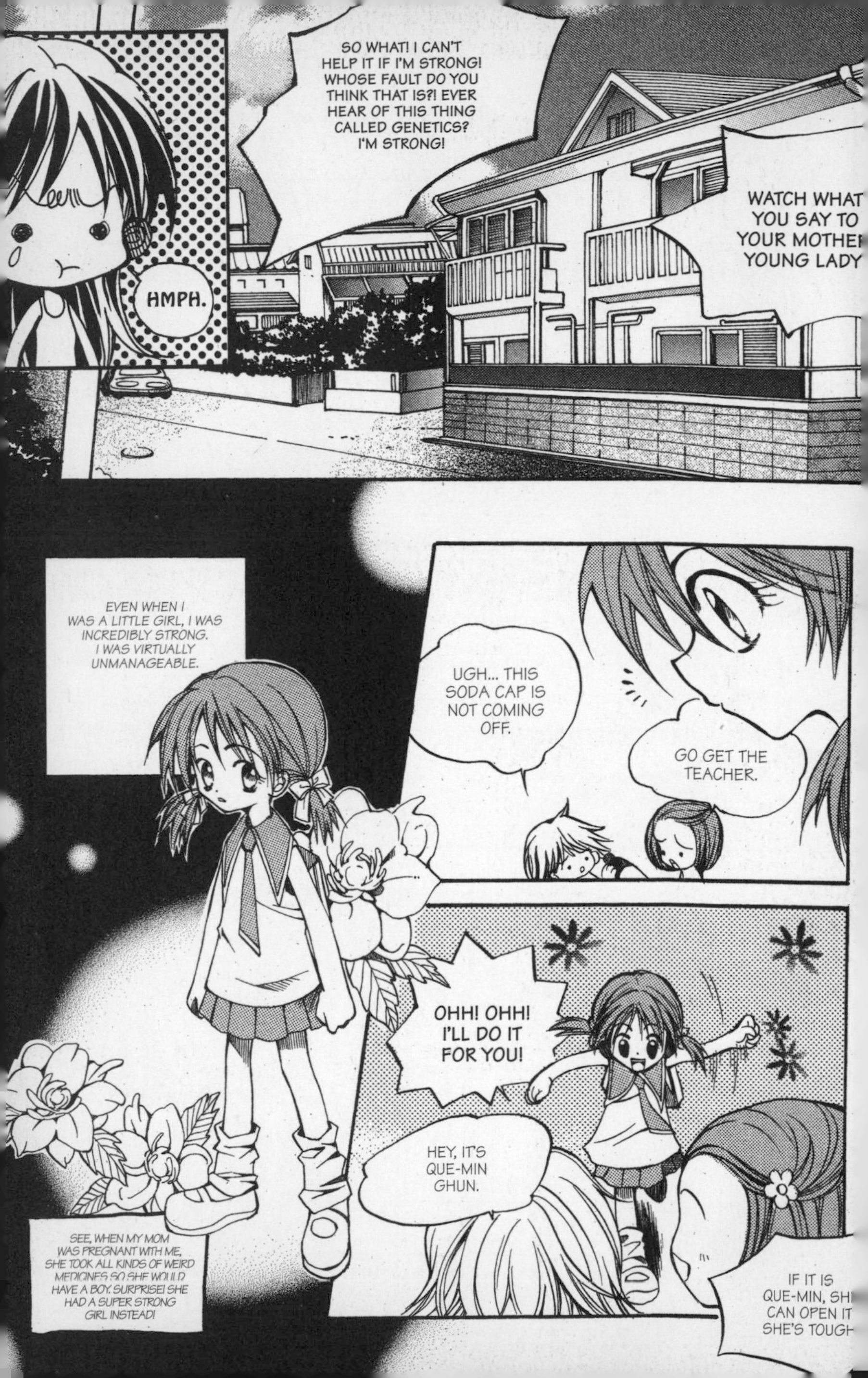
HMPH.
SO WHAT! I CAN'T HELP IT IF I'M STRONG! WHOSE FAULT DO YOU THINK THAT IS?! EVER HEAR OF THIS THING CALLED GENETICS? I'M STRONG!
WATCH WHAT YOU SAY TO YOUR MOTHE YOUNG LADY
EVEN WHEN I WAS A LITTLE GIRL, I WAS INCREDIBLY STRONG. I WAS VIRTUALLY UNMANAGEABLE.
SEE, WHEN MY MOM WAS PREGNANT WITH ME, SHE TOOK ALL KINDS OF WEIRD MEDICINES SO SHE WOULD HAVE A BOY. SURPRISE! SHE HAD A SUPER STRONG GIRL INSTEAD!
UGH... THIS SODA CAP IS NOT COMING OFF.
GO GET THE TEACHER.
OHH! OHH! I'LL DO IT FOR YOU!
HEY, IT'S QUE-MIN GHUN.
IF IT IS QUE-MIN, SH CAN OPEN IT SHE'S TOUGH

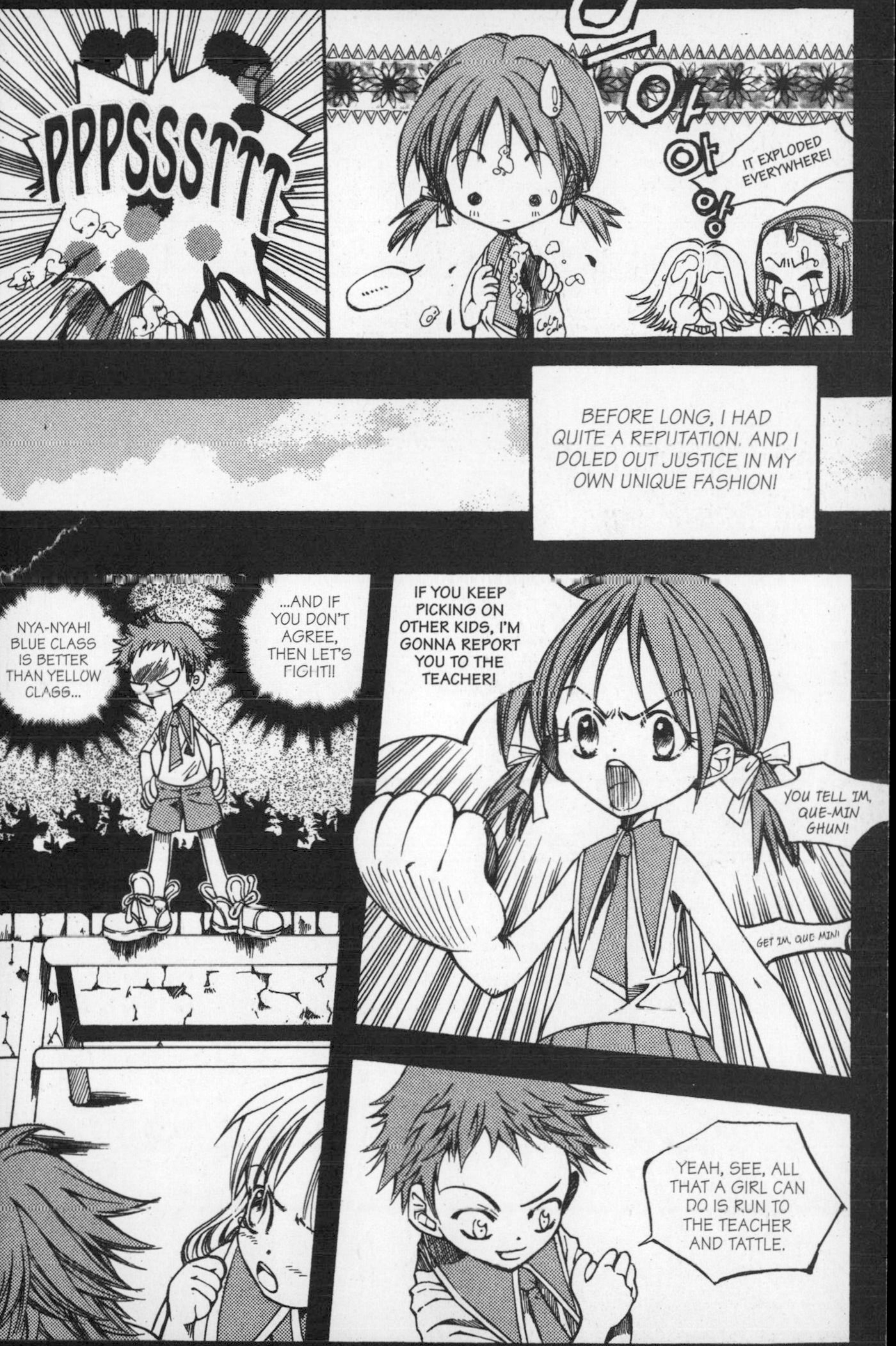
PPPSSSTTT
으아아앙
......
IT EXPLODED EVERYWHERE!
BEFORE LONG, I HAD QUITE A REPUTATION. AND I DOLED OUT JUSTICE IN MY OWN UNIQUE FASHION!
NYA-NYAH! BLUE CLASS IS BETTER THAN YELLOW CLASS...
...AND IF YOU DON'T AGREE, THEN LET'S FIGHT!!
IF YOU KEEP PICKING ON OTHER KIDS, I'M GONNA REPORT YOU TO THE TEACHER!
YOU TELL 'IM, QUE-MIN GHUN!
GET 'IM, QUE MIN!
YEAH, SEE, ALL THAT A GIRL CAN DO IS RUN TO THE TEACHER AND TATTLE.

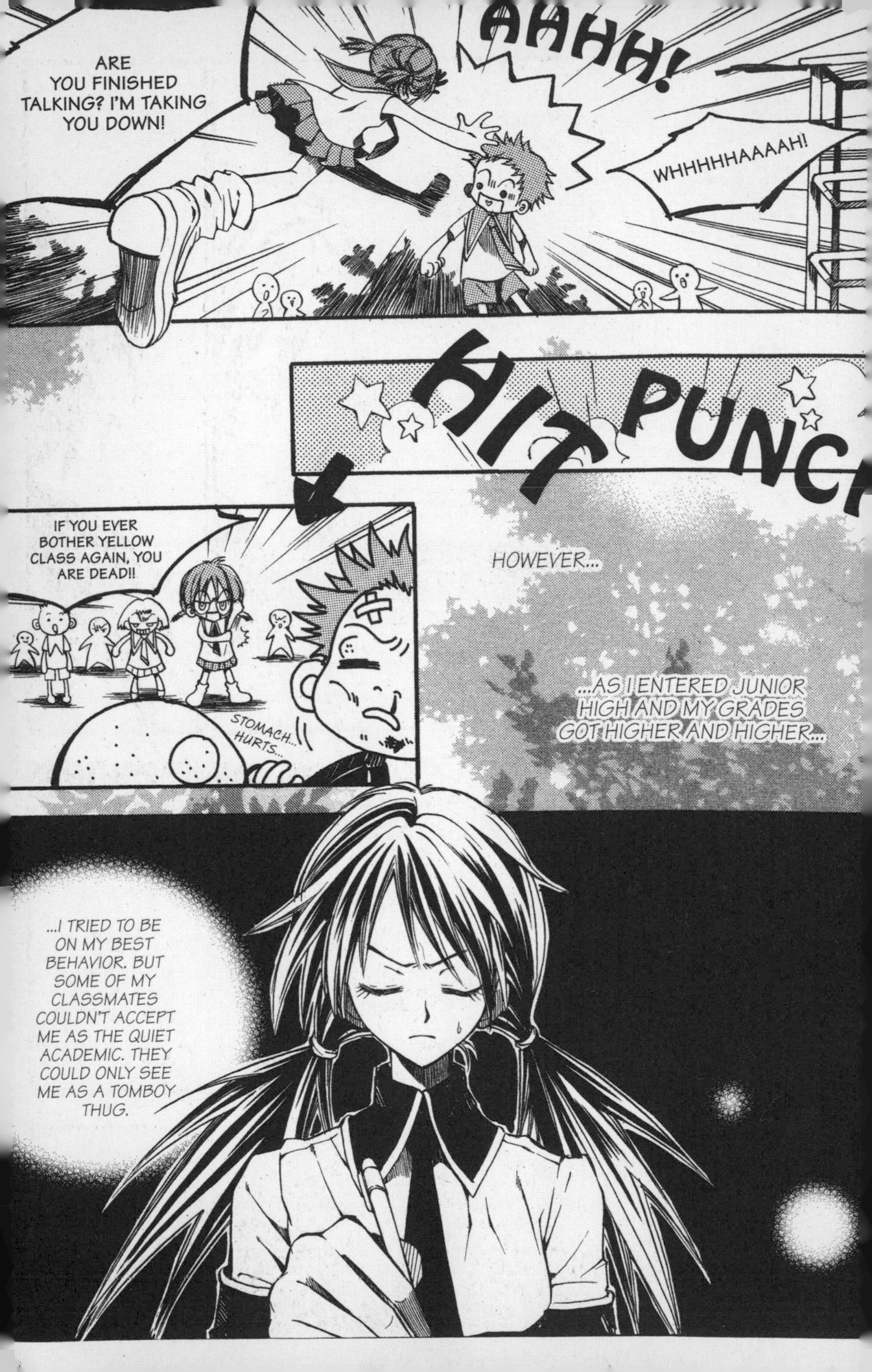
ARE YOU FINISHED TALKING? I'M TAKING YOU DOWN!
AAHH!
WHHHHHAAAAAH!
HIT
PUNC
IF YOU EVER BOTHER YELLOW CLASS AGAIN, YOU ARE DEAD!!
STOMACH... HURTS...
HOWEVER...
...AS I ENTERED JUNIOR HIGH AND MY GRADES GOT HIGHER AND HIGHER...
...I TRIED TO BE ON MY BEST BEHAVIOR. BUT SOME OF MY CLASSMATES COULDN'T ACCEPT ME AS THE QUIET ACADEMIC. THEY COULD ONLY SEE ME AS A TOMBOY THUG.

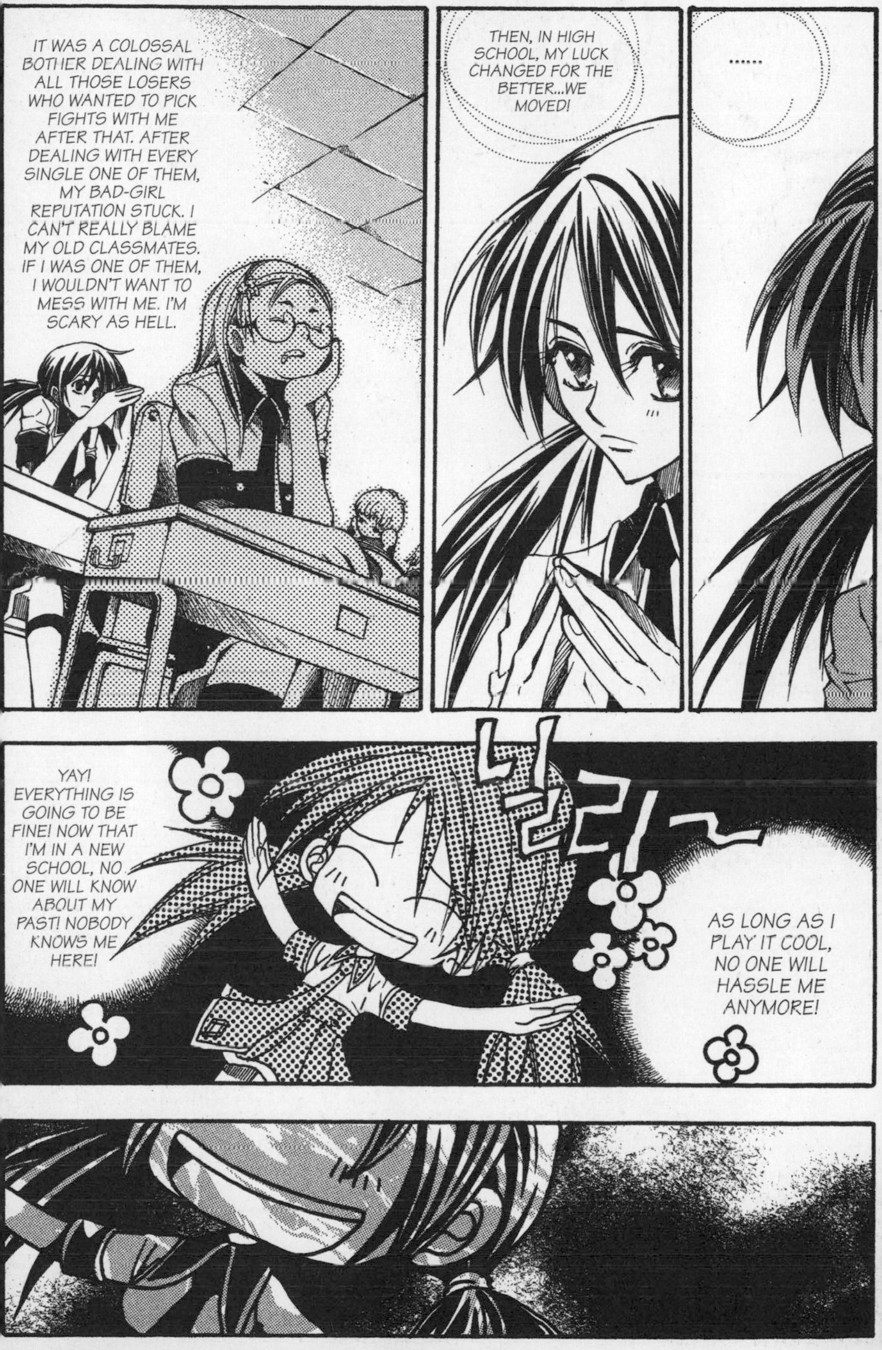
IT WAS A COLOSSAL BOTHER DEALING WITH ALL THOSE LOSERS WHO WANTED TO PICK FIGHTS WITH ME AFTER THAT. AFTER DEALING WITH EVERY SINGLE ONE OF THEM, MY BAD-GIRL REPUTATION STUCK. I CAN'T REALLY BLAME MY OLD CLASSMATES. IF I WAS ONE OF THEM, I WOULDN'T WANT TO MESS WITH ME. I'M SCARY AS HELL.
THEN, IN HIGH SCHOOL, MY LUCK CHANGED FOR THE BETTER...WE MOVED!
......
YAY! EVERYTHING IS GOING TO BE FINE! NOW THAT I'M IN A NEW SCHOOL, NO ONE WILL KNOW ABOUT MY PAST! NOBODY KNOWS ME HERE!
AS LONG AS I PLAY IT COOL, NO ONE WILL HASSLE ME ANYMORE!

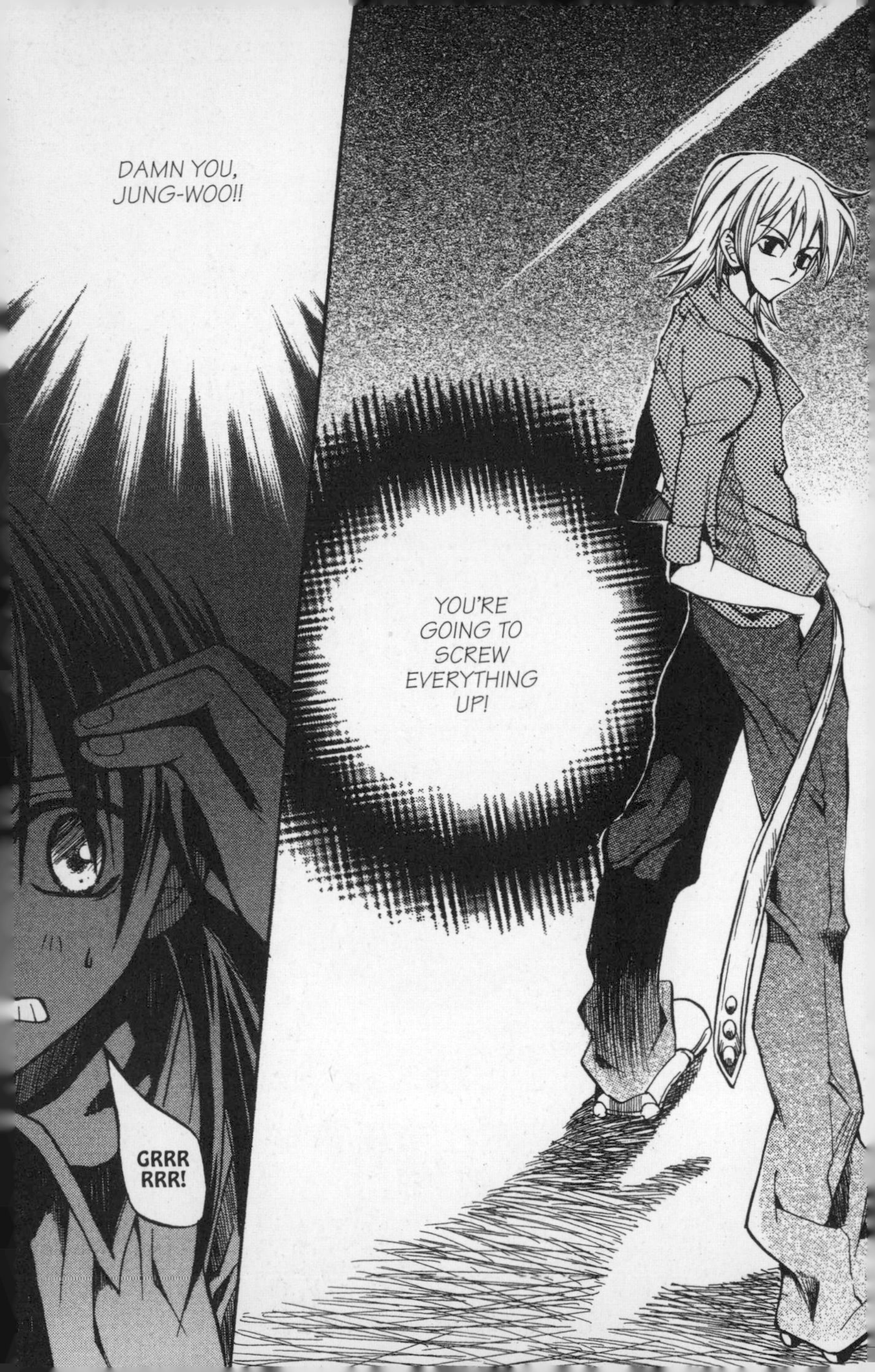
YOU'RE GOING TO SCREW EVERYTHING UP!
DAMN YOU, JUNG-WOO!!
GRRR RRR!

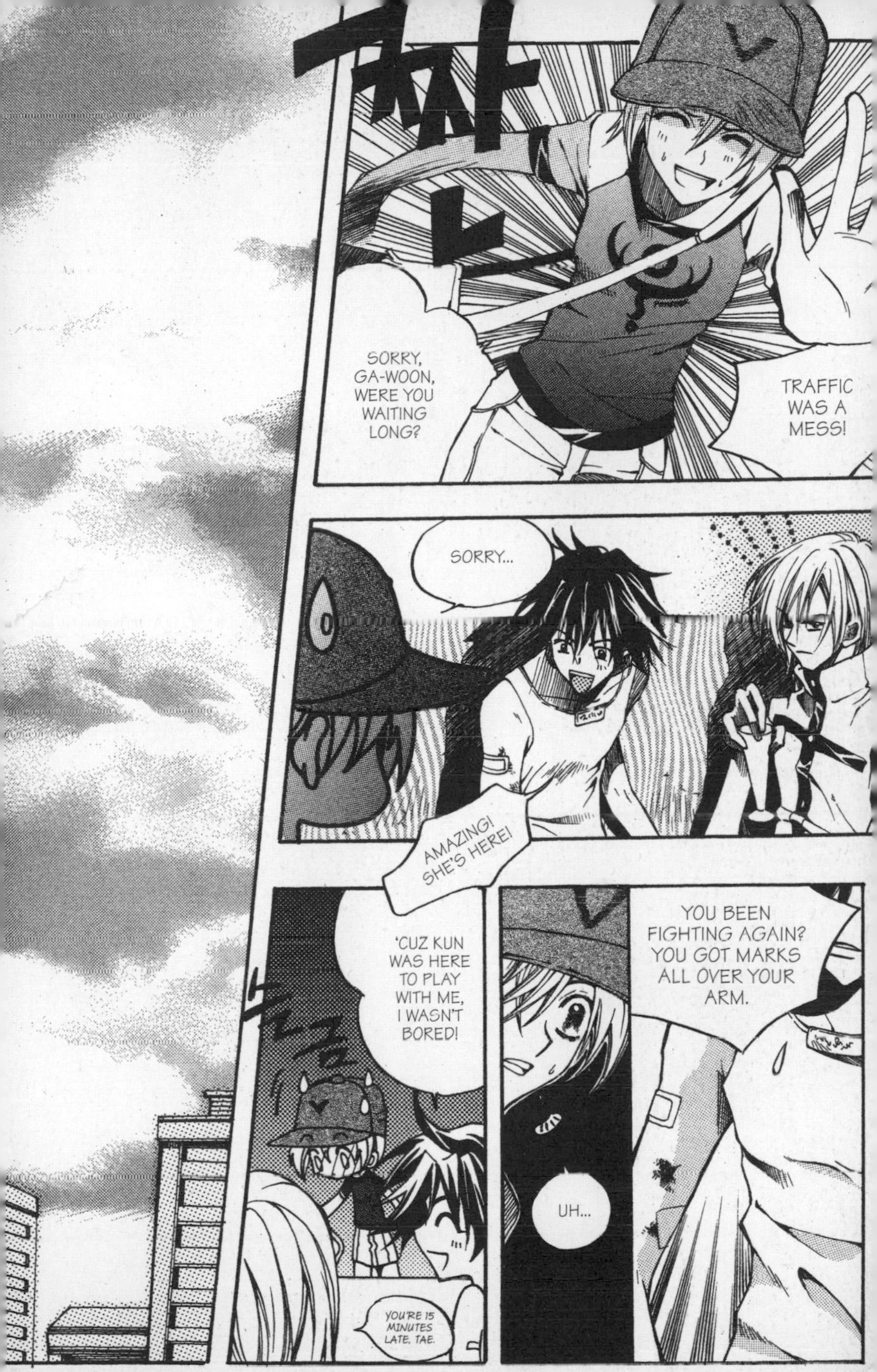
SORRY, GA-WOON, WERE YOU WAITING LONG?
TRAFFIC WAS A MESS!
SORRY...
AMAZING! SHE'S HERE!
'CUZ KUN WAS HERE TO PLAY WITH ME, I WASN'T BORED!
YOU'RE 15 MINUTES LATE, TAE.
YOU BEEN FIGHTING AGAIN? YOU GOT MARKS ALL OVER YOUR ARM.
UH...

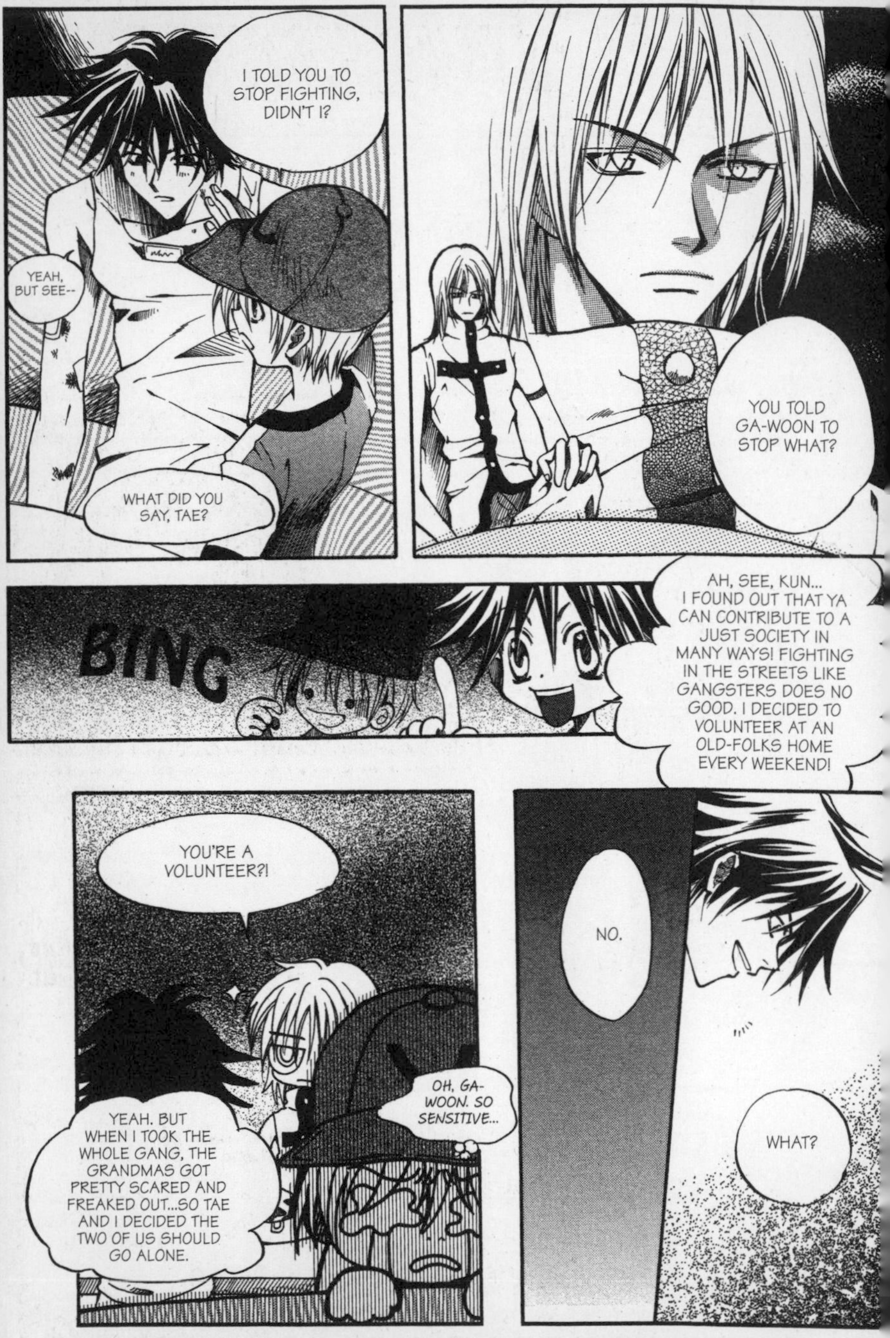
I TOLD YOU TO STOP FIGHTING, DIDN'T I?
YEAH, BUT SEE--
WHAT DID YOU SAY, TAE?
YOU TOLD GA-WOON TO STOP WHAT?
BING
AH, SEE, KUN... I FOUND OUT THAT YA CAN CONTRIBUTE TO A JUST SOCIETY IN MANY WAYS! FIGHTING IN THE STREETS LIKE GANGSTERS DOES NO GOOD. I DECIDED TO VOLUNTEER AT AN OLD-FOLKS HOME EVERY WEEKEND!
YOU'RE A VOLUNTEER?!
YEAH. BUT WHEN I TOOK THE WHOLE GANG, THE GRANDMAS GOT PRETTY SCARED AND FREAKED OUT...SO TAE AND I DECIDED THE TWO OF US SHOULD GO ALONE.
OH, GA-WOON. SO SENSITIVE...
NO.
WHAT?

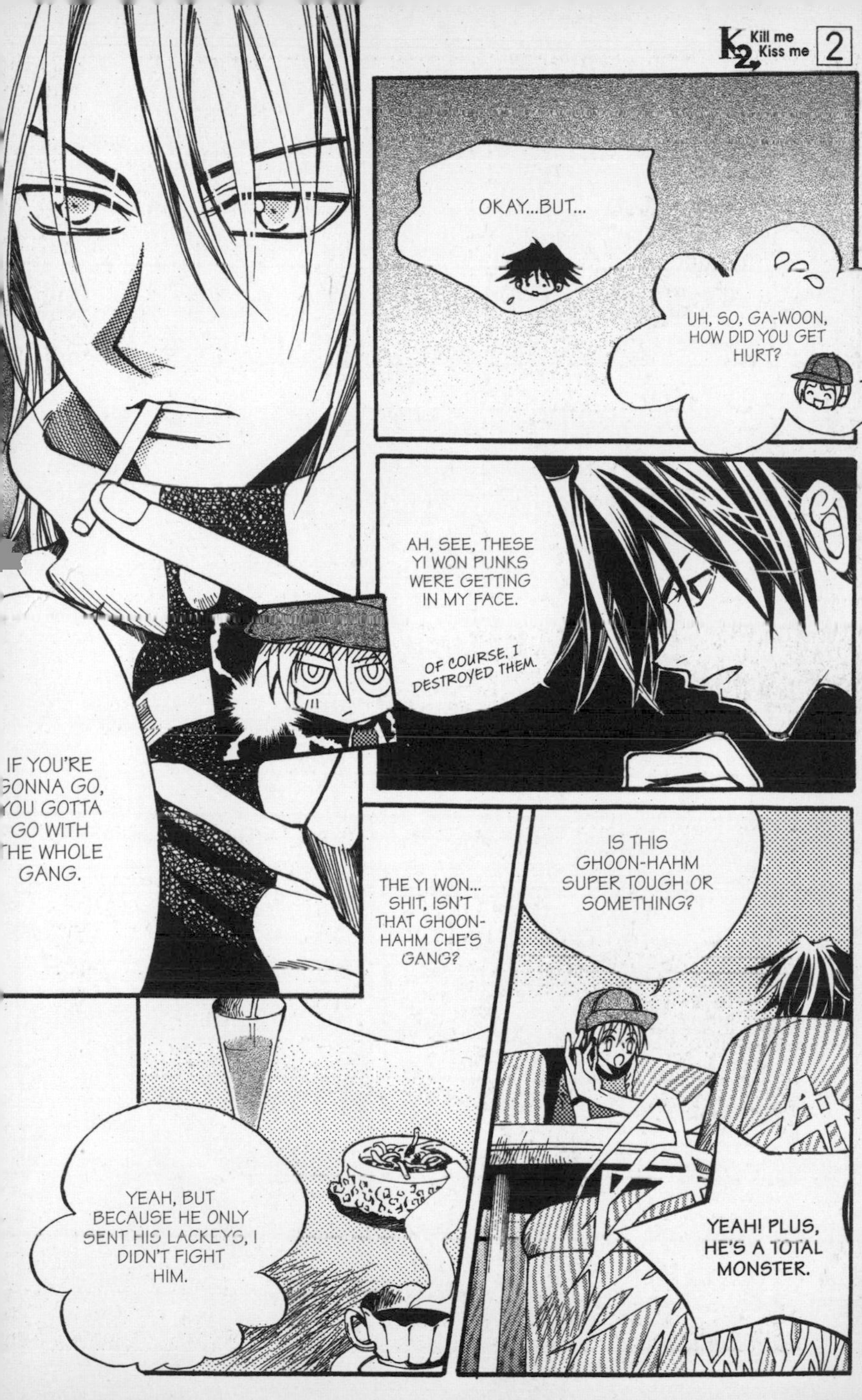
IF YOU'RE GONNA GO, YOU GOTTA GO WITH THE WHOLE GANG.
OKAY...BUT...
UH, SO, GA-WOON, HOW DID YOU GET HURT?
AH, SEE, THESE YI WON PUNKS WERE GETTING IN MY FACE.
OF COURSE, I DESTROYED THEM.
THE YI WON... SHIT, ISN'T THAT GHOON-HAHM CHE'S GANG?
YEAH, BUT BECAUSE HE ONLY SENT HIS LACKEYS, I DIDN'T FIGHT HIM.
IS THIS GHOON-HAHM SUPER TOUGH OR SOMETHING?
YEAH! PLUS, HE'S A TOTAL MONSTER.

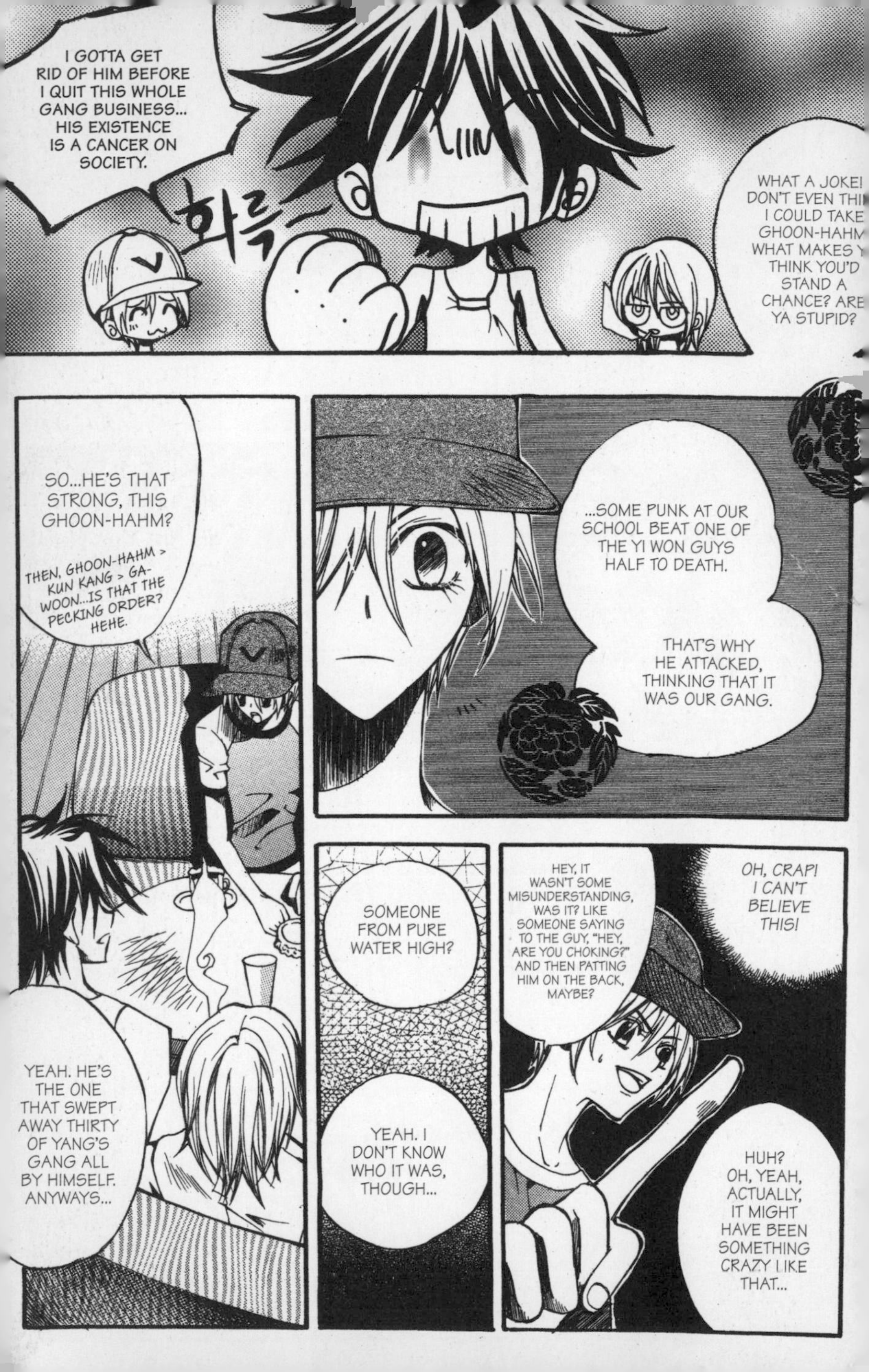
I GOTTA GET RID OF HIM BEFORE I QUIT THIS WHOLE GANG BUSINESS... HIS EXISTENCE IS A CANCER ON SOCIETY.
화륵
WHAT A JOKE! DON'T EVEN THI I COULD TAKE GHOON-HAHM WHAT MAKES Y THINK YOU'D STAND A CHANCE? ARE YA STUPID?
SO...HE'S THAT STRONG, THIS GHOON-HAHM?
THEN, GHOON-HAHM > KUN KANG > GA-WOON...IS THAT THE PECKING ORDER? HEHE.
YEAH. HE'S THE ONE THAT SWEPT AWAY THIRTY OF YANG'S GANG ALL BY HIMSELF. ANYWAYS...
...SOME PUNK AT OUR SCHOOL BEAT ONE OF THE YI WON GUYS HALF TO DEATH.
THAT'S WHY HE ATTACKED, THINKING THAT IT WAS OUR GANG.
SOMEONE FROM PURE WATER HIGH?
YEAH. I DON'T KNOW WHO IT WAS, THOUGH...
HEY, IT WASN'T SOME MISUNDERSTANDING, WAS IT? LIKE SOMEONE SAYING TO THE GUY, "HEY, ARE YOU CHOKING?" AND THEN PATTING HIM ON THE BACK, MAYBE?
OH, CRAP! I CAN'T BELIEVE THIS!
HUH? OH, YEAH, ACTUALLY, IT MIGHT HAVE BEEN SOMETHING CRAZY LIKE THAT...

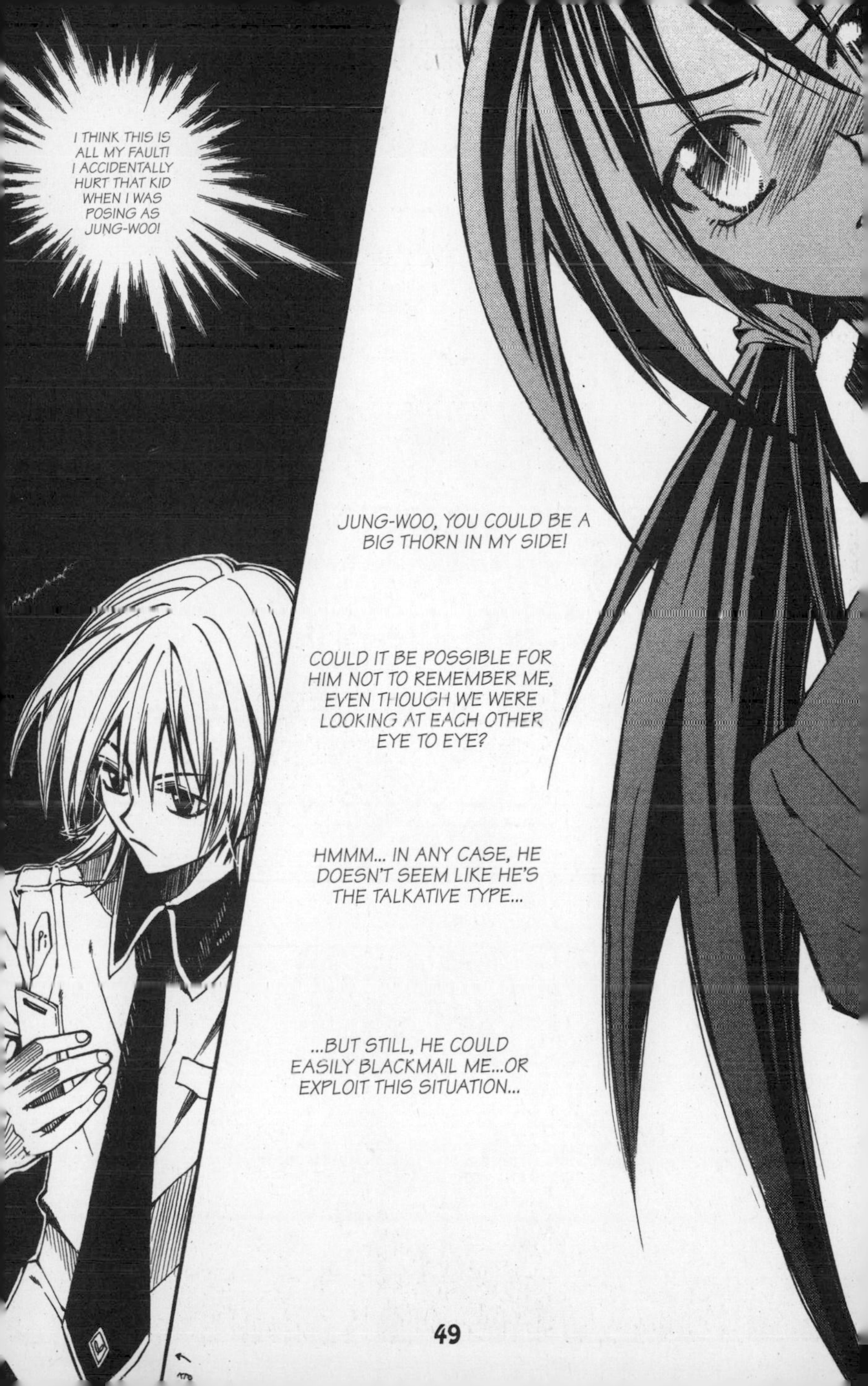
I THINK THIS IS ALL MY FAULT! I ACCIDENTALLY HURT THAT KID WHEN I WAS POSING AS JUNG-WOO!
JUNG-WOO, YOU COULD BE A BIG THORN IN MY SIDE!
COULD IT BE POSSIBLE FOR HIM NOT TO REMEMBER ME, EVEN THOUGH WE WERE LOOKING AT EACH OTHER EYE TO EYE?
HMMM... IN ANY CASE, HE DOESN'T SEEM LIKE HE'S THE TALKATIVE TYPE...
...BUT STILL, HE COULD EASILY BLACKMAIL ME...OR EXPLOIT THIS SITUATION...

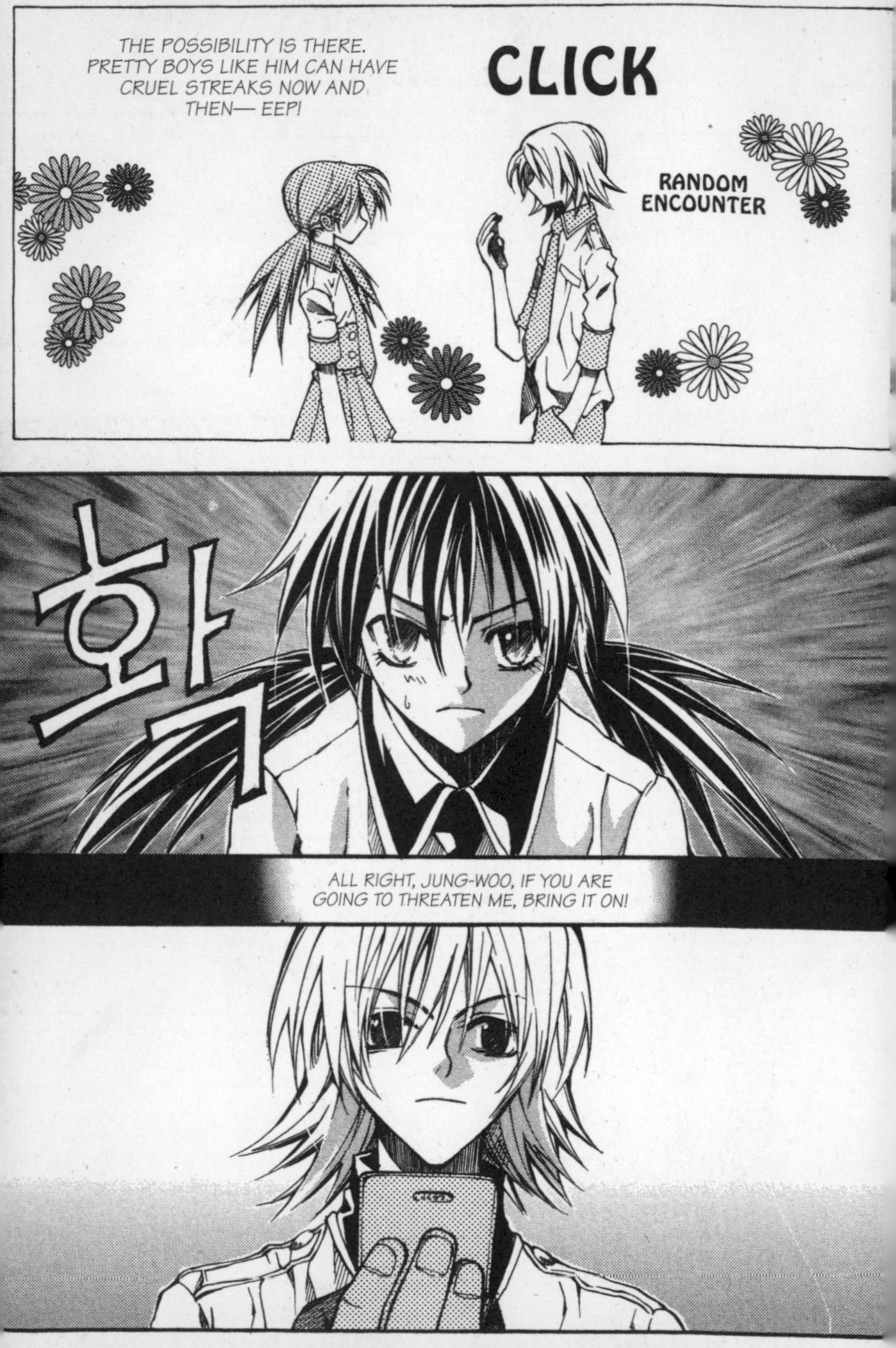
THE POSSIBILITY IS THERE. PRETTY BOYS LIKE HIM CAN HAVE CRUEL STREAKS NOW AND THEN— EEP!
CLICK
RANDOM ENCOUNTER
화
ALL RIGHT, JUNG-WOO, IF YOU ARE GOING TO THREATEN ME, BRING IT ON!

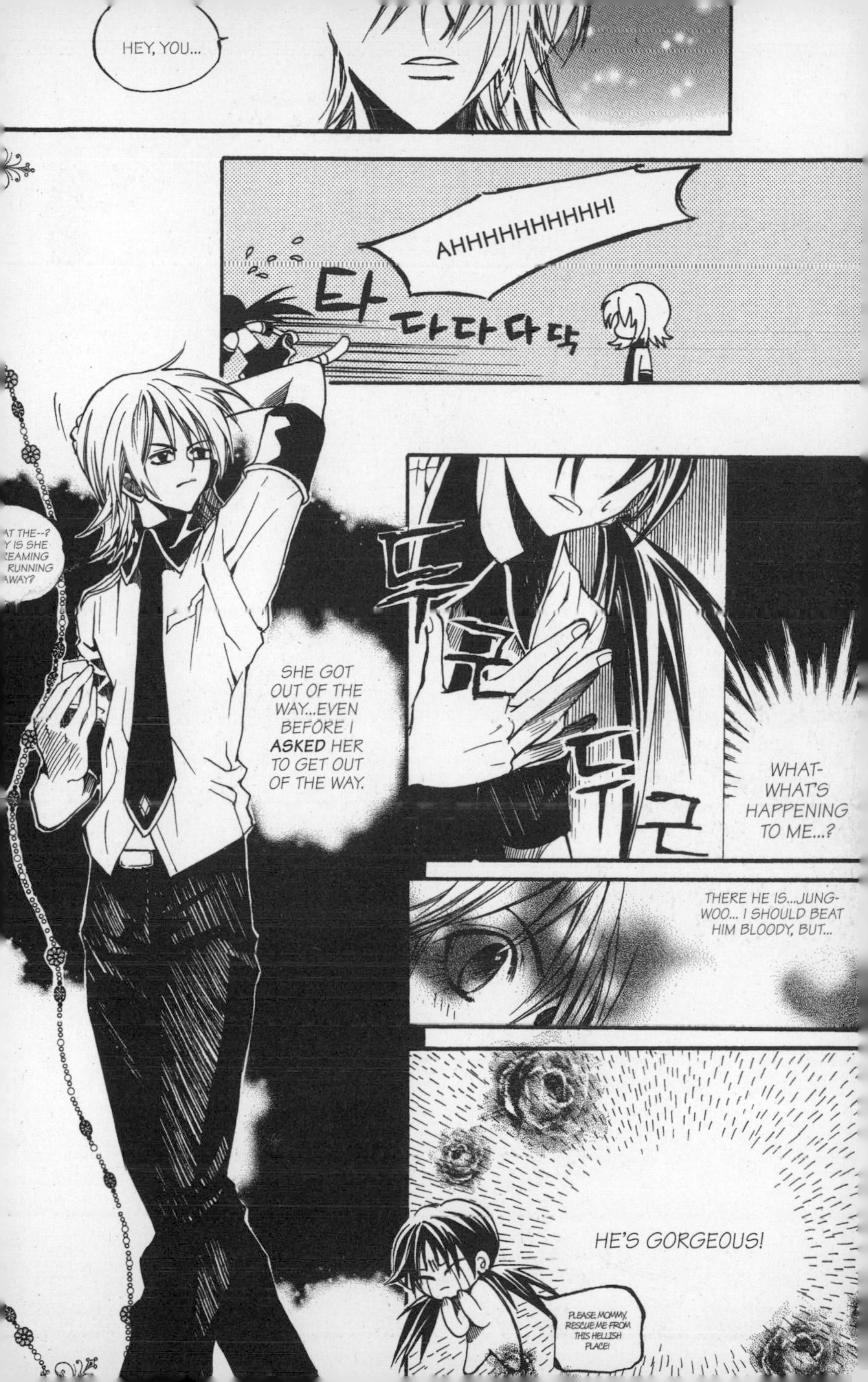
HEY, YOU...
AHHHHHHHHHH!
타다다다다닥
AT THE--? Y IS SHE REAMING RUNNING AWAY?
SHE GOT OUT OF THE WAY...EVEN BEFORE I **ASKED** HER TO GET OUT OF THE WAY.
두근 두근
WHAT-WHAT'S HAPPENING TO ME...?
THERE HE IS...JUNG-WOO... I SHOULD BEAT HIM BLOODY, BUT...
HE'S GORGEOUS!
PLEASE, MOMMY, RESCUE ME FROM THIS HELLISH PLACE!

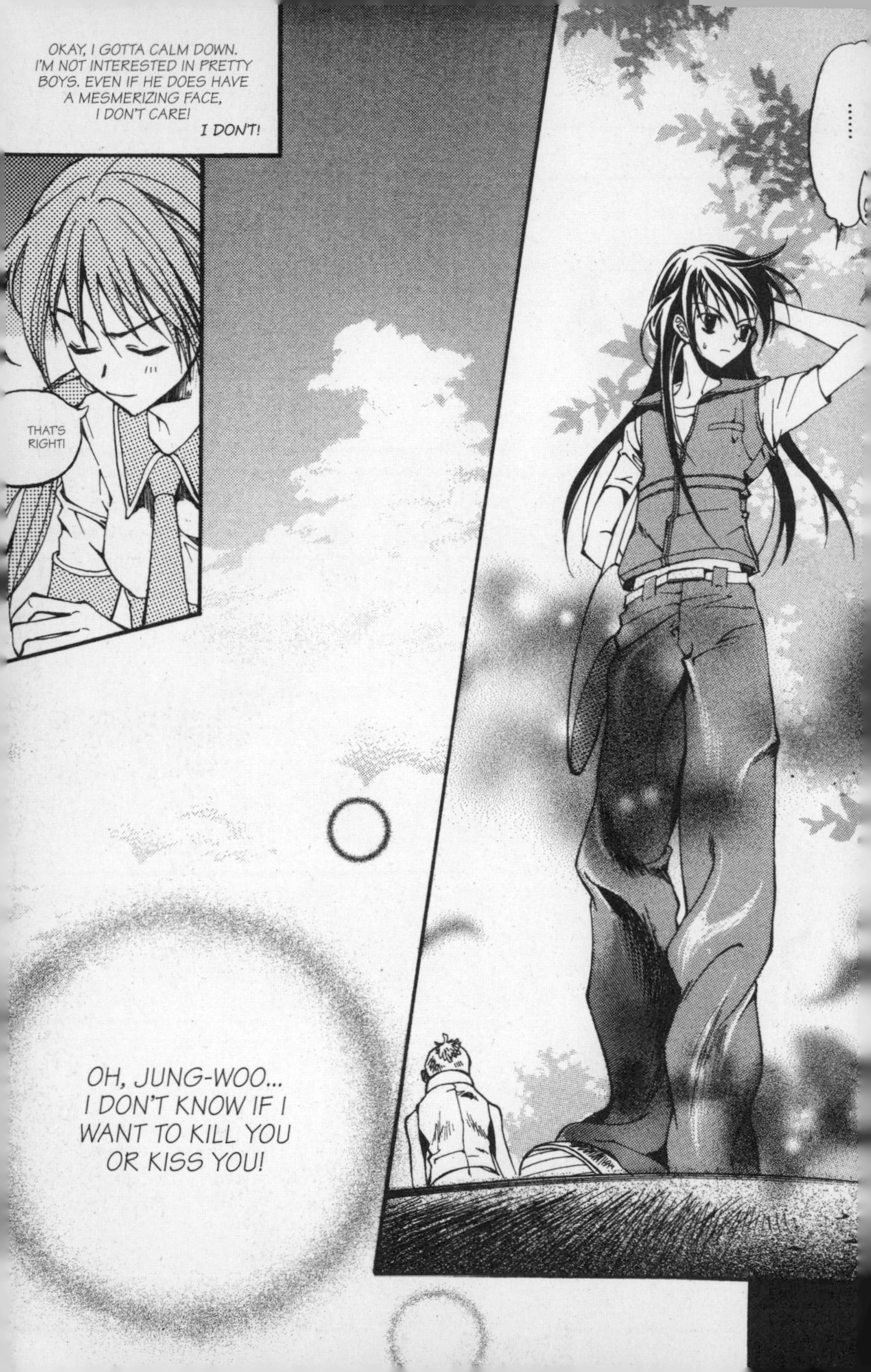
......
OKAY, I GOTTA CALM DOWN. I'M NOT INTERESTED IN PRETTY BOYS. EVEN IF HE DOES HAVE A MESMERIZING FACE, I DON'T CARE!
I DON'T!
THAT'S RIGHT!
OH, JUNG-WOO... I DON'T KNOW IF I WANT TO KILL YOU OR KISS YOU!

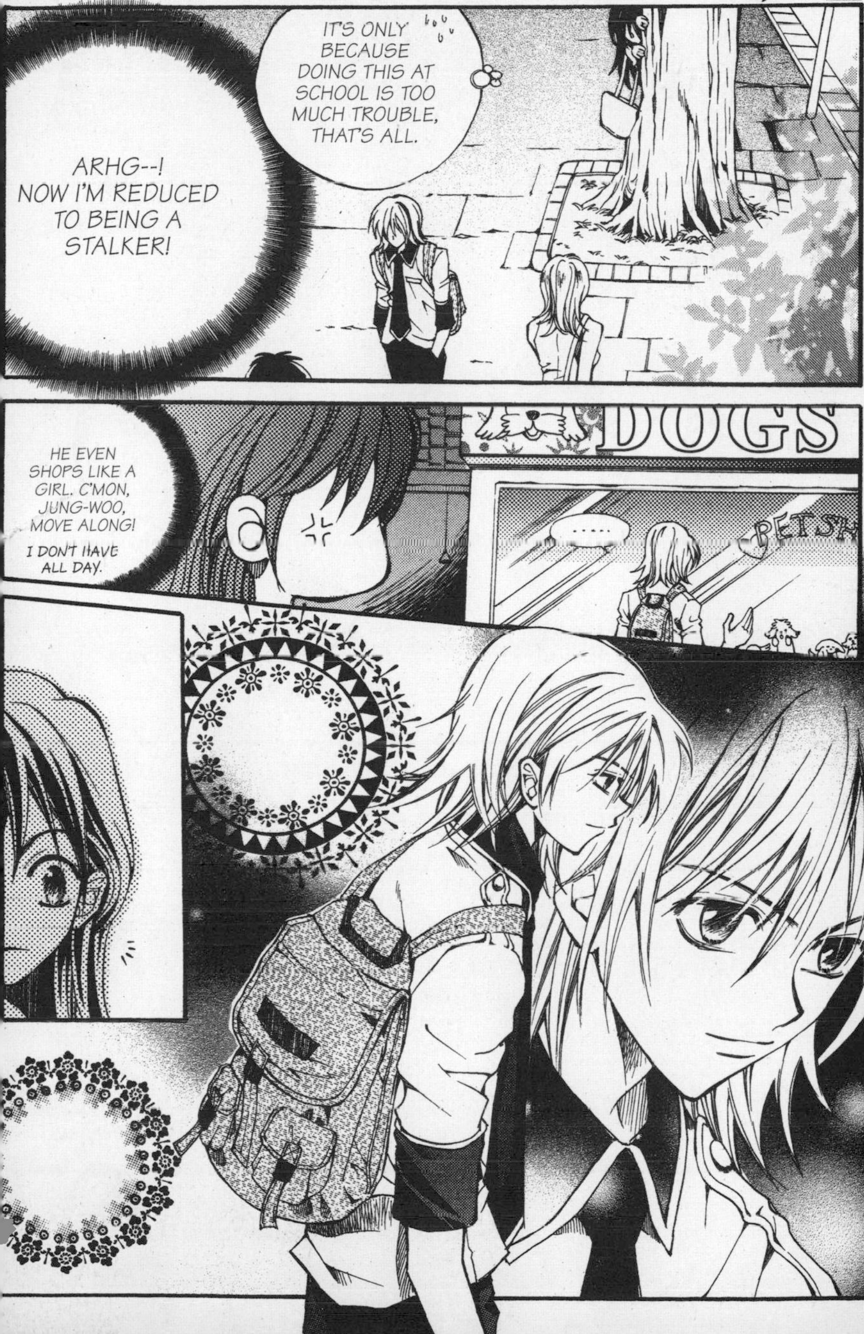
ARHG--! NOW I'M REDUCED TO BEING A STALKER!
IT'S ONLY BECAUSE DOING THIS AT SCHOOL IS TOO MUCH TROUBLE, THAT'S ALL.
DOGS
HE EVEN SHOPS LIKE A GIRL. C'MON, JUNG-WOO, MOVE ALONG!
I DON'T HAVE ALL DAY.
.....

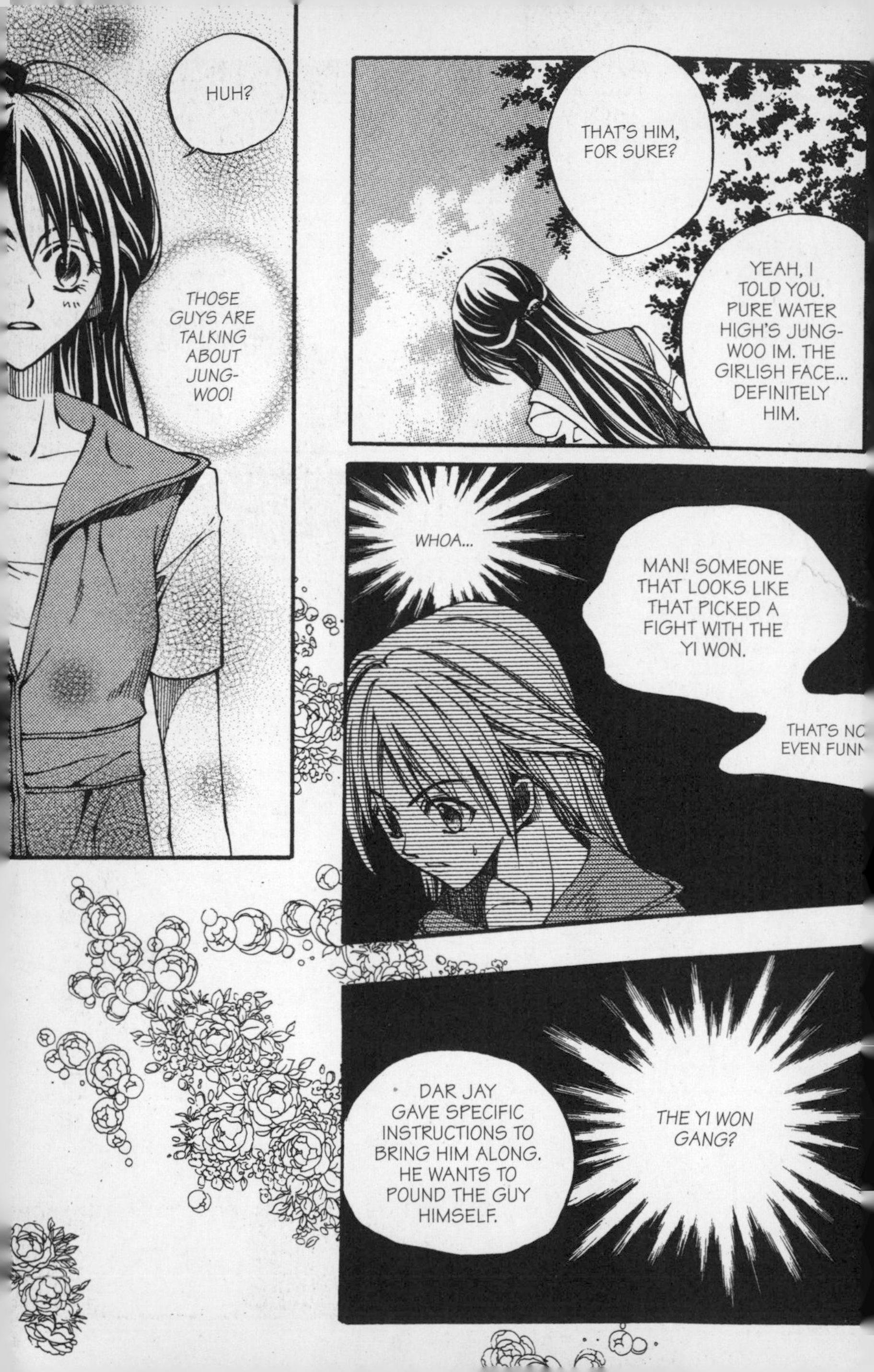
HUH?
THOSE GUYS ARE TALKING ABOUT JUNG-WOO!
THAT'S HIM, FOR SURE?
YEAH, I TOLD YOU. PURE WATER HIGH'S JUNG-WOO IM. THE GIRLISH FACE... DEFINITELY HIM.
WHOA...
MAN! SOMEONE THAT LOOKS LIKE THAT PICKED A FIGHT WITH THE YI WON.
DAR JAY GAVE SPECIFIC INSTRUCTIONS TO BRING HIM ALONG. HE WANTS TO POUND THE GUY HIMSELF.
THE YI WON GANG?

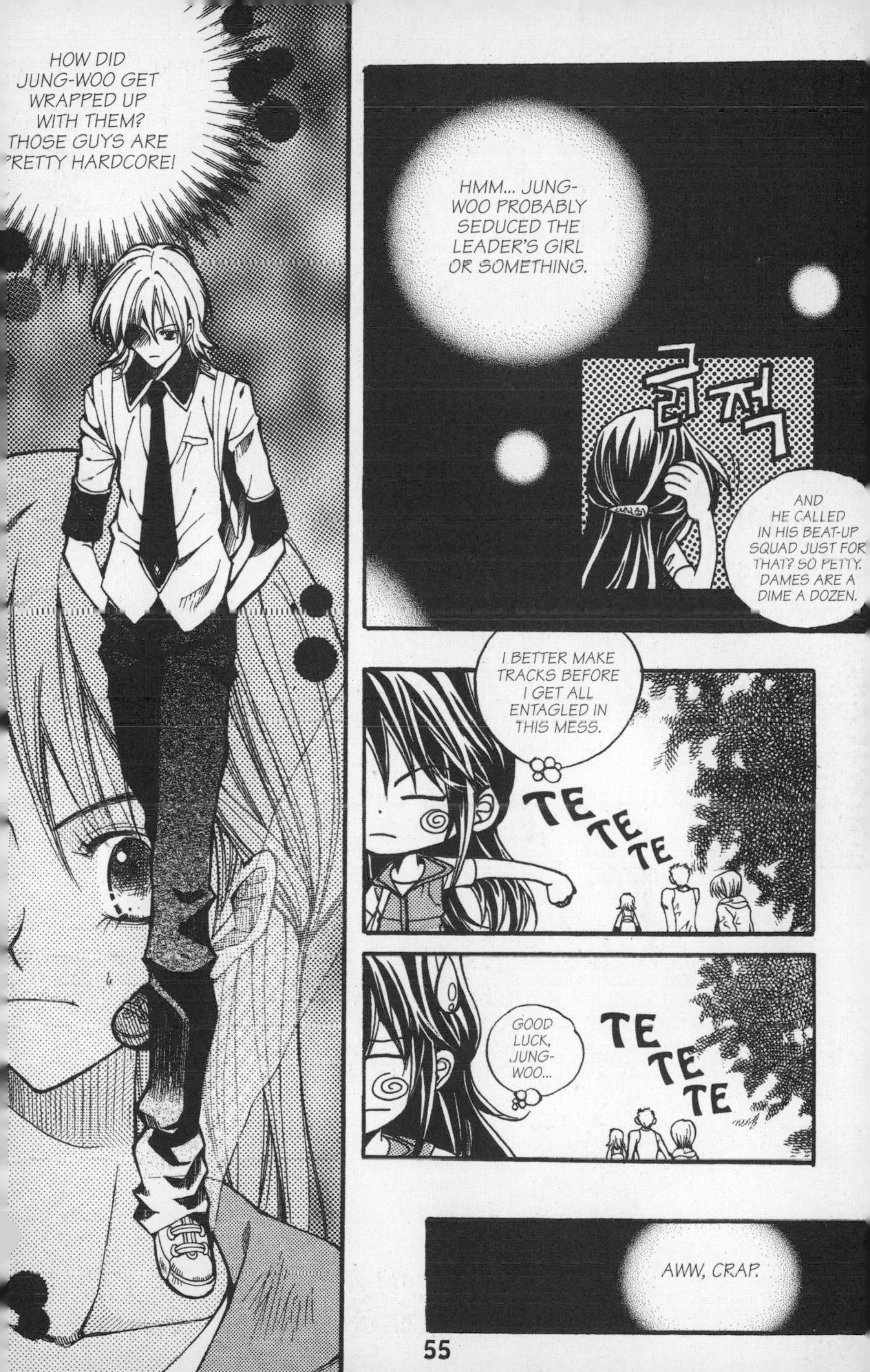
HOW DID JUNG-WOO GET WRAPPED UP WITH THEM? THOSE GUYS ARE PRETTY HARDCORE!
HMM... JUNG-WOO PROBABLY SEDUCED THE LEADER'S GIRL OR SOMETHING.
긁적
AND HE CALLED IN HIS BEAT-UP SQUAD JUST FOR THAT? SO PETTY. DAMES ARE A DIME A DOZEN.
I BETTER MAKE TRACKS BEFORE I GET ALL ENTAGLED IN THIS MESS.
TE TE TE TE
GOOD LUCK, JUNG-WOO...
TE TE TE TE
AWW, CRAP.

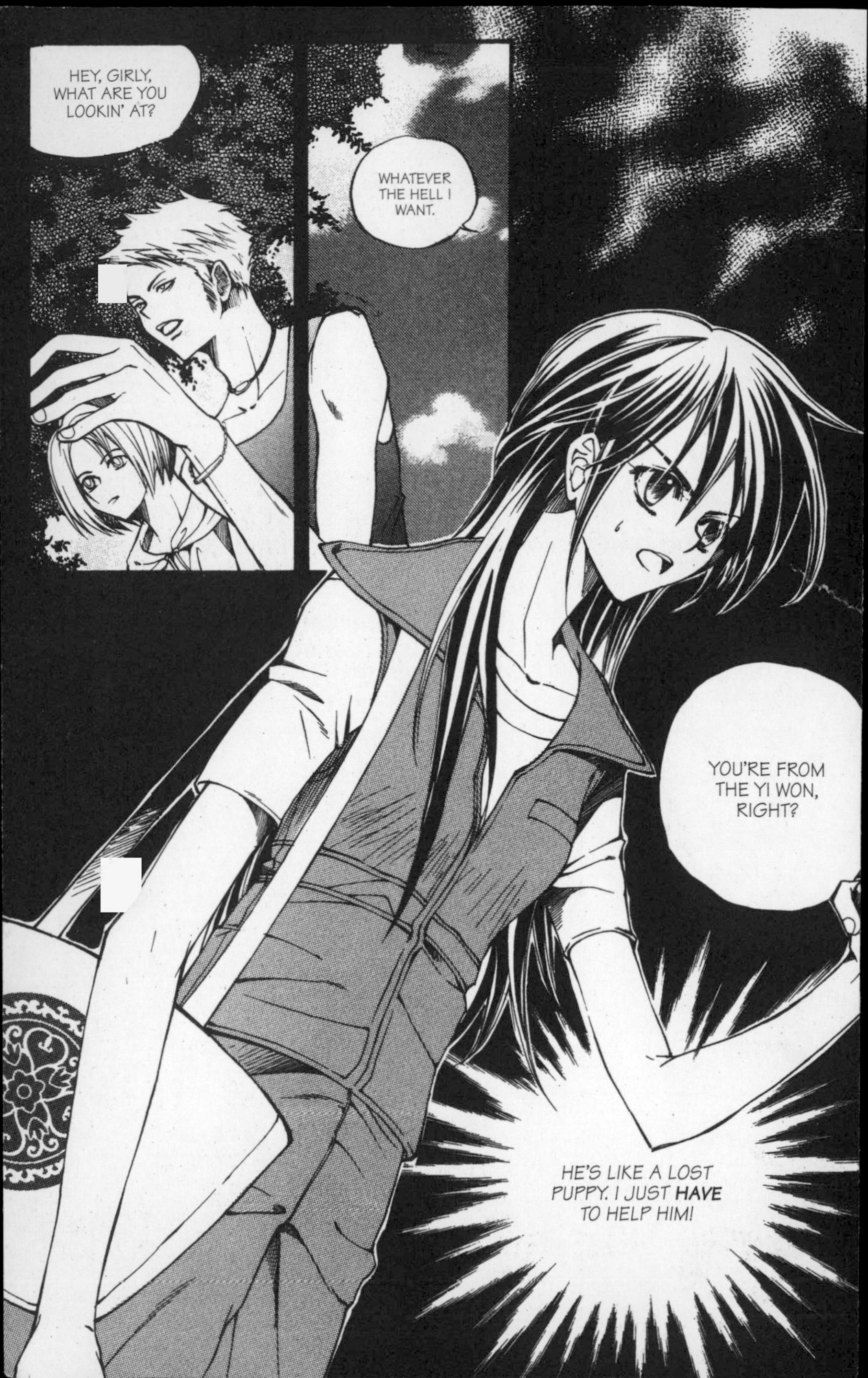
HEY, GIRLY, WHAT ARE YOU LOOKIN' AT?
WHATEVER THE HELL I WANT.
YOU'RE FROM THE YI WON, RIGHT?
HE'S LIKE A LOST PUPPY. I JUST **HAVE** TO HELP HIM!

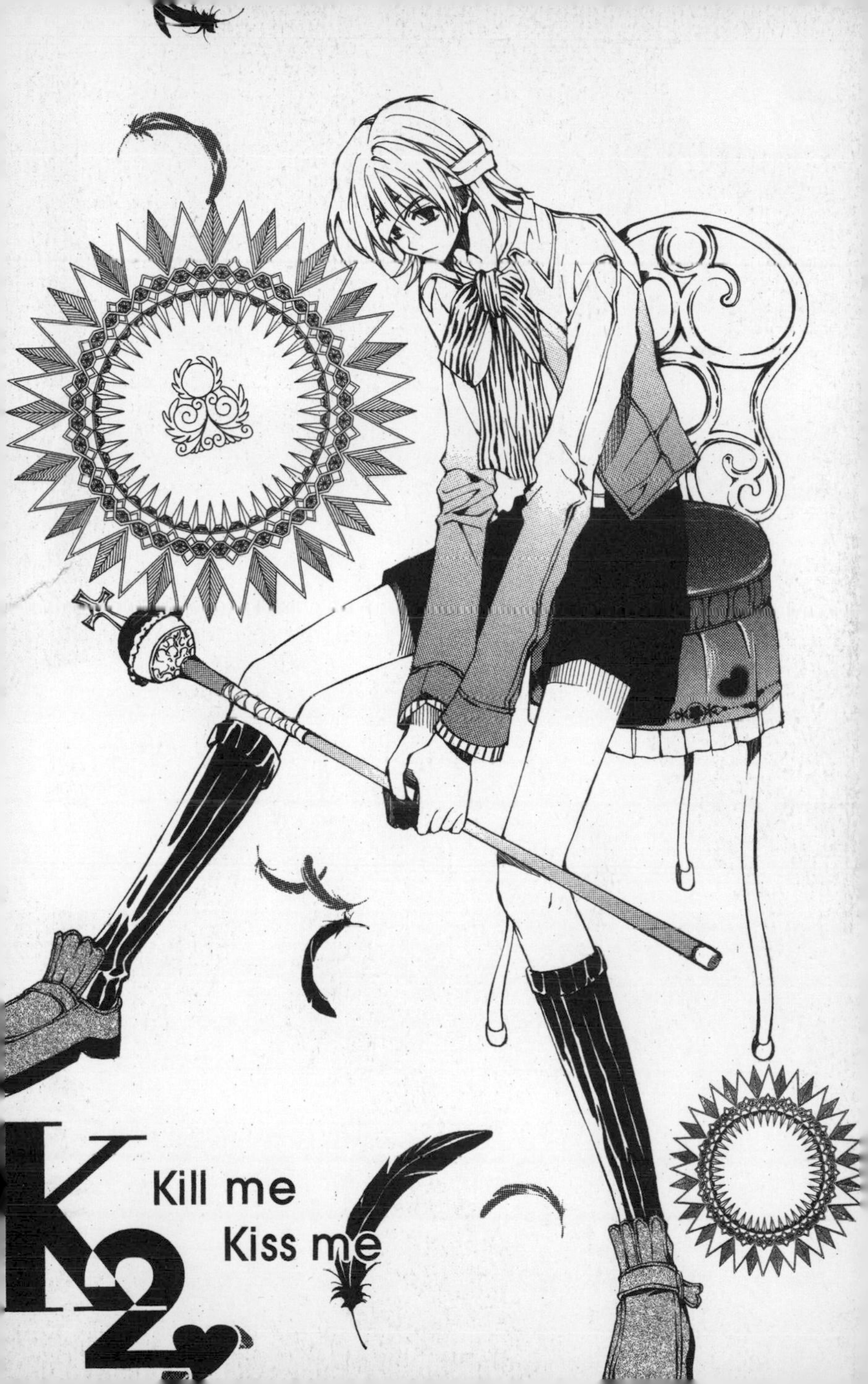
K2
Kill me
Kiss me

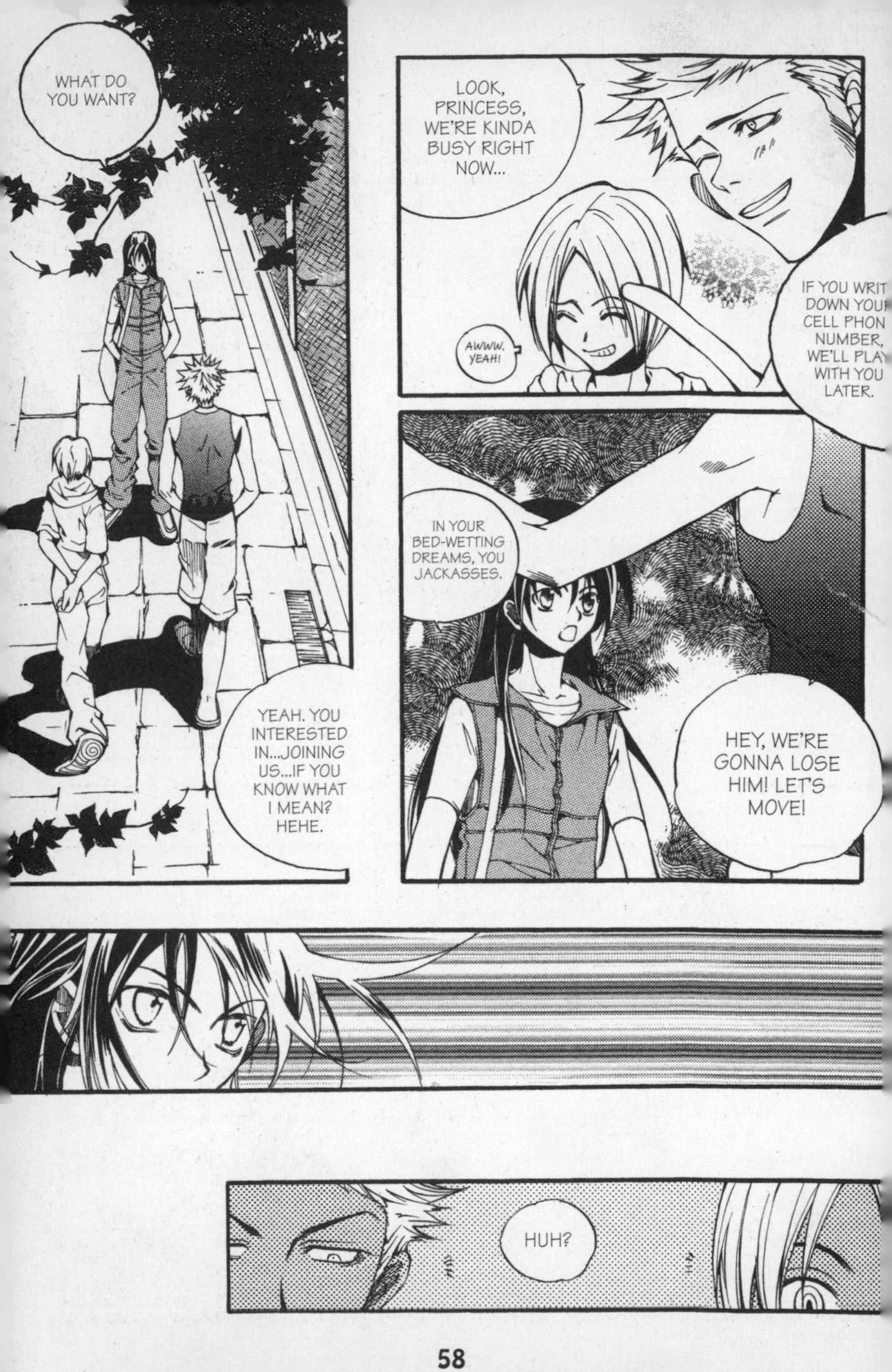
WHAT DO YOU WANT?
YEAH. YOU INTERESTED IN...JOINING US...IF YOU KNOW WHAT I MEAN? HEHE.
LOOK, PRINCESS, WE'RE KINDA BUSY RIGHT NOW...
AWWW, YEAH!
IF YOU WRIT DOWN YOUR CELL PHON NUMBER, WE'LL PLAY WITH YOU LATER.
IN YOUR BED-WETTING DREAMS, YOU JACKASSES.
HEY, WE'RE GONNA LOSE HIM! LET'S MOVE!
HUH?

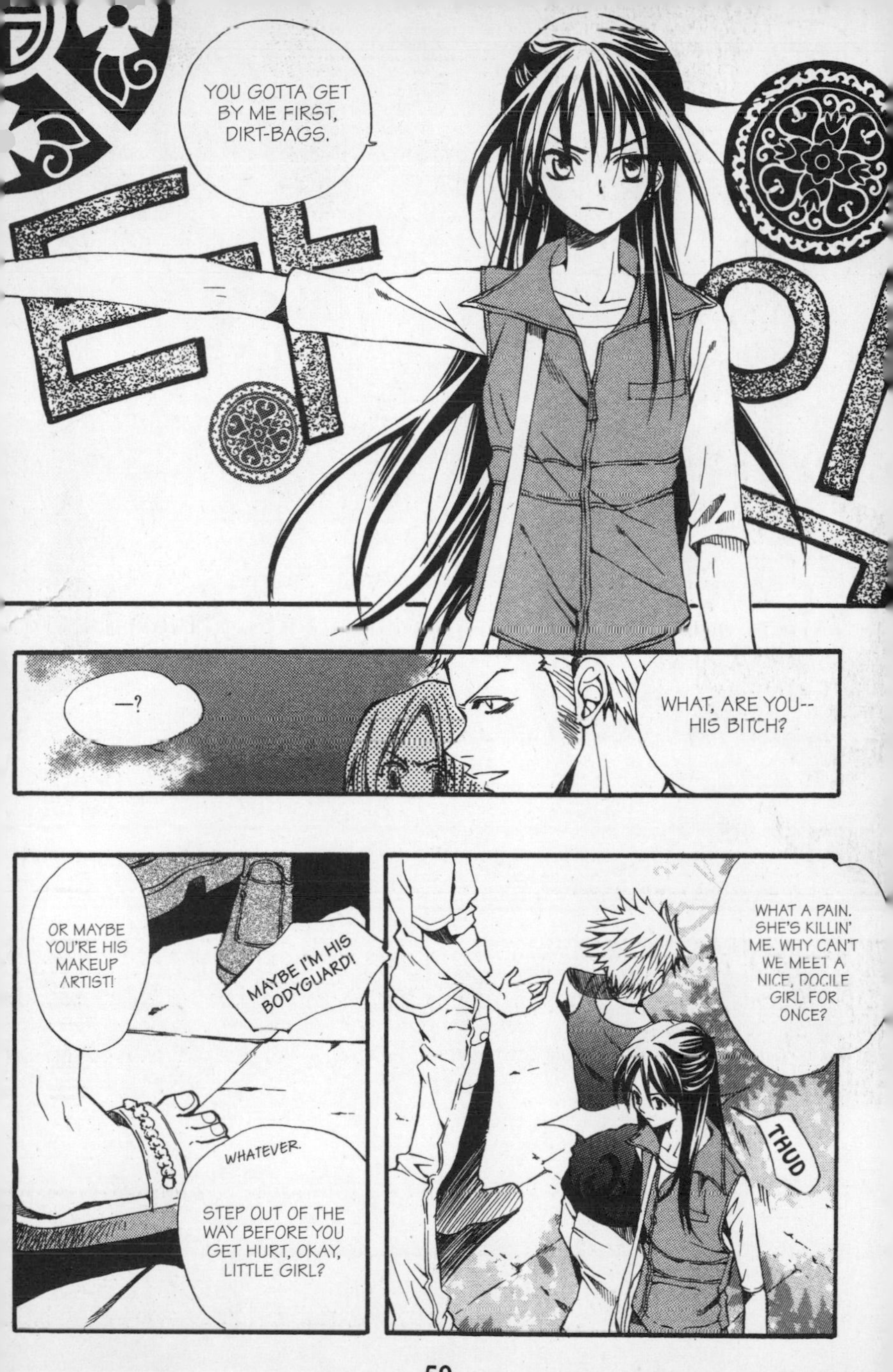
YOU GOTTA GET BY ME FIRST, DIRT-BAGS.
—?
WHAT, ARE YOU-- HIS BITCH?
OR MAYBE YOU'RE HIS MAKEUP ARTIST!
MAYBE I'M HIS BODYGUARD!
WHATEVER.
STEP OUT OF THE WAY BEFORE YOU GET HURT, OKAY, LITTLE GIRL?
WHAT A PAIN. SHE'S KILLIN' ME. WHY CAN'T WE MEET A NICE, DOCILE GIRL FOR ONCE?
THUD

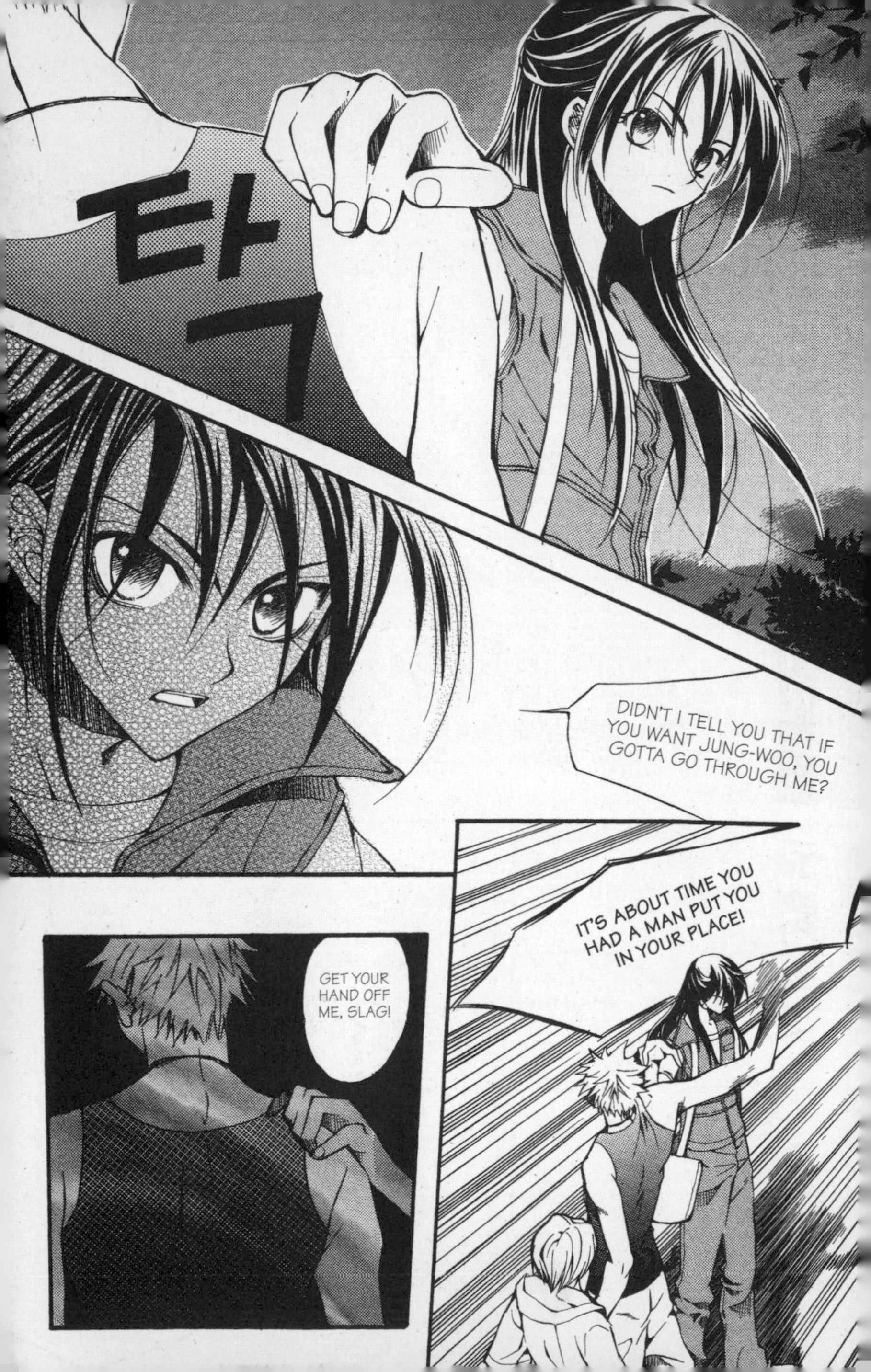
탁
DIDN'T I TELL YOU THAT IF YOU WANT JUNG-WOO, YOU GOTTA GO THROUGH ME?
GET YOUR HAND OFF ME, SLAG!
IT'S ABOUT TIME YOU HAD A MAN PUT YOU IN YOUR PLACE!

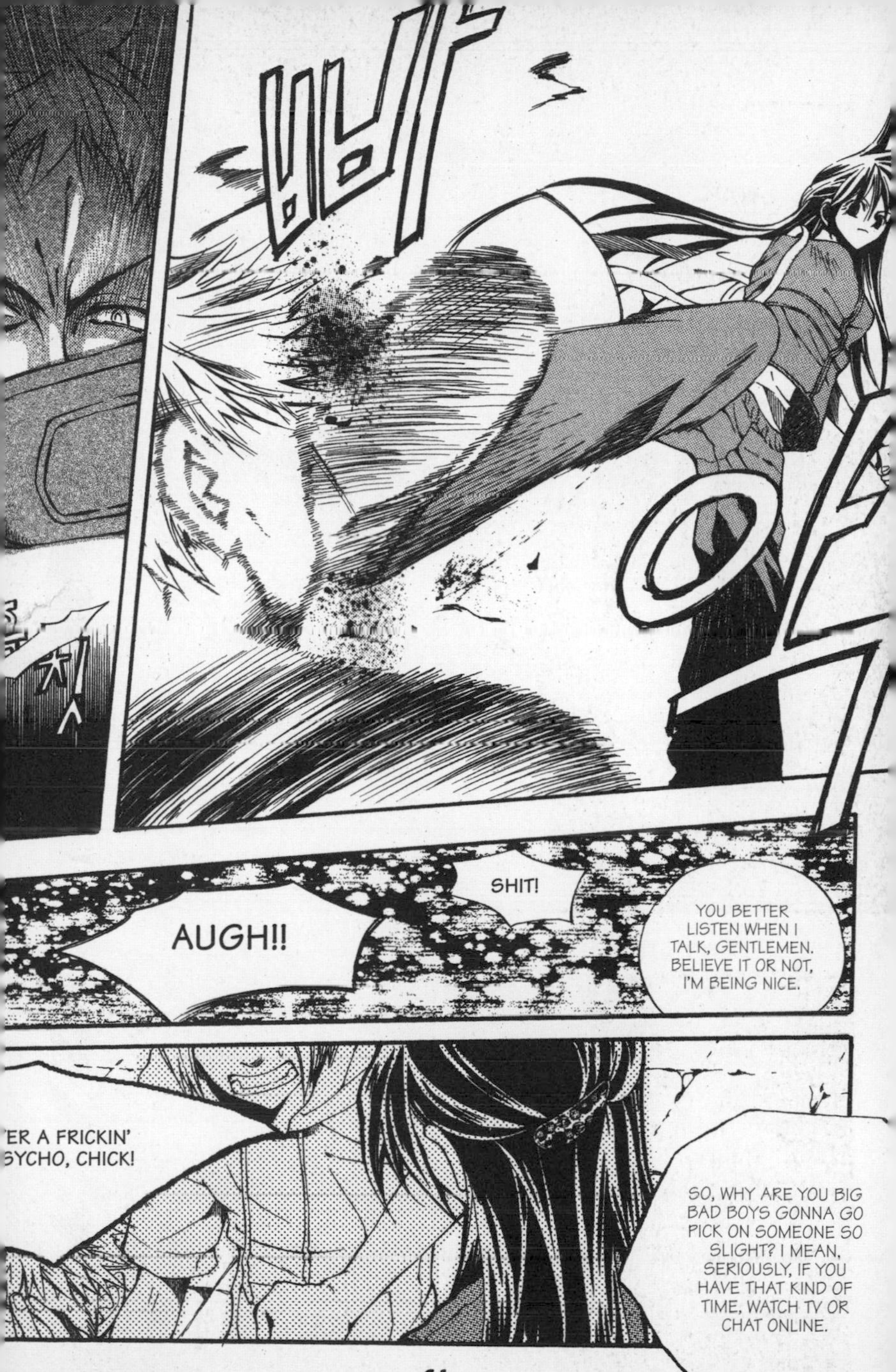
AUGH!!
SHIT!
YOU BETTER LISTEN WHEN I TALK, GENTLEMEN. BELIEVE IT OR NOT, I'M BEING NICE.
'ER A FRICKIN' SYCHO, CHICK!
SO, WHY ARE YOU BIG BAD BOYS GONNA GO PICK ON SOMEONE SO SLIGHT? I MEAN, SERIOUSLY, IF YOU HAVE THAT KIND OF TIME, WATCH TV OR CHAT ONLINE.

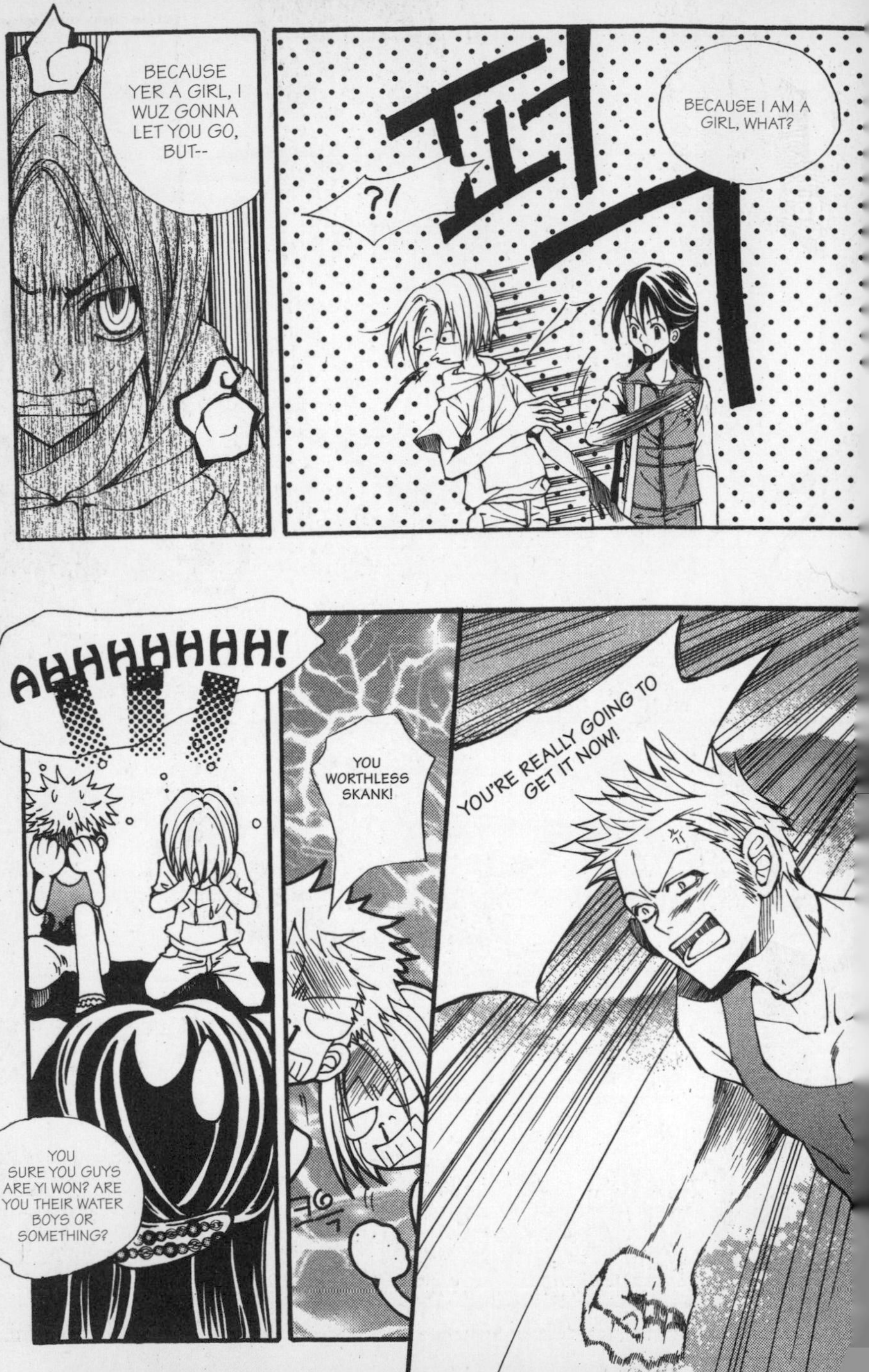
BECAUSE YER A GIRL, I WUZ GONNA LET YOU GO, BUT--
?!
BECAUSE I AM A GIRL, WHAT?
AHHHHHHH!
YOU SURE YOU GUYS ARE YI WON? ARE YOU THEIR WATER BOYS OR SOMETHING?
YOU WORTHLESS SKANK!
YOU'RE REALLY GOING TO GET IT NOW!

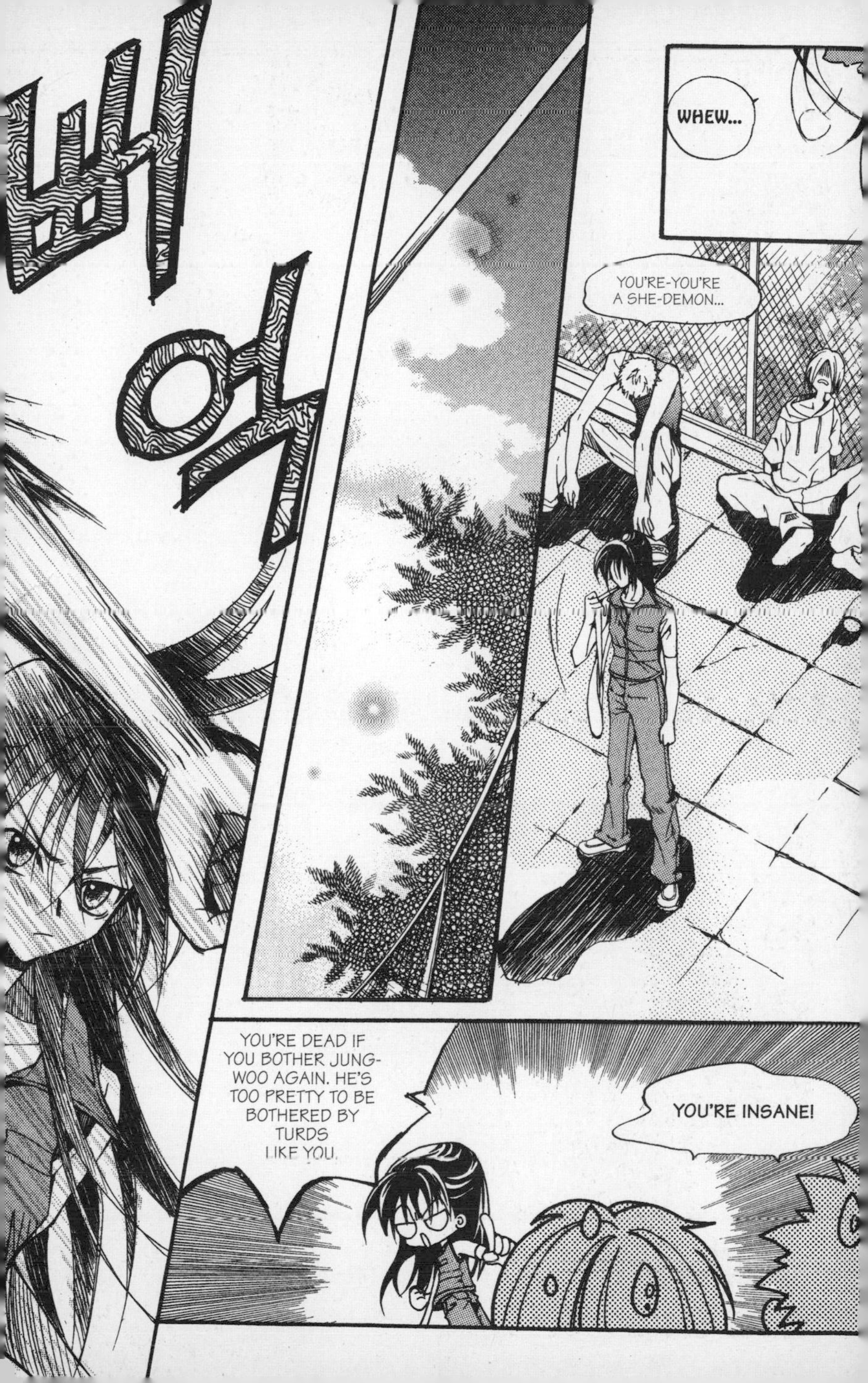
WHEW...
YOU'RE-YOU'RE A SHE-DEMON...
YOU'RE DEAD IF YOU BOTHER JUNG-WOO AGAIN. HE'S TOO PRETTY TO BE BOTHERED BY TURDS LIKE YOU.
YOU'RE INSANE!

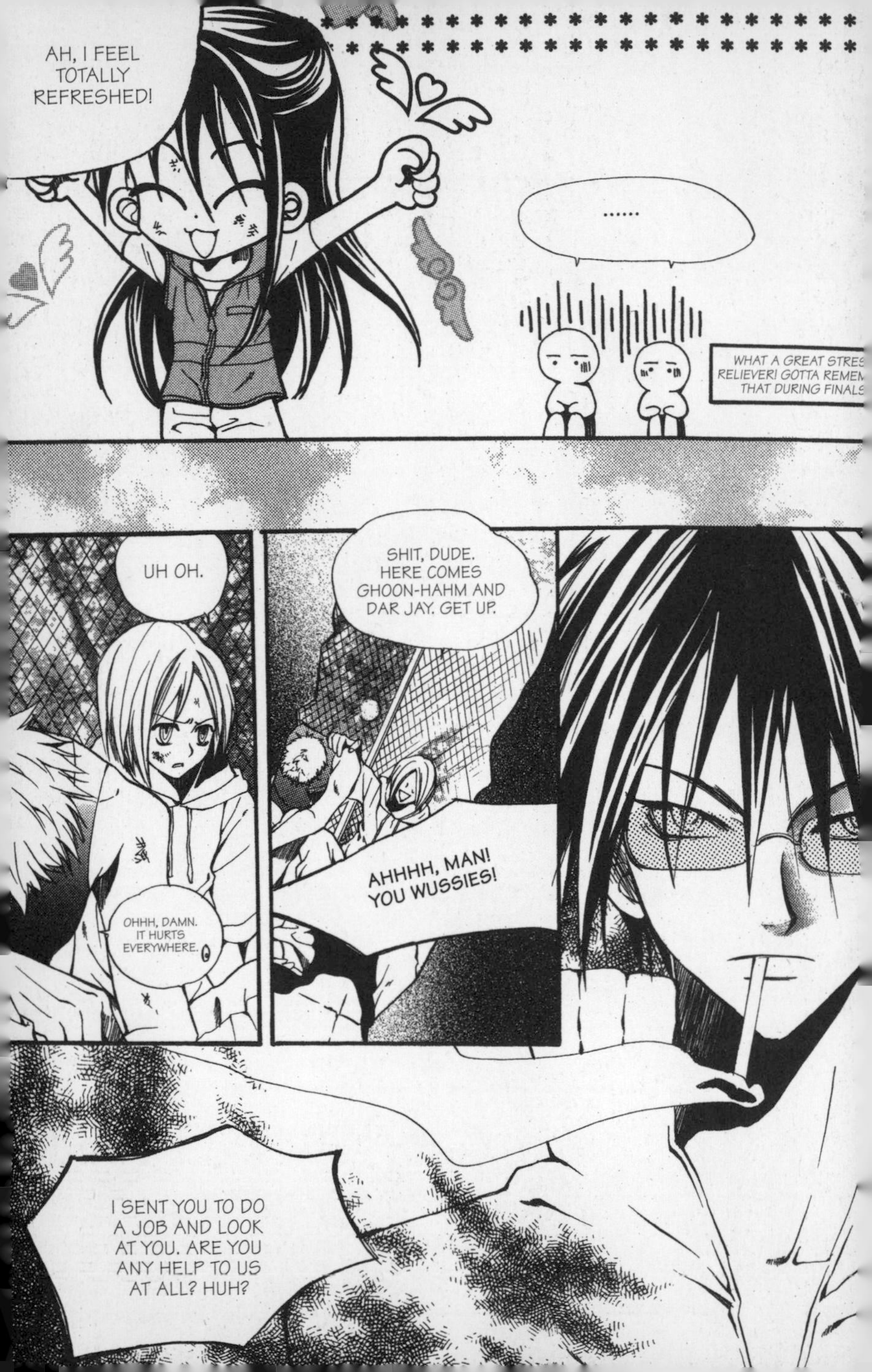
AH, I FEEL TOTALLY REFRESHED!
......
WHAT A GREAT STRES RELIEVER! GOTTA REMEM THAT DURING FINALS
UH OH.
OHHH, DAMN. IT HURTS EVERYWHERE.
SHIT, DUDE. HERE COMES GHOON-HAHM AND DAR JAY. GET UP.
AHHHH, MAN! YOU WUSSIES!
I SENT YOU TO DO A JOB AND LOOK AT YOU. ARE YOU ANY HELP TO US AT ALL? HUH?

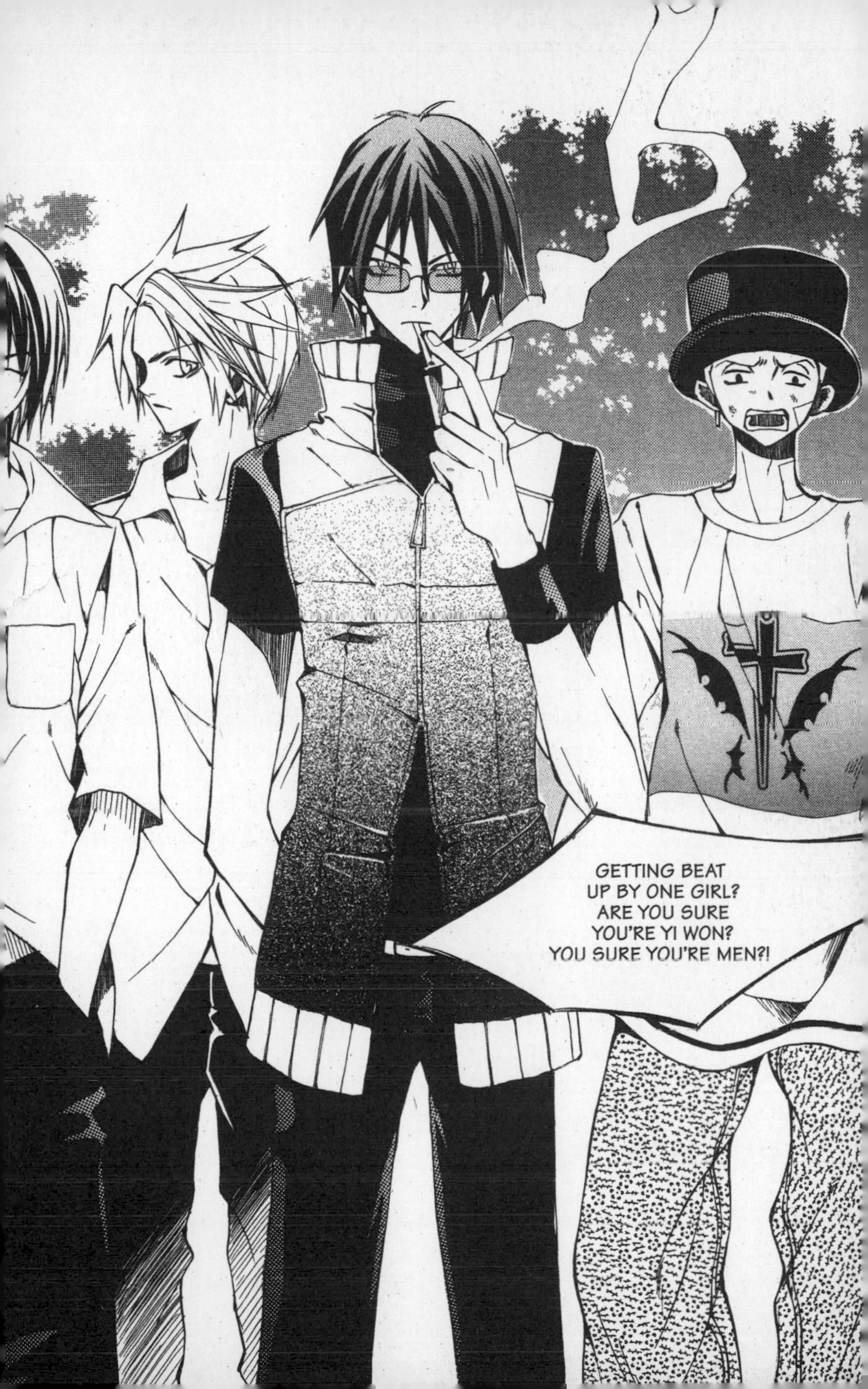
GETTING BEAT UP BY ONE GIRL? ARE YOU SURE YOU'RE YI WON? YOU SURE YOU'RE MEN?!

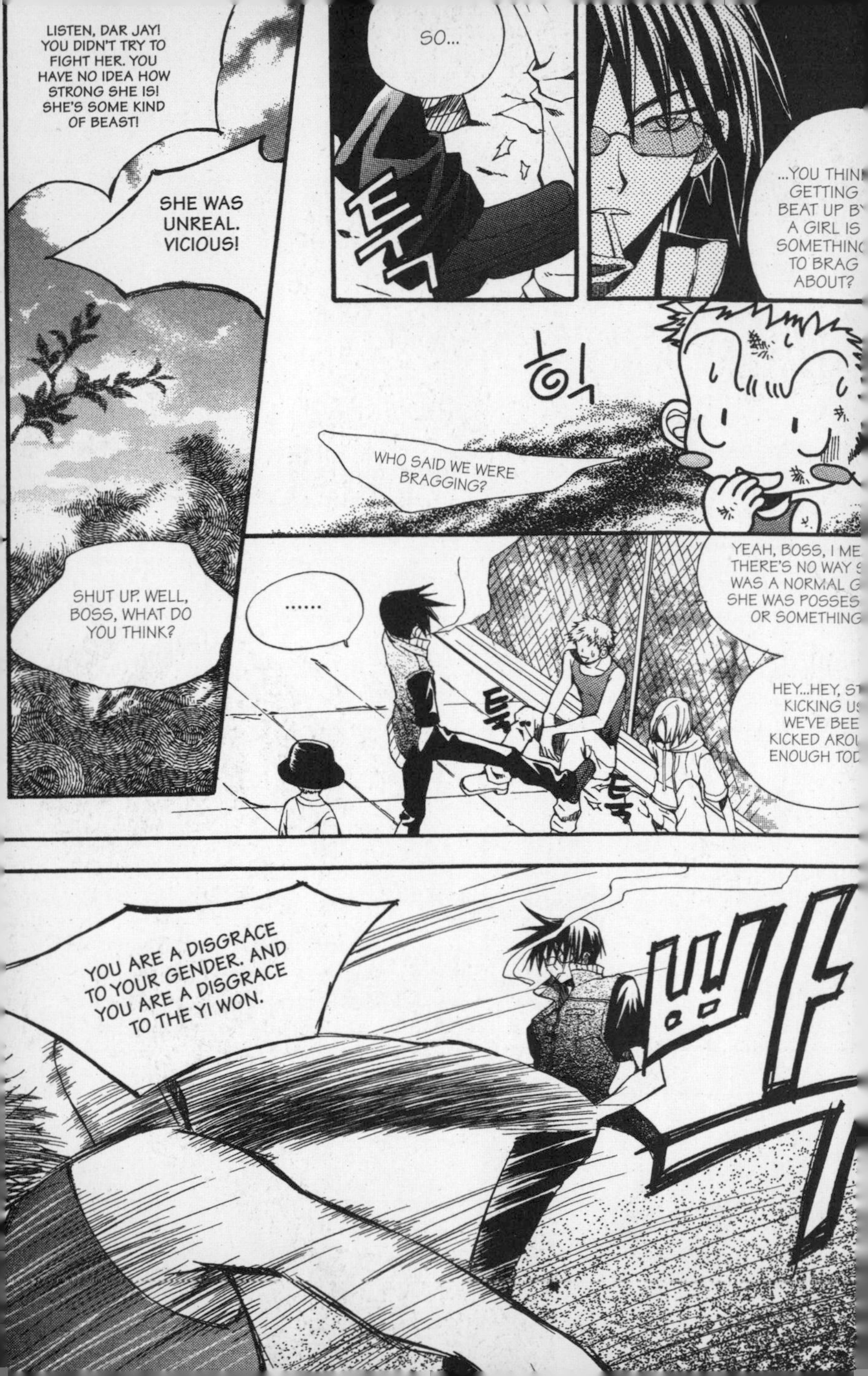
LISTEN, DAR JAY! YOU DIDN'T TRY TO FIGHT HER. YOU HAVE NO IDEA HOW STRONG SHE IS! SHE'S SOME KIND OF BEAST!
SHE WAS UNREAL. VICIOUS!
SO...
...YOU THIN GETTING BEAT UP B A GIRL IS SOMETHIN TO BRAG ABOUT?
흥
WHO SAID WE WERE BRAGGING?
SHUT UP. WELL, BOSS, WHAT DO YOU THINK?
....
YEAH, BOSS, I ME THERE'S NO WAY S WAS A NORMAL G SHE WAS POSSES OR SOMETHING
툭
툭
HEY...HEY, ST KICKING US WE'VE BEE KICKED ARO ENOUGH TOD
YOU ARE A DISGRACE TO YOUR GENDER. AND YOU ARE A DISGRACE TO THE YI WON.

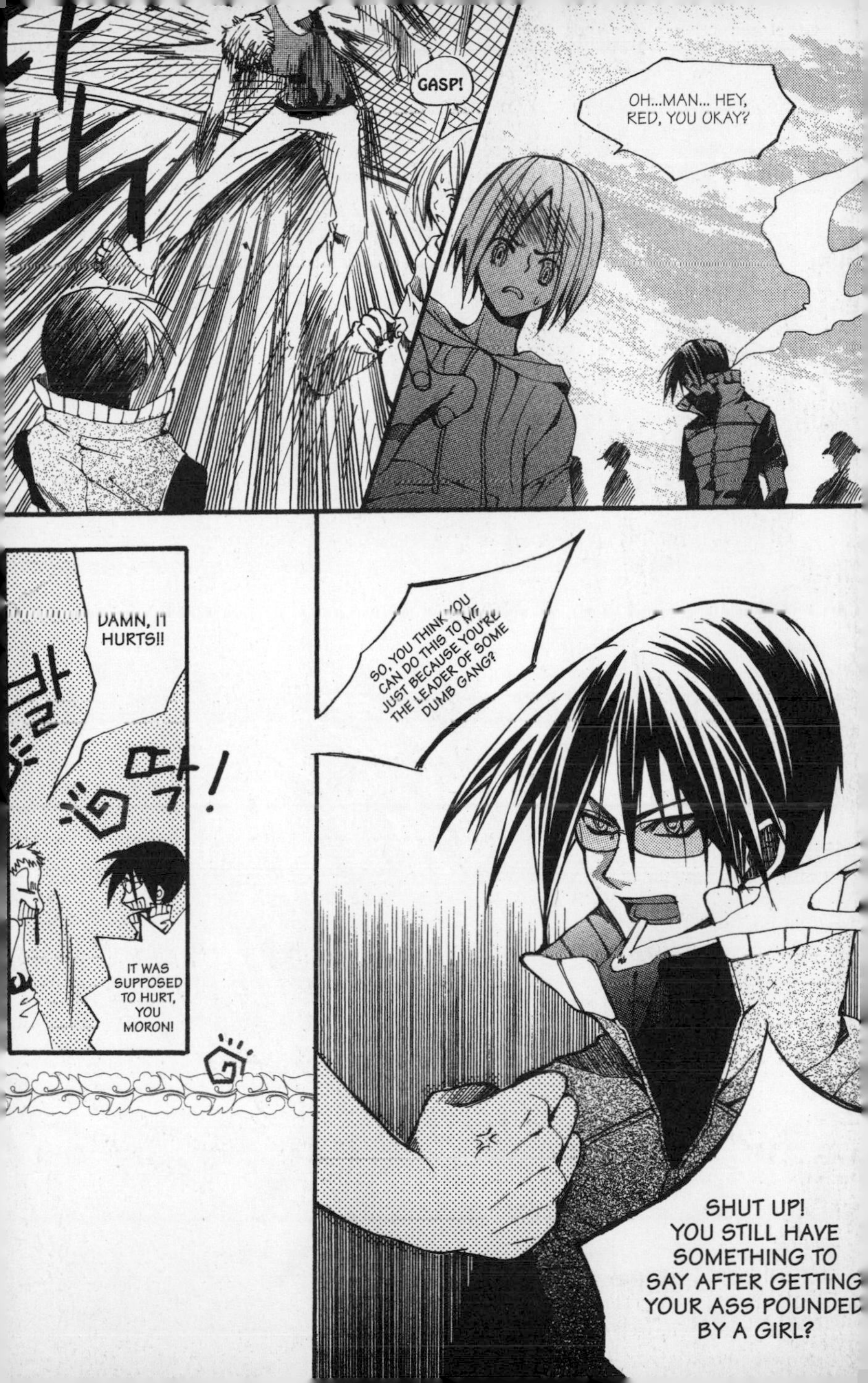
GASP!
OH...MAN... HEY, RED, YOU OKAY?
DAMN, IT HURTS!!
IT WAS SUPPOSED TO HURT, YOU MORON!
SO, YOU THINK YOU CAN DO THIS TO ME JUST BECAUSE YOU'RE THE LEADER OF SOME DUMB GANG?
SHUT UP! YOU STILL HAVE SOMETHING TO SAY AFTER GETTING YOUR ASS POUNDED BY A GIRL?

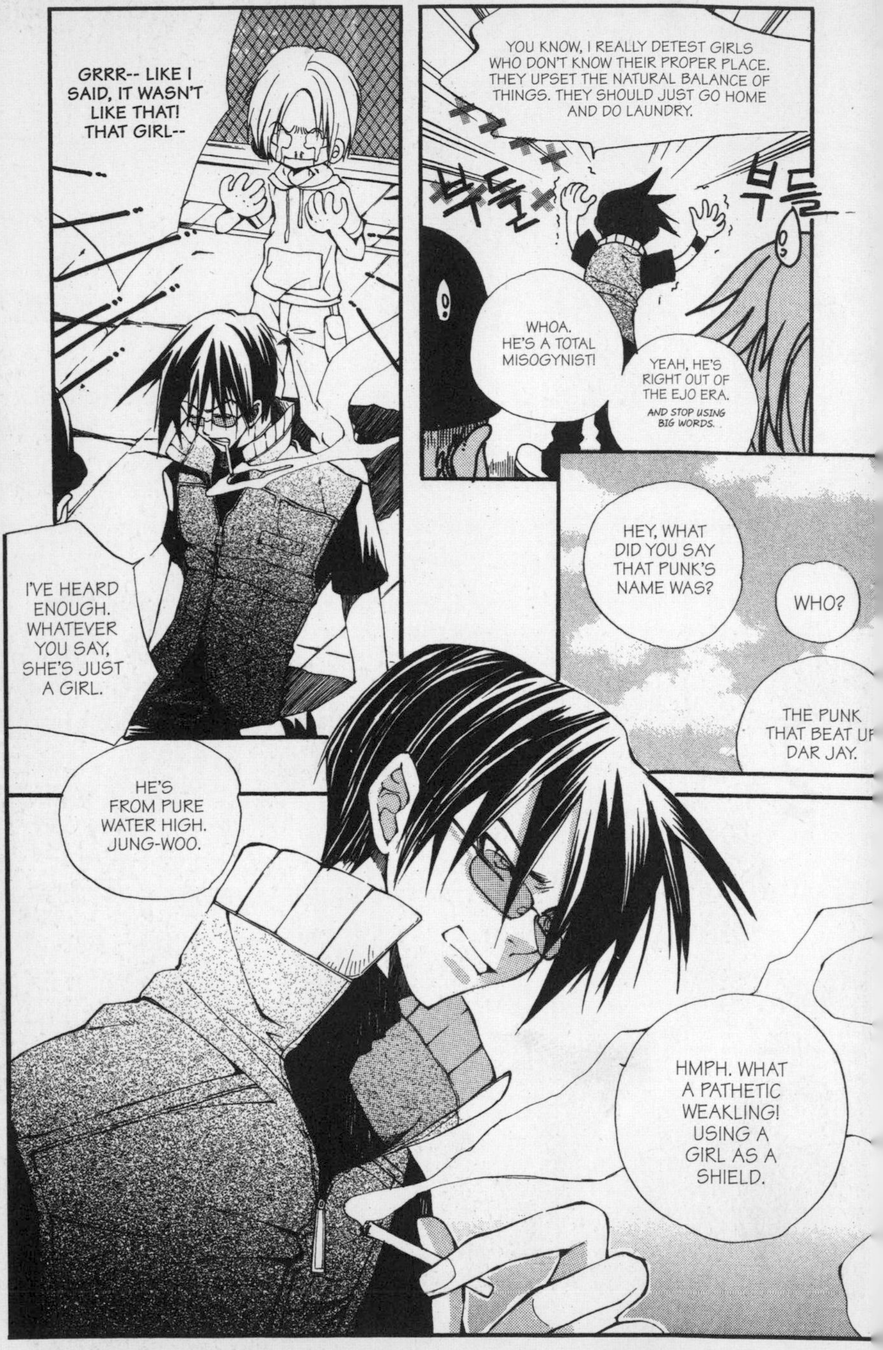
GRRR-- LIKE I SAID, IT WASN'T LIKE THAT! THAT GIRL--
I'VE HEARD ENOUGH. WHATEVER YOU SAY, SHE'S JUST A GIRL.
YOU KNOW, I REALLY DETEST GIRLS WHO DON'T KNOW THEIR PROPER PLACE. THEY UPSET THE NATURAL BALANCE OF THINGS. THEY SHOULD JUST GO HOME AND DO LAUNDRY.
부들
부들
WHOA. HE'S A TOTAL MISOGYNIST!
YEAH, HE'S RIGHT OUT OF THE EJO ERA.
AND STOP USING BIG WORDS.
HEY, WHAT DID YOU SAY THAT PUNK'S NAME WAS?
WHO?
THE PUNK THAT BEAT U DAR JAY.
HE'S FROM PURE WATER HIGH. JUNG-WOO.
HMPH. WHAT A PATHETIC WEAKLING! USING A GIRL AS A SHIELD.

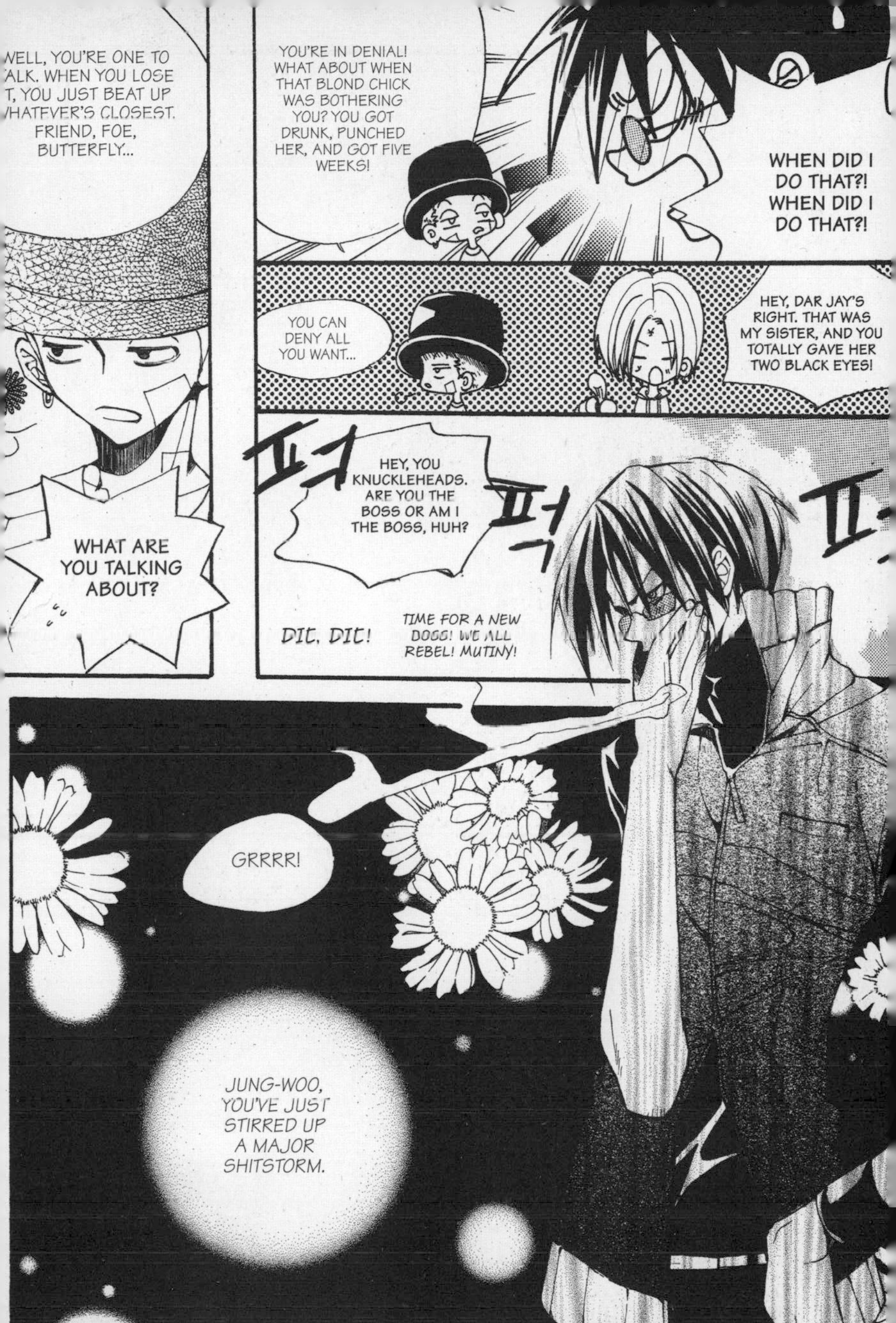
VELL, YOU'RE ONE TO ALK. WHEN YOU LOSE T, YOU JUST BEAT UP VHATEVER'S CLOSEST. FRIEND, FOE, BUTTERFLY...
WHAT ARE YOU TALKING ABOUT?
YOU'RE IN DENIAL! WHAT ABOUT WHEN THAT BLOND CHICK WAS BOTHERING YOU? YOU GOT DRUNK, PUNCHED HER, AND GOT FIVE WEEKS!
WHEN DID I DO THAT?! WHEN DID I DO THAT?!
YOU CAN DENY ALL YOU WANT...
HEY, DAR JAY'S RIGHT. THAT WAS MY SISTER, AND YOU TOTALLY GAVE HER TWO BLACK EYES!
퍽
HEY, YOU KNUCKLEHEADS. ARE YOU THE BOSS OR AM I THE BOSS, HUH?
퍽
DIT, DIT!
TIME FOR A NEW BOSS! WE ALL REBEL! MUTINY!
GRRRR!
JUNG-WOO, YOU'VE JUST STIRRED UP A MAJOR SHITSTORM.

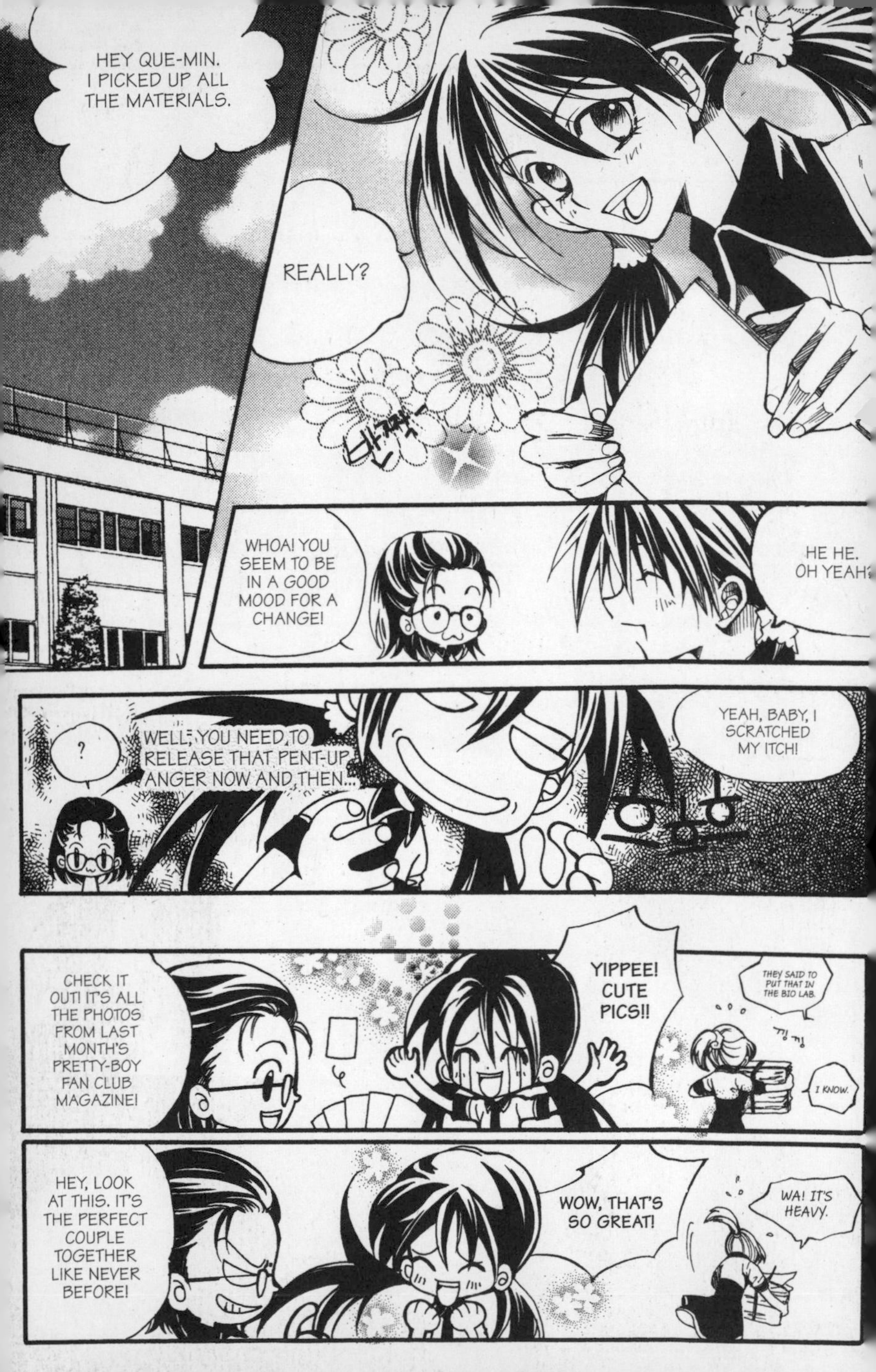

HEY QUE-MIN. I PICKED UP ALL THE MATERIALS.
REALLY?
WHOA! YOU SEEM TO BE IN A GOOD MOOD FOR A CHANGE!
HE HE. OH YEAH?
?
WELL, YOU NEED TO RELEASE THAT PENT-UP ANGER NOW AND THEN...
YEAH, BABY, I SCRATCHED MY ITCH!
CHECK IT OUT! IT'S ALL THE PHOTOS FROM LAST MONTH'S PRETTY-BOY FAN CLUB MAGAZINE!
YIPPEE! CUTE PICS!!
THEY SAID TO PUT THAT IN THE BIO LAB.
I KNOW.
HEY, LOOK AT THIS. IT'S THE PERFECT COUPLE TOGETHER LIKE NEVER BEFORE!
WOW, THAT'S SO GREAT!
WA! IT'S HEAVY.

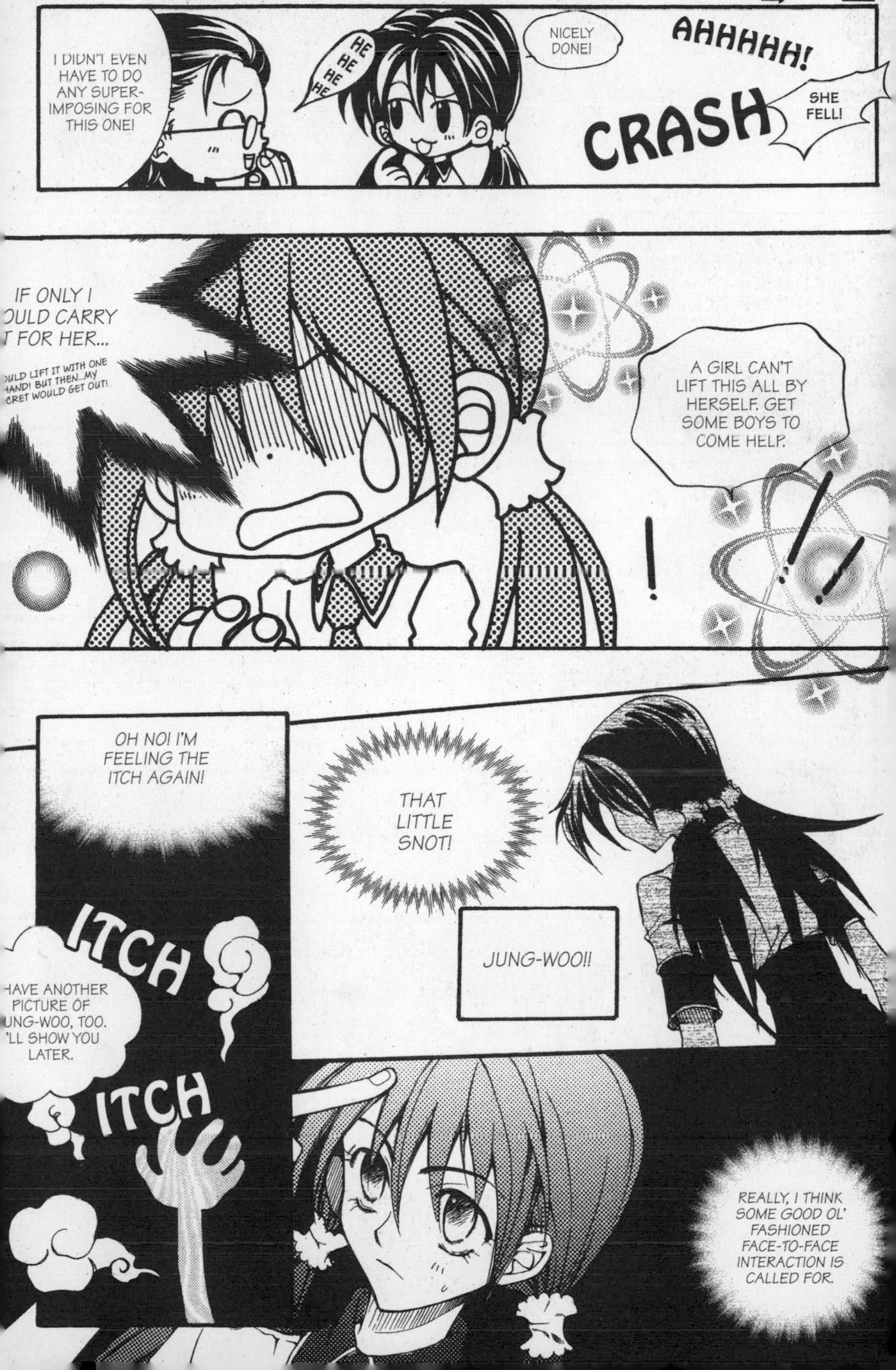
I DIDN'T EVEN HAVE TO DO ANY SUPER-IMPOSING FOR THIS ONE!
HE HE HE HE
NICELY DONE!
AHHHHH!
CRASH
SHE FELL!
IF ONLY I OULD CARRY T FOR HER...
OULD LIFT IT WITH ONE HAND! BUT THEN...MY CRET WOULD GET OUT!
A GIRL CAN'T LIFT THIS ALL BY HERSELF. GET SOME BOYS TO COME HELP.
!
!!
OH NO! I'M FEELING THE ITCH AGAIN!
THAT LITTLE SNOT!
JUNG-WOO!!
ITCH
HAVE ANOTHER PICTURE OF UNG-WOO, TOO. 'LL SHOW YOU LATER.
ITCH
REALLY, I THINK SOME GOOD OL' FASHIONED FACE-TO-FACE INTERACTION IS CALLED FOR.

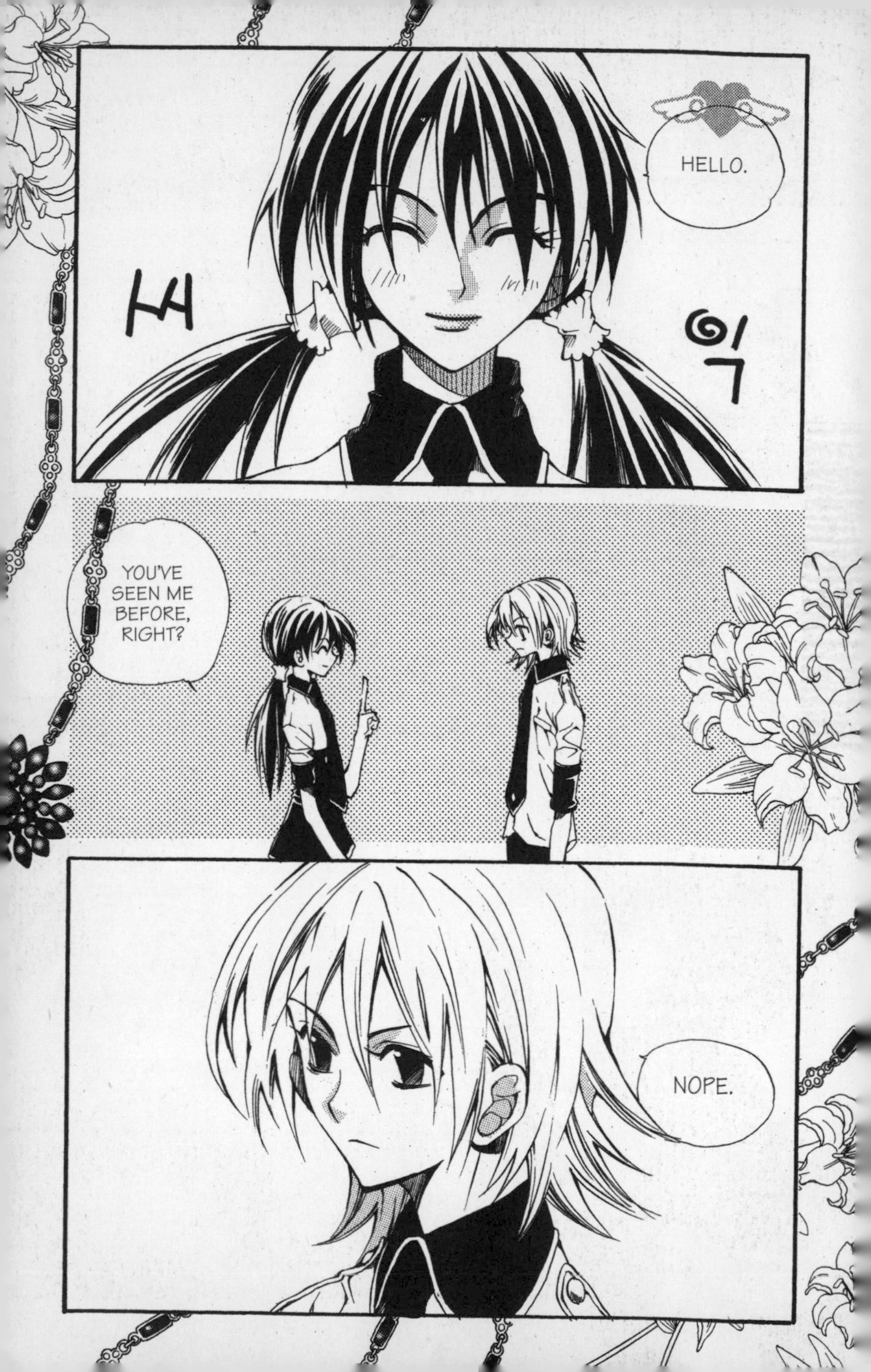
HELLO.
YOU'VE SEEN ME BEFORE, RIGHT?
NOPE.

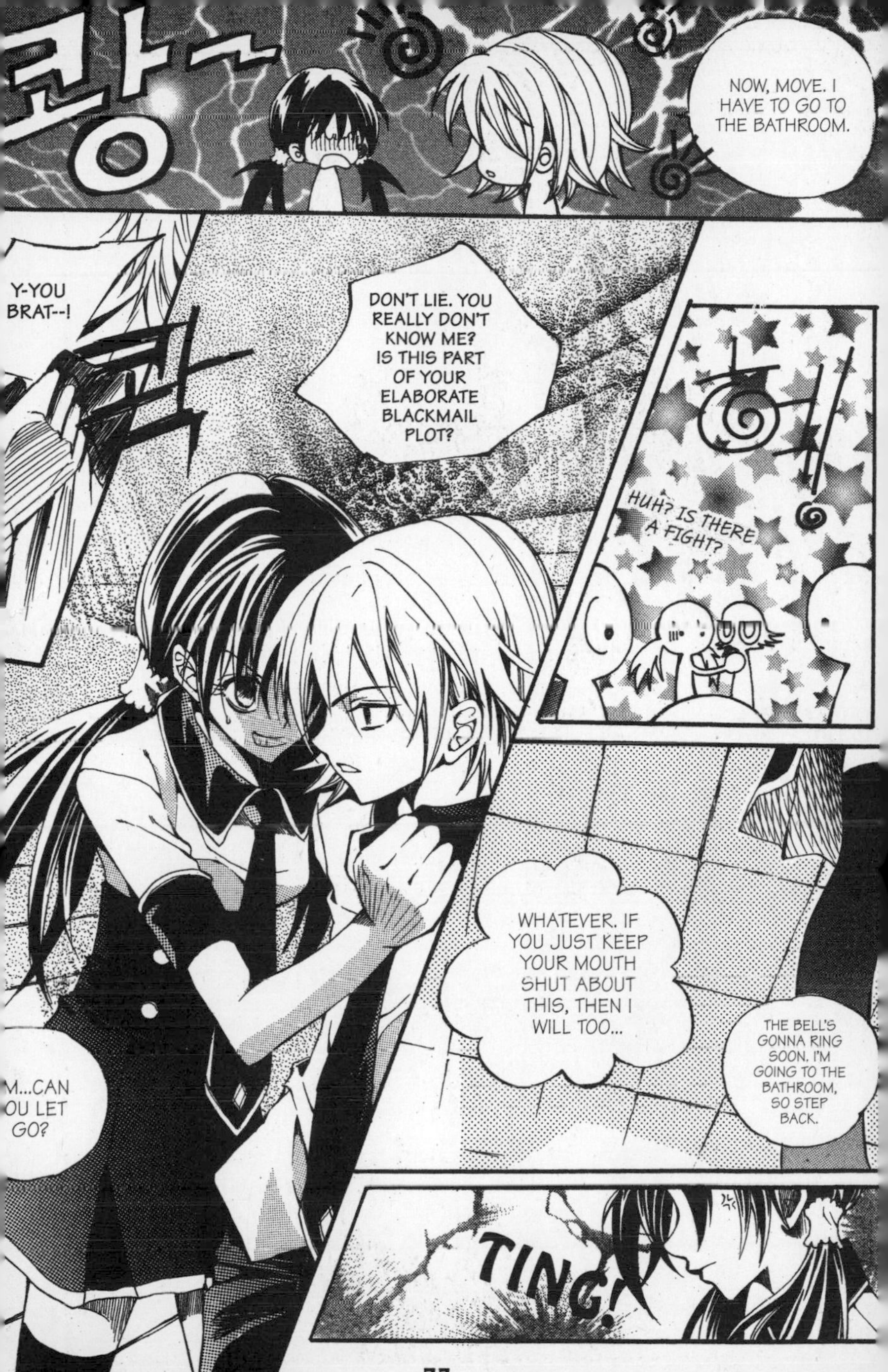
NOW, MOVE. I HAVE TO GO TO THE BATHROOM.
Y-YOU BRAT--!
M...CAN OU LET GO?
DON'T LIE. YOU REALLY DON'T KNOW ME? IS THIS PART OF YOUR ELABORATE BLACKMAIL PLOT?
HUH? IS THERE A FIGHT?
WHATEVER. IF YOU JUST KEEP YOUR MOUTH SHUT ABOUT THIS, THEN I WILL TOO...
THE BELL'S GONNA RING SOON. I'M GOING TO THE BATHROOM, SO STEP BACK.
TING!

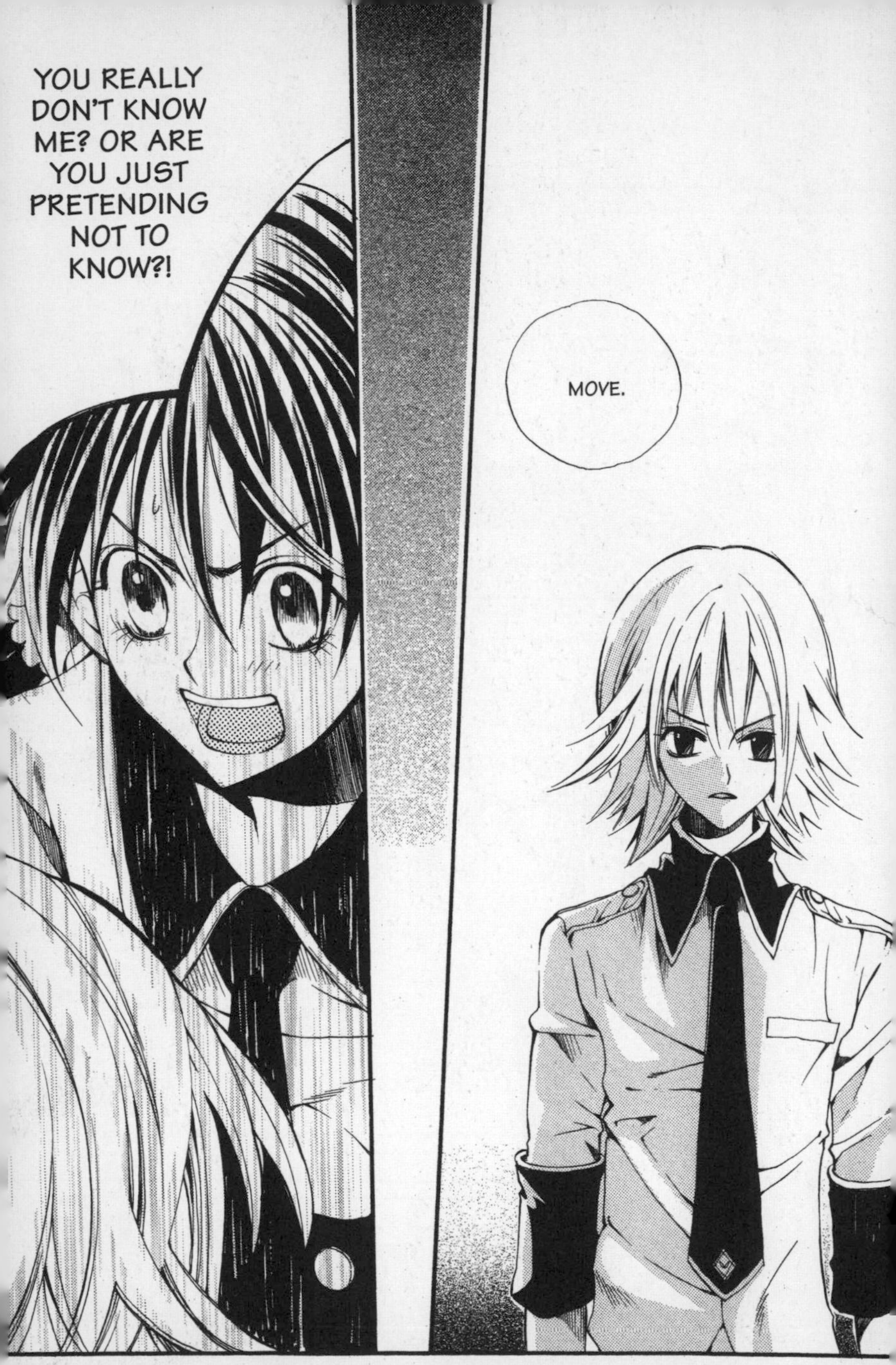
YOU REALLY DON'T KNOW ME? OR ARE YOU JUST PRETENDING NOT TO KNOW?!
MOVE.

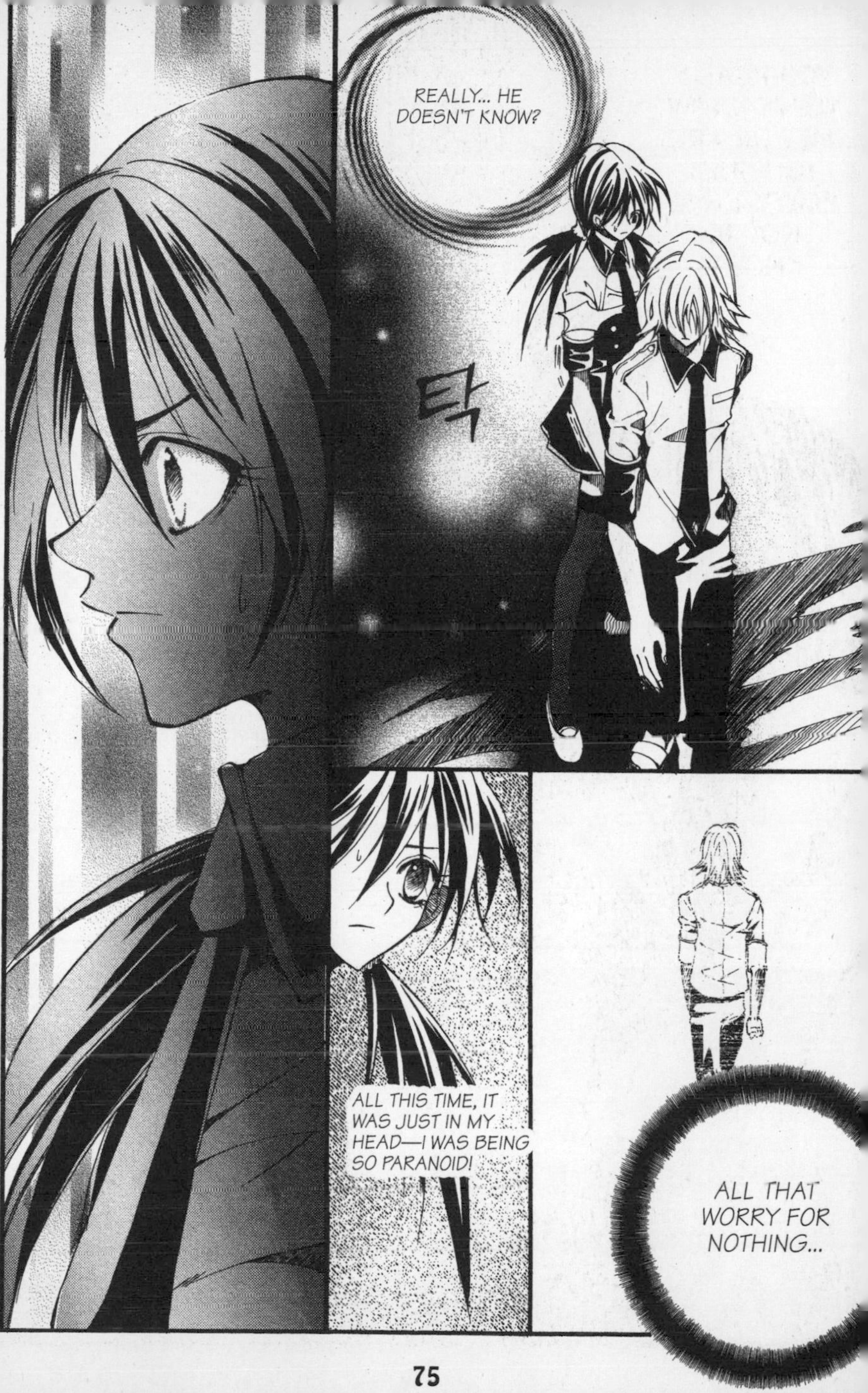
REALLY... HE DOESN'T KNOW?
탁
ALL THIS TIME, IT WAS JUST IN MY HEAD—I WAS BEING SO PARANOID!
ALL THAT WORRY FOR NOTHING...

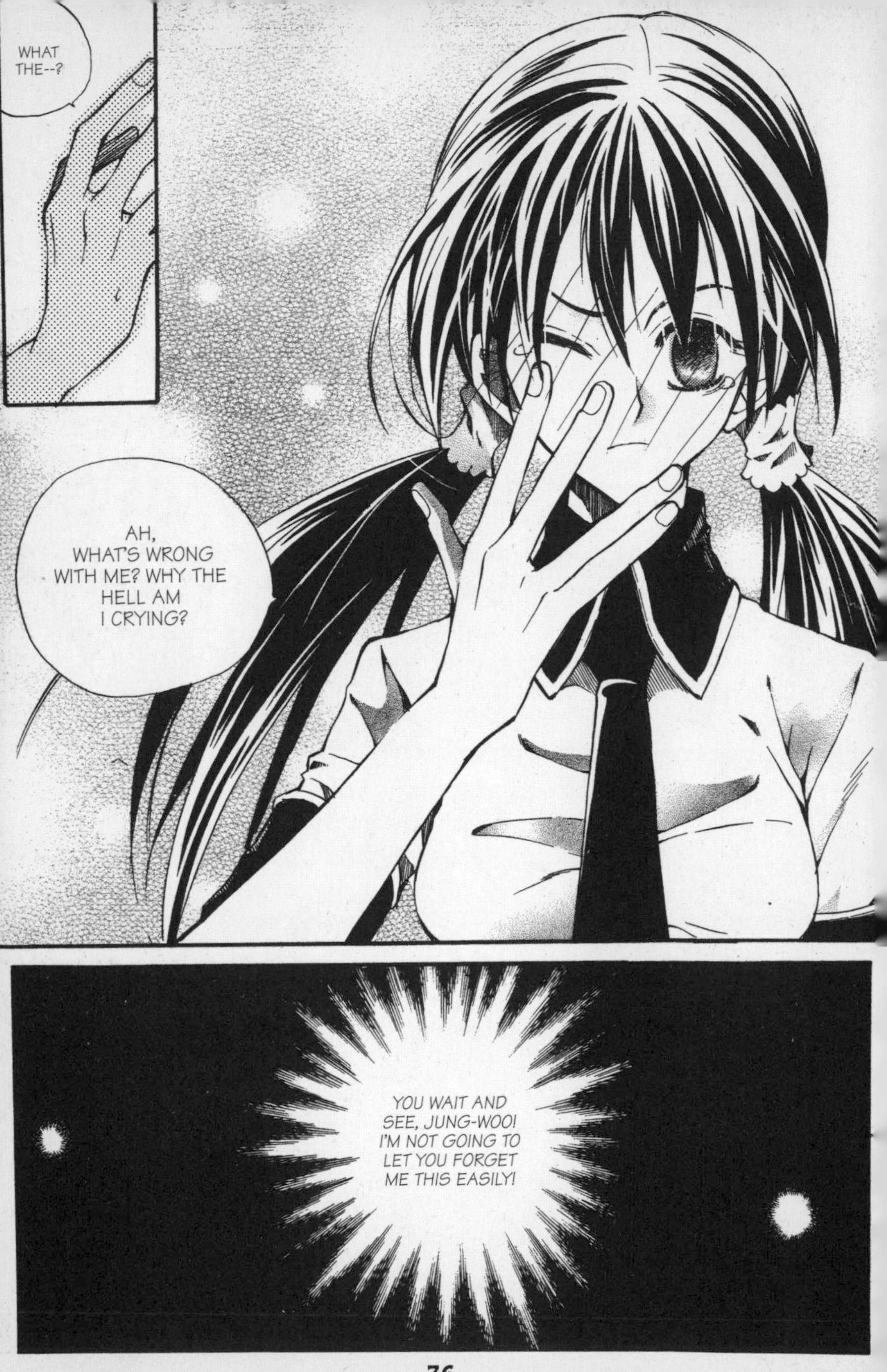
WHAT THE--?
AH, WHAT'S WRONG WITH ME? WHY THE HELL AM I CRYING?
YOU WAIT AND SEE, JUNG-WOO! I'M NOT GOING TO LET YOU FORGET ME THIS EASILY!

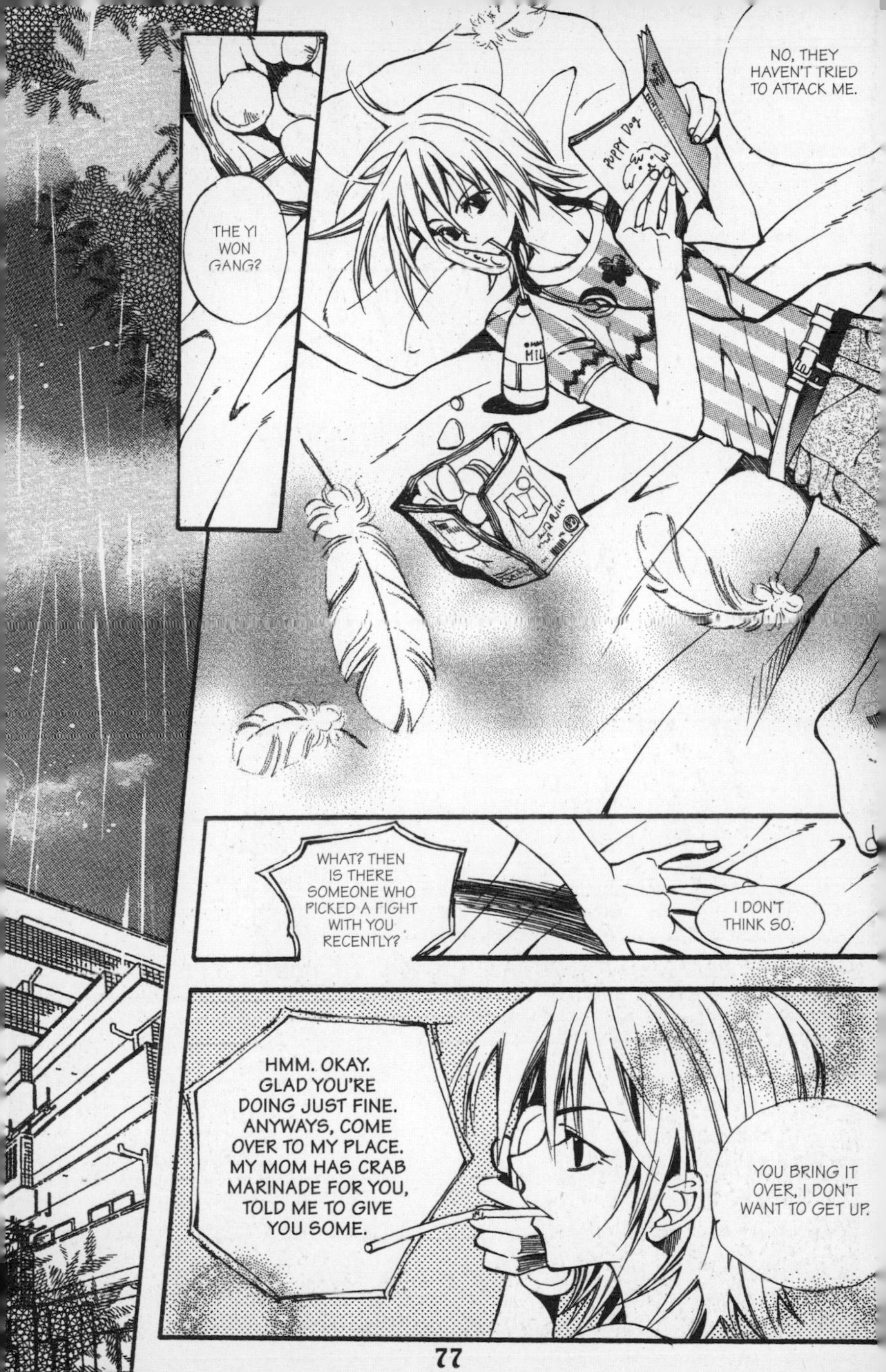
THE YI WON GANG?
NO, THEY HAVEN'T TRIED TO ATTACK ME.
PUPPY Dog
WHAT? THEN IS THERE SOMEONE WHO PICKED A FIGHT WITH YOU RECENTLY?
I DON'T THINK SO.
HMM. OKAY. GLAD YOU'RE DOING JUST FINE. ANYWAYS, COME OVER TO MY PLACE. MY MOM HAS CRAB MARINADE FOR YOU, TOLD ME TO GIVE YOU SOME.
YOU BRING IT OVER, I DON'T WANT TO GET UP.

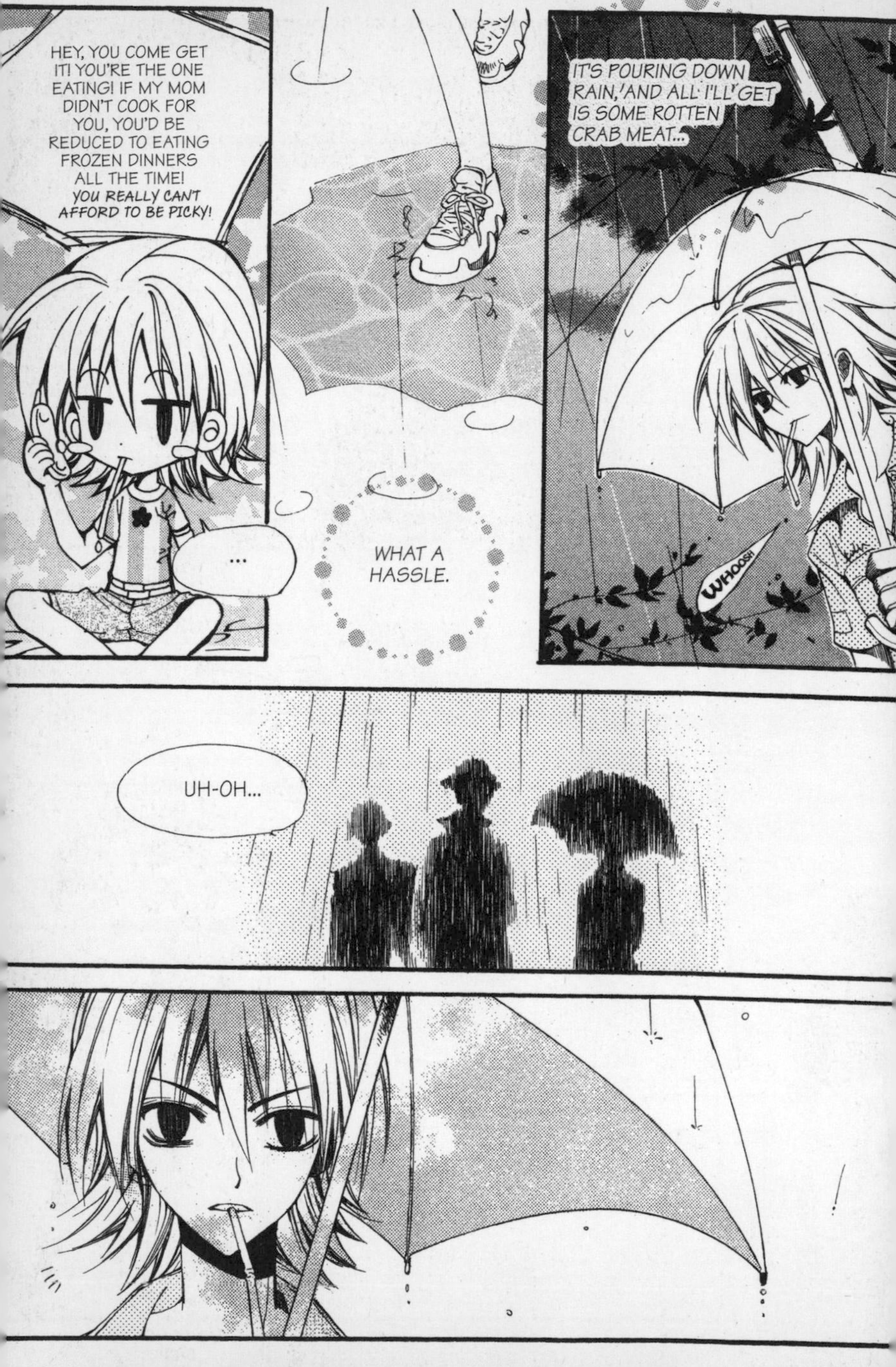
HEY, YOU COME GET IT! YOU'RE THE ONE EATING! IF MY MOM DIDN'T COOK FOR YOU, YOU'D BE REDUCED TO EATING FROZEN DINNERS ALL THE TIME!
YOU REALLY CAN'T AFFORD TO BE PICKY!
...
WHAT A HASSLE.
IT'S POURING DOWN RAIN, AND ALL I'LL GET IS SOME ROTTEN CRAB MEAT...
WHOOSH
UH-OH...

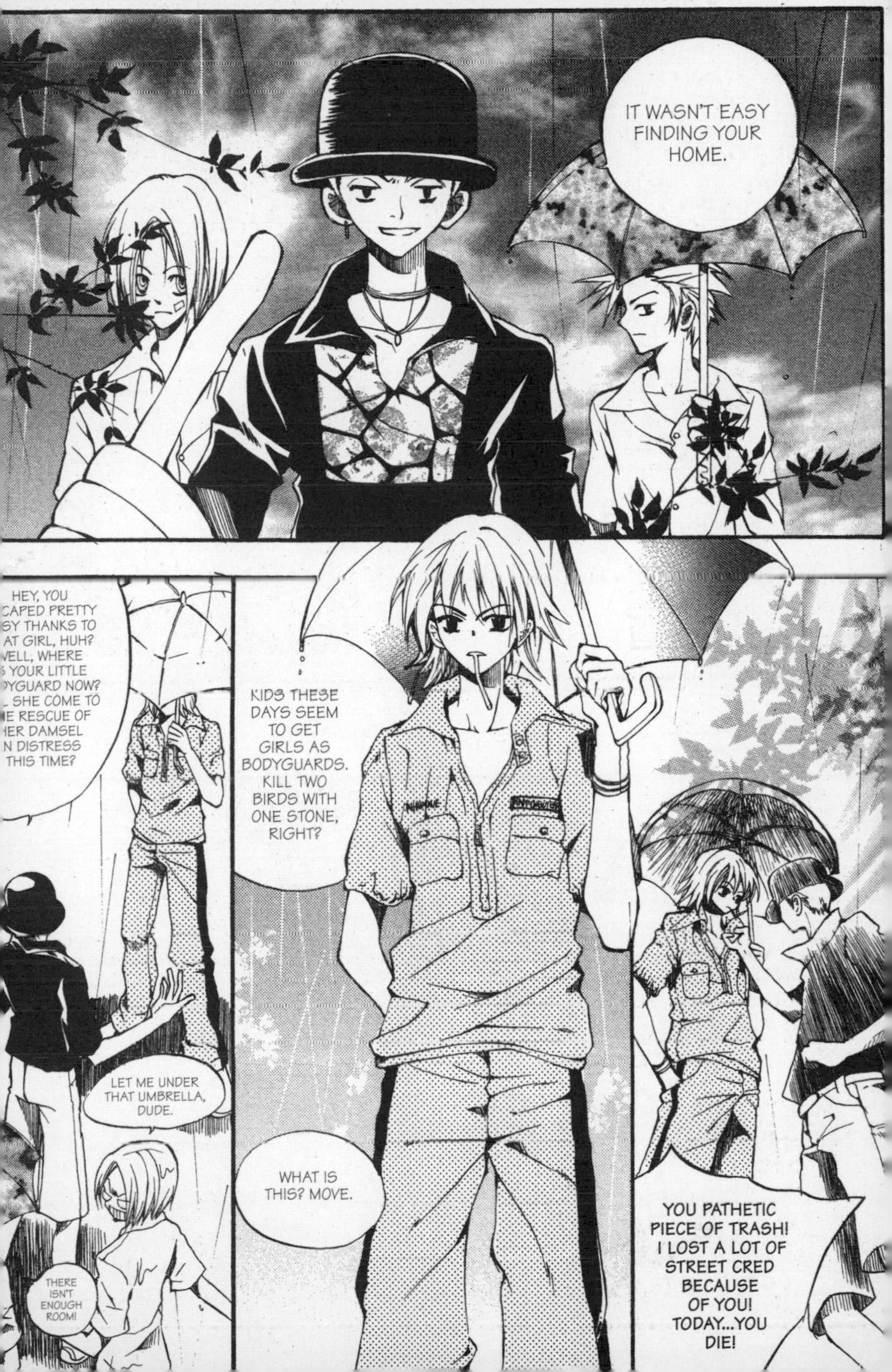
IT WASN'T EASY FINDING YOUR HOME.
HEY, YOU CAPED PRETTY SY THANKS TO AT GIRL, HUH? WELL, WHERE S YOUR LITTLE DYGUARD NOW? L SHE COME TO E RESCUE OF HER DAMSEL N DISTRESS THIS TIME?
LET ME UNDER THAT UMBRELLA, DUDE.
THERE ISN'T ENOUGH ROOM!
KIDS THESE DAYS SEEM TO GET GIRLS AS BODYGUARDS. KILL TWO BIRDS WITH ONE STONE, RIGHT?
WHAT IS THIS? MOVE.
YOU PATHETIC PIECE OF TRASH! I LOST A LOT OF STREET CRED BECAUSE OF YOU! TODAY...YOU DIE!

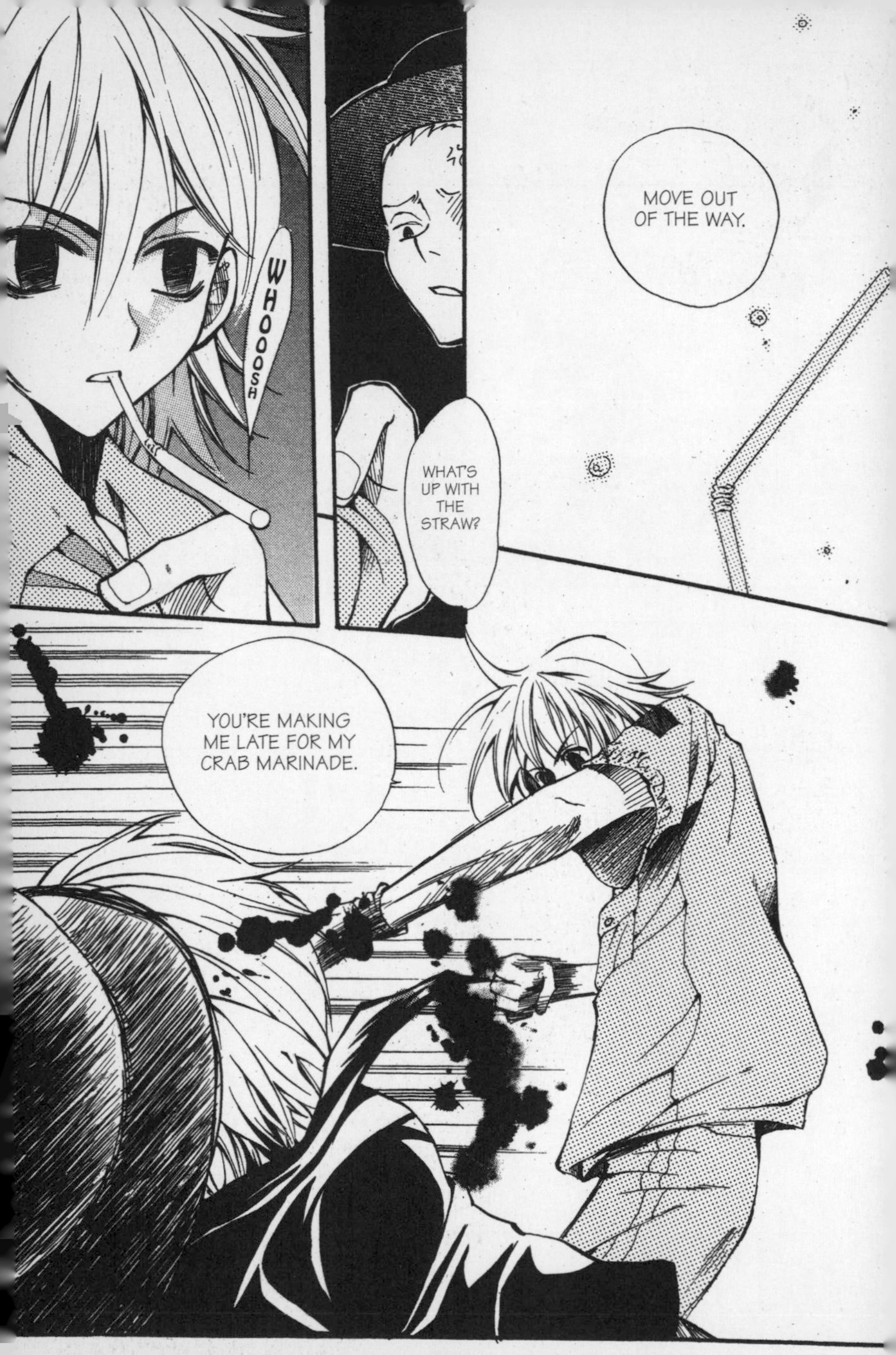
WHOOOOSH
WHAT'S UP WITH THE STRAW?
MOVE OUT OF THE WAY.
YOU'RE MAKING ME LATE FOR MY CRAB MARINADE.

K2 Kill me Kiss me

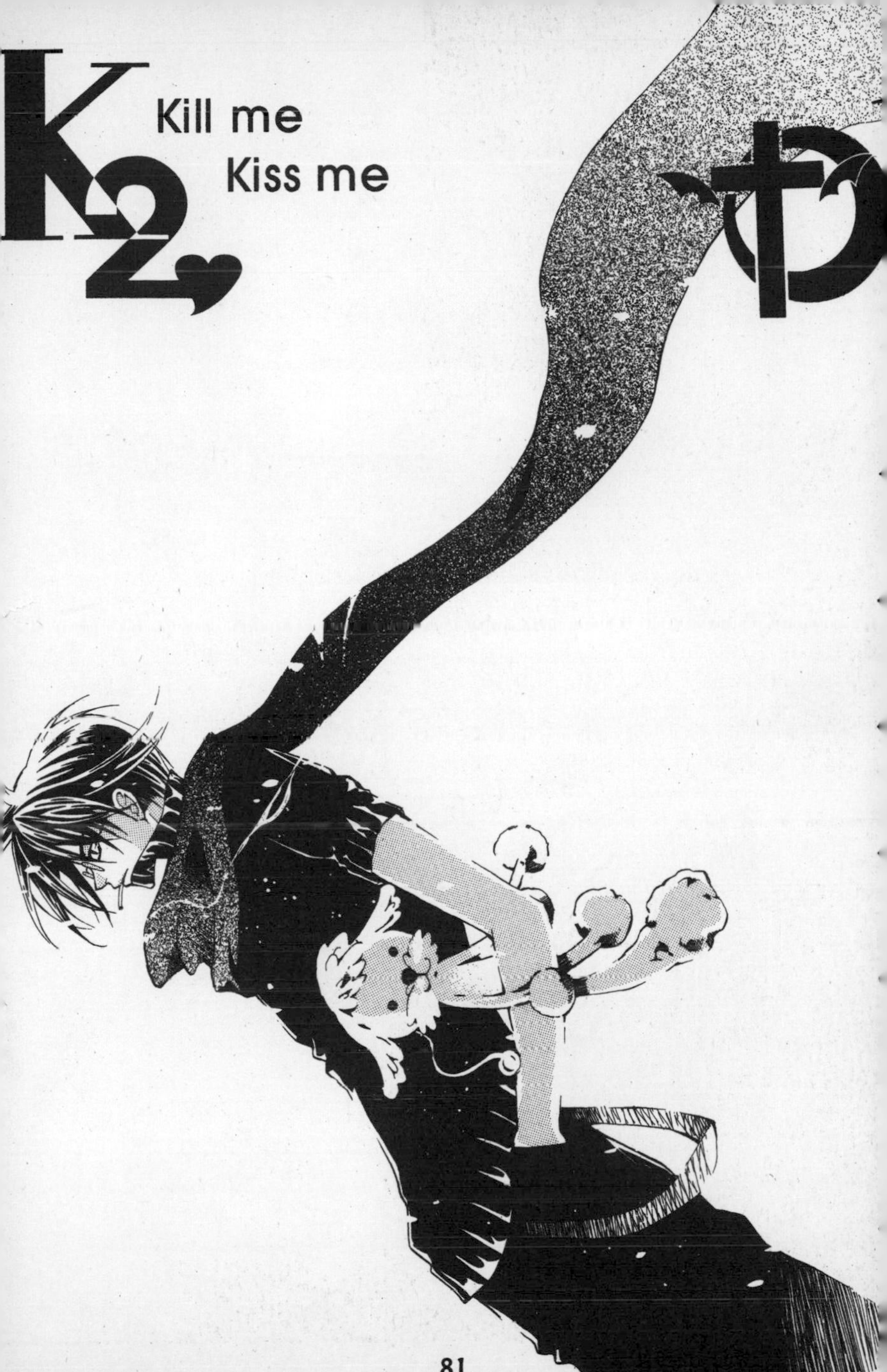

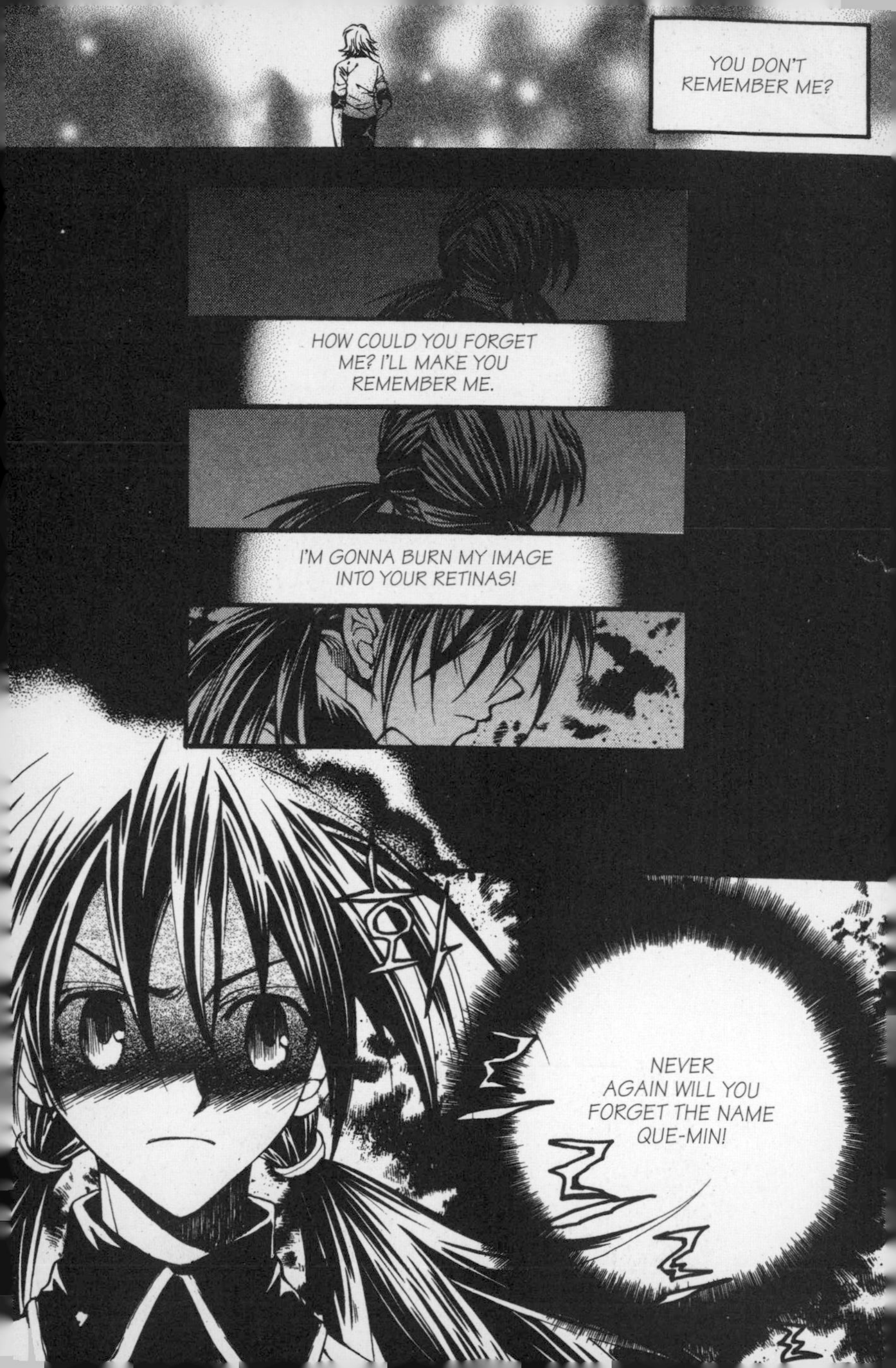
YOU DON'T REMEMBER ME?
HOW COULD YOU FORGET ME? I'LL MAKE YOU REMEMBER ME.
I'M GONNA BURN MY IMAGE INTO YOUR RETINAS!
NEVER AGAIN WILL YOU FORGET THE NAME QUE-MIN!

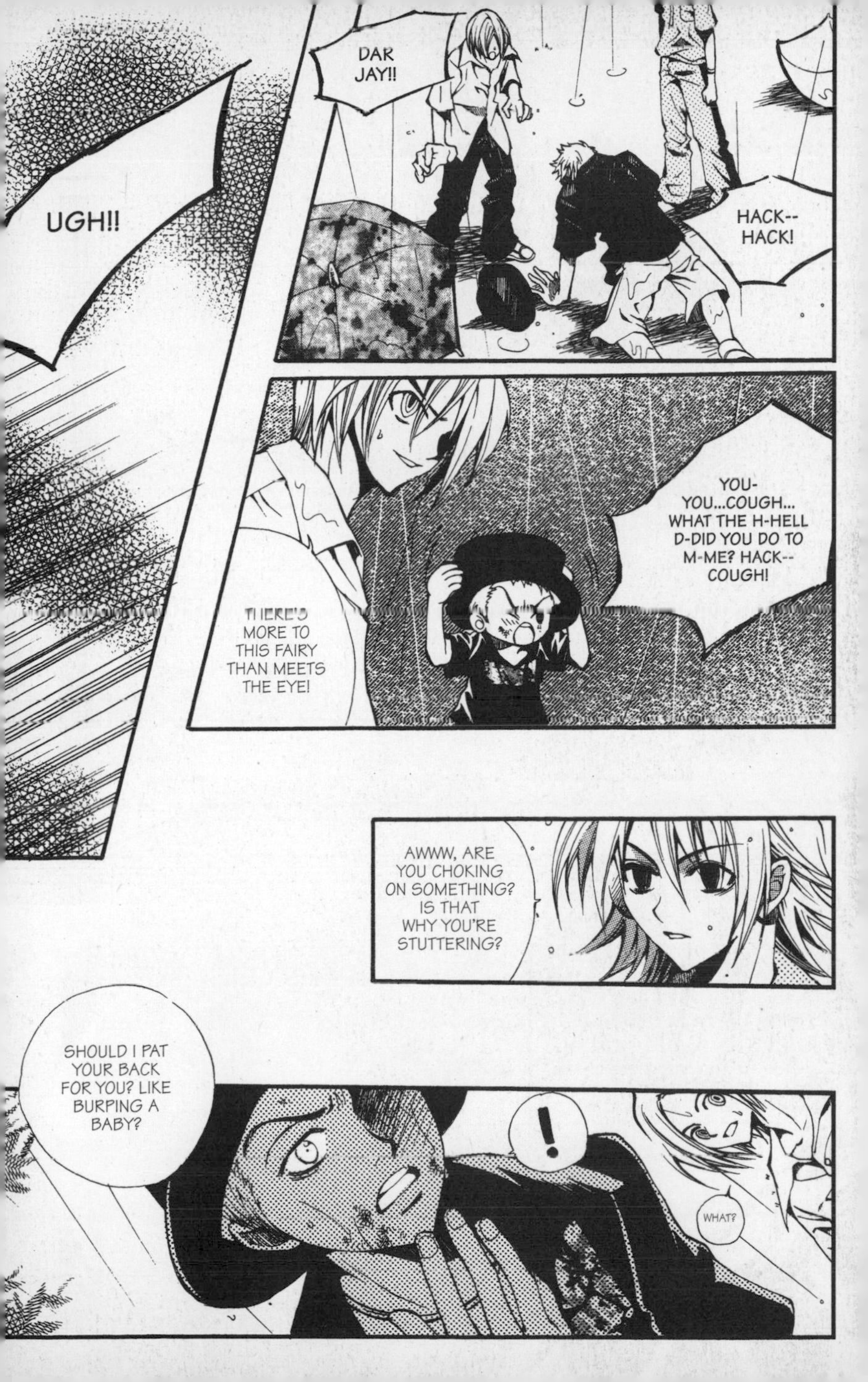
UGH!!
DAR JAY!!
HACK-- HACK!
THERE'S MORE TO THIS FAIRY THAN MEETS THE EYE!
YOU- YOU...COUGH... WHAT THE H-HELL D-DID YOU DO TO M-ME? HACK-- COUGH!
AWWW, ARE YOU CHOKING ON SOMETHING? IS THAT WHY YOU'RE STUTTERING?
SHOULD I PAT YOUR BACK FOR YOU? LIKE BURPING A BABY?
!
WHAT?

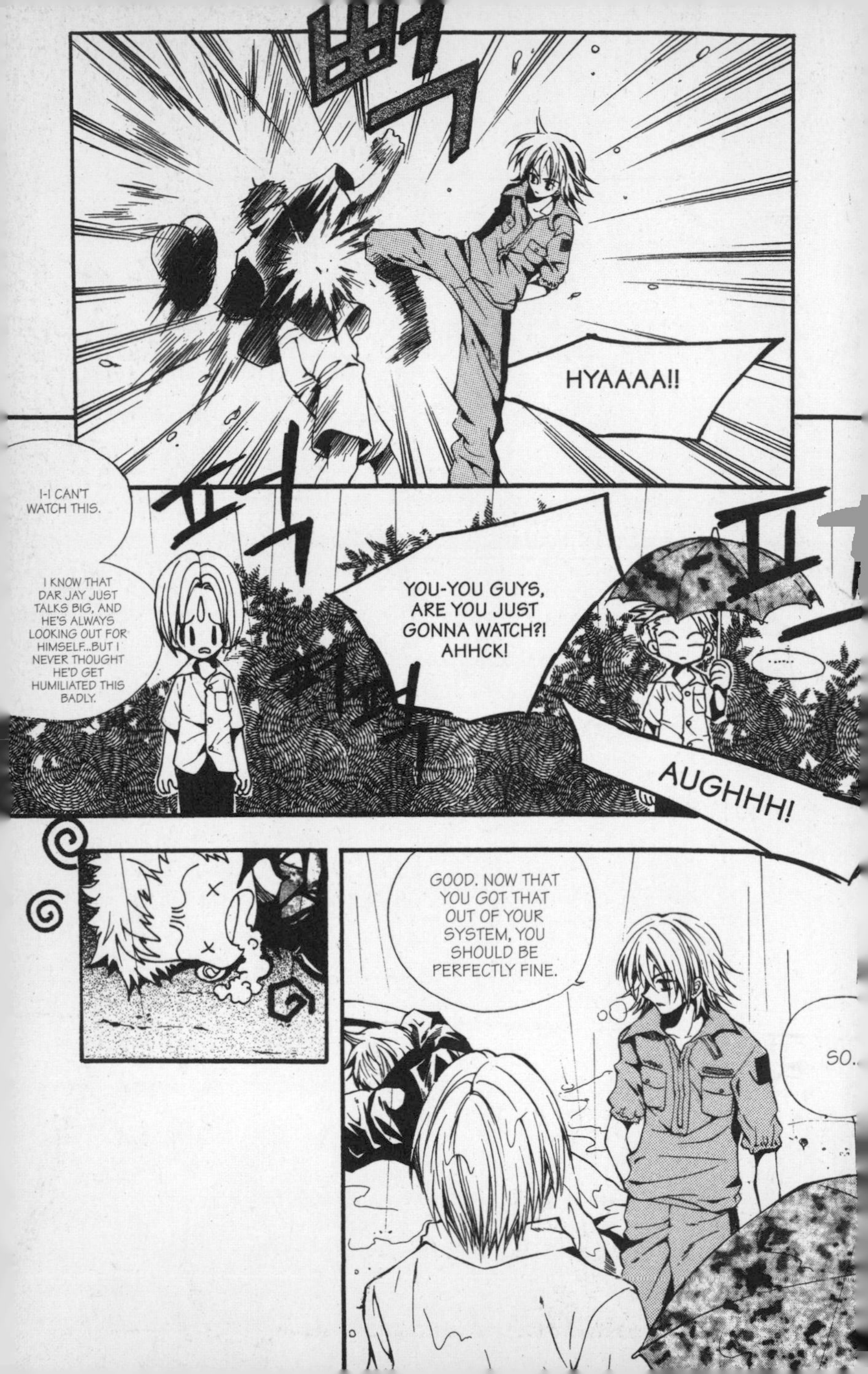
뻑
HYAAAA!!
I-I CAN'T WATCH THIS.
I KNOW THAT DAR JAY JUST TALKS BIG, AND HE'S ALWAYS LOOKING OUT FOR HIMSELF...BUT I NEVER THOUGHT HE'D GET HUMILIATED THIS BADLY.
퍽
YOU-YOU GUYS, ARE YOU JUST GONNA WATCH?! AHHCK!
......
AUGHHH!
GOOD. NOW THAT YOU GOT THAT OUT OF YOUR SYSTEM, YOU SHOULD BE PERFECTLY FINE.
SO...

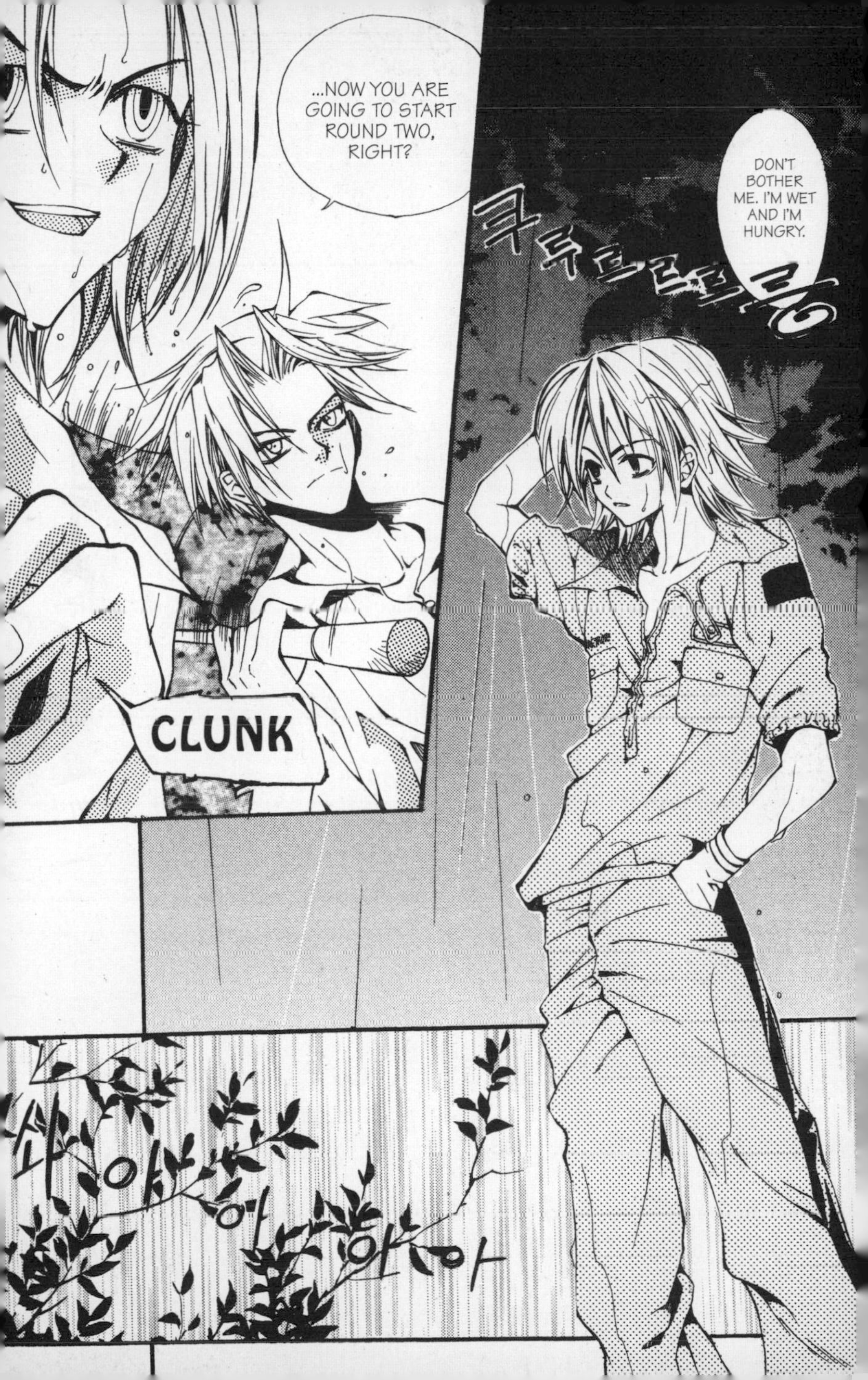
...NOW YOU ARE GOING TO START ROUND TWO, RIGHT?
CLUNK
DON'T BOTHER ME. I'M WET AND I'M HUNGRY.

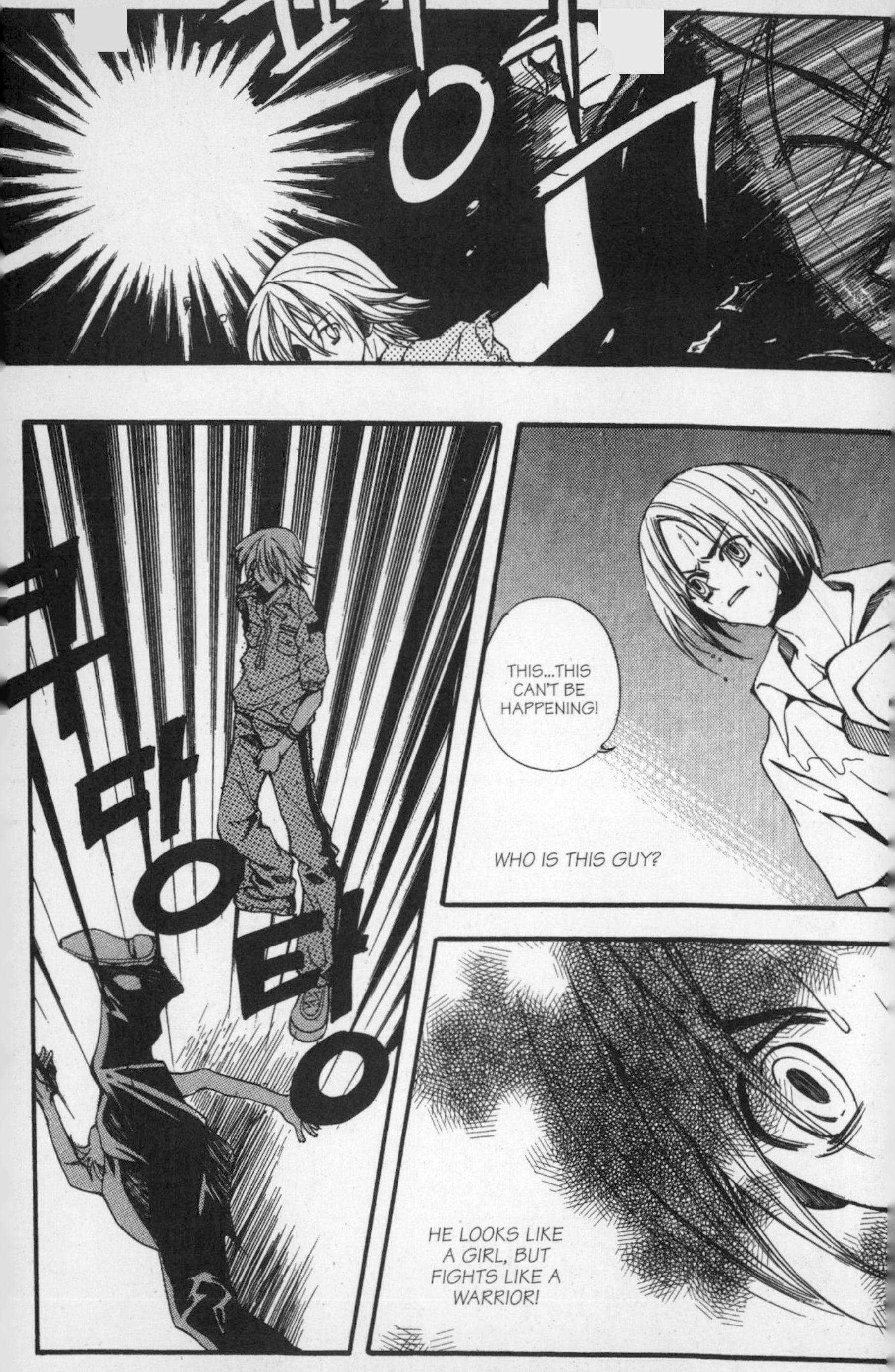
THIS...THIS CAN'T BE HAPPENING!
WHO IS THIS GUY?
HE LOOKS LIKE A GIRL, BUT FIGHTS LIKE A WARRIOR!

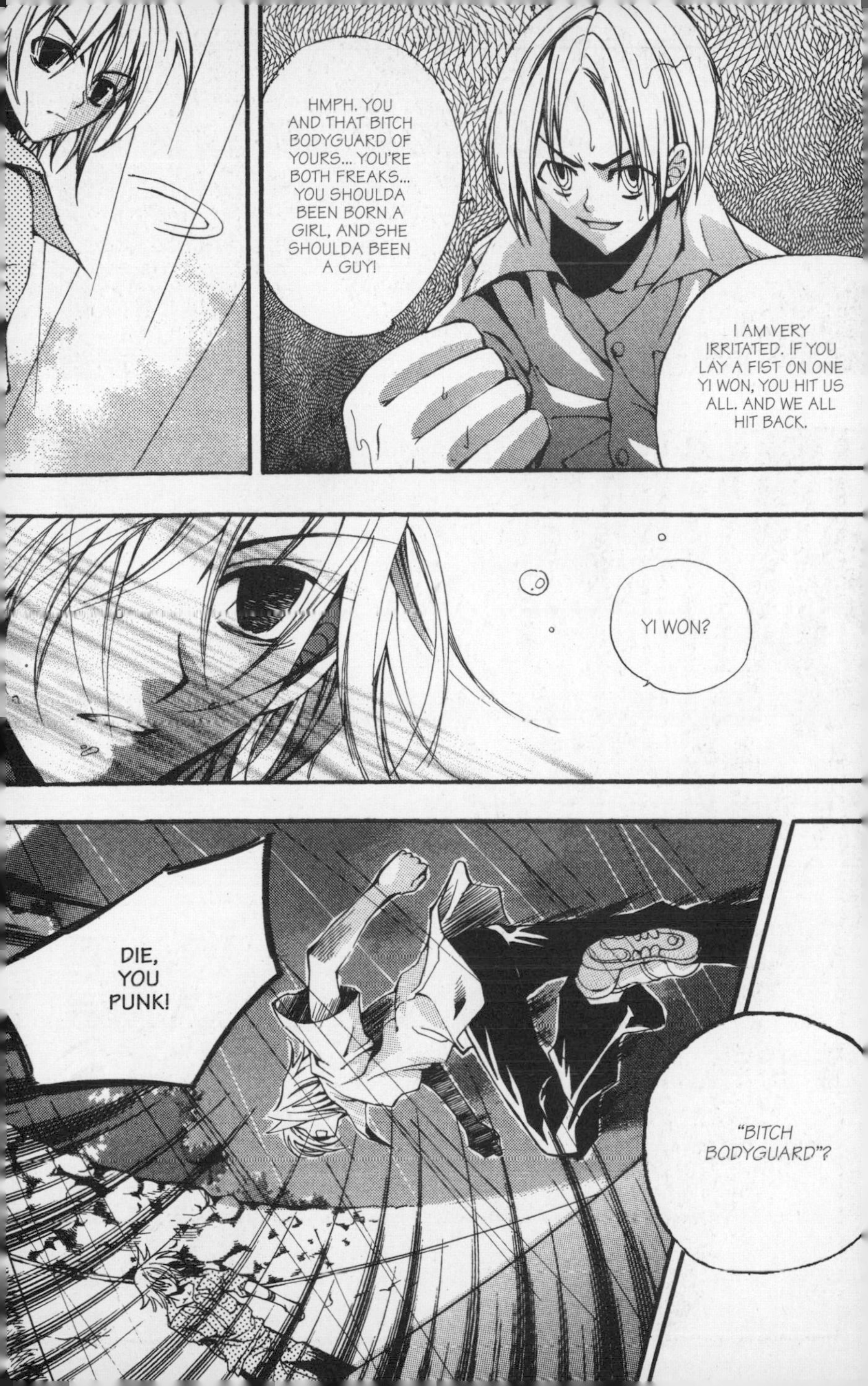
HMPH. YOU AND THAT BITCH BODYGUARD OF YOURS... YOU'RE BOTH FREAKS... YOU SHOULDA BEEN BORN A GIRL, AND SHE SHOULDA BEEN A GUY!
I AM VERY IRRITATED. IF YOU LAY A FIST ON ONE YI WON, YOU HIT US ALL. AND WE ALL HIT BACK.
YI WON?
DIE, YOU PUNK!
"BITCH BODYGUARD"?

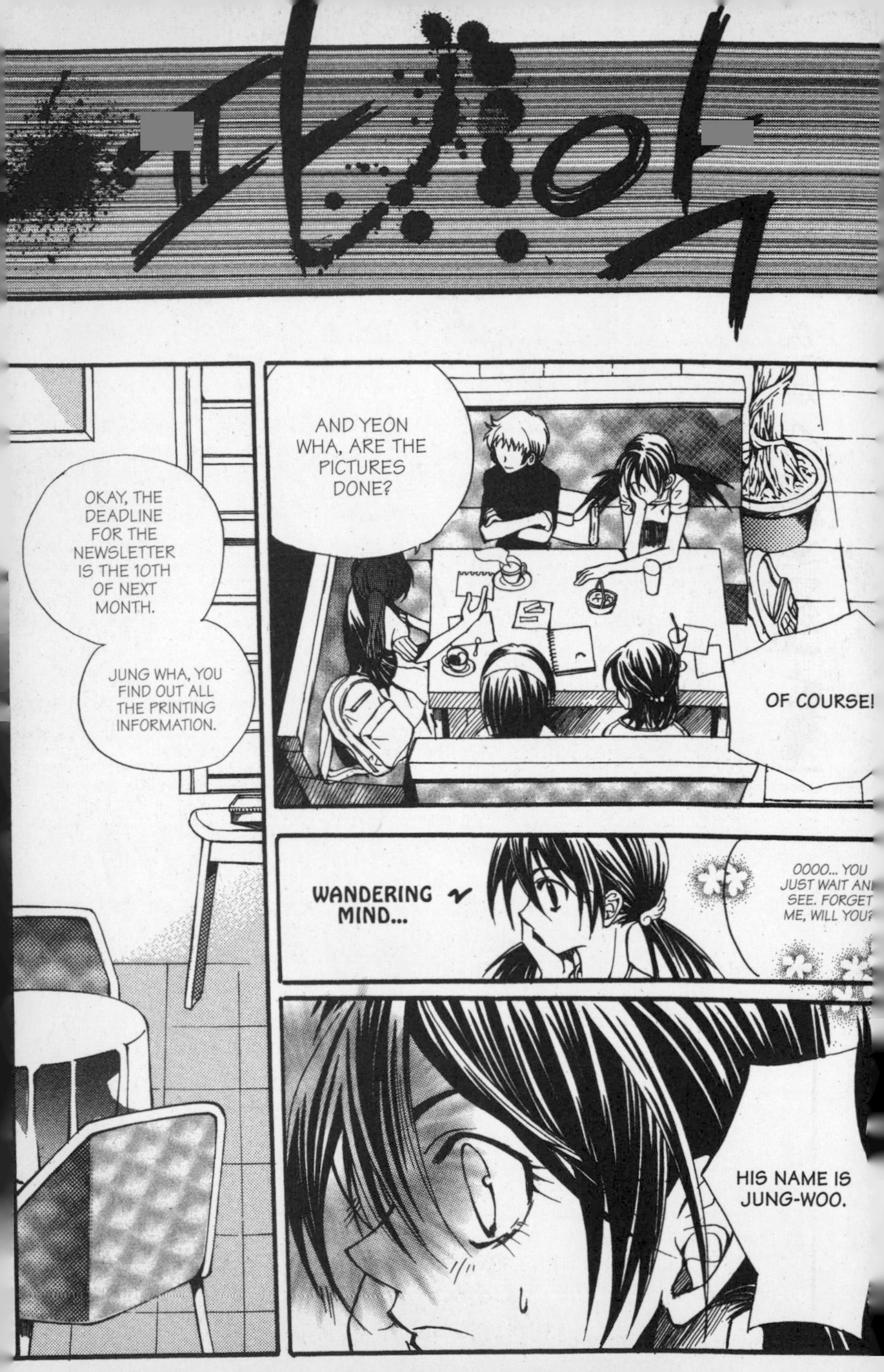
OKAY, THE DEADLINE FOR THE NEWSLETTER IS THE 10TH OF NEXT MONTH.
JUNG WHA, YOU FIND OUT ALL THE PRINTING INFORMATION.
AND YEON WHA, ARE THE PICTURES DONE?
OF COURSE!
WANDERING MIND...
OOOO... YOU JUST WAIT AN SEE. FORGET ME, WILL YOU
HIS NAME IS JUNG-WOO.

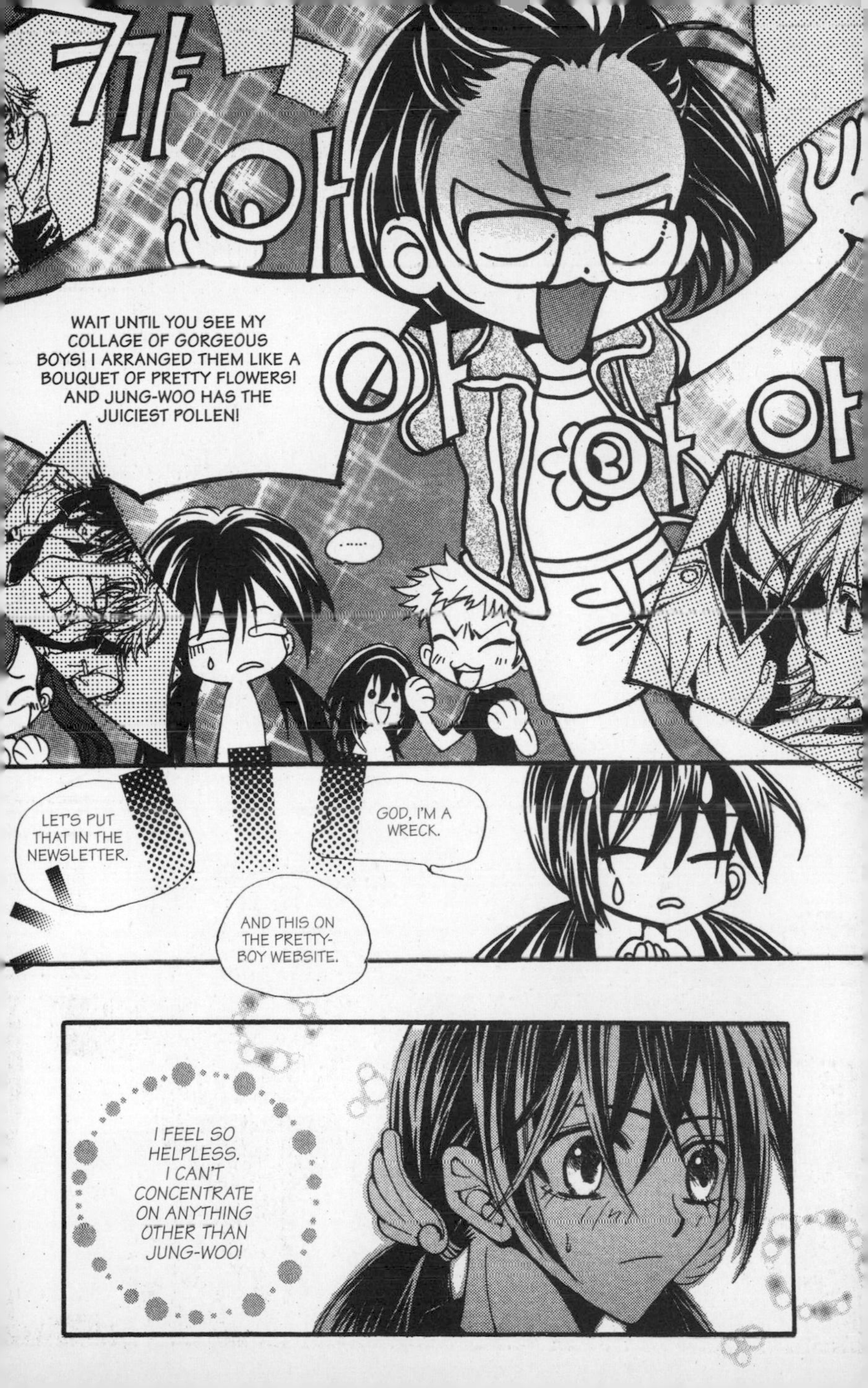
까아아아아
WAIT UNTIL YOU SEE MY COLLAGE OF GORGEOUS BOYS! I ARRANGED THEM LIKE A BOUQUET OF PRETTY FLOWERS! AND JUNG-WOO HAS THE JUICIEST POLLEN!
......
LET'S PUT THAT IN THE NEWSLETTER.
GOD, I'M A WRECK.
AND THIS ON THE PRETTY-BOY WEBSITE.
I FEEL SO HELPLESS. I CAN'T CONCENTRATE ON ANYTHING OTHER THAN JUNG-WOO!

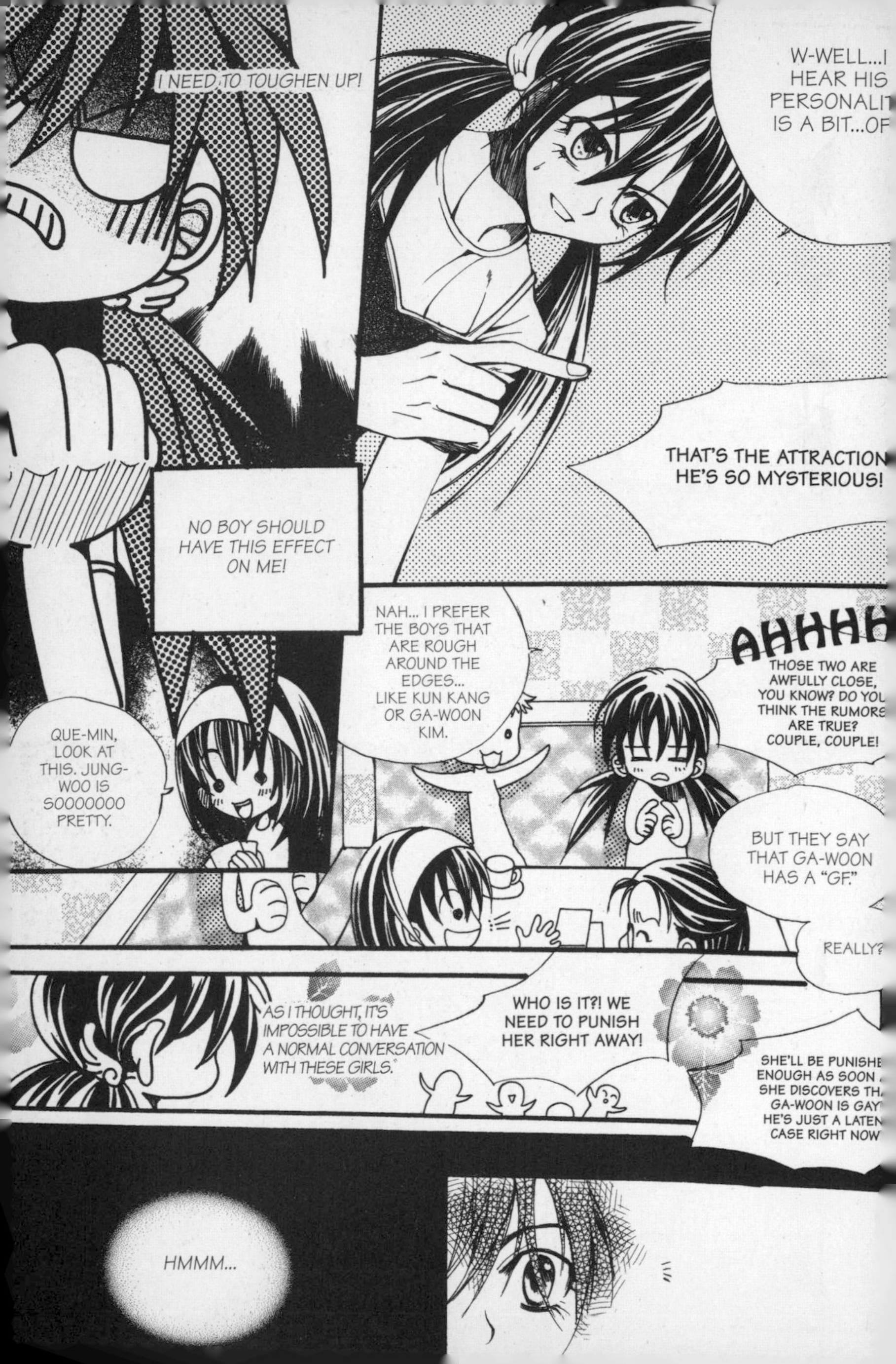
I NEED TO TOUGHEN UP!
NO BOY SHOULD HAVE THIS EFFECT ON ME!
W-WELL...I HEAR HIS PERSONALIT IS A BIT...OF
THAT'S THE ATTRACTION HE'S SO MYSTERIOUS!
QUE-MIN, LOOK AT THIS. JUNG-WOO IS SOOOOOOO PRETTY.
NAH... I PREFER THE BOYS THAT ARE ROUGH AROUND THE EDGES... LIKE KUN KANG OR GA-WOON KIM.
AHHHH
THOSE TWO ARE AWFULLY CLOSE, YOU KNOW? DO YOU THINK THE RUMORS ARE TRUE? COUPLE, COUPLE!
BUT THEY SAY THAT GA-WOON HAS A "GF."
REALLY?
AS I THOUGHT, IT'S IMPOSSIBLE TO HAVE A NORMAL CONVERSATION WITH THESE GIRLS.
WHO IS IT?! WE NEED TO PUNISH HER RIGHT AWAY!
SHE'LL BE PUNISHE ENOUGH AS SOON SHE DISCOVERS TH GA-WOON IS GAY HE'S JUST A LATEN CASE RIGHT NOW
HMMM...

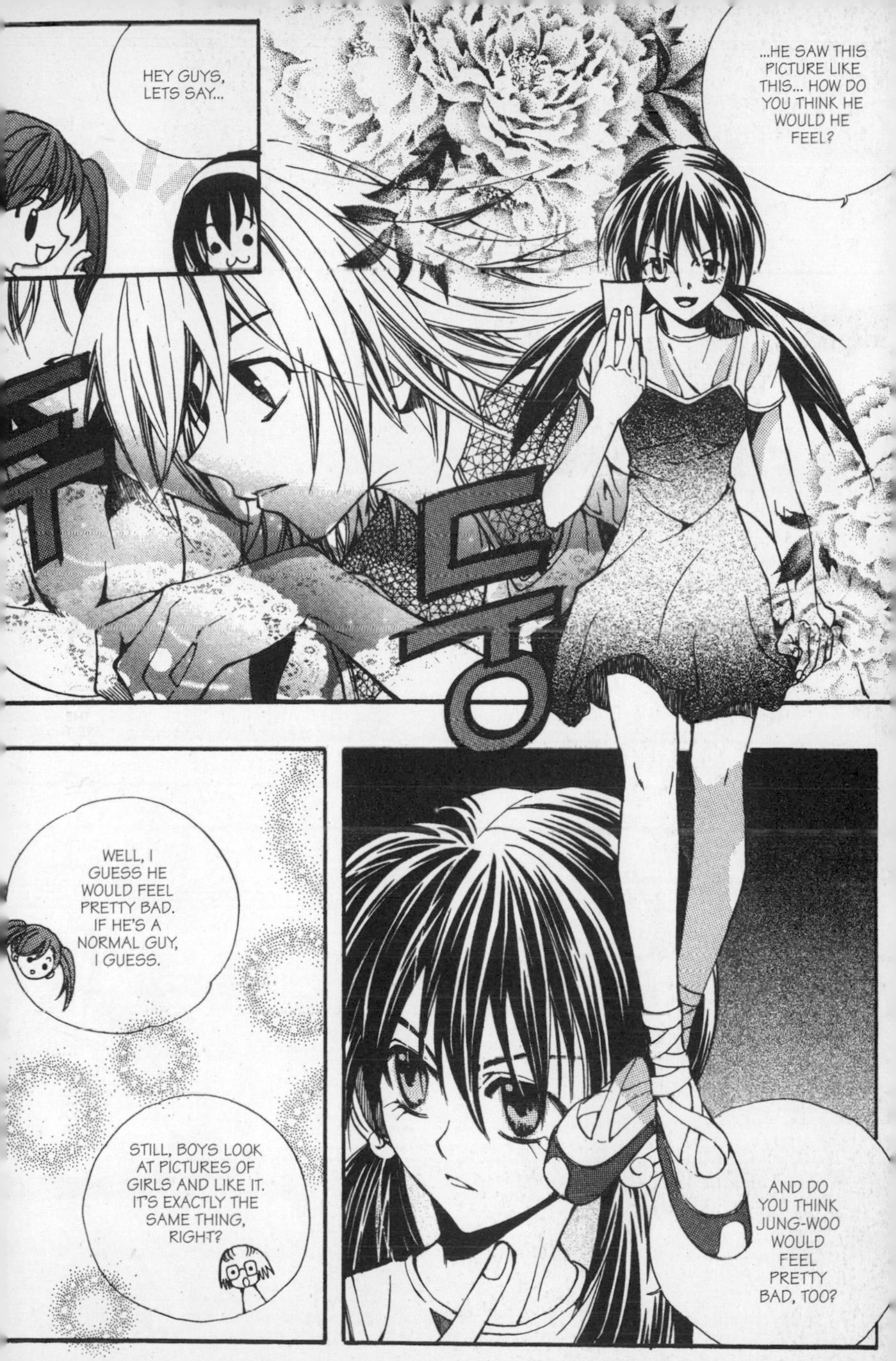
HEY GUYS, LETS SAY...
...HE SAW THIS PICTURE LIKE THIS... HOW DO YOU THINK HE WOULD HE FEEL?
WELL, I GUESS HE WOULD FEEL PRETTY BAD. IF HE'S A NORMAL GUY, I GUESS.
STILL, BOYS LOOK AT PICTURES OF GIRLS AND LIKE IT. IT'S EXACTLY THE SAME THING, RIGHT?
AND DO YOU THINK JUNG-WOO WOULD FEEL PRETTY BAD, TOO?

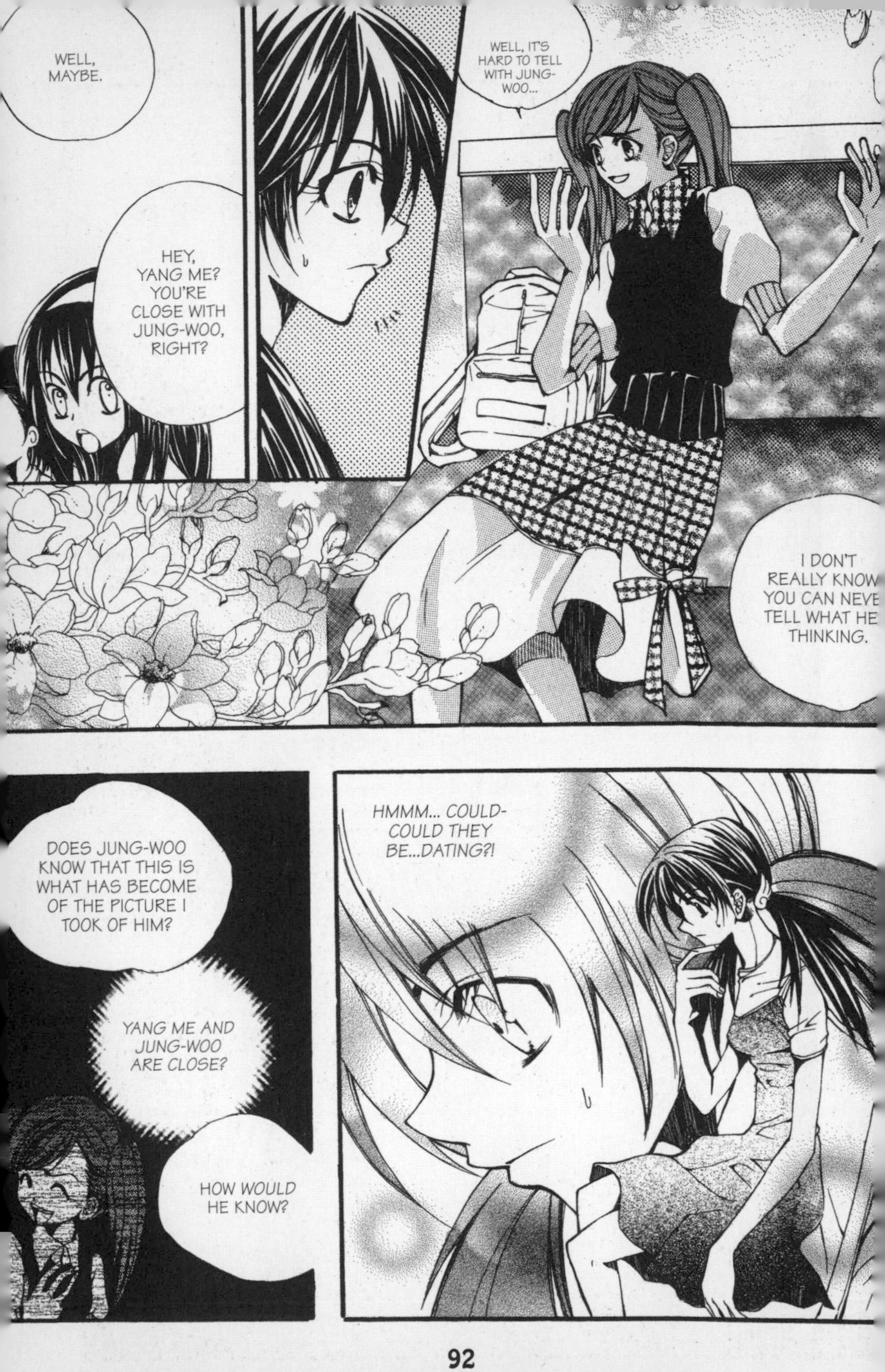
WELL, MAYBE.
HEY, YANG ME? YOU'RE CLOSE WITH JUNG-WOO, RIGHT?
WELL, IT'S HARD TO TELL WITH JUNG-WOO...
I DON'T REALLY KNOW YOU CAN NEVE TELL WHAT HE THINKING.
DOES JUNG-WOO KNOW THAT THIS IS WHAT HAS BECOME OF THE PICTURE I TOOK OF HIM?
YANG ME AND JUNG-WOO ARE CLOSE?
HOW WOULD HE KNOW?
HMMM... COULD-COULD THEY BE...DATING?!

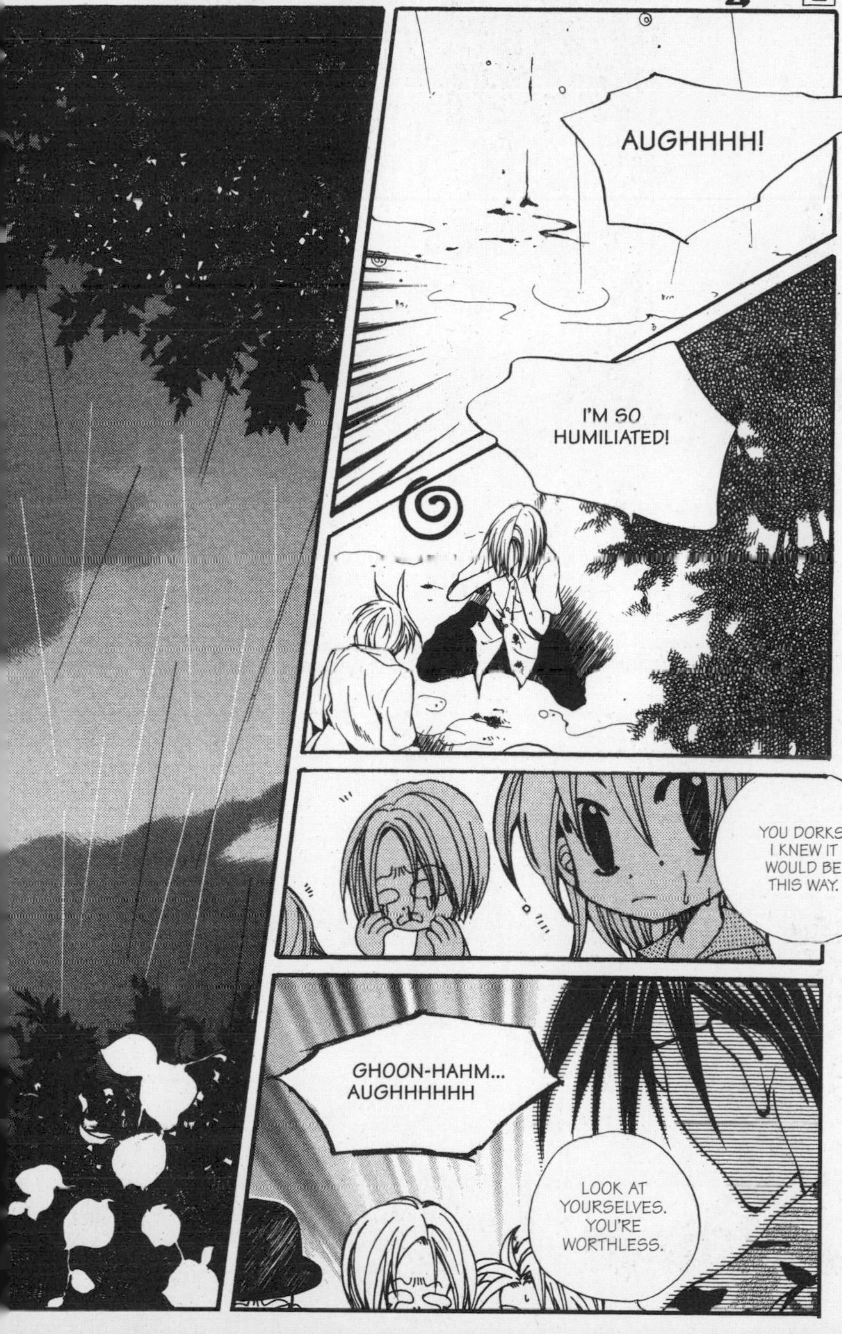
AUGHHHH!
I'M SO HUMILIATED!
YOU DORKS. I KNEW IT WOULD BE THIS WAY.
GHOON-HAHM... AUGHHHHHH
LOOK AT YOURSELVES. YOU'RE WORTHLESS.

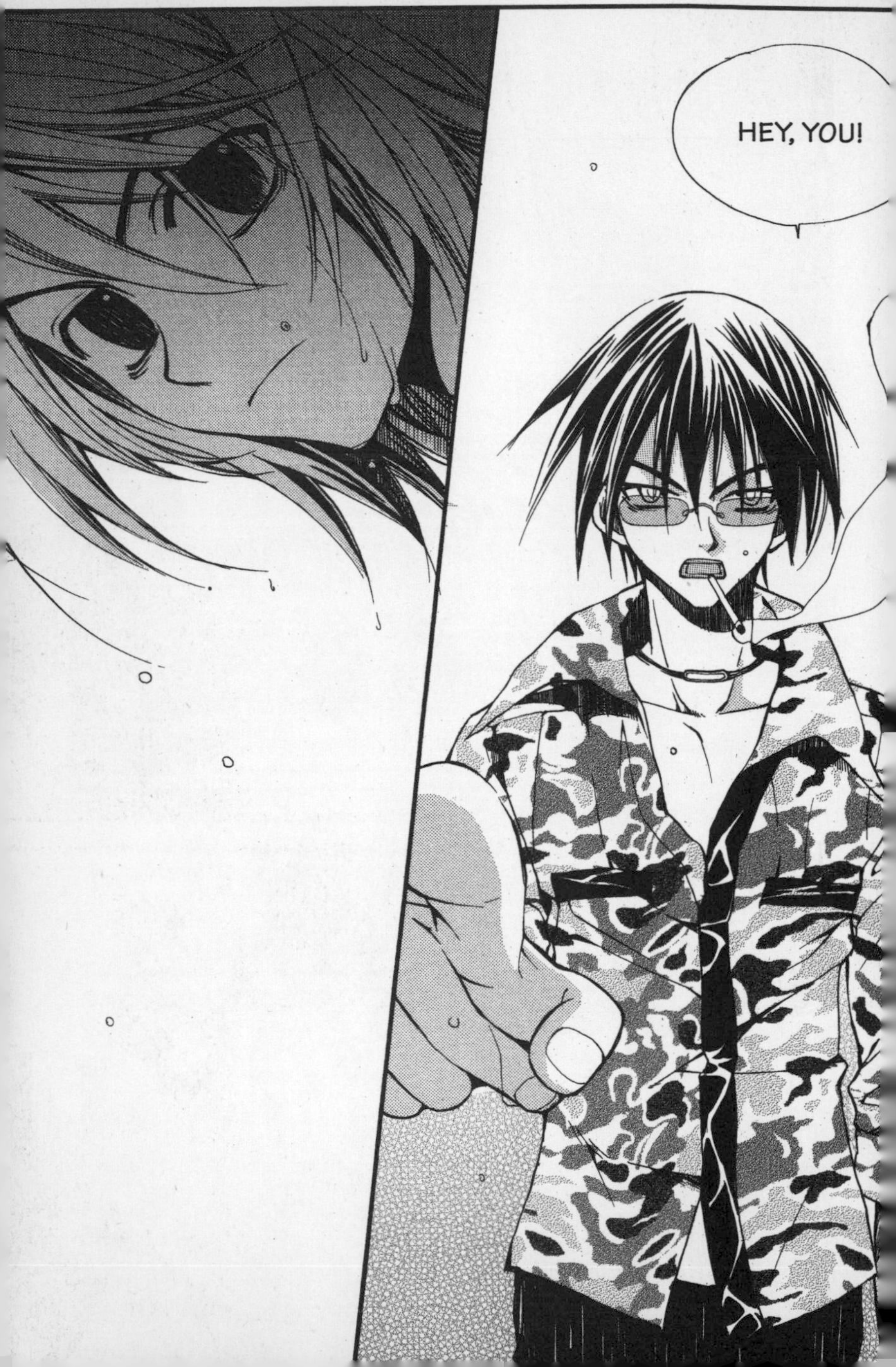
HEY, YOU!

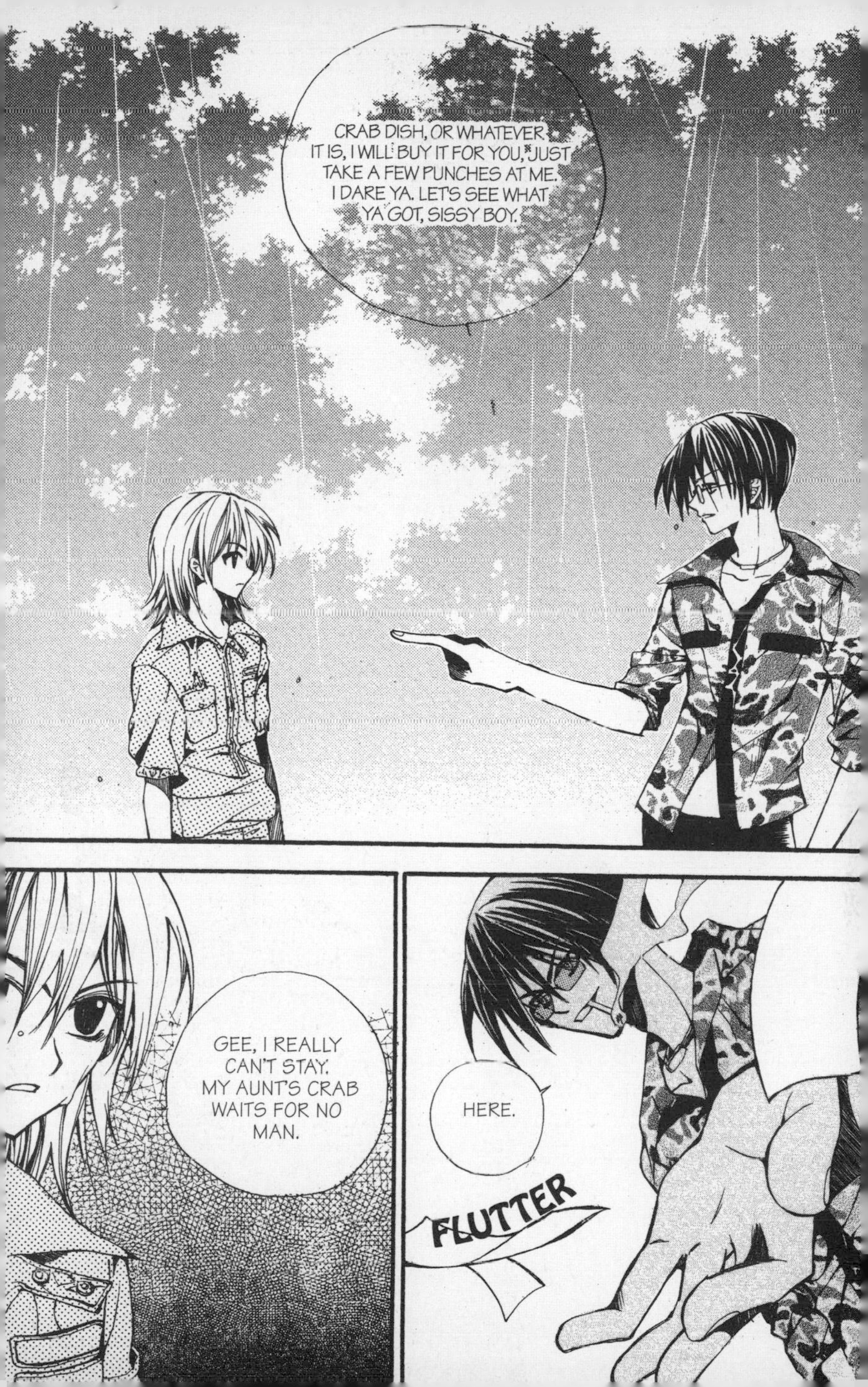
CRAB DISH, OR WHATEVER IT IS, I WILL BUY IT FOR YOU, JUST TAKE A FEW PUNCHES AT ME. I DARE YA. LET'S SEE WHAT YA GOT, SISSY BOY.
GEE, I REALLY CAN'T STAY. MY AUNT'S CRAB WAITS FOR NO MAN.
HERE.
FLUTTER

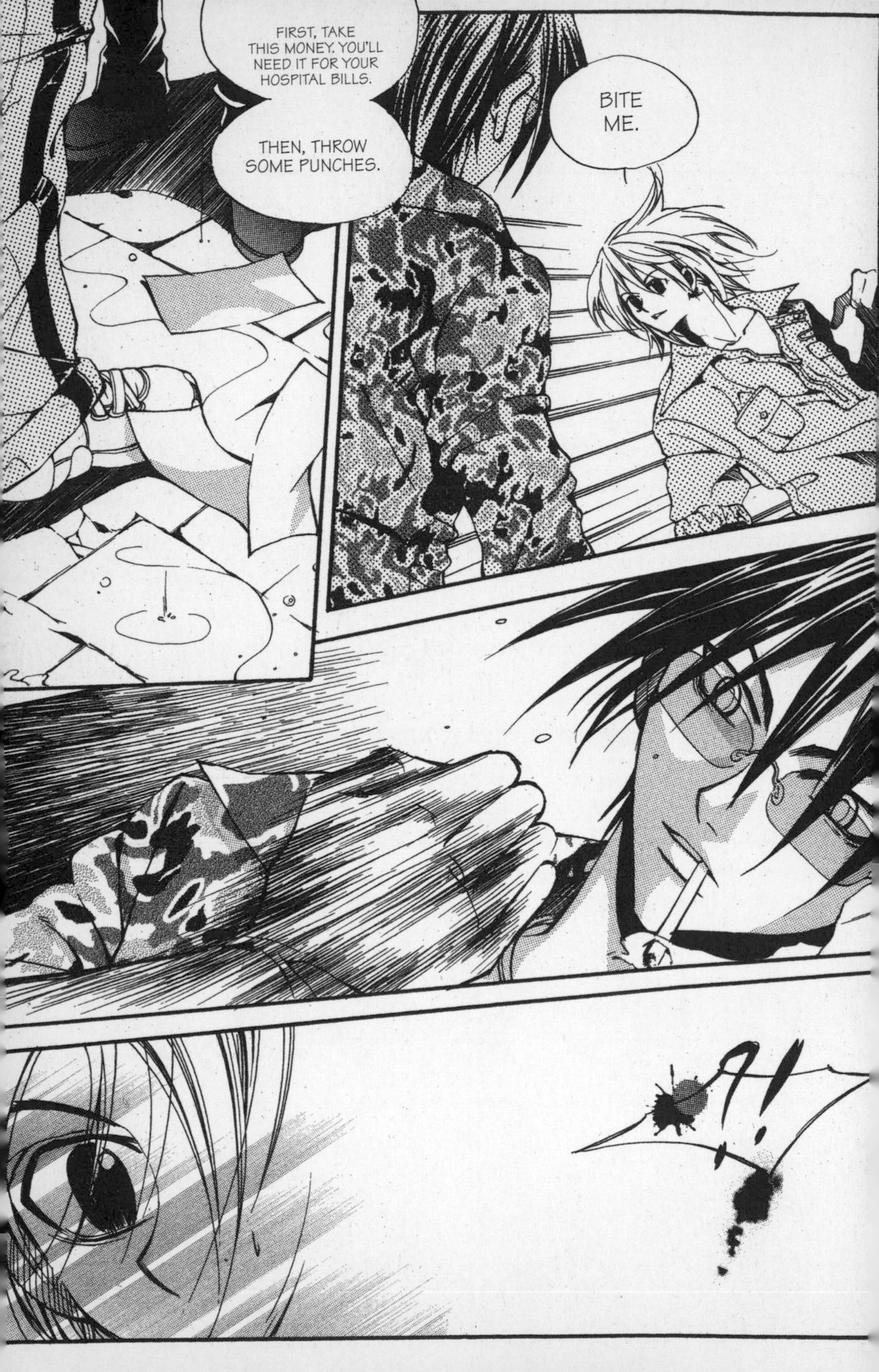
FIRST, TAKE THIS MONEY. YOU'LL NEED IT FOR YOUR HOSPITAL BILLS.
THEN, THROW SOME PUNCHES.
BITE ME.
?!

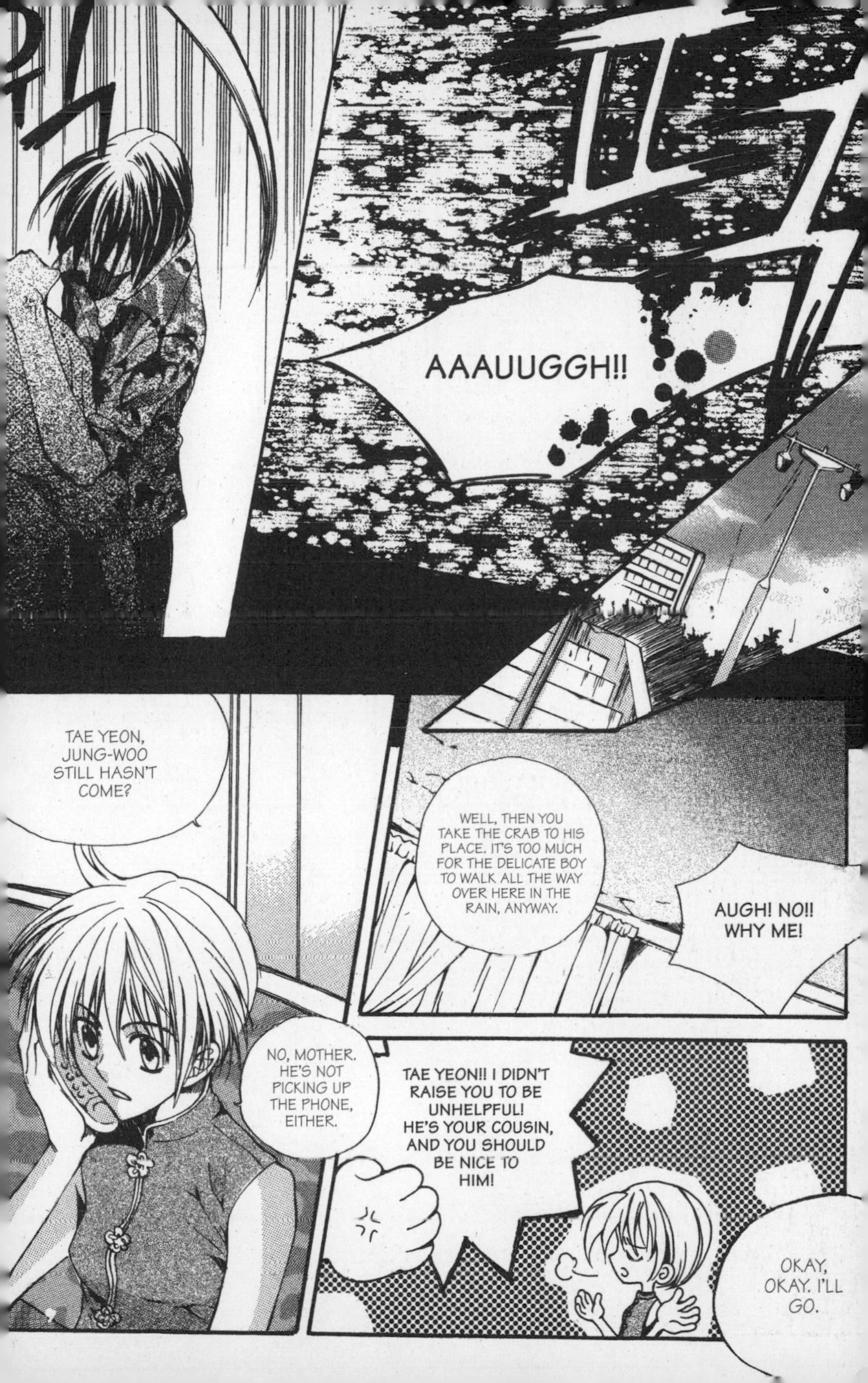
AAAUUGGH!!
TAE YEON, JUNG-WOO STILL HASN'T COME?
WELL, THEN YOU TAKE THE CRAB TO HIS PLACE. IT'S TOO MUCH FOR THE DELICATE BOY TO WALK ALL THE WAY OVER HERE IN THE RAIN, ANYWAY.
AUGH! NO!! WHY ME!
NO, MOTHER. HE'S NOT PICKING UP THE PHONE, EITHER.
TAE YEON!! I DIDN'T RAISE YOU TO BE UNHELPFUL! HE'S YOUR COUSIN, AND YOU SHOULD BE NICE TO HIM!
OKAY, OKAY. I'LL GO.

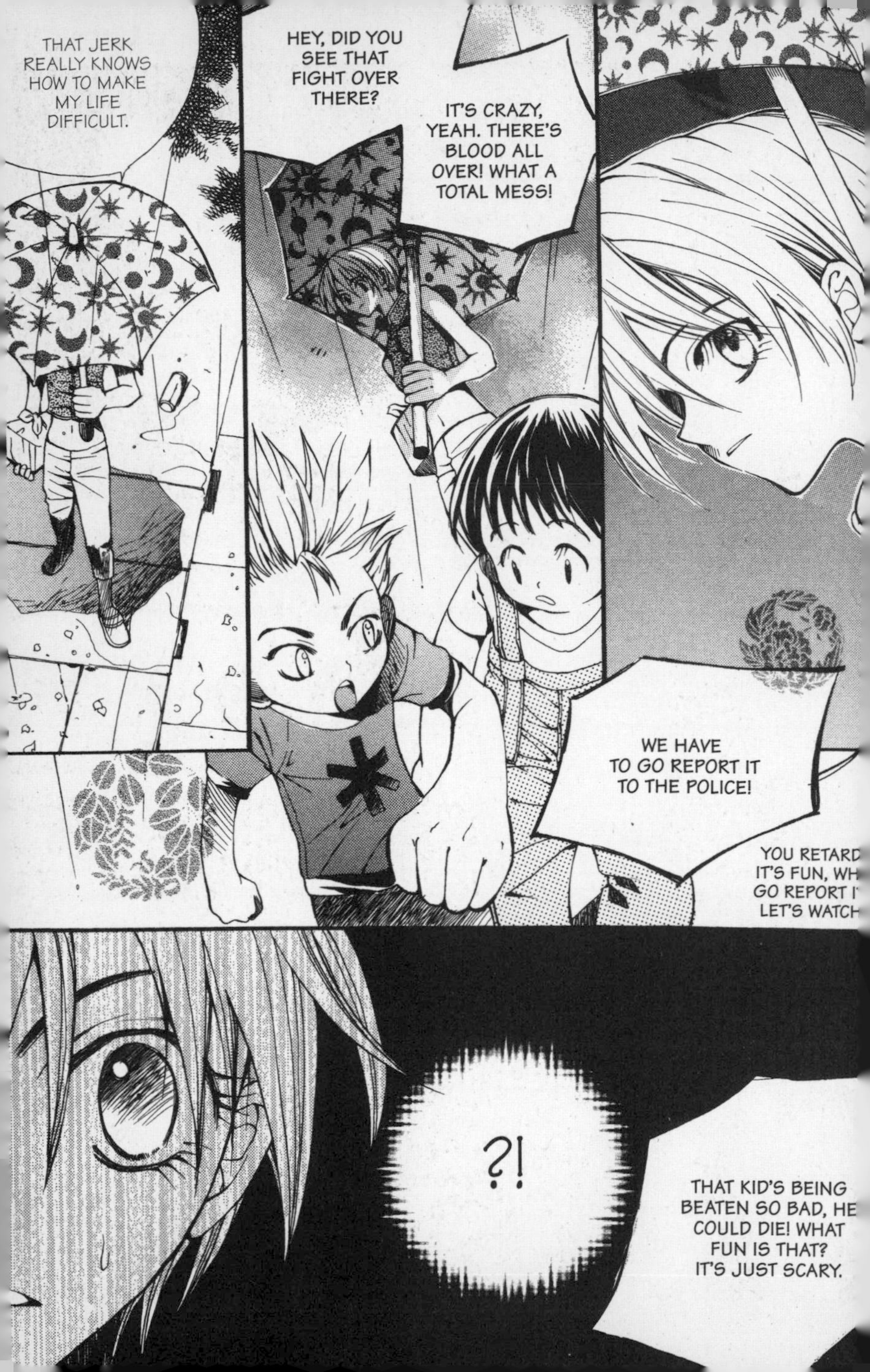
THAT JERK REALLY KNOWS HOW TO MAKE MY LIFE DIFFICULT.
HEY, DID YOU SEE THAT FIGHT OVER THERE?
IT'S CRAZY, YEAH. THERE'S BLOOD ALL OVER! WHAT A TOTAL MESS!
WE HAVE TO GO REPORT IT TO THE POLICE!
YOU RETARD IT'S FUN, WH GO REPORT I LET'S WATCH
?!
THAT KID'S BEING BEATEN SO BAD, HE COULD DIE! WHAT FUN IS THAT? IT'S JUST SCARY.

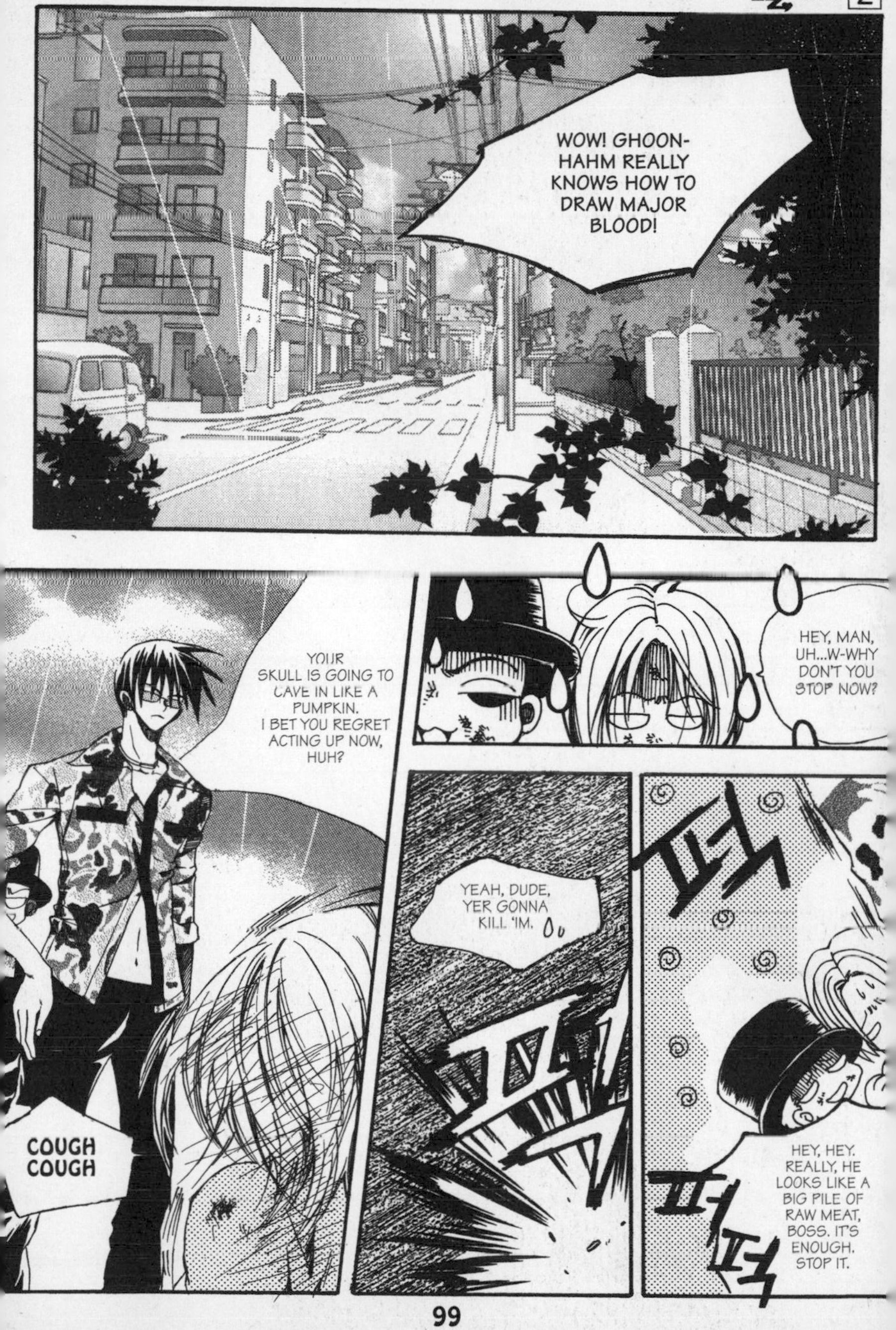
WOW! GHOON-HAHM REALLY KNOWS HOW TO DRAW MAJOR BLOOD!
YOUR SKULL IS GOING TO CAVE IN LIKE A PUMPKIN. I BET YOU REGRET ACTING UP NOW, HUH?
COUGH COUGH
HEY, MAN, UH...W-WHY DON'T YOU STOP NOW?
YEAH, DUDE, YER GONNA KILL 'IM.
HEY, HEY. REALLY, HE LOOKS LIKE A BIG PILE OF RAW MEAT, BOSS. IT'S ENOUGH. STOP IT.

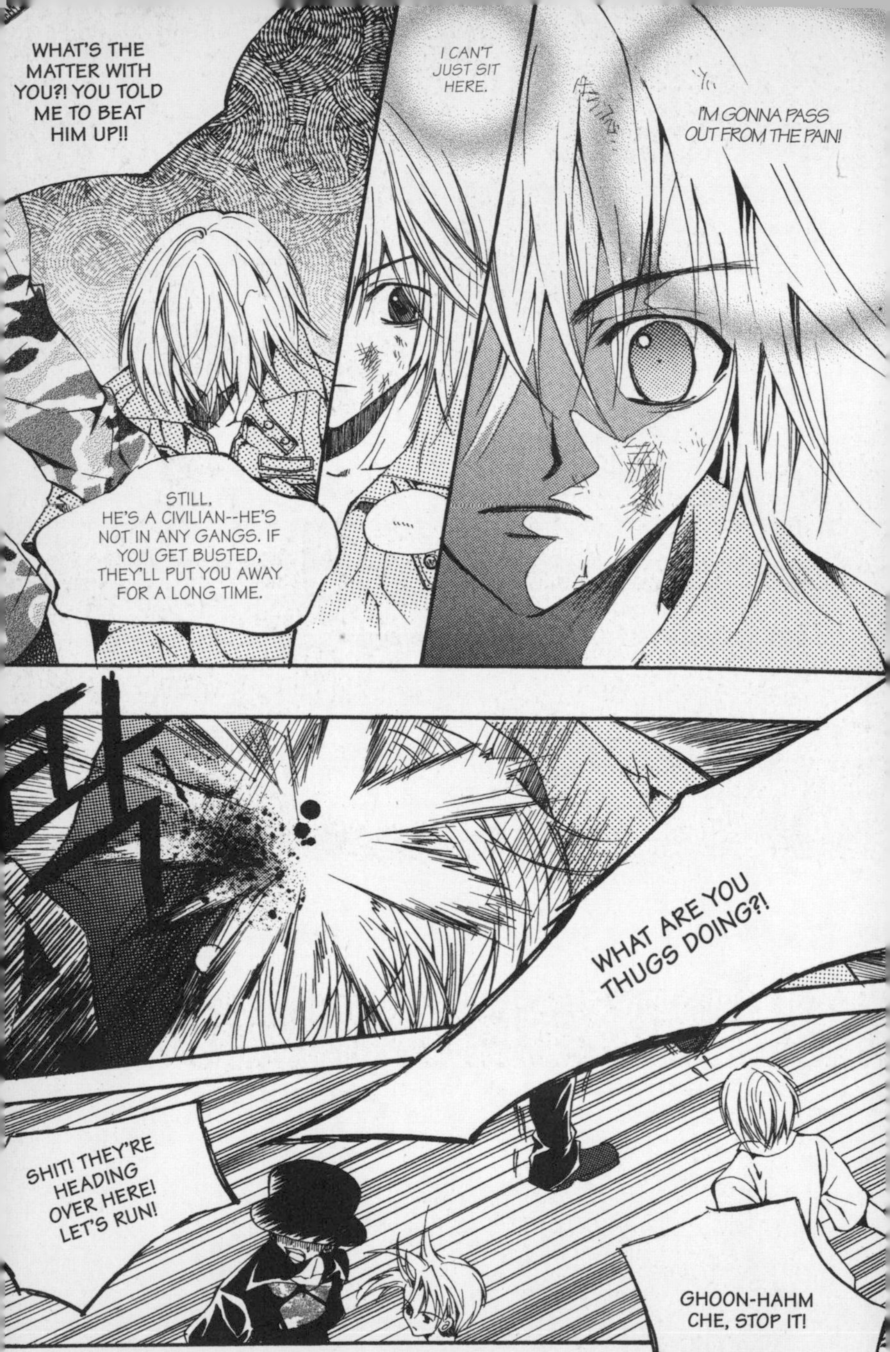
WHAT'S THE MATTER WITH YOU?! YOU TOLD ME TO BEAT HIM UP!!
STILL, HE'S A CIVILIAN--HE'S NOT IN ANY GANGS. IF YOU GET BUSTED, THEY'LL PUT YOU AWAY FOR A LONG TIME.
I CAN'T JUST SIT HERE.
.....
I'M GONNA PASS OUT FROM THE PAIN!
WHAT ARE YOU THUGS DOING?!
SHIT! THEY'RE HEADING OVER HERE! LET'S RUN!
GHOON-HAHM CHE, STOP IT!

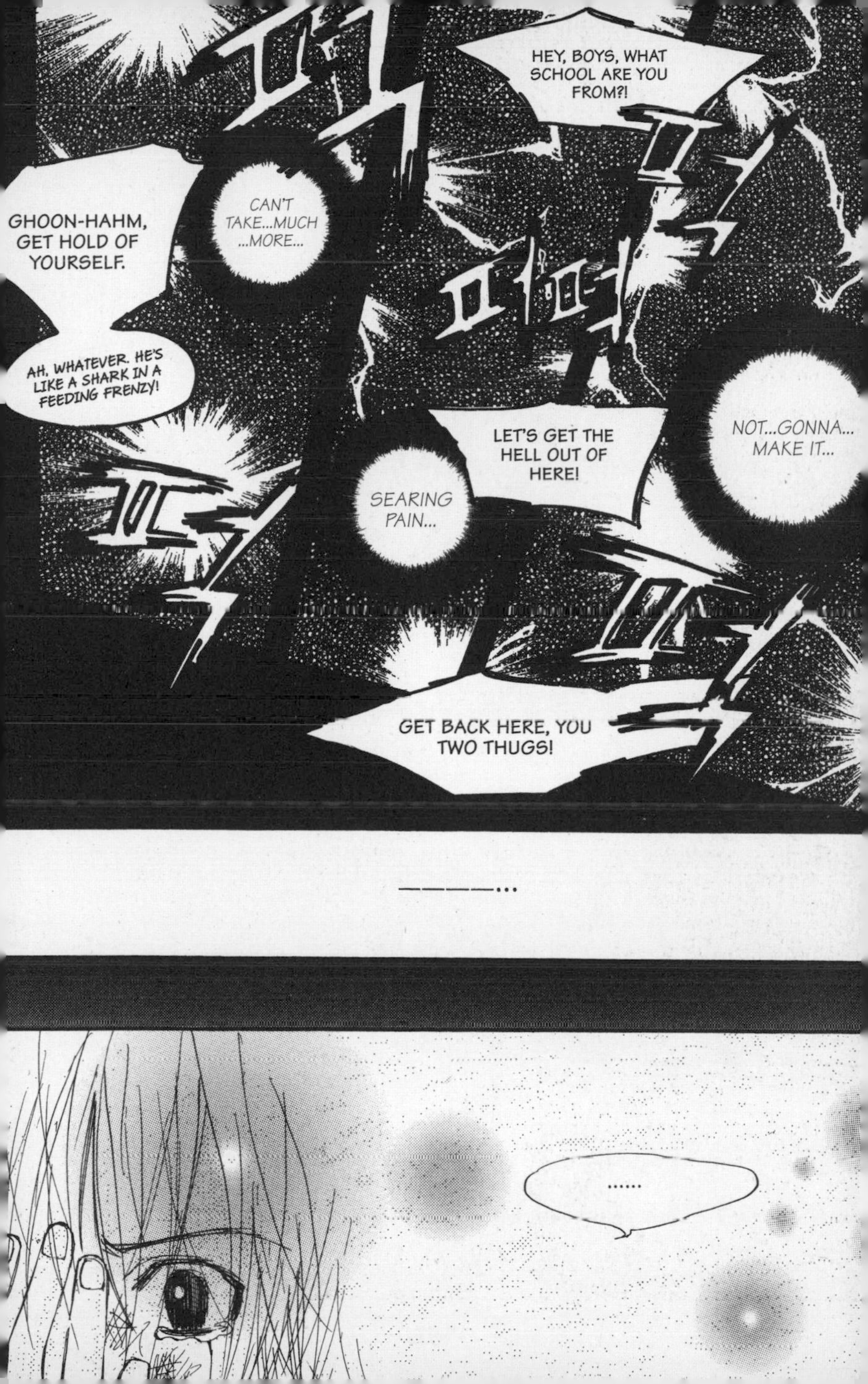
HEY, BOYS, WHAT SCHOOL ARE YOU FROM?!
GHOON-HAHM, GET HOLD OF YOURSELF.
CAN'T TAKE...MUCH ...MORE...
AH, WHATEVER. HE'S LIKE A SHARK IN A FEEDING FRENZY!
LET'S GET THE HELL OUT OF HERE!
NOT...GONNA... MAKE IT...
SEARING PAIN...
GET BACK HERE, YOU TWO THUGS!
———...
......

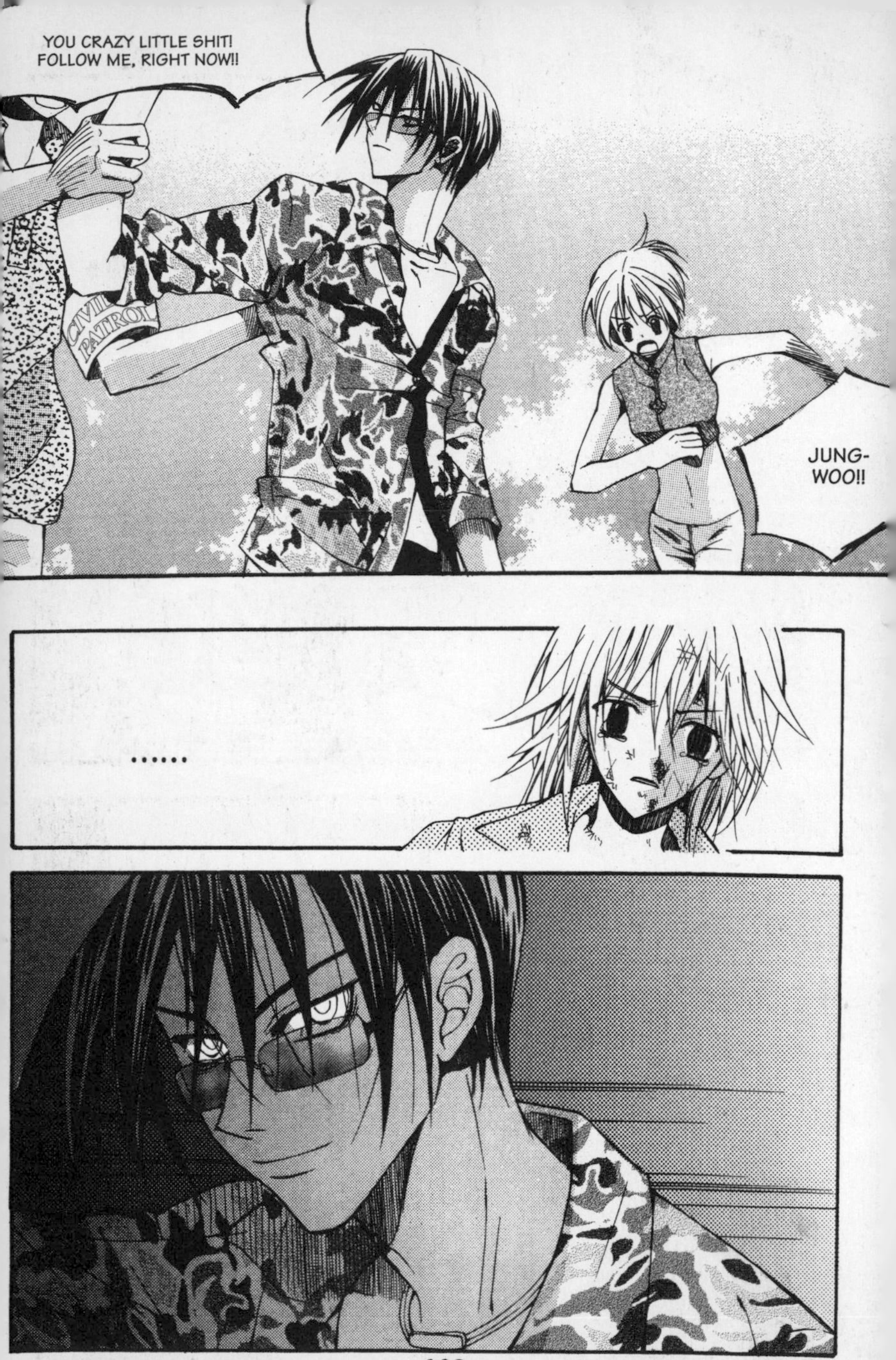
YOU CRAZY LITTLE SHIT! FOLLOW ME, RIGHT NOW!!
CIVIL PATROL
JUNG-WOO!!
......

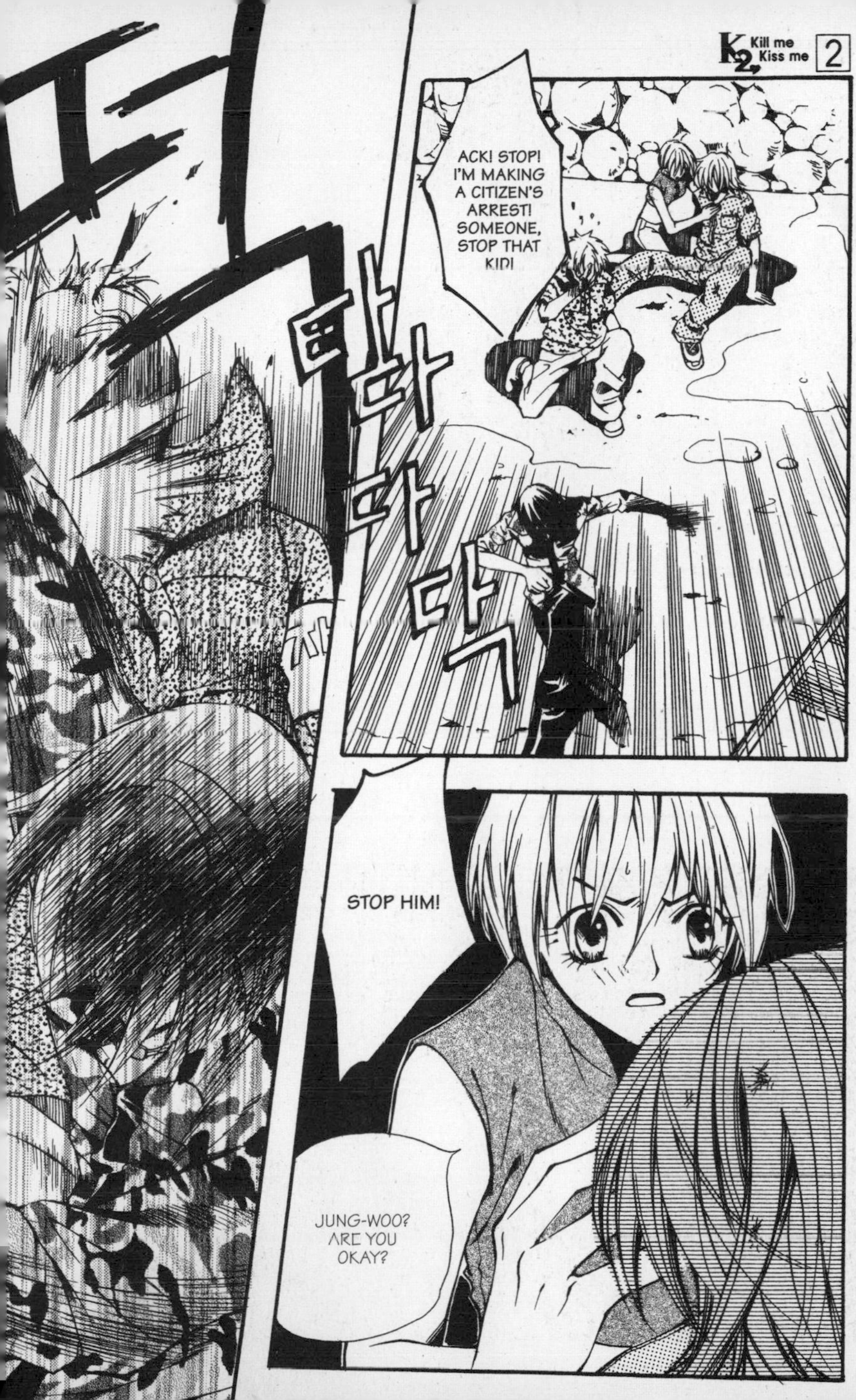
ACK! STOP! I'M MAKING A CITIZEN'S ARREST! SOMEONE, STOP THAT KID!
STOP HIM!
JUNG-WOO? ARE YOU OKAY?

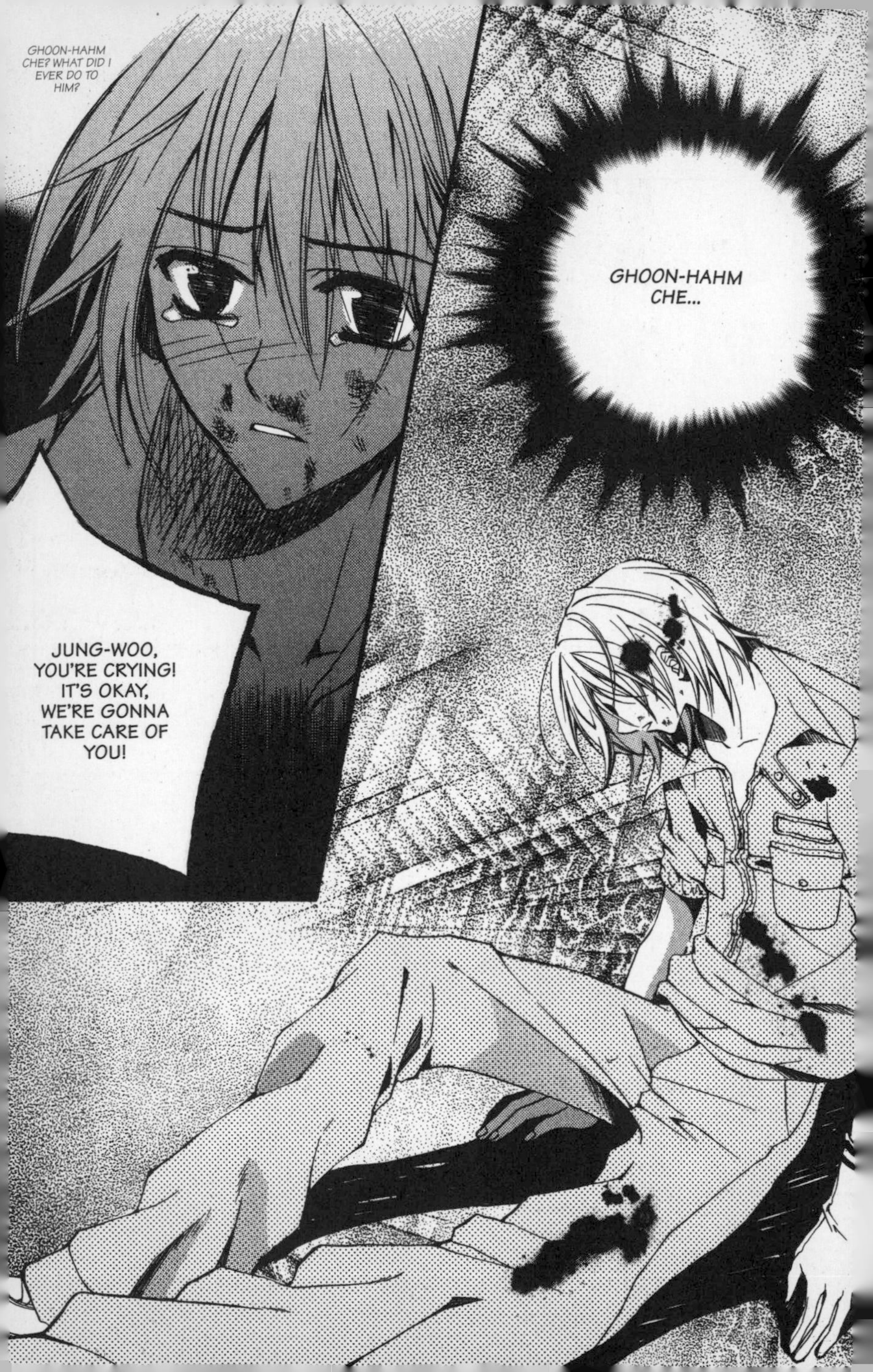
GHOON-HAHM CHE? WHAT DID I EVER DO TO HIM?
GHOON-HAHM CHE...
JUNG-WOO, YOU'RE CRYING! IT'S OKAY, WE'RE GONNA TAKE CARE OF YOU!

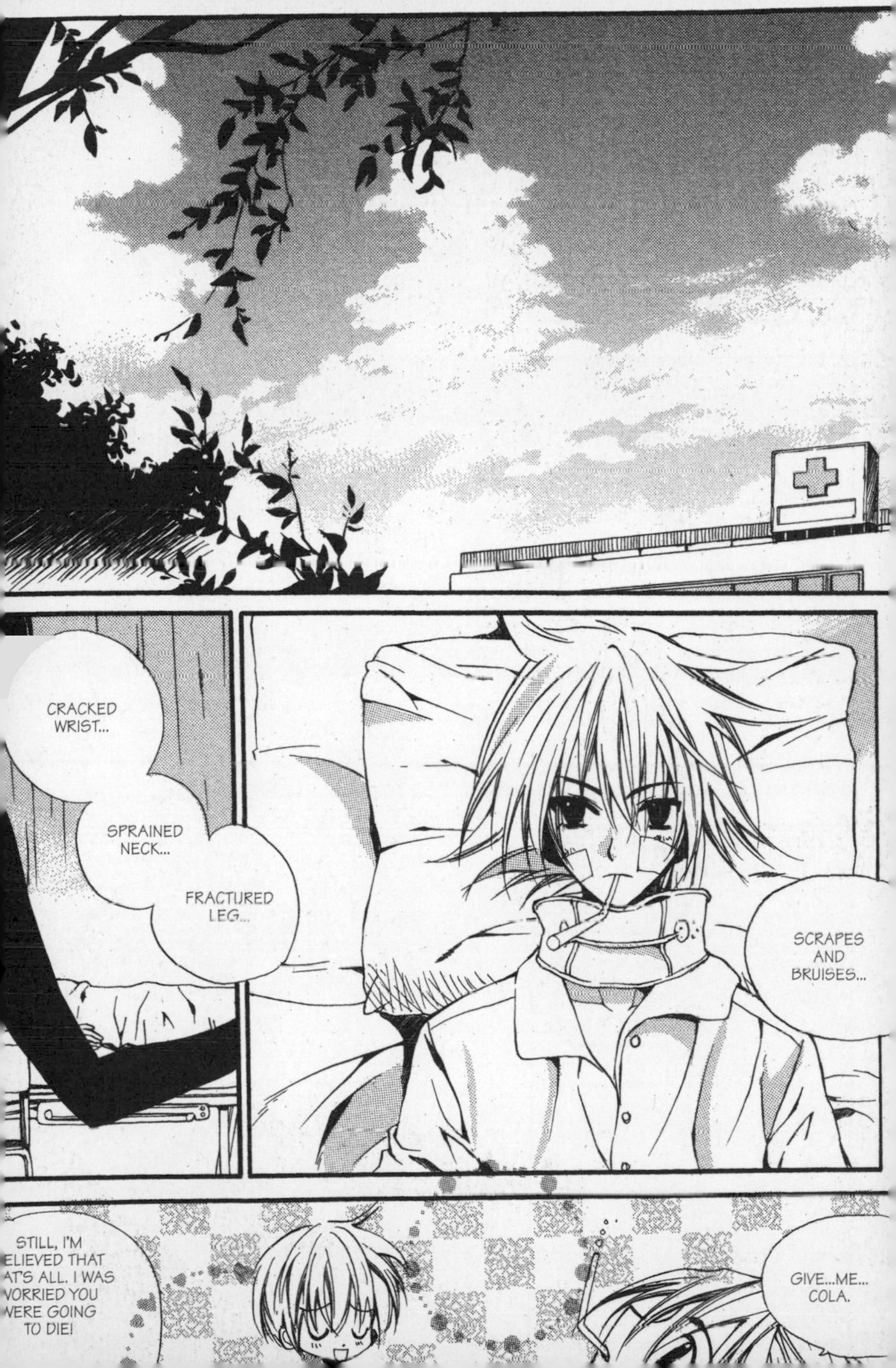
CRACKED WRIST...
SPRAINED NECK...
FRACTURED LEG...
SCRAPES AND BRUISES...
STILL, I'M ELIEVED THAT AT'S ALL. I WAS VORRIED YOU WERE GOING TO DIE!
GIVE...ME... COLA.

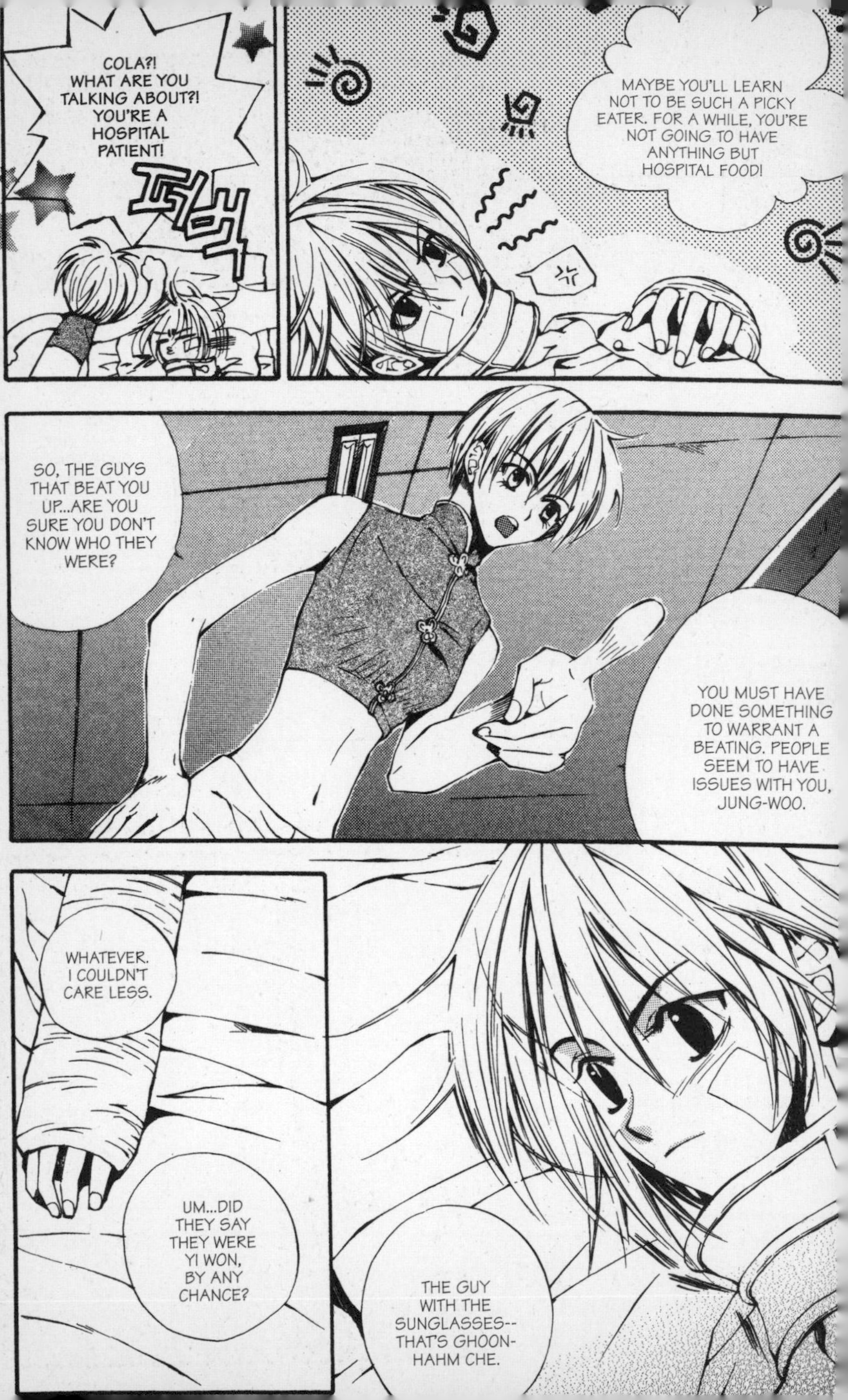
COLA?! WHAT ARE YOU TALKING ABOUT?! YOU'RE A HOSPITAL PATIENT!
MAYBE YOU'LL LEARN NOT TO BE SUCH A PICKY EATER. FOR A WHILE, YOU'RE NOT GOING TO HAVE ANYTHING BUT HOSPITAL FOOD!
SO, THE GUYS THAT BEAT YOU UP...ARE YOU SURE YOU DON'T KNOW WHO THEY WERE?
YOU MUST HAVE DONE SOMETHING TO WARRANT A BEATING. PEOPLE SEEM TO HAVE ISSUES WITH YOU, JUNG-WOO.
WHATEVER. I COULDN'T CARE LESS.
UM...DID THEY SAY THEY WERE YI WON, BY ANY CHANCE?
THE GUY WITH THE SUNGLASSES-- THAT'S GHOON-HAHM CHE.

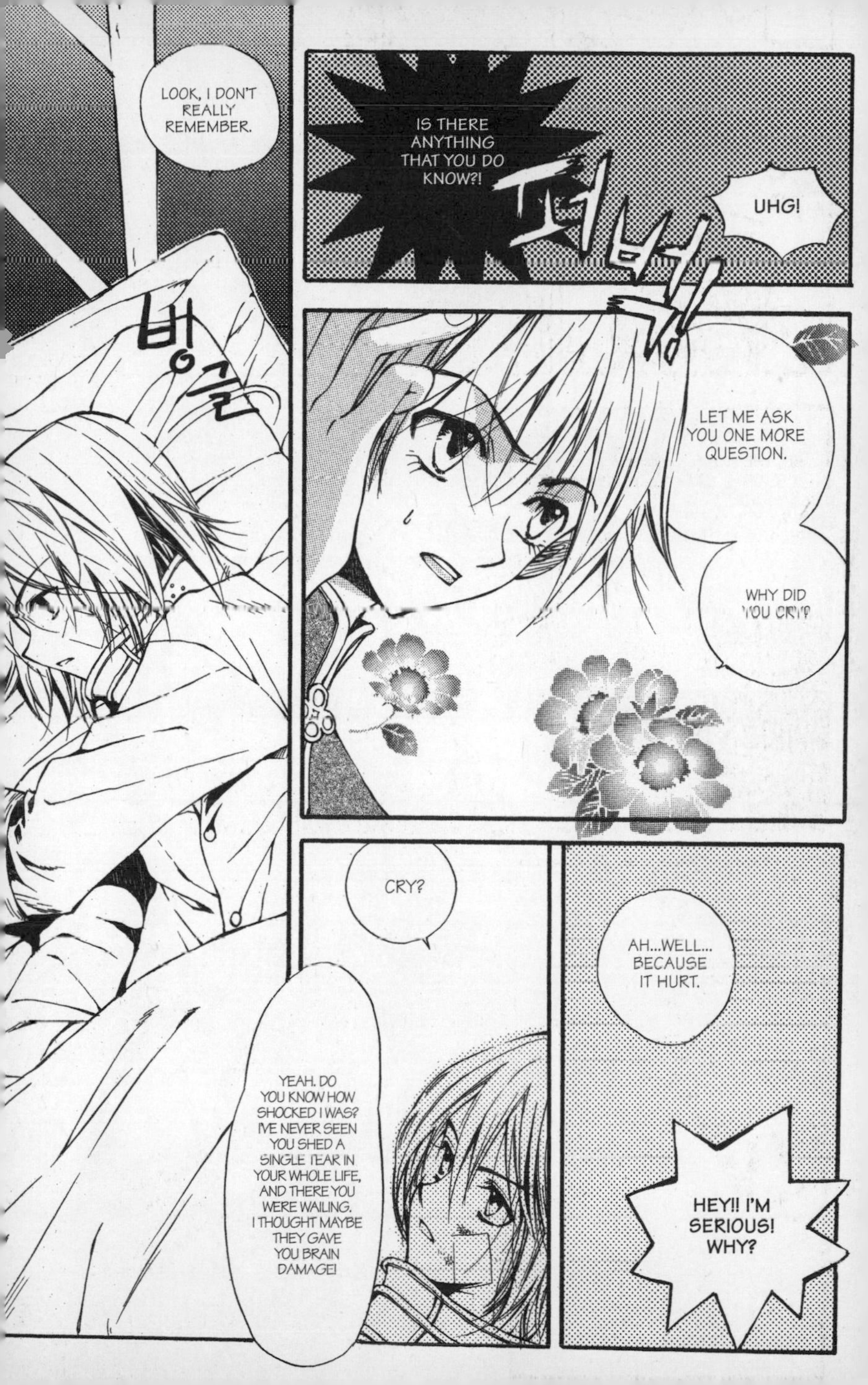
LOOK, I DON'T REALLY REMEMBER.
빙글
IS THERE ANYTHING THAT YOU DO KNOW?!
UHG!
LET ME ASK YOU ONE MORE QUESTION.
WHY DID YOU CRY?
CRY?
YEAH. DO YOU KNOW HOW SHOCKED I WAS? I'VE NEVER SEEN YOU SHED A SINGLE TEAR IN YOUR WHOLE LIFE, AND THERE YOU WERE WAILING. I THOUGHT MAYBE THEY GAVE YOU BRAIN DAMAGE!
AH...WELL... BECAUSE IT HURT.
HEY!! I'M SERIOUS! WHY?

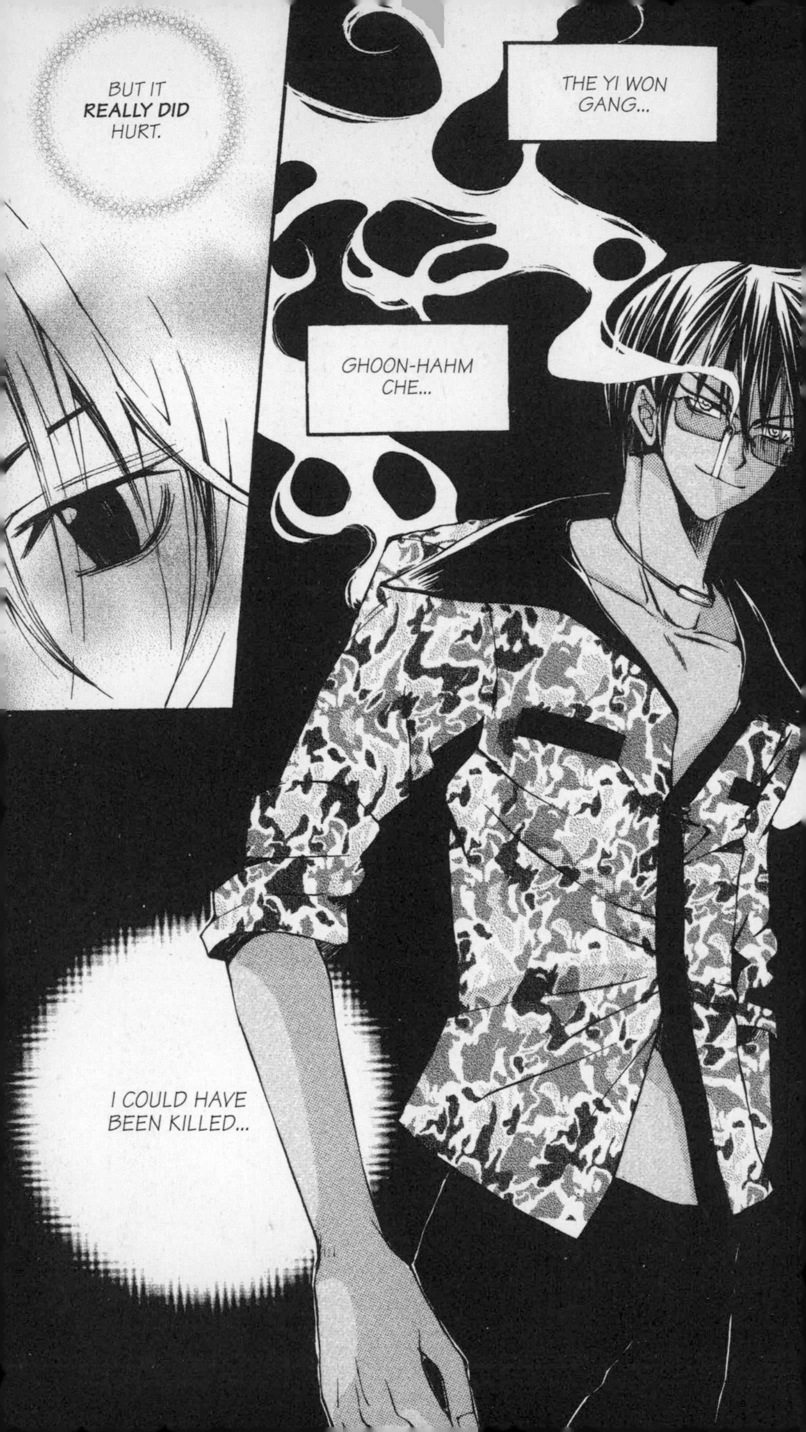
BUT IT **REALLY DID** HURT.
THE YI WON GANG...
GHOON-HAHM CHE...
I COULD HAVE BEEN KILLED...

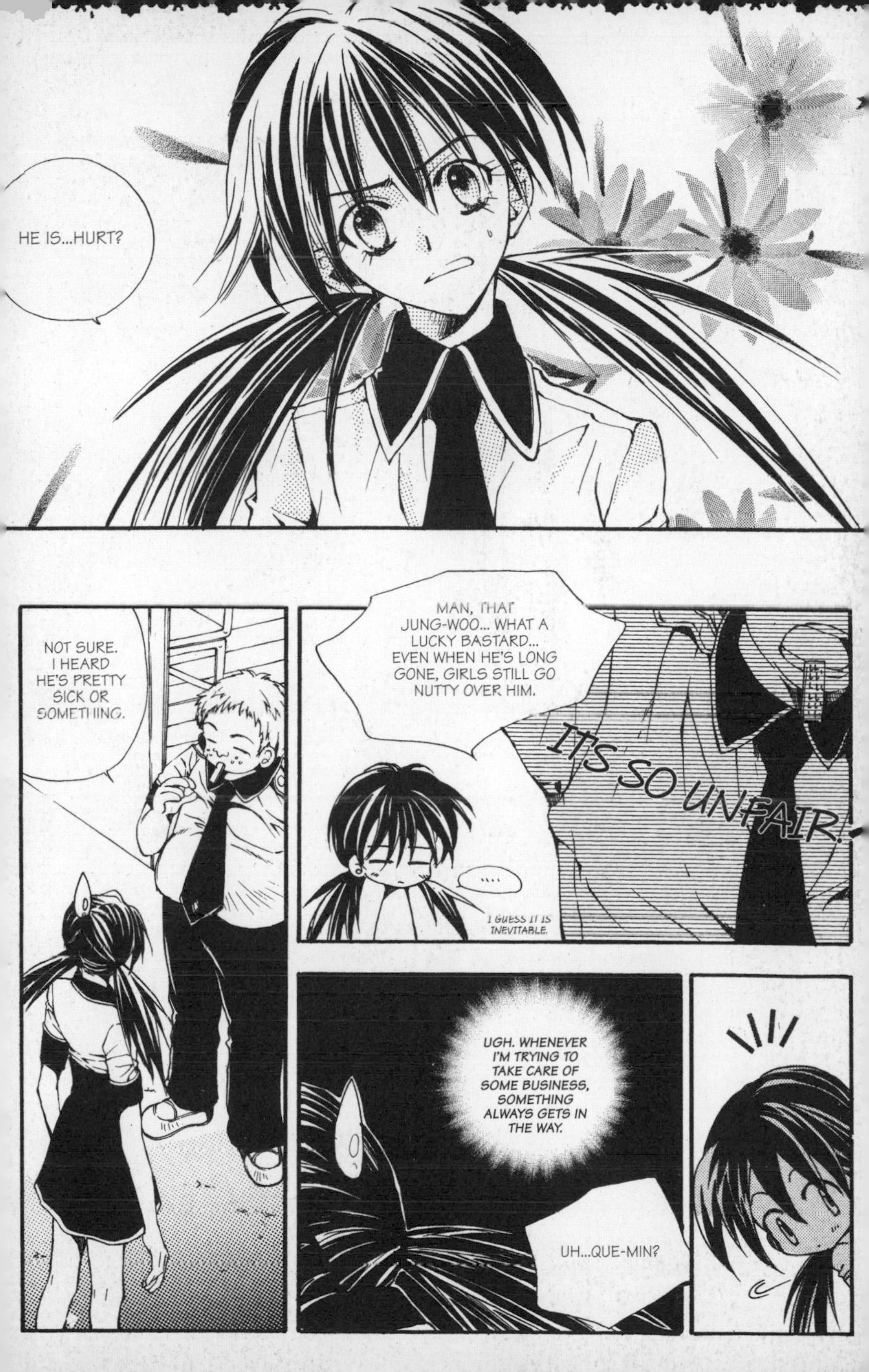
HE IS...HURT?
NOT SURE. I HEARD HE'S PRETTY SICK OR SOMETHING.
MAN, THAT JUNG-WOO... WHAT A LUCKY BASTARD... EVEN WHEN HE'S LONG GONE, GIRLS STILL GO NUTTY OVER HIM.
....
I GUESS IT IS INEVITABLE.
IT'S SO UNFAIR!
UGH. WHENEVER I'M TRYING TO TAKE CARE OF SOME BUSINESS, SOMETHING ALWAYS GETS IN THE WAY.
UH...QUE-MIN?

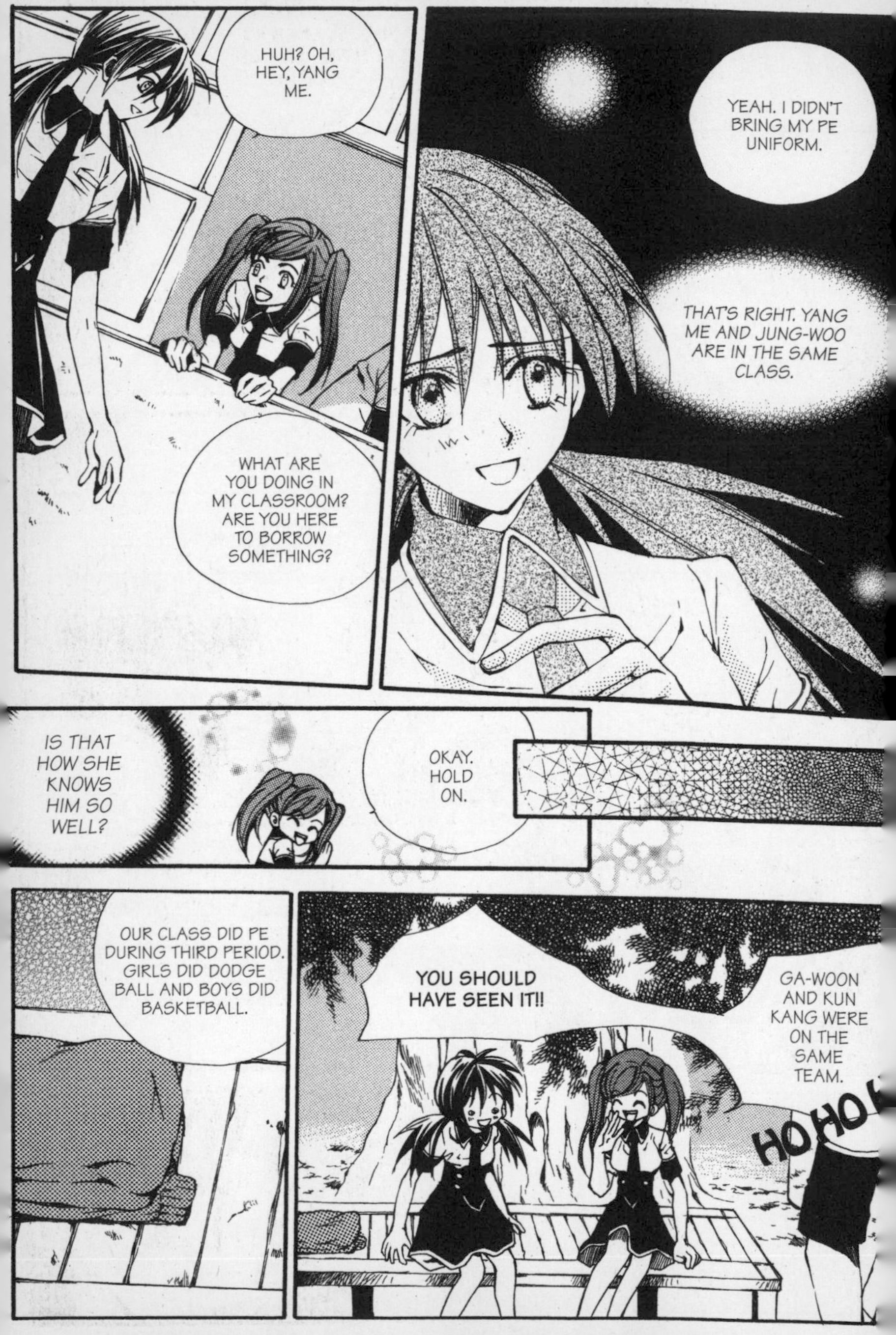
HUH? OH, HEY, YANG ME.
WHAT ARE YOU DOING IN MY CLASSROOM? ARE YOU HERE TO BORROW SOMETHING?
YEAH. I DIDN'T BRING MY PE UNIFORM.
THAT'S RIGHT. YANG ME AND JUNG-WOO ARE IN THE SAME CLASS.
IS THAT HOW SHE KNOWS HIM SO WELL?
OKAY. HOLD ON.
OUR CLASS DID PE DURING THIRD PERIOD. GIRLS DID DODGE BALL AND BOYS DID BASKETBALL.
YOU SHOULD HAVE SEEN IT!!
GA-WOON AND KUN KANG WERE ON THE SAME TEAM.
HO HO

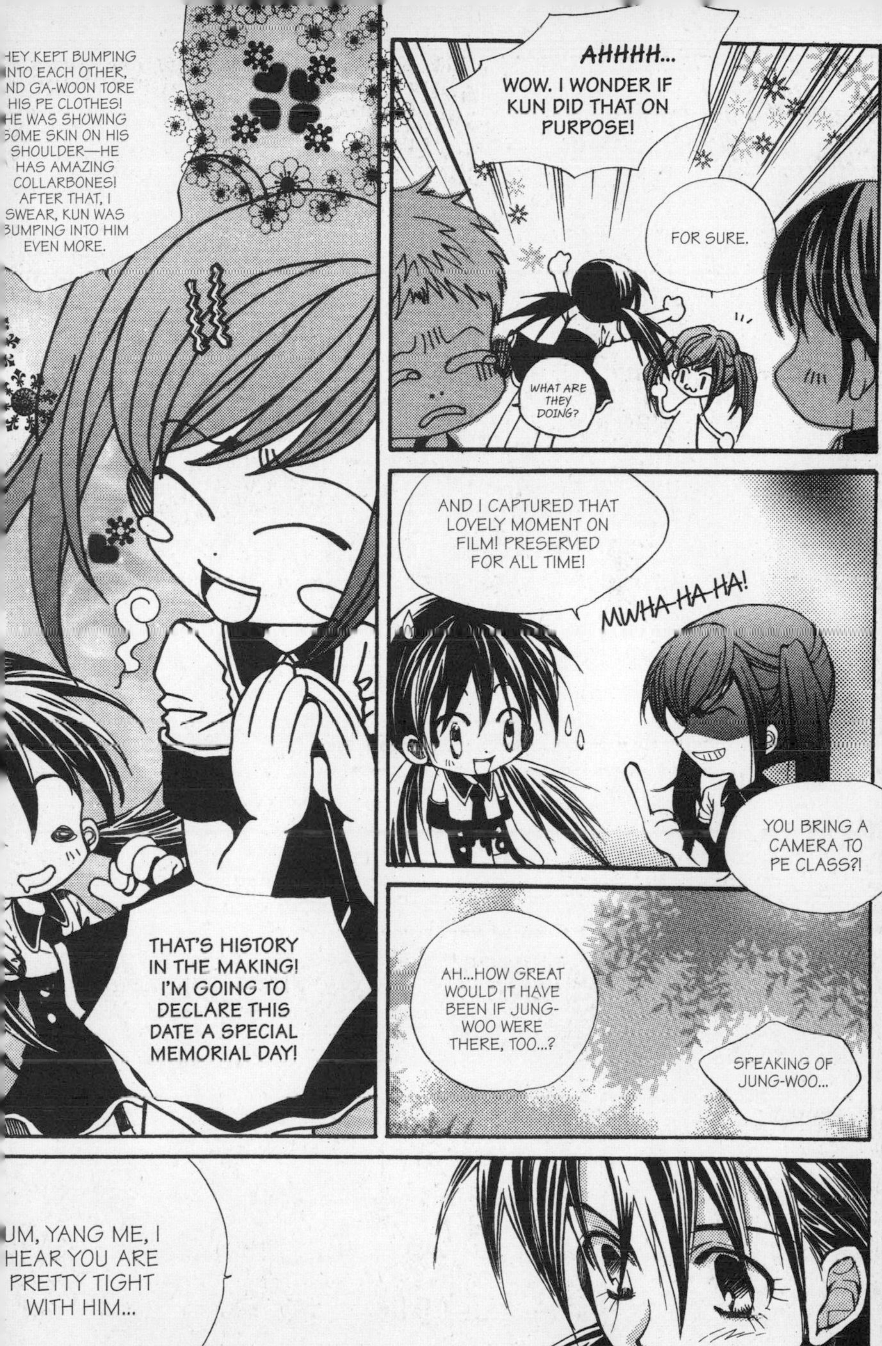

HEY KEPT BUMPING INTO EACH OTHER, ND GA-WOON TORE HIS PE CLOTHES! HE WAS SHOWING SOME SKIN ON HIS SHOULDER—HE HAS AMAZING COLLARBONES! AFTER THAT, I SWEAR, KUN WAS BUMPING INTO HIM EVEN MORE.
THAT'S HISTORY IN THE MAKING! I'M GOING TO DECLARE THIS DATE A SPECIAL MEMORIAL DAY!
AHHHH...
WOW. I WONDER IF KUN DID THAT ON PURPOSE!
FOR SURE.
WHAT ARE THEY DOING?
AND I CAPTURED THAT LOVELY MOMENT ON FILM! PRESERVED FOR ALL TIME!
MWHA-HA-HA!
YOU BRING A CAMERA TO PE CLASS?!
AH...HOW GREAT WOULD IT HAVE BEEN IF JUNG-WOO WERE THERE, TOO...?
SPEAKING OF JUNG-WOO...
UM, YANG ME, I HEAR YOU ARE PRETTY TIGHT WITH HIM...

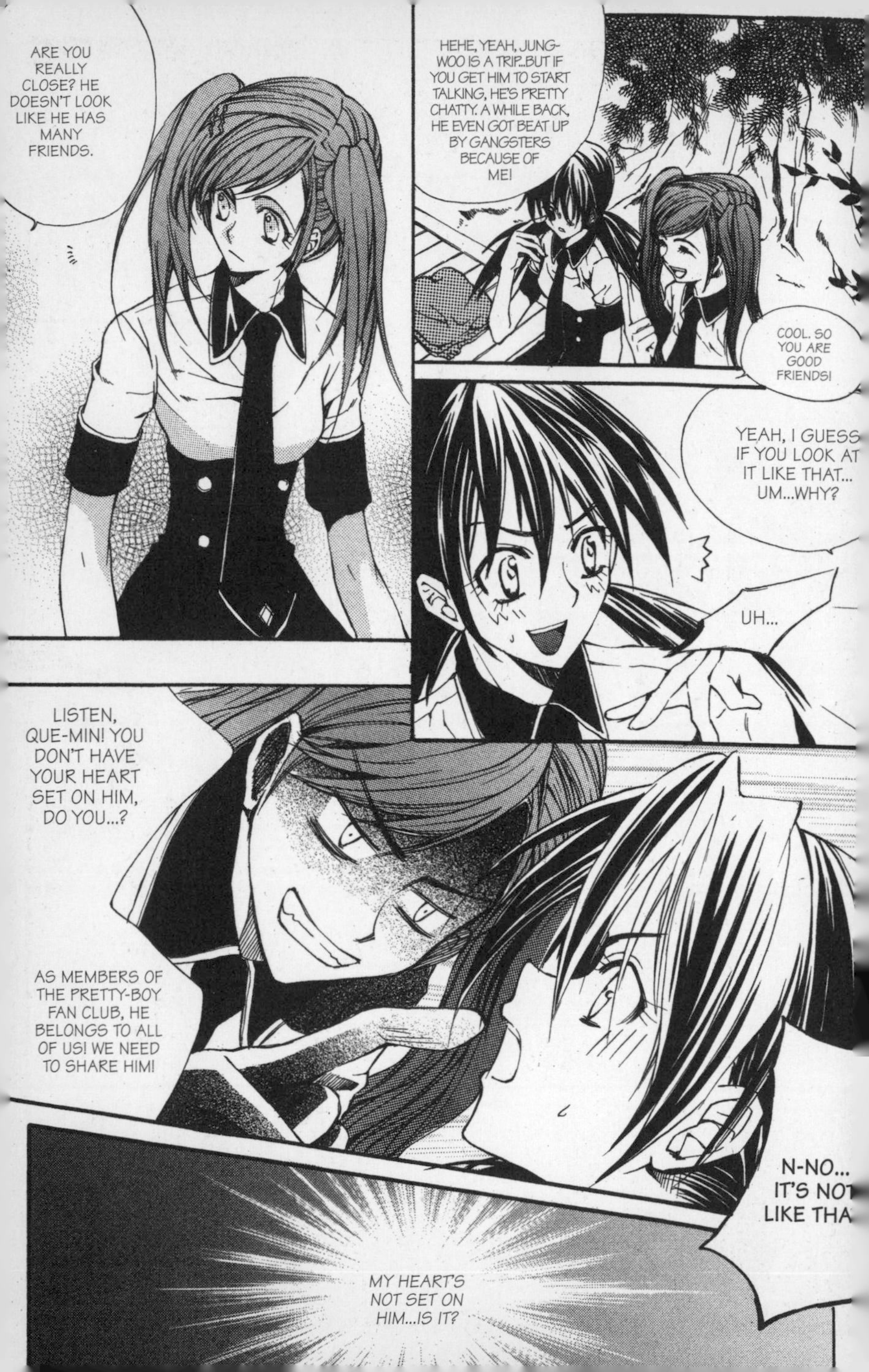
ARE YOU REALLY CLOSE? HE DOESN'T LOOK LIKE HE HAS MANY FRIENDS.
HEHE, YEAH, JUNG-WOO IS A TRIP...BUT IF YOU GET HIM TO START TALKING, HE'S PRETTY CHATTY. A WHILE BACK, HE EVEN GOT BEAT UP BY GANGSTERS BECAUSE OF ME!
COOL. SO YOU ARE GOOD FRIENDS!
YEAH, I GUESS IF YOU LOOK AT IT LIKE THAT... UM...WHY?
UH...
LISTEN, QUE-MIN! YOU DON'T HAVE YOUR HEART SET ON HIM, DO YOU...?
AS MEMBERS OF THE PRETTY-BOY FAN CLUB, HE BELONGS TO ALL OF US! WE NEED TO SHARE HIM!
N-NO... IT'S NOT LIKE THA
MY HEART'S NOT SET ON HIM...IS IT?

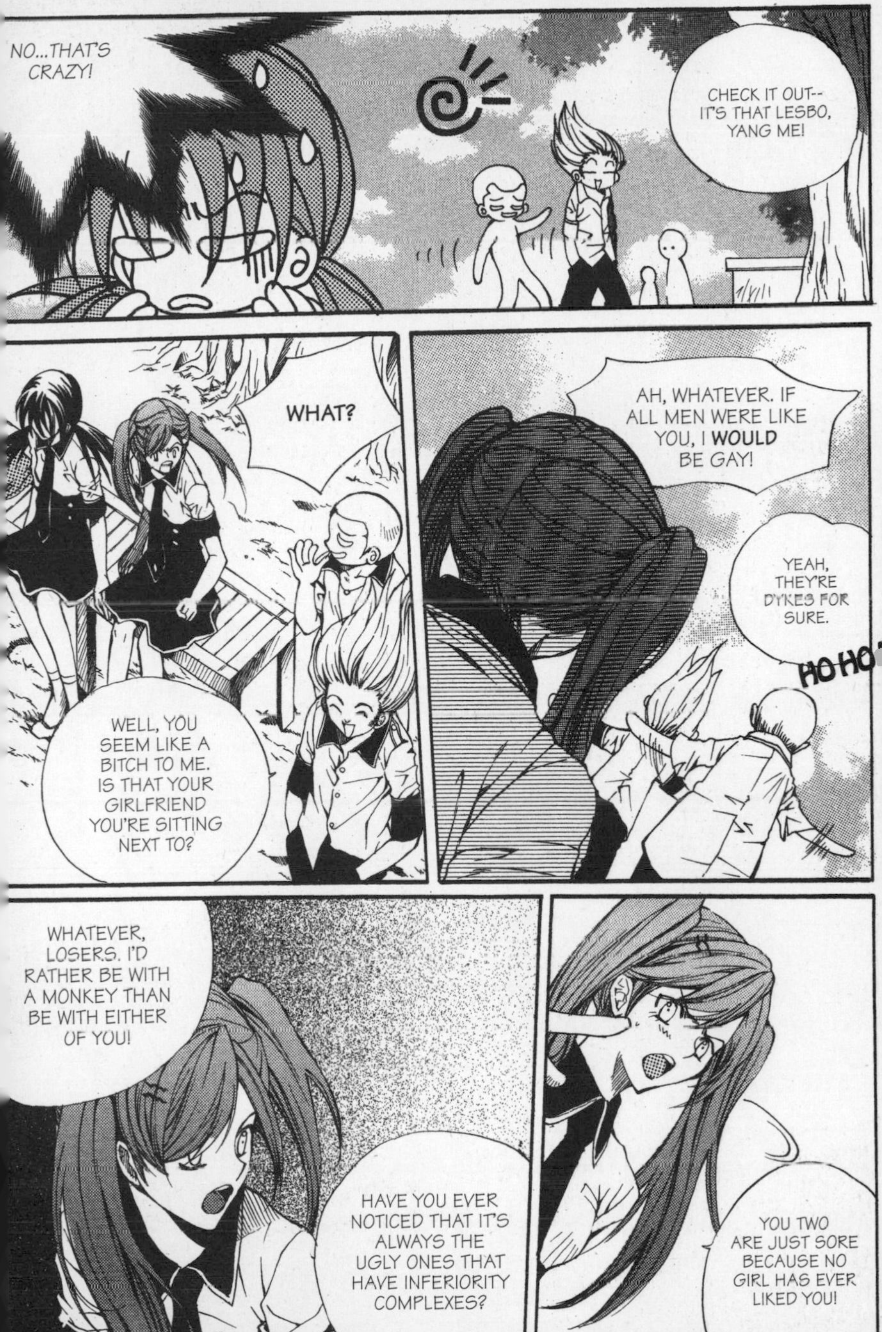
NO...THAT'S CRAZY!
CHECK IT OUT-- IT'S THAT LESBO, YANG ME!
WHAT?
WELL, YOU SEEM LIKE A BITCH TO ME. IS THAT YOUR GIRLFRIEND YOU'RE SITTING NEXT TO?
AH, WHATEVER. IF ALL MEN WERE LIKE YOU, I **WOULD** BE GAY!
YEAH, THEY'RE DYKES FOR SURE.
HO HO
WHATEVER, LOSERS. I'D RATHER BE WITH A MONKEY THAN BE WITH EITHER OF YOU!
HAVE YOU EVER NOTICED THAT IT'S ALWAYS THE UGLY ONES THAT HAVE INFERIORITY COMPLEXES?
YOU TWO ARE JUST SORE BECAUSE NO GIRL HAS EVER LIKED YOU!

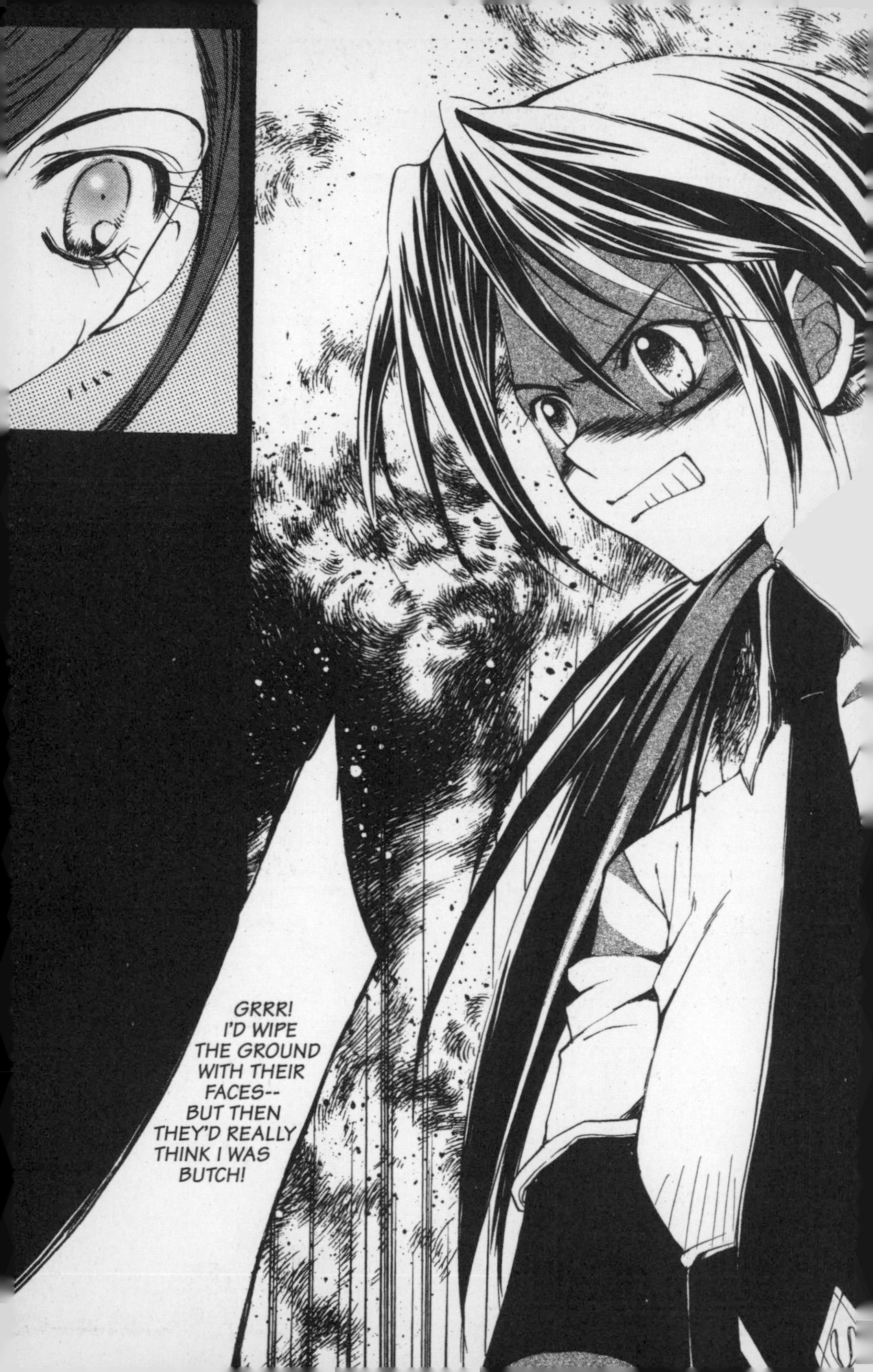
GRRR! I'D WIPE THE GROUND WITH THEIR FACES-- BUT THEN THEY'D REALLY THINK I WAS BUTCH!

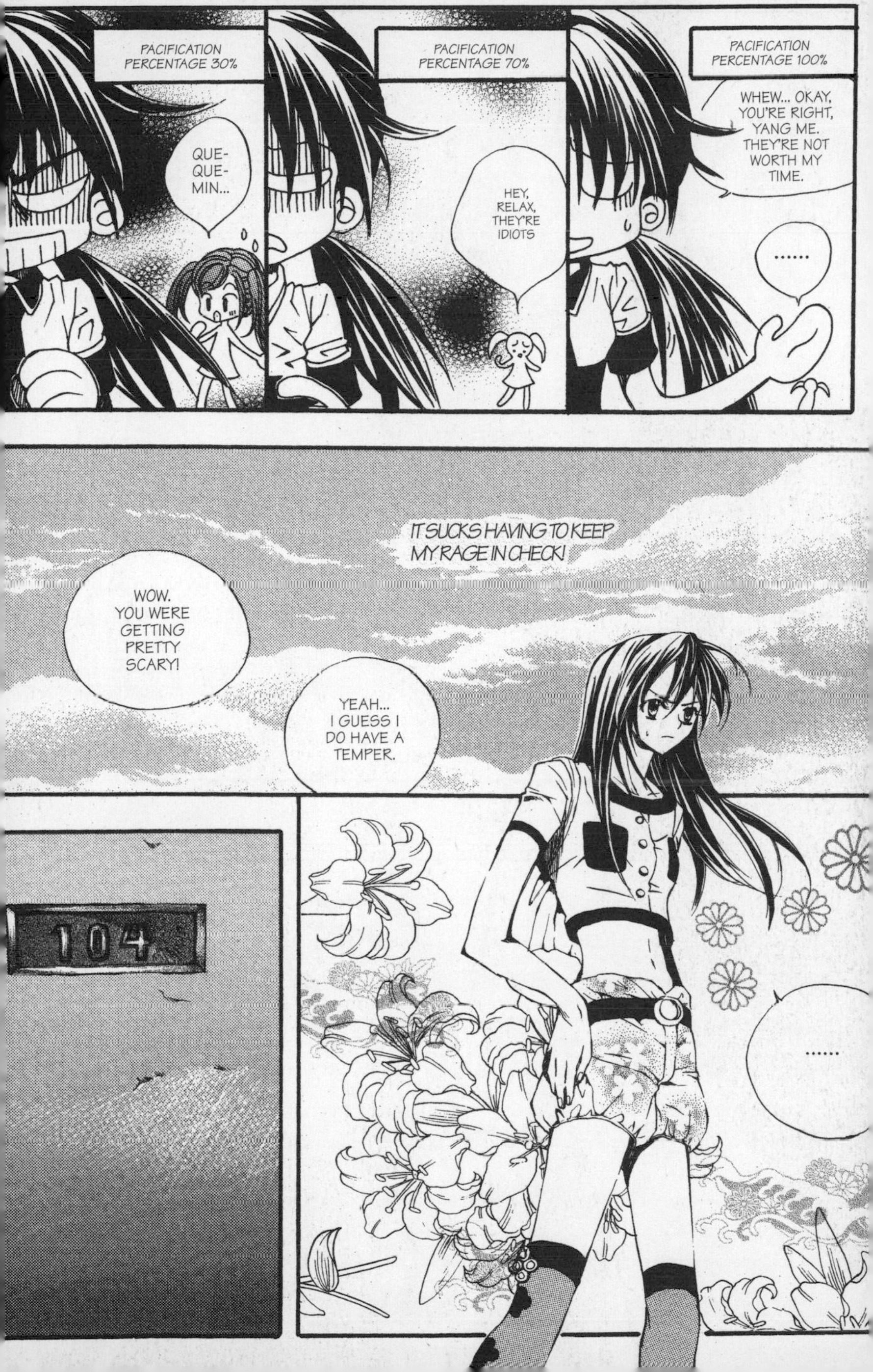
PACIFICATION PERCENTAGE 30%
QUE-QUE-MIN...
PACIFICATION PERCENTAGE 70%
HEY, RELAX, THEY'RE IDIOTS
PACIFICATION PERCENTAGE 100%
WHEW... OKAY, YOU'RE RIGHT, YANG ME. THEY'RE NOT WORTH MY TIME.
......
IT SUCKS HAVING TO KEEP MY RAGE IN CHECK!
WOW. YOU WERE GETTING PRETTY SCARY!
YEAH... I GUESS I DO HAVE A TEMPER.
104
......

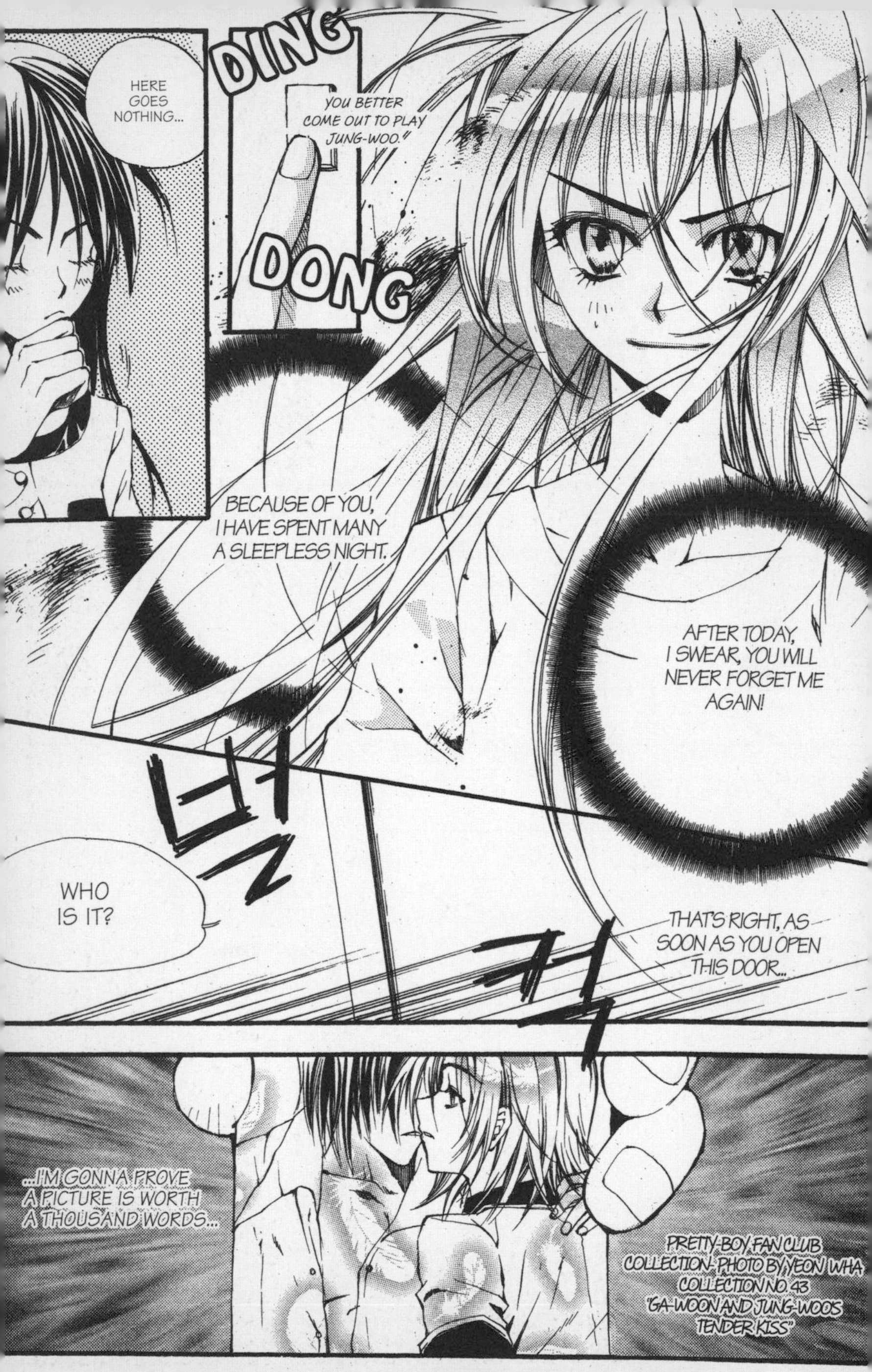
HERE GOES NOTHING...
DING
YOU BETTER COME OUT TO PLAY JUNG-WOO.
DONG
BECAUSE OF YOU, I HAVE SPENT MANY A SLEEPLESS NIGHT.
AFTER TODAY, I SWEAR, YOU WILL NEVER FORGET ME AGAIN!
WHO IS IT?
THAT'S RIGHT, AS SOON AS YOU OPEN THIS DOOR...
...I'M GONNA PROVE A PICTURE IS WORTH A THOUSAND WORDS...
PRETTY-BOY FAN CLUB COLLECTION- PHOTO BY YEON WHA COLLECTION NO. 43 "GA-WOON AND JUNG-WOO'S TENDER KISS"

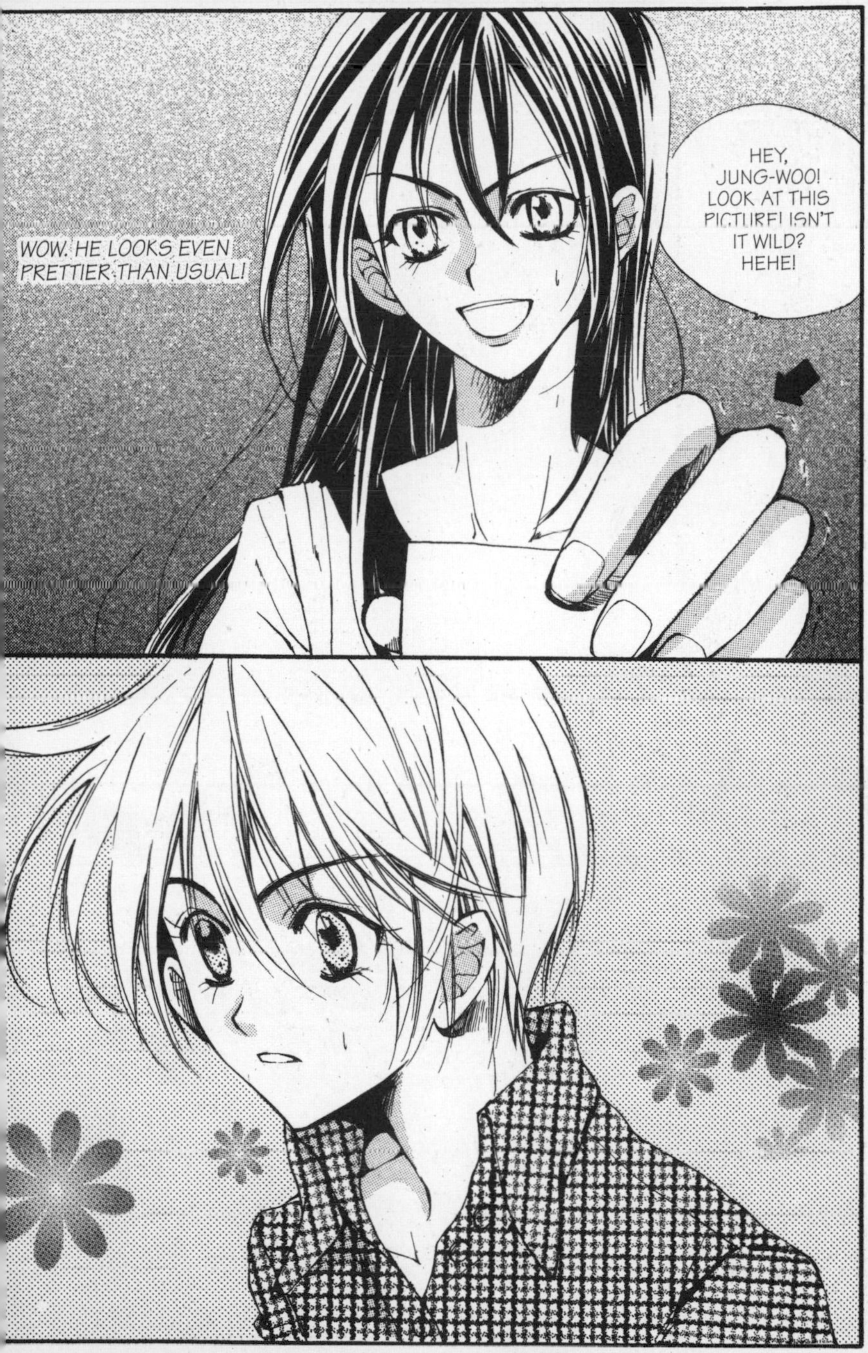

WOW. HE LOOKS EVEN PRETTIER THAN USUAL!
HEY, JUNG-WOO! LOOK AT THIS PICTURE! ISN'T IT WILD? HEHE!

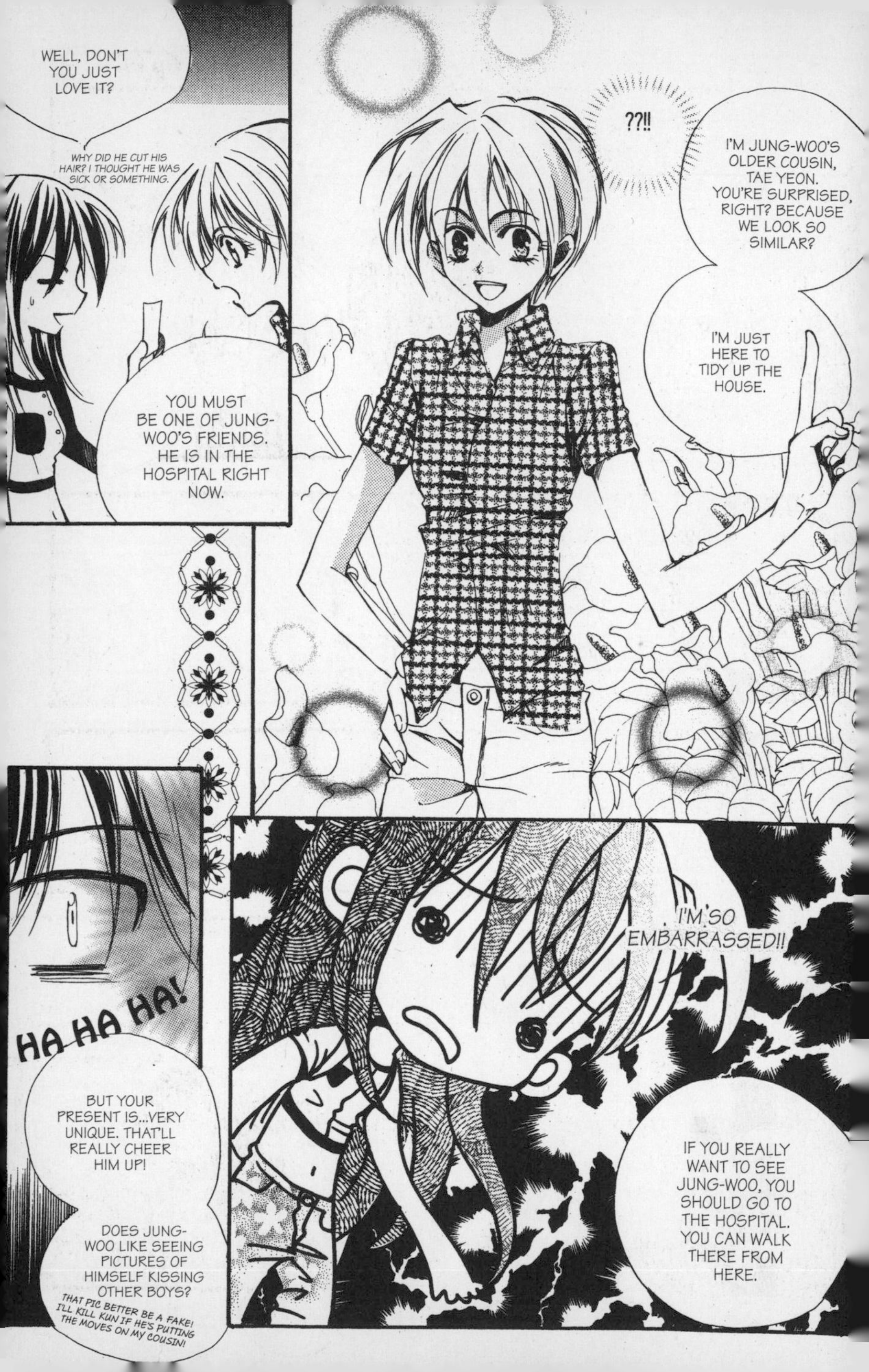
WELL, DON'T YOU JUST LOVE IT?
WHY DID HE CUT HIS HAIR? I THOUGHT HE WAS SICK OR SOMETHING.
YOU MUST BE ONE OF JUNG-WOO'S FRIENDS. HE IS IN THE HOSPITAL RIGHT NOW.
??!!
I'M JUNG-WOO'S OLDER COUSIN, TAE YEON. YOU'RE SURPRISED, RIGHT? BECAUSE WE LOOK SO SIMILAR?
I'M JUST HERE TO TIDY UP THE HOUSE.
HA HA HA!
BUT YOUR PRESENT IS...VERY UNIQUE. THAT'LL REALLY CHEER HIM UP!
DOES JUNG-WOO LIKE SEEING PICTURES OF HIMSELF KISSING OTHER BOYS?
THAT PIC BETTER BE A FAKE! I'LL KILL KUN IF HE'S PUTTING THE MOVES ON MY COUSIN!
I'M SO EMBARRASSED!!
IF YOU REALLY WANT TO SEE JUNG-WOO, YOU SHOULD GO TO THE HOSPITAL. YOU CAN WALK THERE FROM HERE.

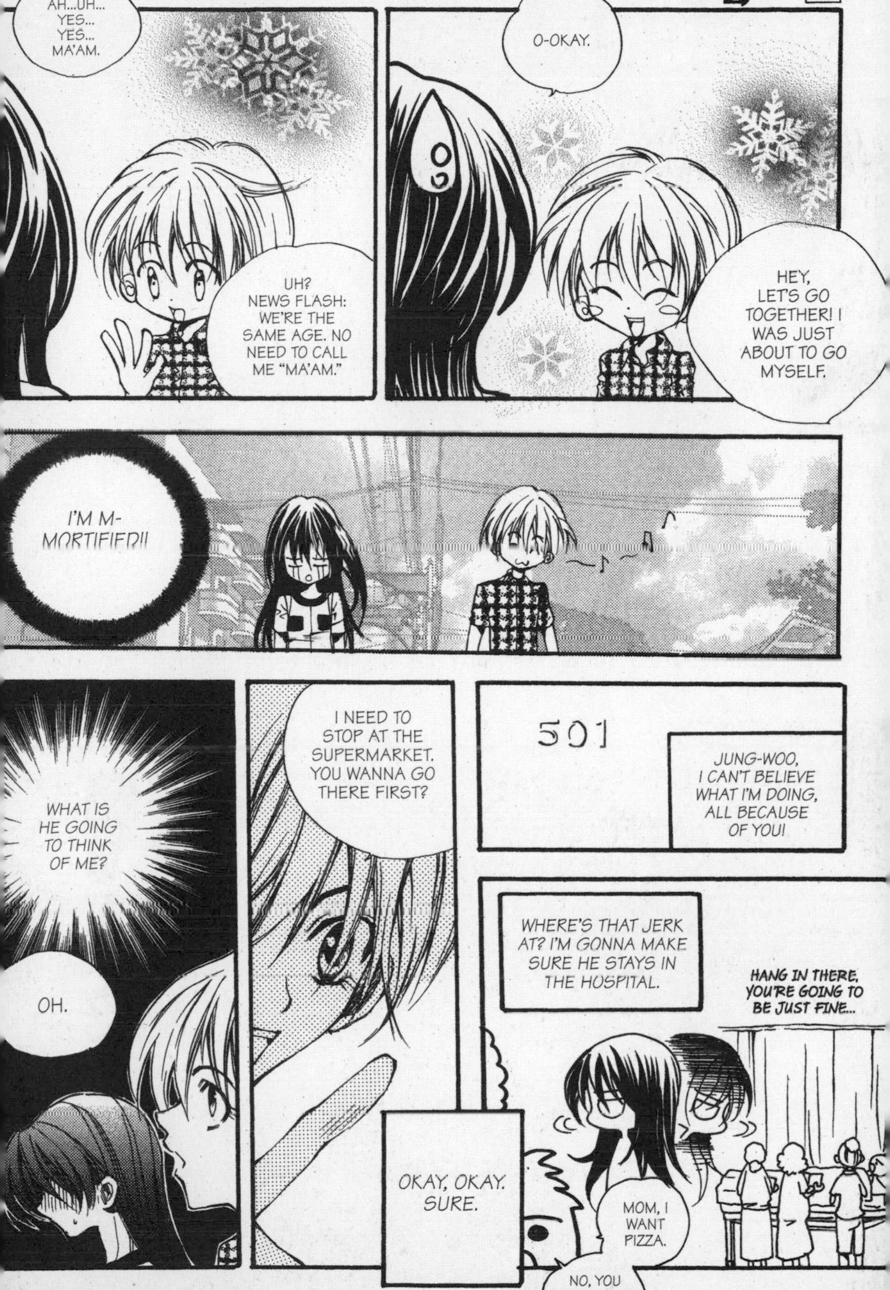
AH...UH... YES... YES... MA'AM.
UH? NEWS FLASH: WE'RE THE SAME AGE. NO NEED TO CALL ME "MA'AM."
O-OKAY.
HEY, LET'S GO TOGETHER! I WAS JUST ABOUT TO GO MYSELF.
I'M M-MORTIFIED!!
WHAT IS HE GOING TO THINK OF ME?
OH.
I NEED TO STOP AT THE SUPERMARKET. YOU WANNA GO THERE FIRST?
OKAY, OKAY. SURE.
501
JUNG-WOO, I CAN'T BELIEVE WHAT I'M DOING, ALL BECAUSE OF YOU!
WHERE'S THAT JERK AT? I'M GONNA MAKE SURE HE STAYS IN THE HOSPITAL.
HANG IN THERE. YOU'RE GOING TO BE JUST FINE...
MOM, I WANT PIZZA.
NO, YOU HURT YOUR NECK.

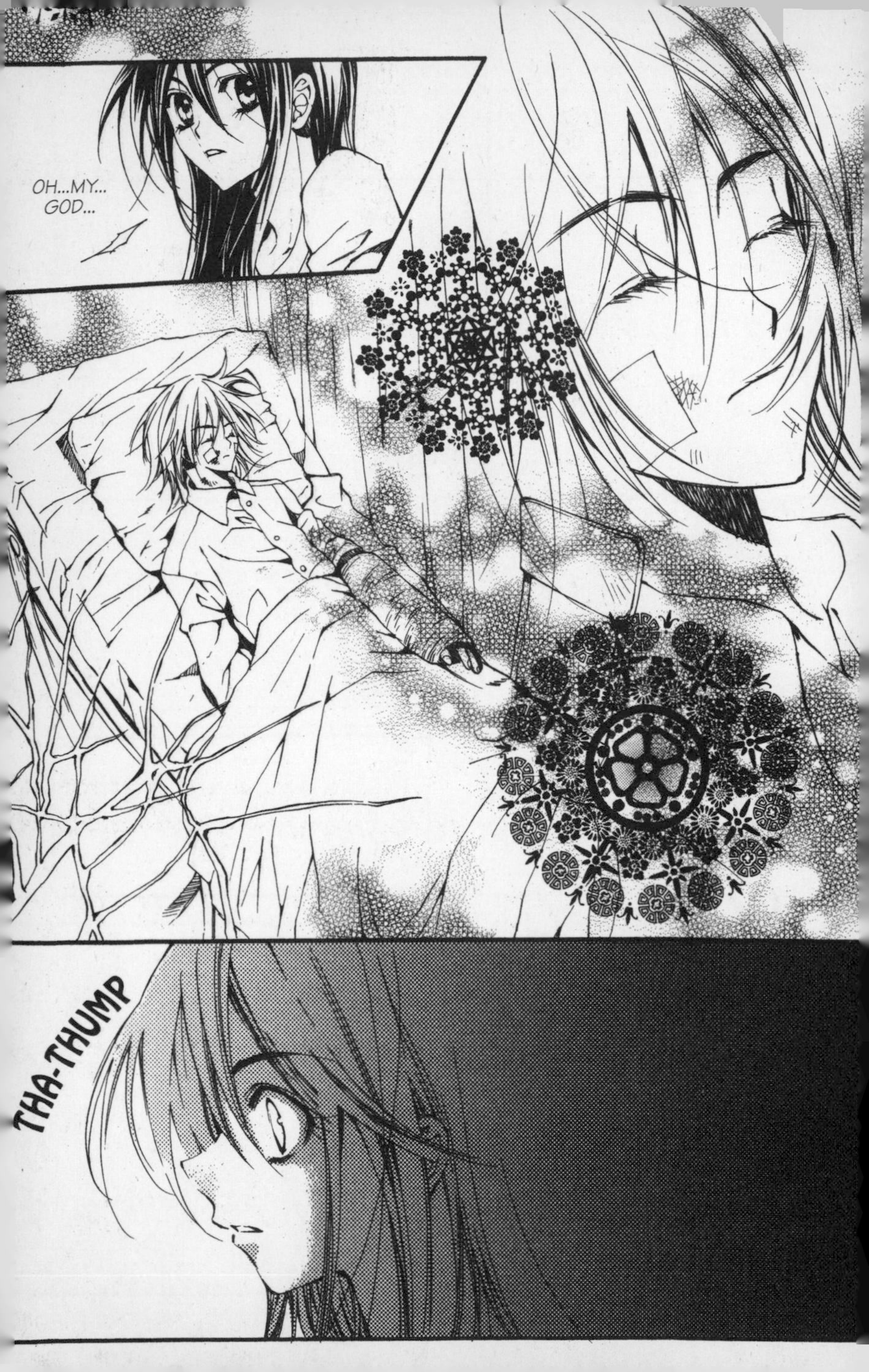
OH...MY... GOD...
THA-THUMP

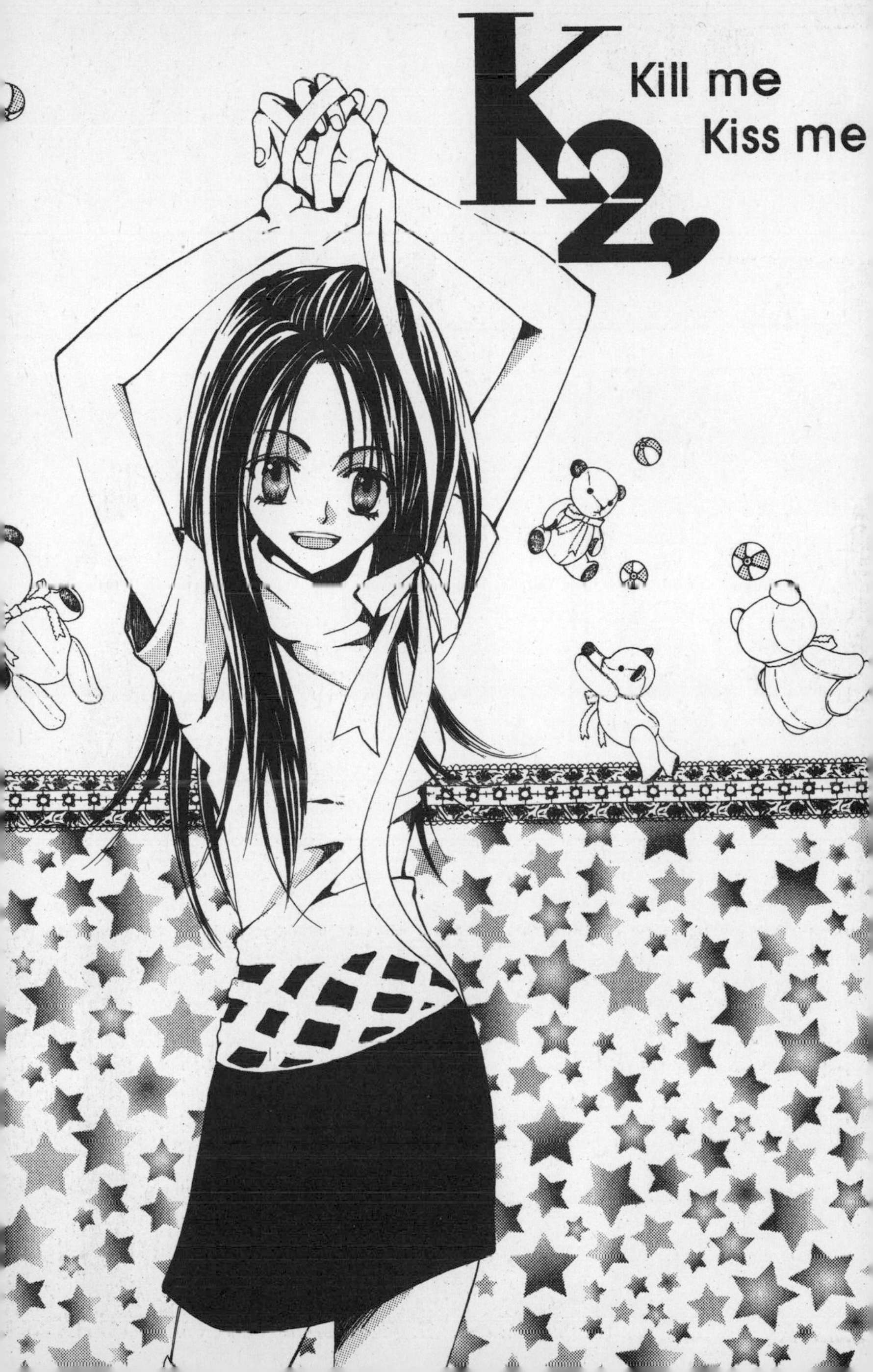
K2
Kill me
Kiss me

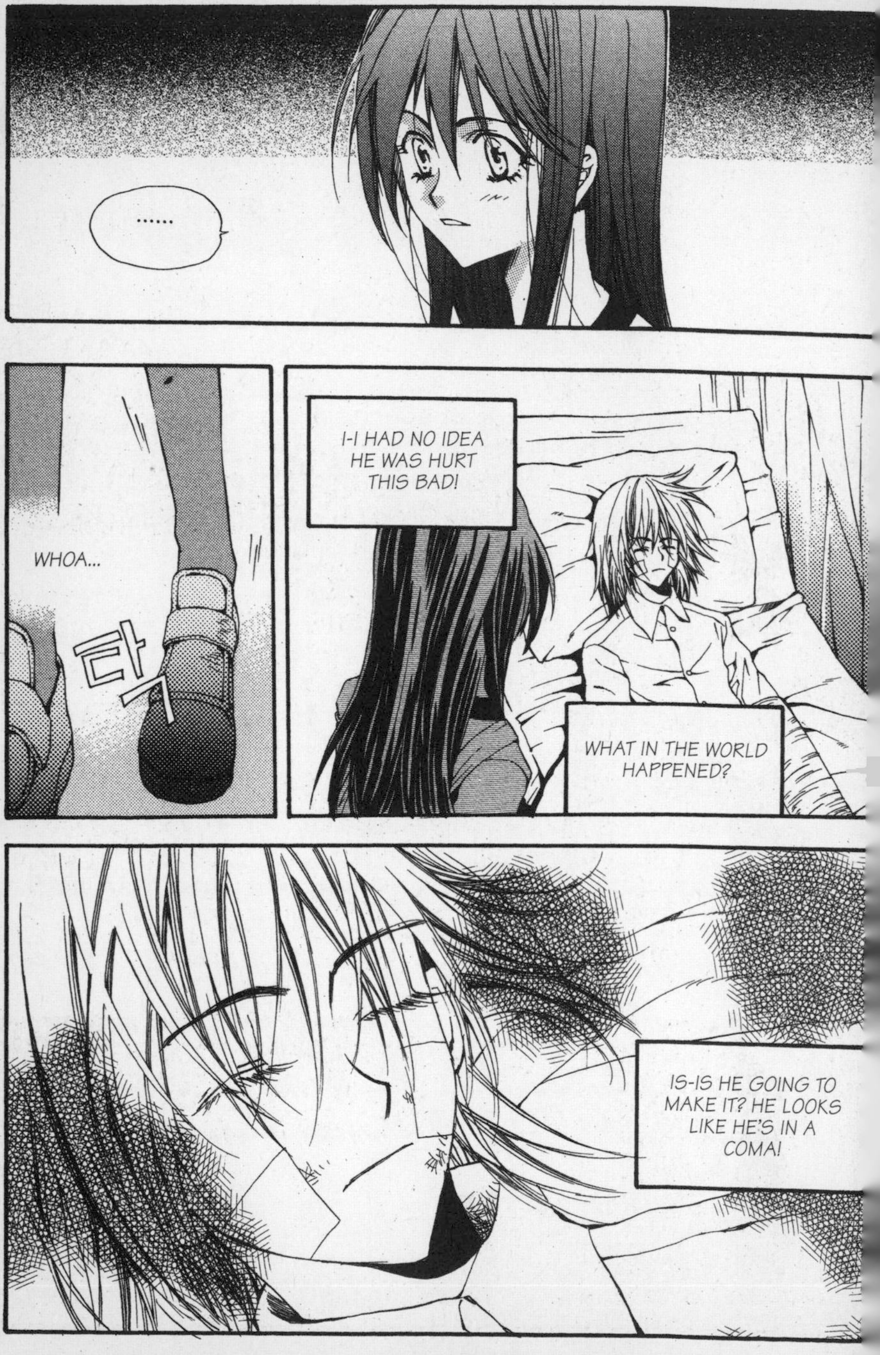
......
WHOA...
타
I-I HAD NO IDEA HE WAS HURT THIS BAD!
WHAT IN THE WORLD HAPPENED?
IS-IS HE GOING TO MAKE IT? HE LOOKS LIKE HE'S IN A COMA!

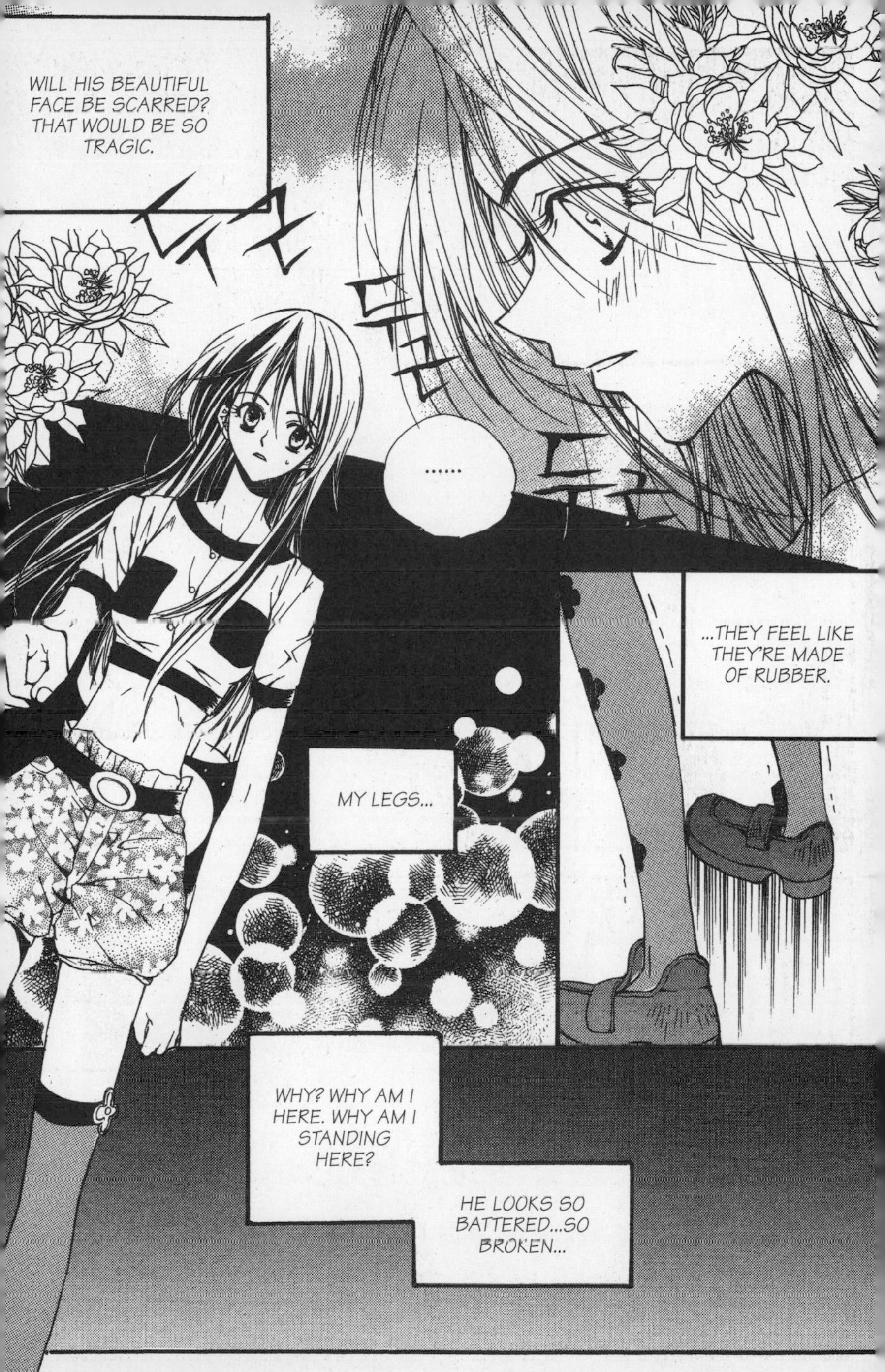
WILL HIS BEAUTIFUL FACE BE SCARRED? THAT WOULD BE SO TRAGIC.
......
MY LEGS...
...THEY FEEL LIKE THEY'RE MADE OF RUBBER.
WHY? WHY AM I HERE. WHY AM I STANDING HERE?
HE LOOKS SO BATTERED...SO BROKEN...

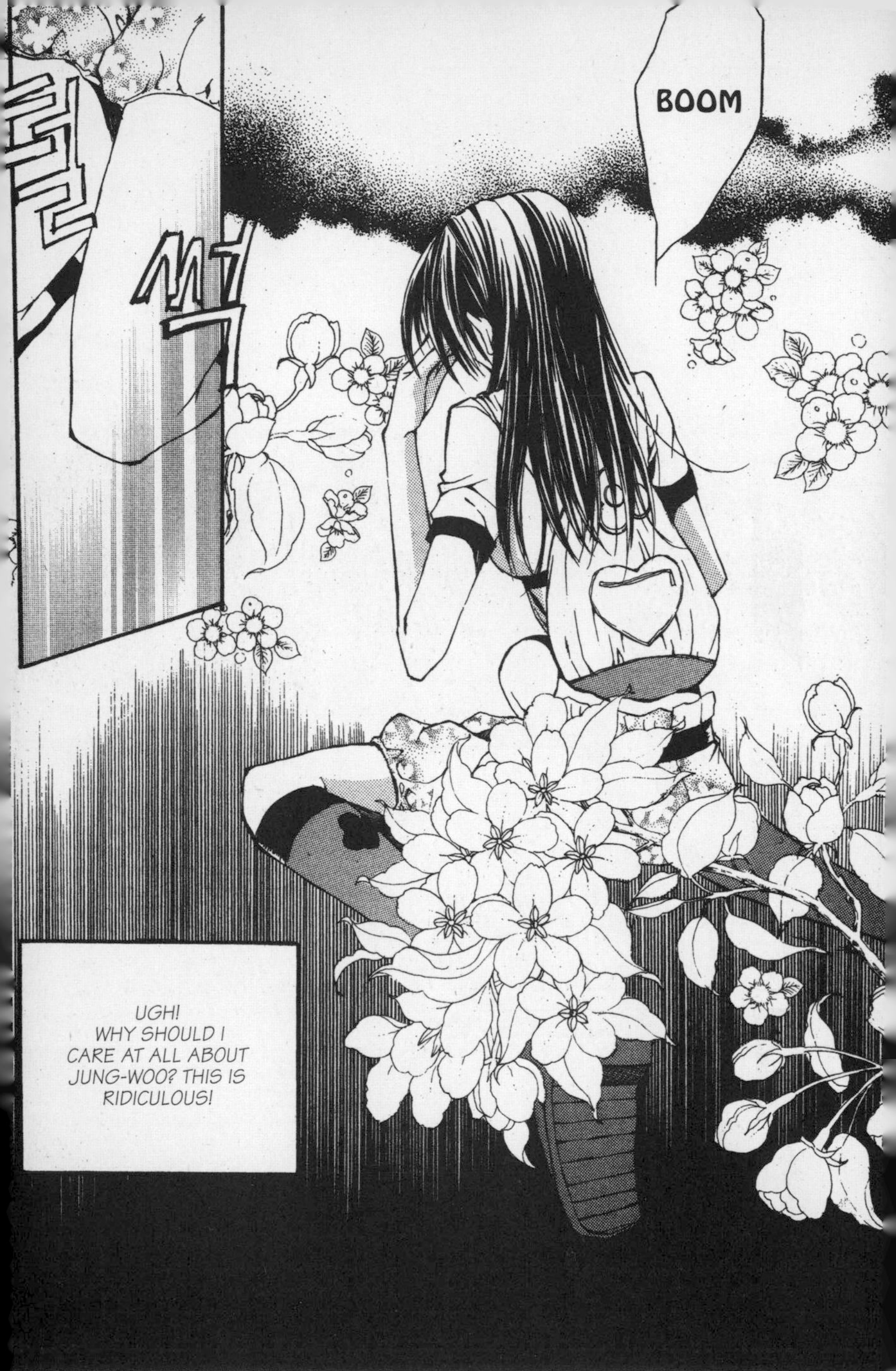
BOOM
UGH! WHY SHOULD I CARE AT ALL ABOUT JUNG-WOO? THIS IS RIDICULOUS!

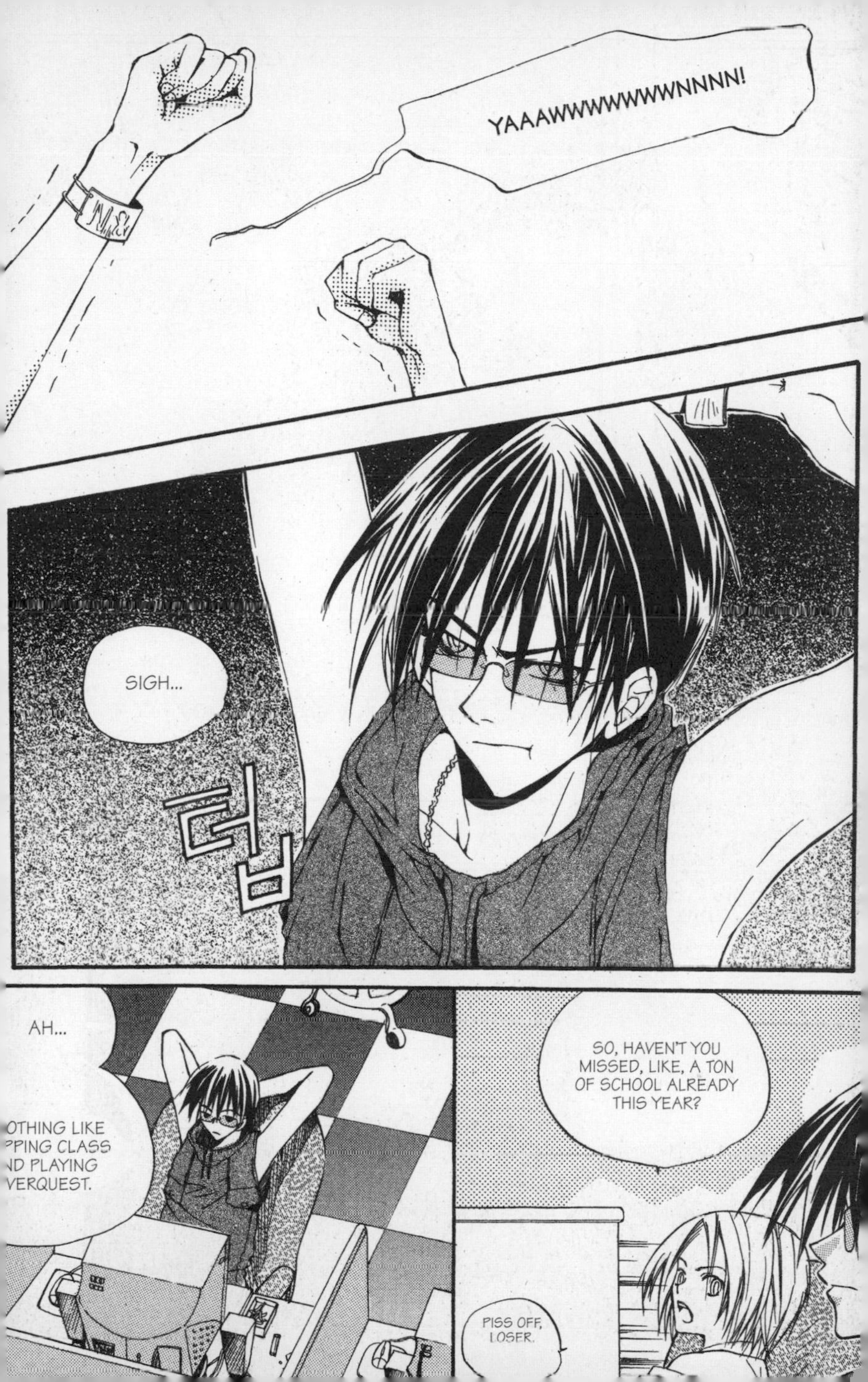
YAAAWWWWWWWNNNN!
SIGH...
AH...
OTHING LIKE
PPING CLASS
ND PLAYING
VERQUEST.
SO, HAVEN'T YOU MISSED, LIKE, A TON OF SCHOOL ALREADY THIS YEAR?
PISS OFF, LOSER.

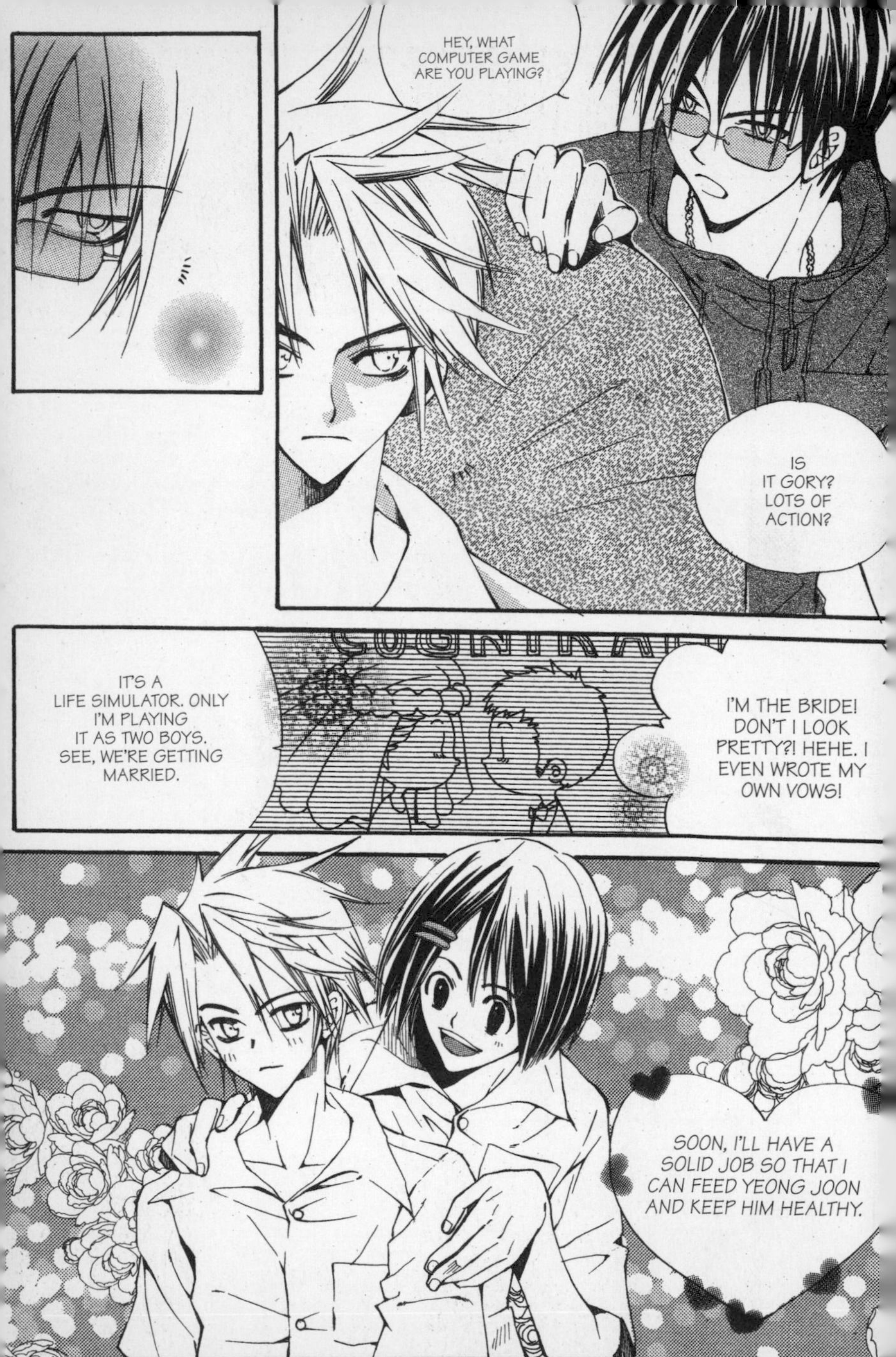
HEY, WHAT COMPUTER GAME ARE YOU PLAYING?
IS IT GORY? LOTS OF ACTION?
IT'S A LIFE SIMULATOR. ONLY I'M PLAYING IT AS TWO BOYS. SEE, WE'RE GETTING MARRIED.
I'M THE BRIDE! DON'T I LOOK PRETTY?! HEHE. I EVEN WROTE MY OWN VOWS!
SOON, I'LL HAVE A SOLID JOB SO THAT I CAN FEED YEONG JOON AND KEEP HIM HEALTHY.

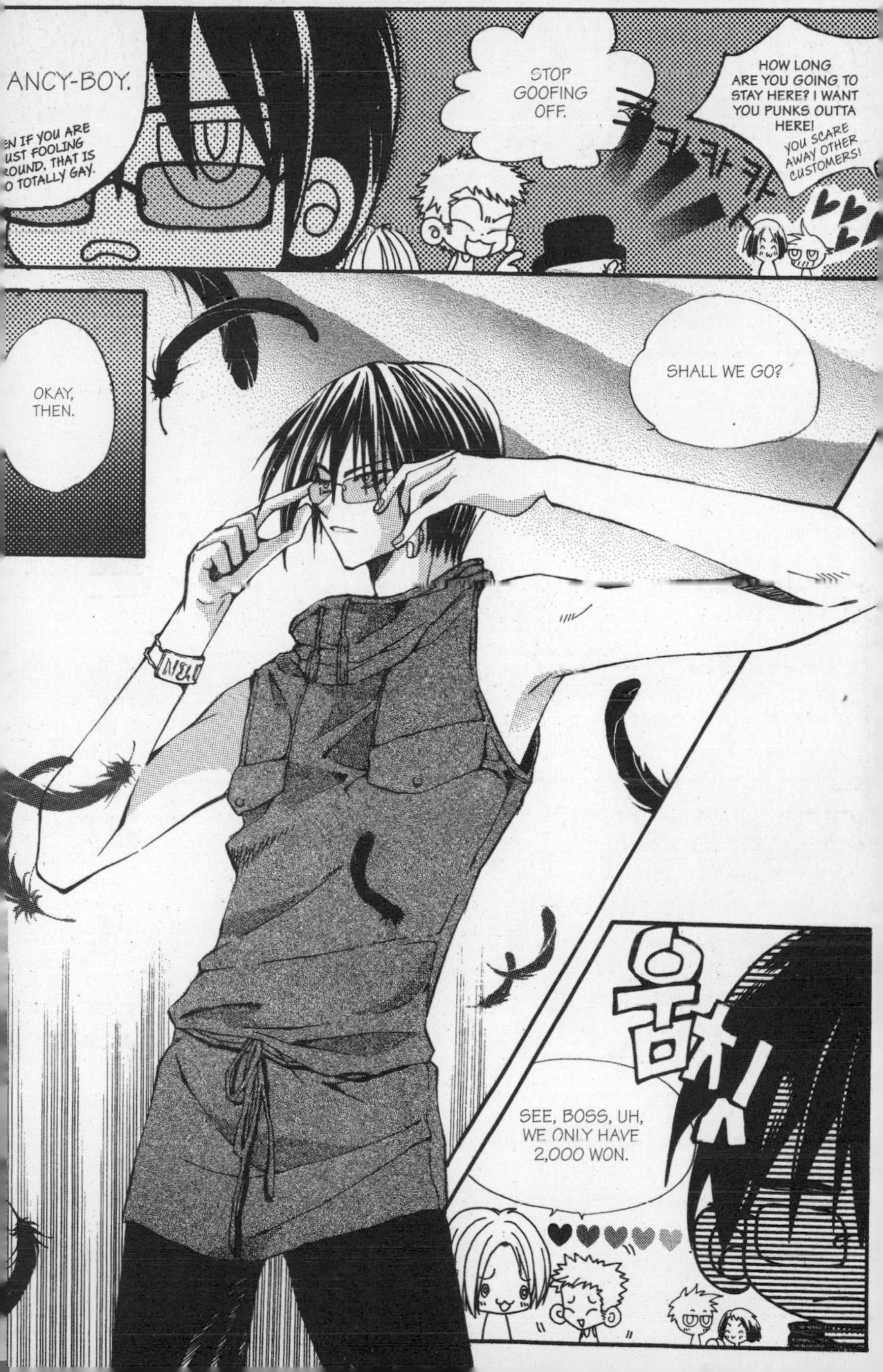
ANCY-BOY.
EN IF YOU ARE
UST FOOLING
ROUND, THAT IS
O TOTALLY GAY.
STOP GOOFING OFF.
HOW LONG ARE YOU GOING TO STAY HERE? I WANT YOU PUNKS OUTTA HERE!
YOU SCARE AWAY OTHER CUSTOMERS!
OKAY, THEN.
SHALL WE GO?
SEE, BOSS, UH, WE ONLY HAVE 2,000 WON.

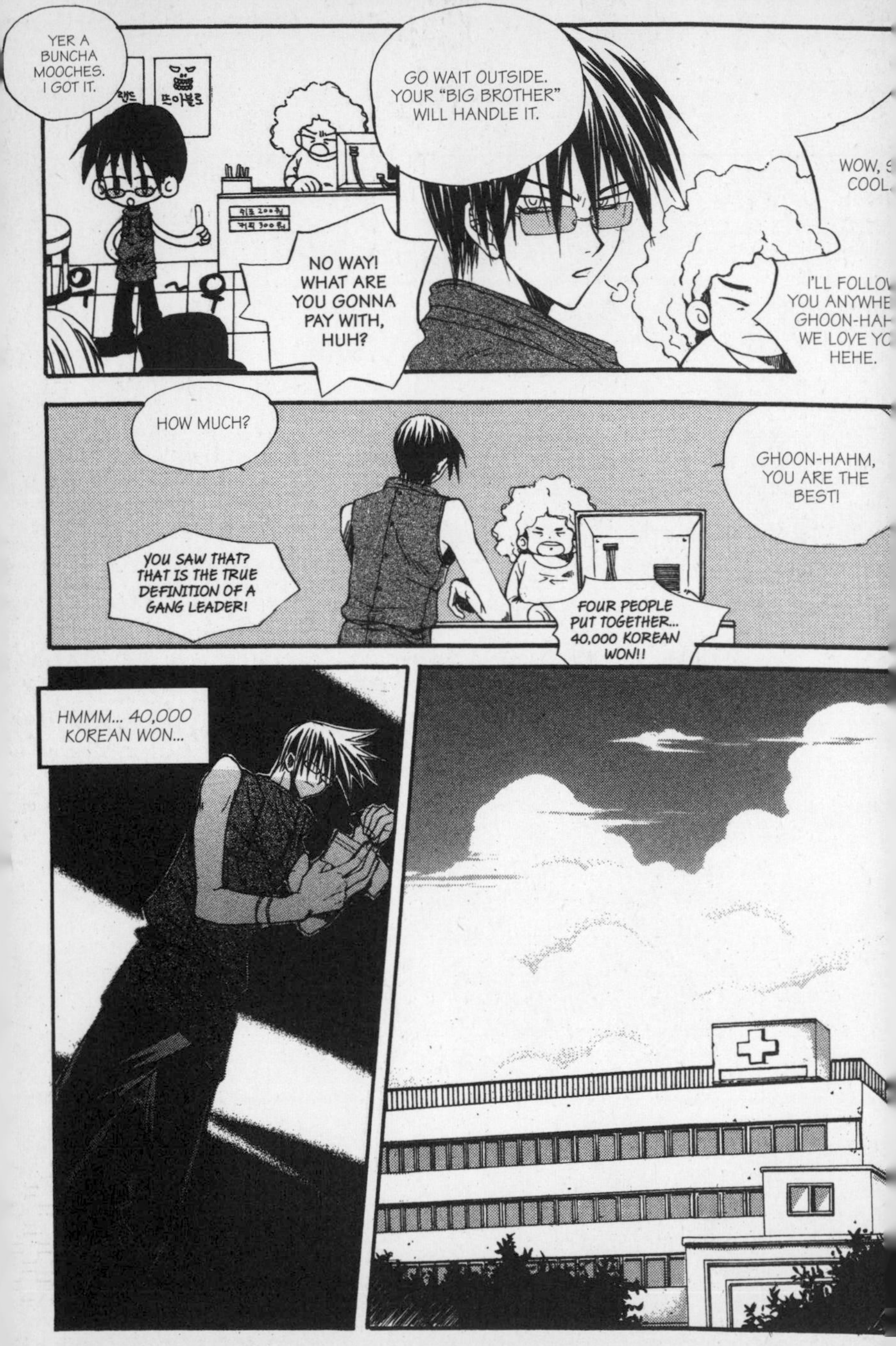
YER A BUNCHA MOOCHES. I GOT IT.
뜨아블로
NO WAY! WHAT ARE YOU GONNA PAY WITH, HUH?
GO WAIT OUTSIDE. YOUR "BIG BROTHER" WILL HANDLE IT.
WOW, S COOL.
I'LL FOLLOW YOU ANYWHE GHOON-HAH WE LOVE YO HEHE.
HOW MUCH?
YOU SAW THAT? THAT IS THE TRUE DEFINITION OF A GANG LEADER!
FOUR PEOPLE PUT TOGETHER... 40,000 KOREAN WON!!
GHOON-HAHM, YOU ARE THE BEST!
HMMM... 40,000 KOREAN WON...

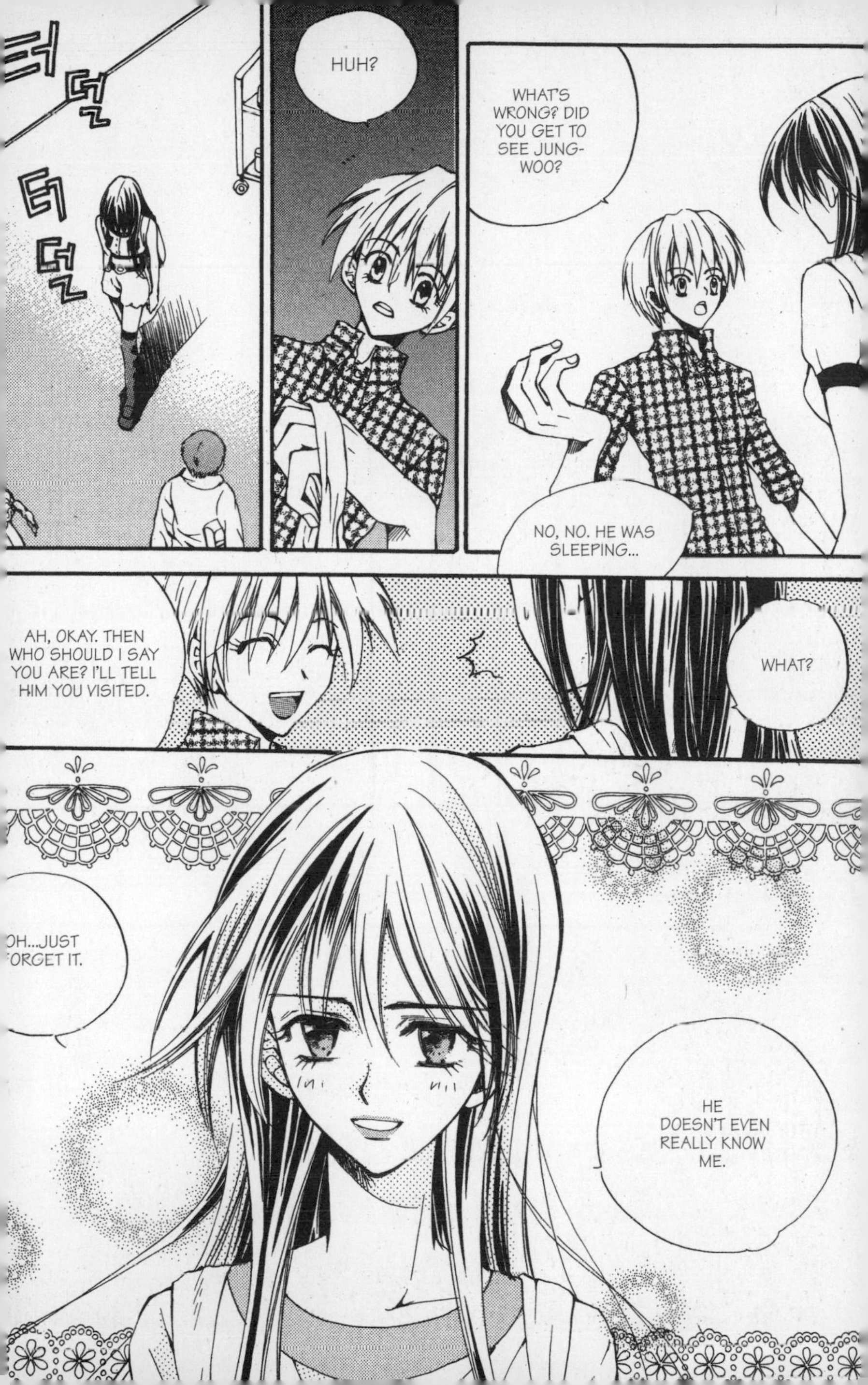
터덜
터덜
HUH?
WHAT'S WRONG? DID YOU GET TO SEE JUNG-WOO?
NO, NO. HE WAS SLEEPING...
AH, OKAY. THEN WHO SHOULD I SAY YOU ARE? I'LL TELL HIM YOU VISITED.
WHAT?
OH...JUST FORGET IT.
HE DOESN'T EVEN REALLY KNOW ME.

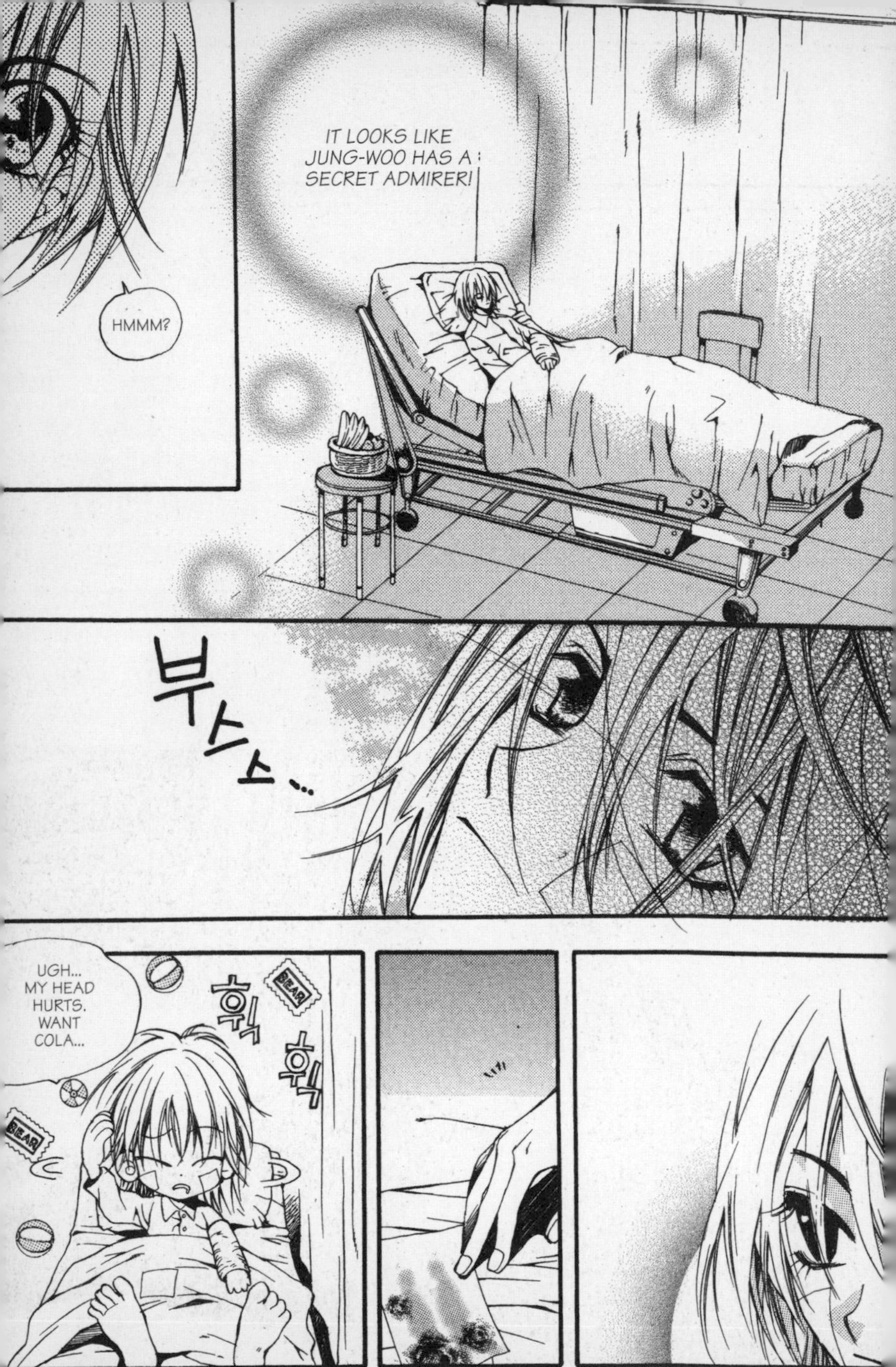
HMMM?
IT LOOKS LIKE JUNG-WOO HAS A SECRET ADMIRER!
부스스...
UGH... MY HEAD HURTS. WANT COLA...
훅 훅

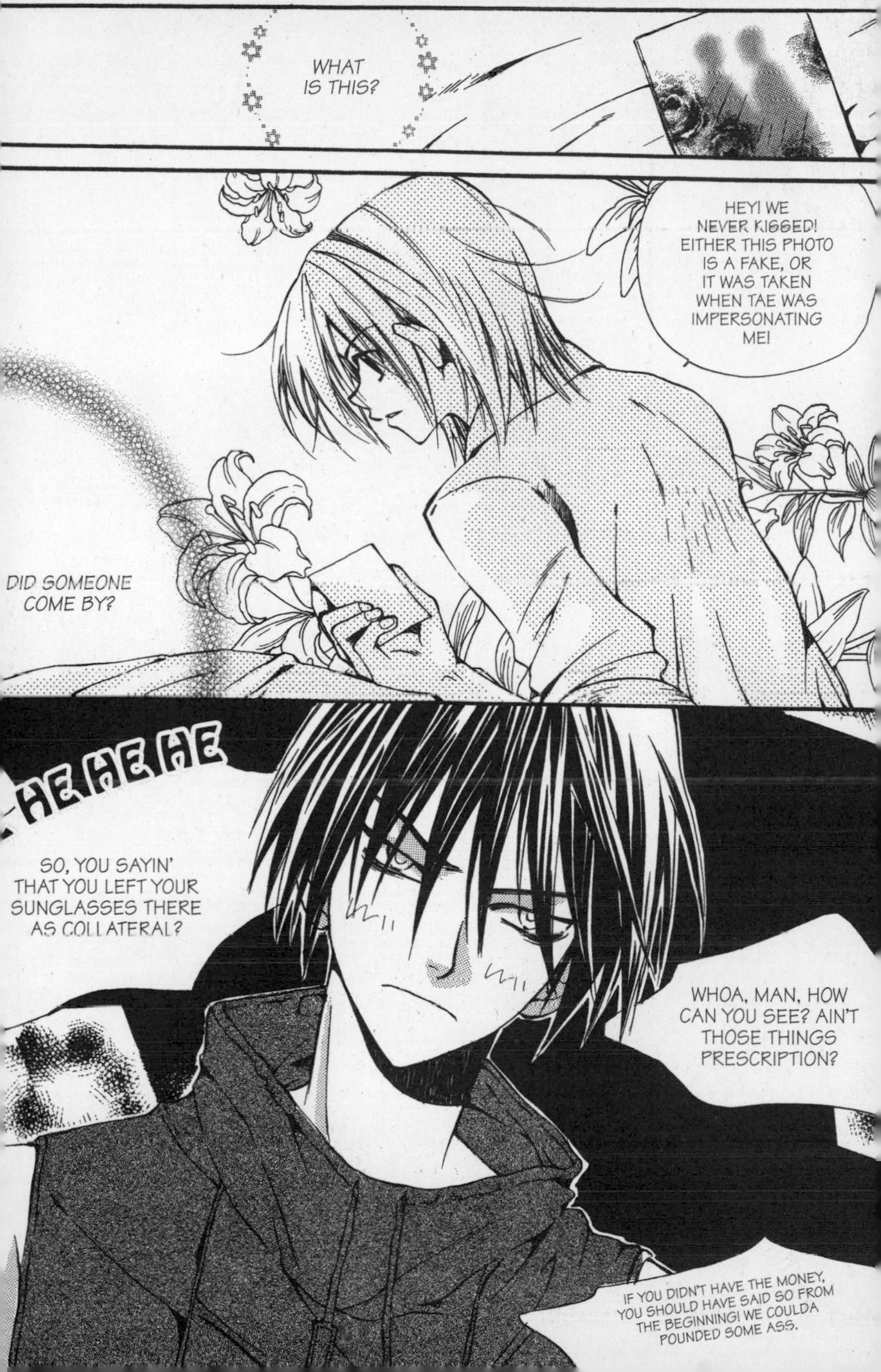
WHAT IS THIS?
DID SOMEONE COME BY?
HEY! WE NEVER KISSED! EITHER THIS PHOTO IS A FAKE, OR IT WAS TAKEN WHEN TAE WAS IMPERSONATING ME!
HE HE HE
SO, YOU SAYIN' THAT YOU LEFT YOUR SUNGLASSES THERE AS COLLATERAL?
WHOA, MAN, HOW CAN YOU SEE? AIN'T THOSE THINGS PRESCRIPTION?
IF YOU DIDN'T HAVE THE MONEY, YOU SHOULD HAVE SAID SO FROM THE BEGINNING! WE COULDA POUNDED SOME ASS.

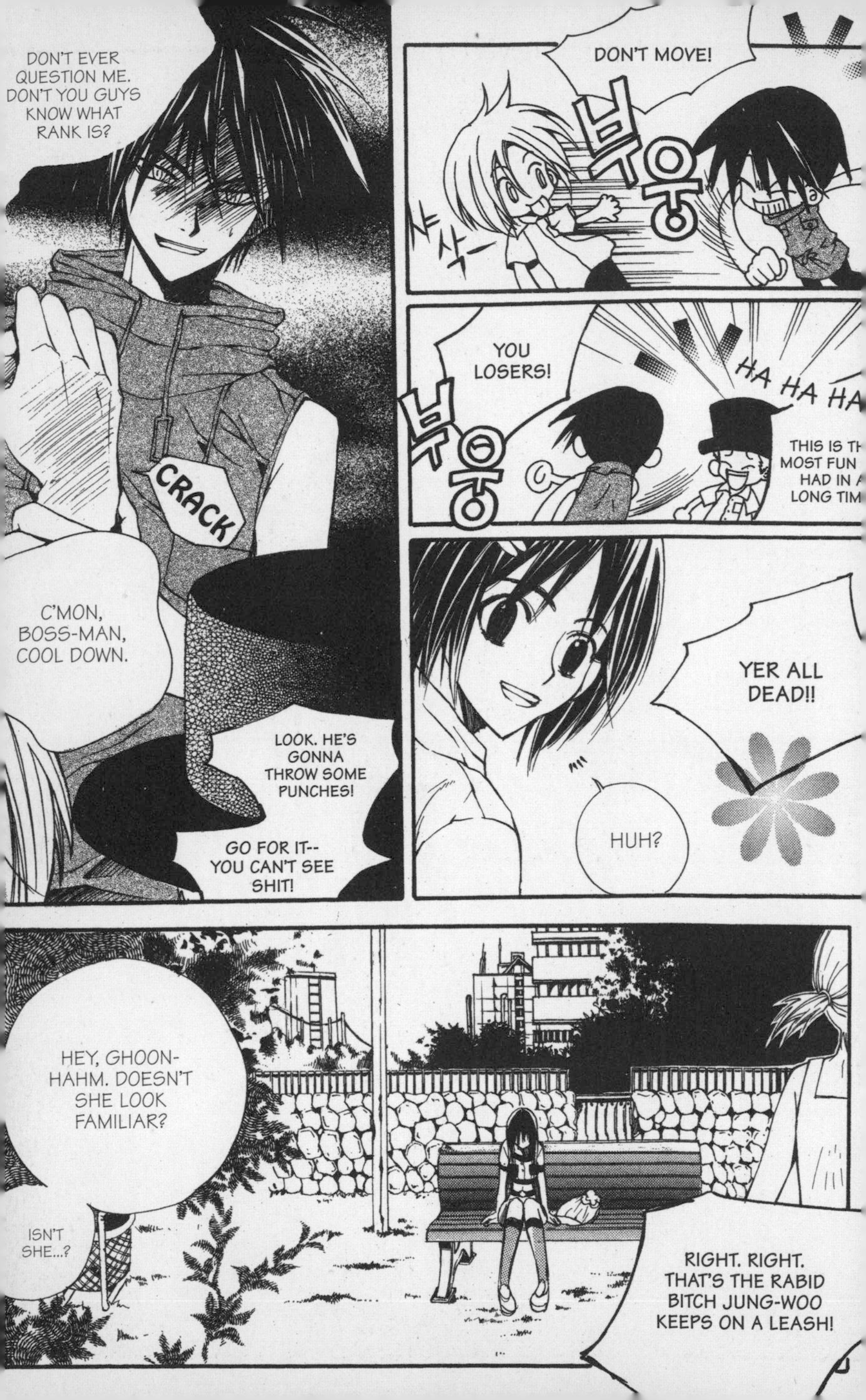
DON'T EVER QUESTION ME. DON'T YOU GUYS KNOW WHAT RANK IS?
CRACK
C'MON, BOSS-MAN, COOL DOWN.
LOOK. HE'S GONNA THROW SOME PUNCHES!
GO FOR IT-- YOU CAN'T SEE SHIT!
DON'T MOVE!
YOU LOSERS!
HA HA HA
THIS IS TH MOST FUN HAD IN A LONG TIM
YER ALL DEAD!!
HUH?
HEY, GHOON-HAHM. DOESN'T SHE LOOK FAMILIAR?
ISN'T SHE...?
RIGHT. RIGHT. THAT'S THE RABID BITCH JUNG-WOO KEEPS ON A LEASH!

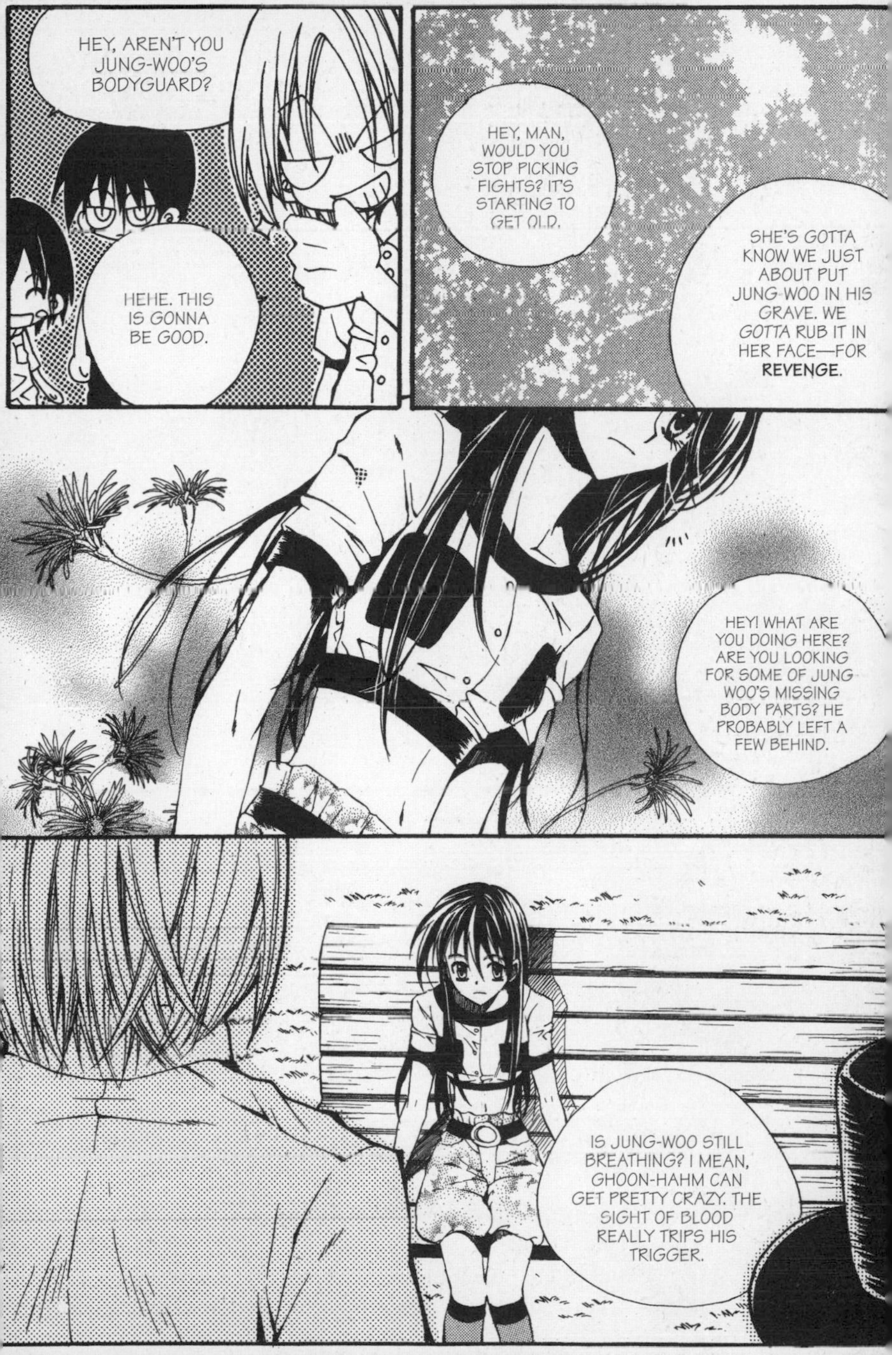
HEY, AREN'T YOU JUNG-WOO'S BODYGUARD?
HEHE. THIS IS GONNA BE GOOD.
HEY, MAN, WOULD YOU STOP PICKING FIGHTS? IT'S STARTING TO GET OLD.
SHE'S GOTTA KNOW WE JUST ABOUT PUT JUNG-WOO IN HIS GRAVE. WE GOTTA RUB IT IN HER FACE—FOR **REVENGE**.
HEY! WHAT ARE YOU DOING HERE? ARE YOU LOOKING FOR SOME OF JUNG WOO'S MISSING BODY PARTS? HE PROBABLY LEFT A FEW BEHIND.
IS JUNG-WOO STILL BREATHING? I MEAN, GHOON-HAHM CAN GET PRETTY CRAZY. THE SIGHT OF BLOOD REALLY TRIPS HIS TRIGGER.

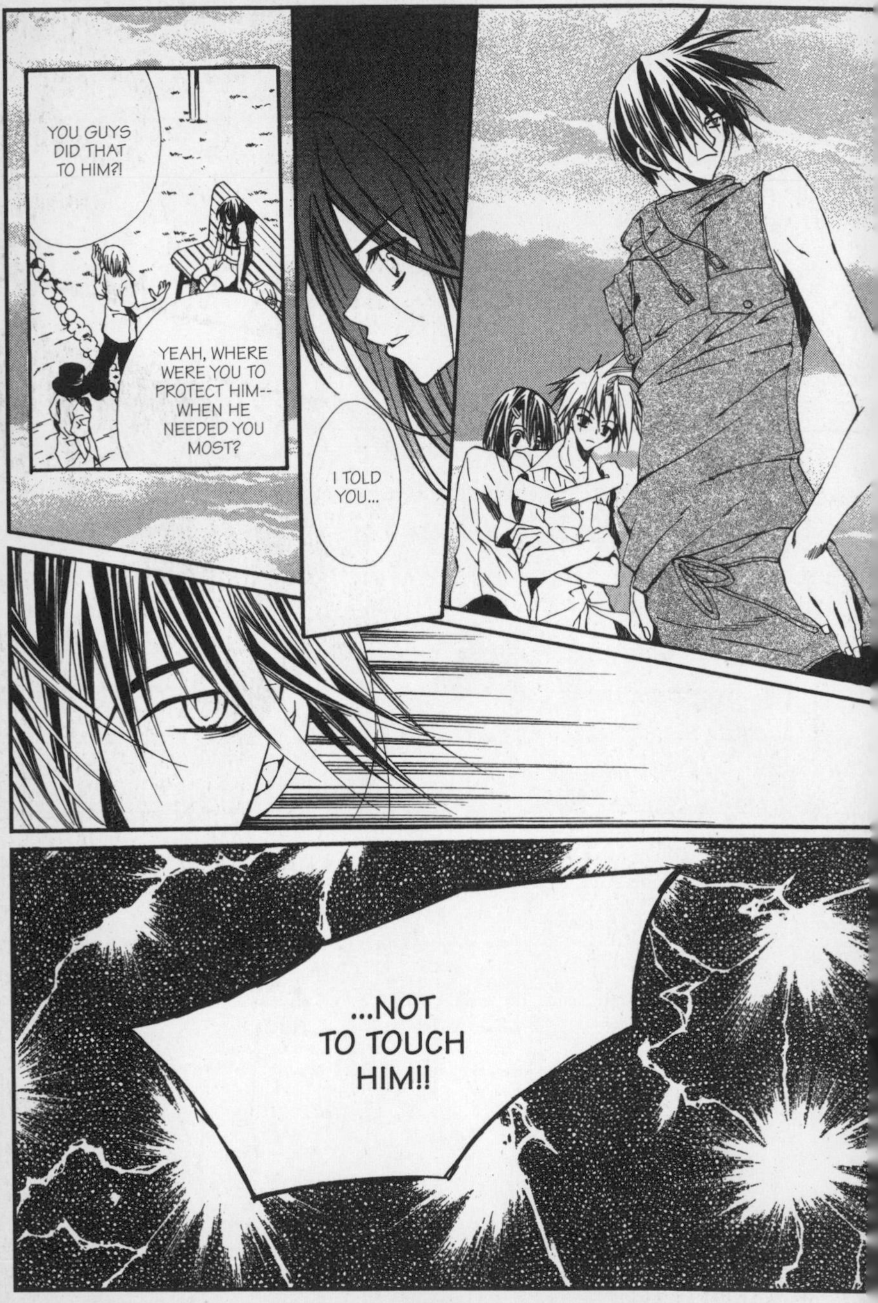
YOU GUYS DID THAT TO HIM?!
YEAH, WHERE WERE YOU TO PROTECT HIM-- WHEN HE NEEDED YOU MOST?
I TOLD YOU...
...NOT TO TOUCH HIM!!

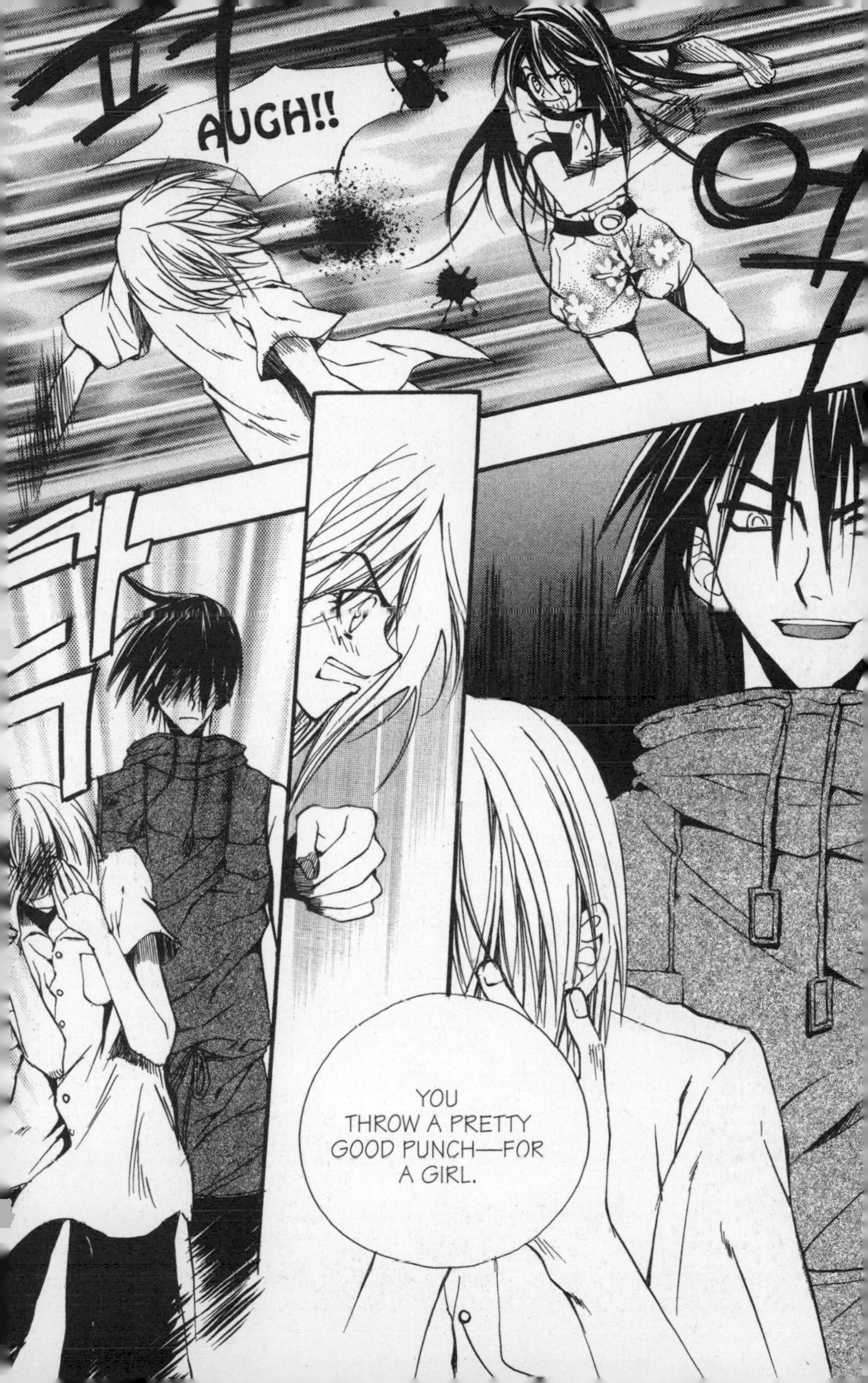
AUGH!!
YOU THROW A PRETTY GOOD PUNCH—FOR A GIRL.

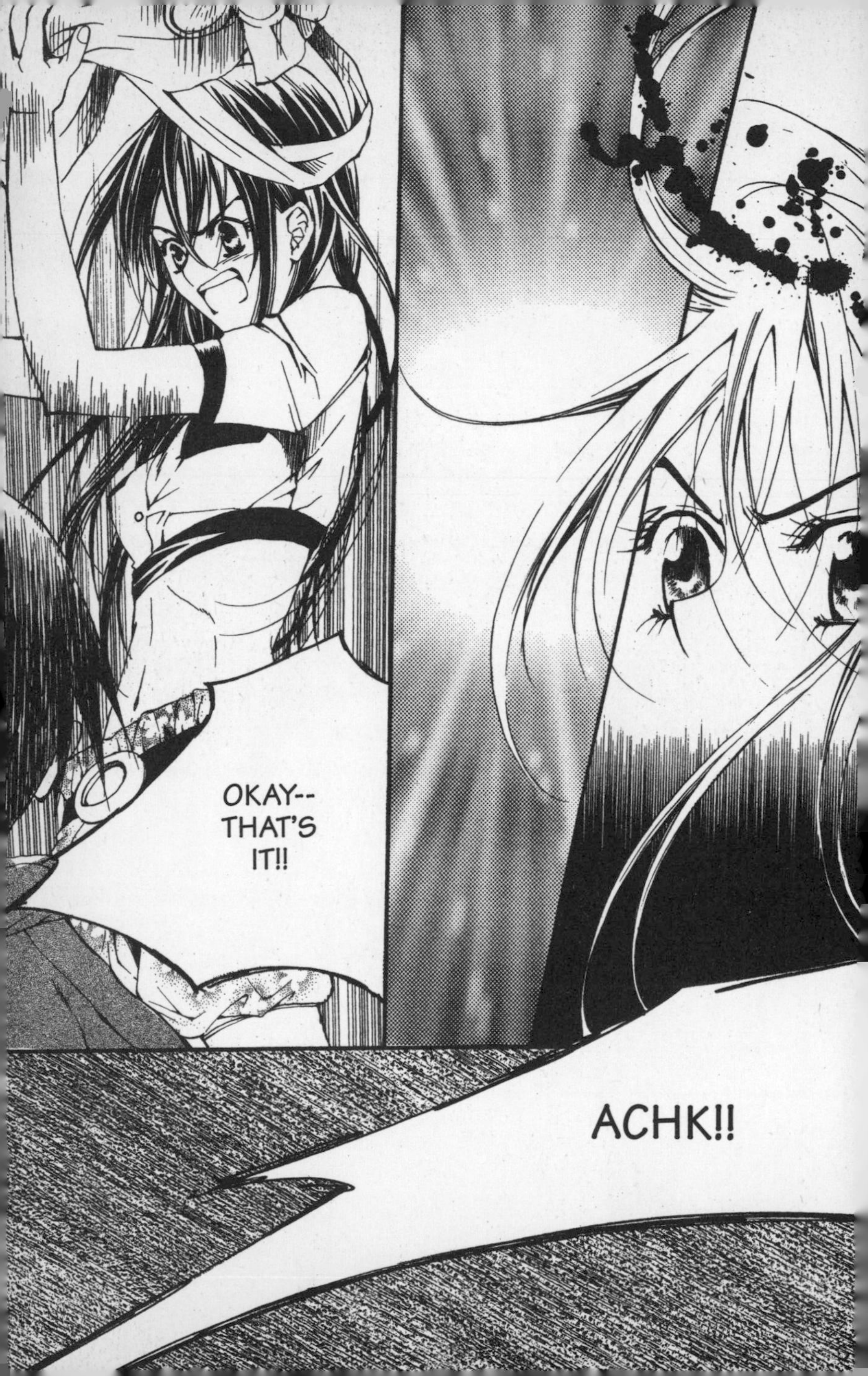
OKAY-- THAT'S IT!!
ACHK!!

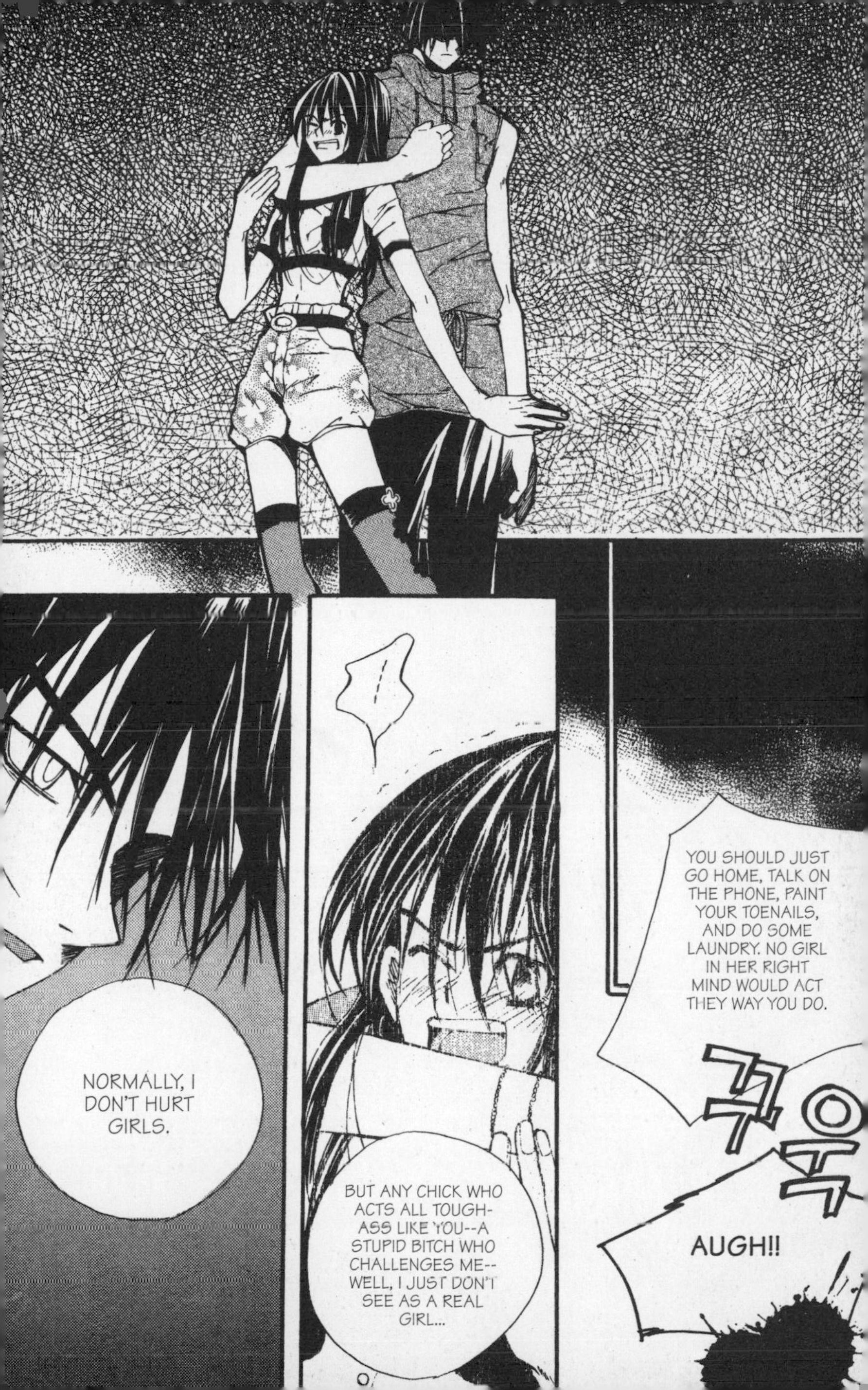
NORMALLY, I DON'T HURT GIRLS.
BUT ANY CHICK WHO ACTS ALL TOUGH-ASS LIKE YOU--A STUPID BITCH WHO CHALLENGES ME--WELL, I JUST DON'T SEE AS A REAL GIRL...
YOU SHOULD JUST GO HOME, TALK ON THE PHONE, PAINT YOUR TOENAILS, AND DO SOME LAUNDRY. NO GIRL IN HER RIGHT MIND WOULD ACT THEY WAY YOU DO.
꾸욱
AUGH!!

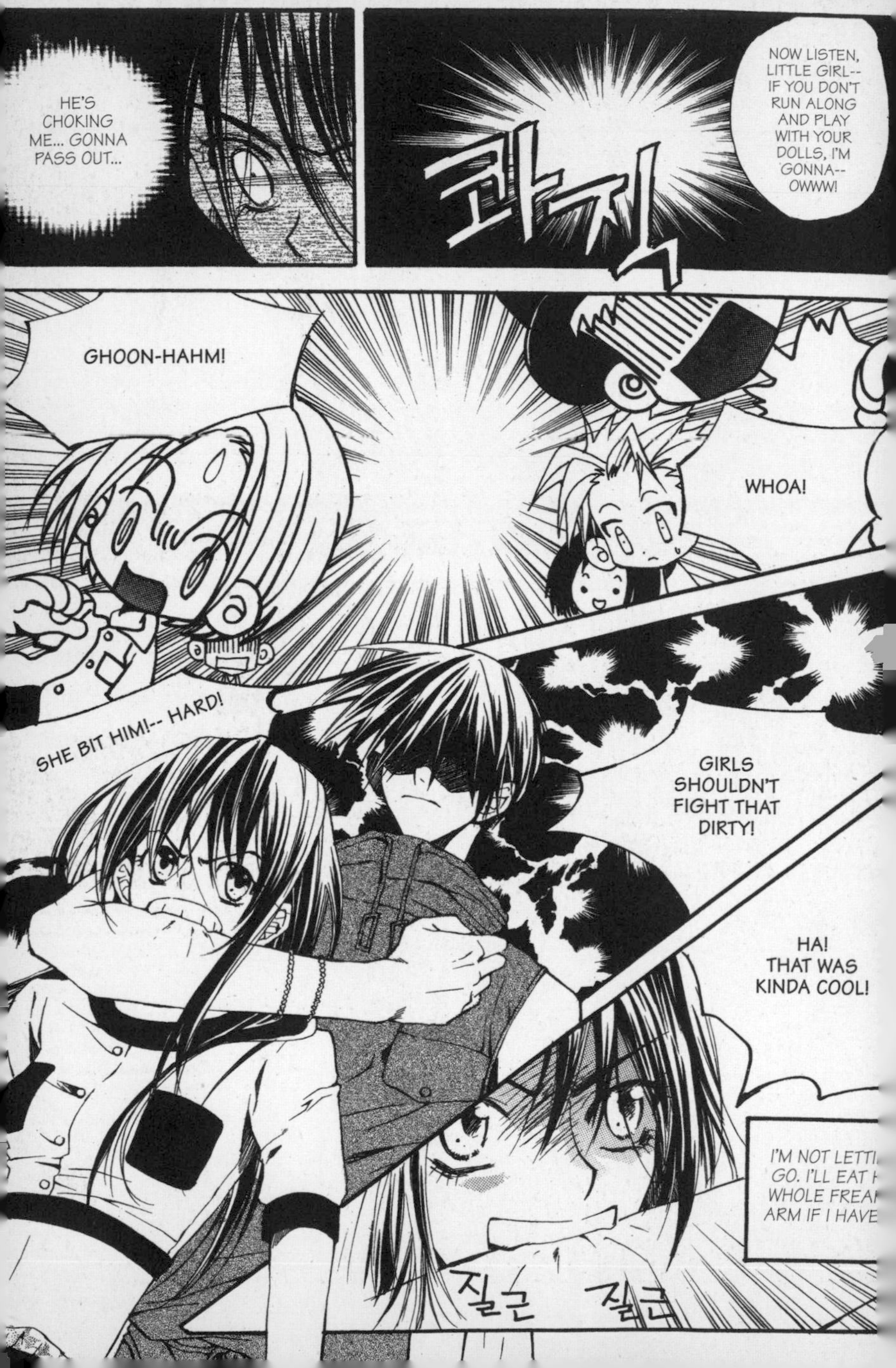
HE'S CHOKING ME... GONNA PASS OUT...
NOW LISTEN, LITTLE GIRL-- IF YOU DON'T RUN ALONG AND PLAY WITH YOUR DOLLS, I'M GONNA-- OWWW!
콰직
GHOON-HAHM!
WHOA!
SHE BIT HIM!-- HARD!
GIRLS SHOULDN'T FIGHT THAT DIRTY!
HA! THAT WAS KINDA COOL!
I'M NOT LETTI GO. I'LL EAT H WHOLE FREA ARM IF I HAVE
질근 질근

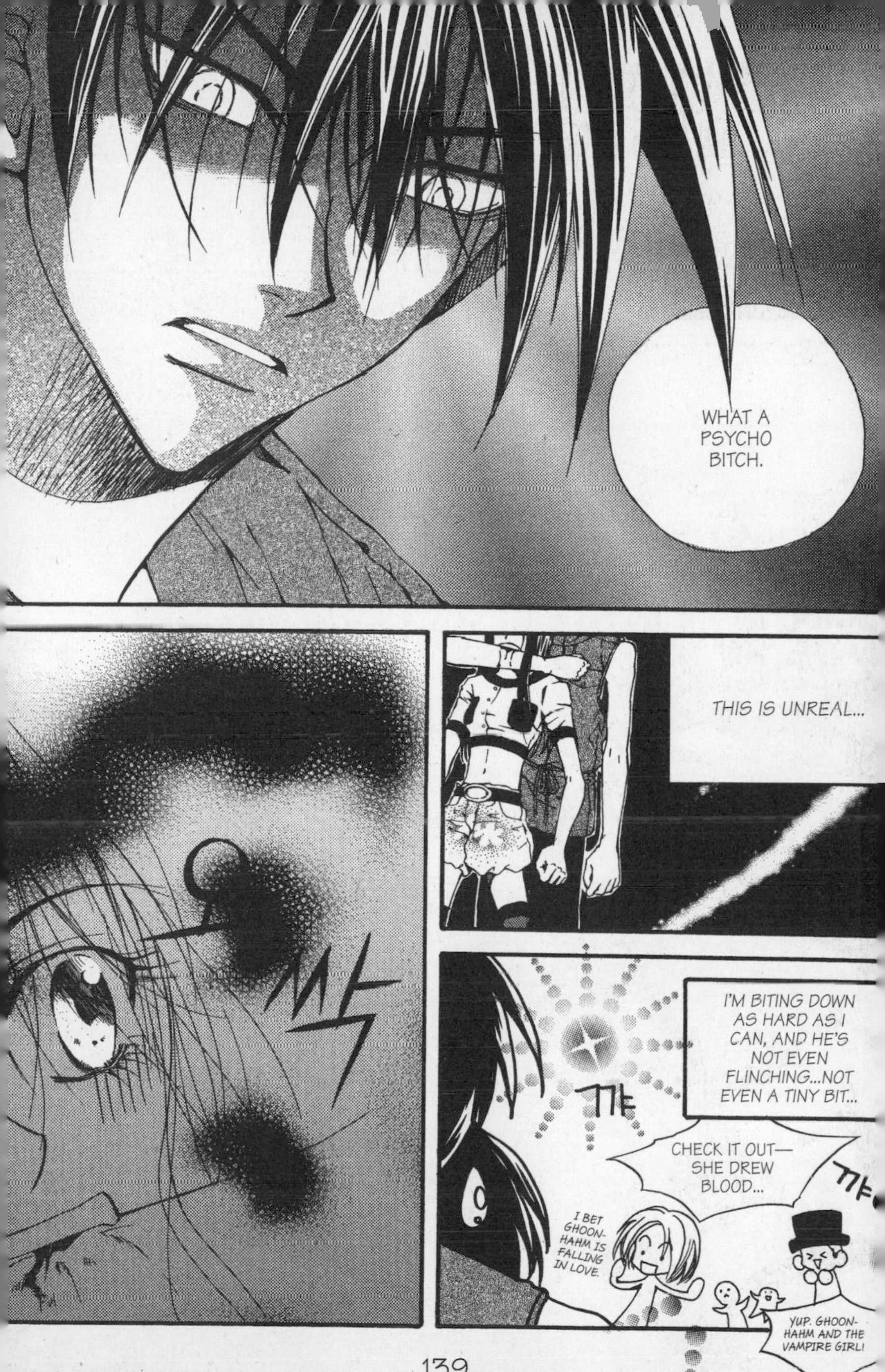
WHAT A PSYCHO BITCH.
THIS IS UNREAL...
I'M BITING DOWN AS HARD AS I CAN, AND HE'S NOT EVEN FLINCHING...NOT EVEN A TINY BIT...
CHECK IT OUT— SHE DREW BLOOD...
I BET GHOON-HAHM IS FALLING IN LOVE.
YUP. GHOON-HAHM AND THE VAMPIRE GIRL!

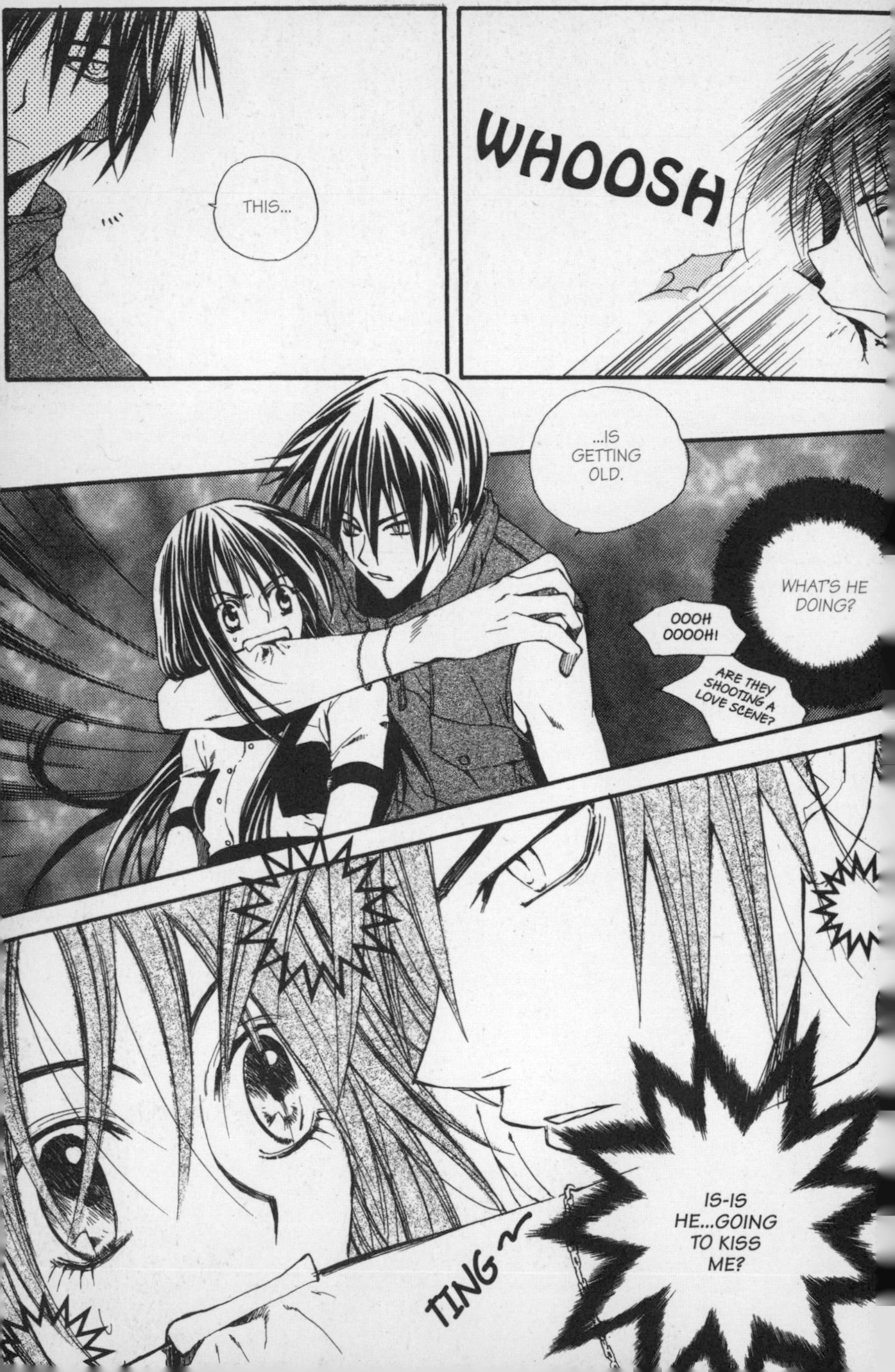
THIS...
WHOOSH
...IS GETTING OLD.
OOOH OOOOH!
WHAT'S HE DOING?
ARE THEY SHOOTING A LOVE SCENE?
TING~
IS-IS HE...GOING TO KISS ME?

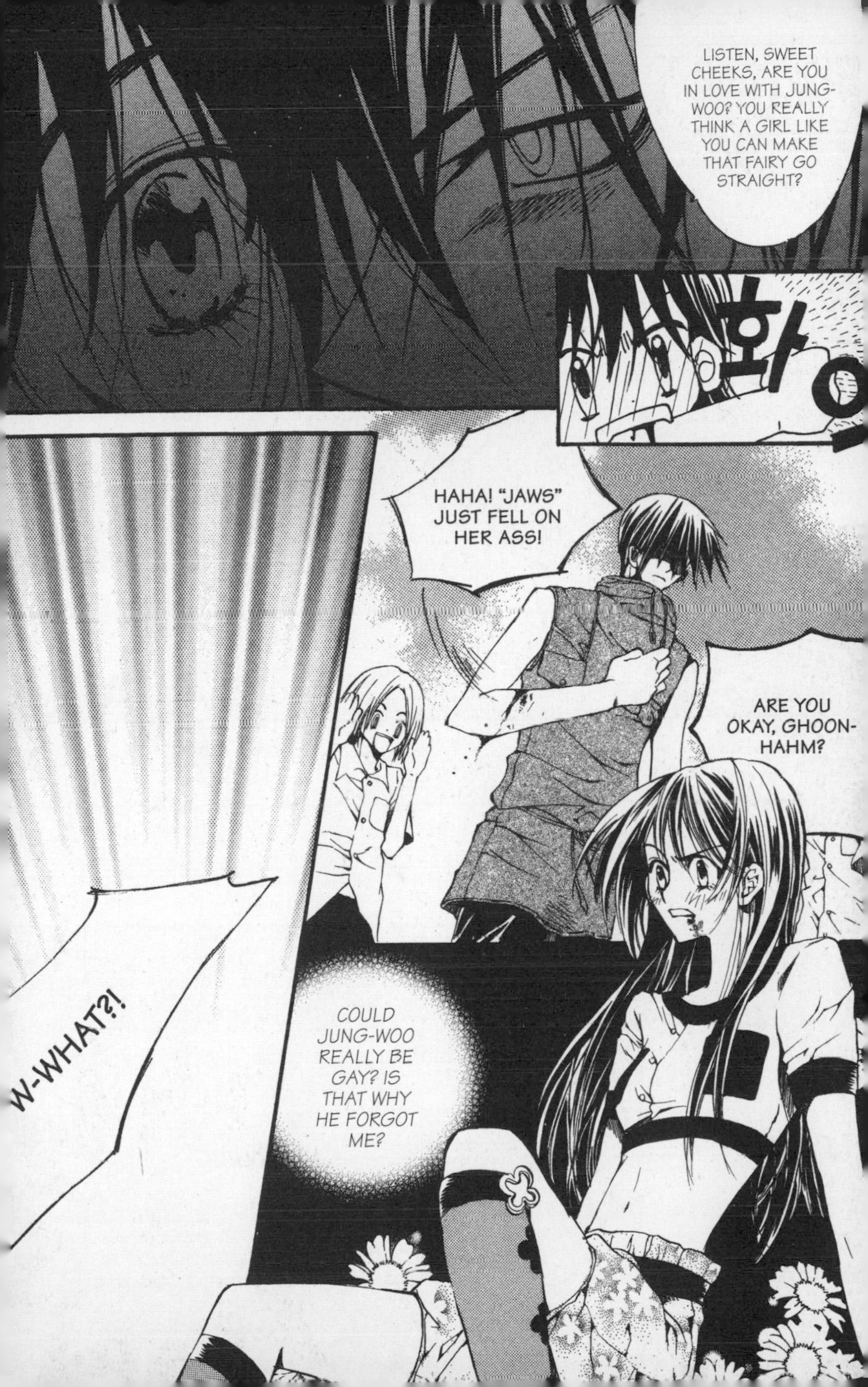

LISTEN, SWEET CHEEKS, ARE YOU IN LOVE WITH JUNG-WOO? YOU REALLY THINK A GIRL LIKE YOU CAN MAKE THAT FAIRY GO STRAIGHT?
화
W-WHAT?!
HAHA! "JAWS" JUST FELL ON HER ASS!
ARE YOU OKAY, GHOON-HAHM?
COULD JUNG-WOO REALLY BE GAY? IS THAT WHY HE FORGOT ME?

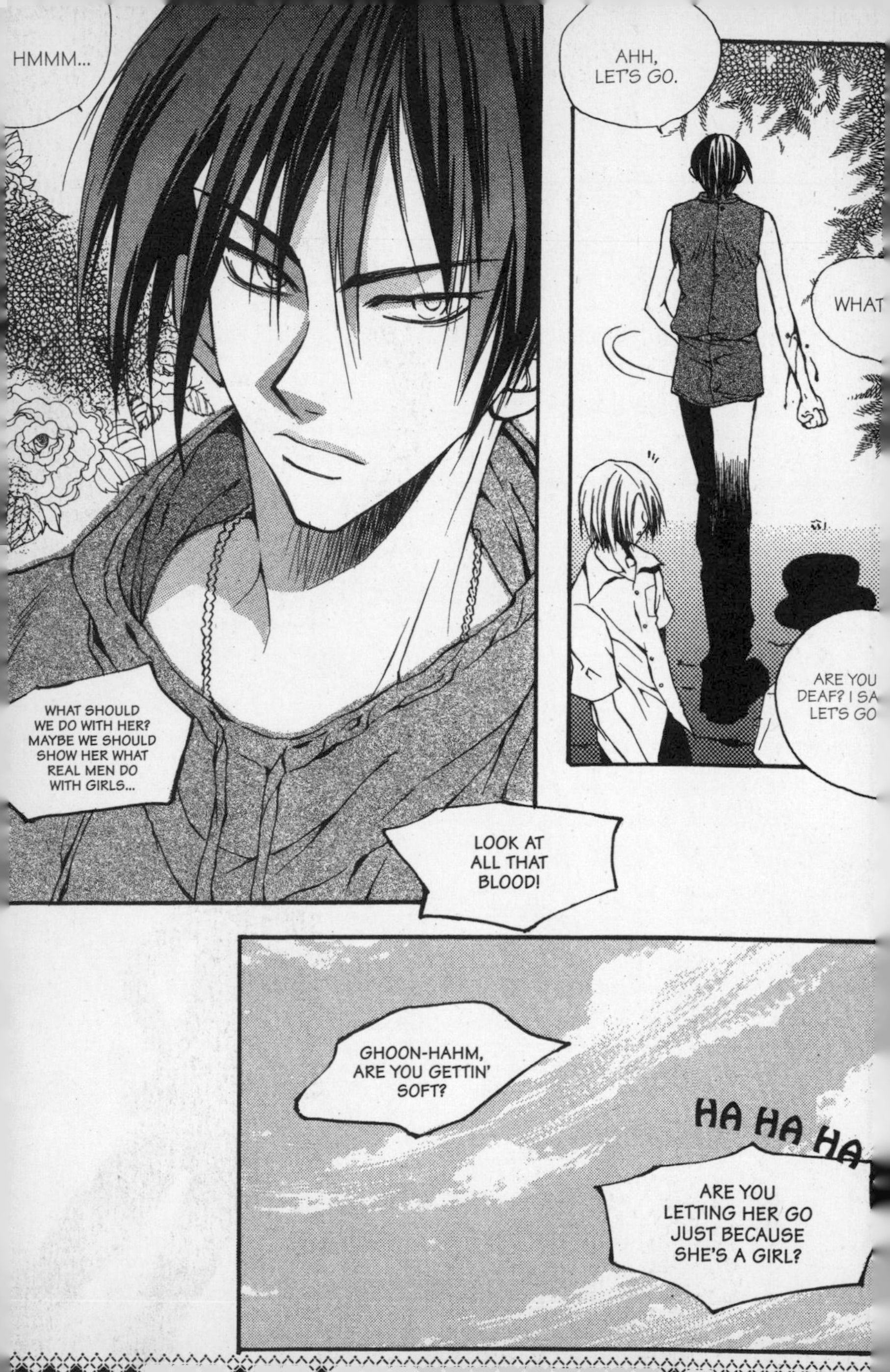
HMMM...
WHAT SHOULD WE DO WITH HER? MAYBE WE SHOULD SHOW HER WHAT REAL MEN DO WITH GIRLS...
LOOK AT ALL THAT BLOOD!
AHH, LET'S GO.
WHAT
ARE YOU DEAF? I SA LET'S GO
GHOON-HAHM, ARE YOU GETTIN' SOFT?
HA HA HA
ARE YOU LETTING HER GO JUST BECAUSE SHE'S A GIRL?

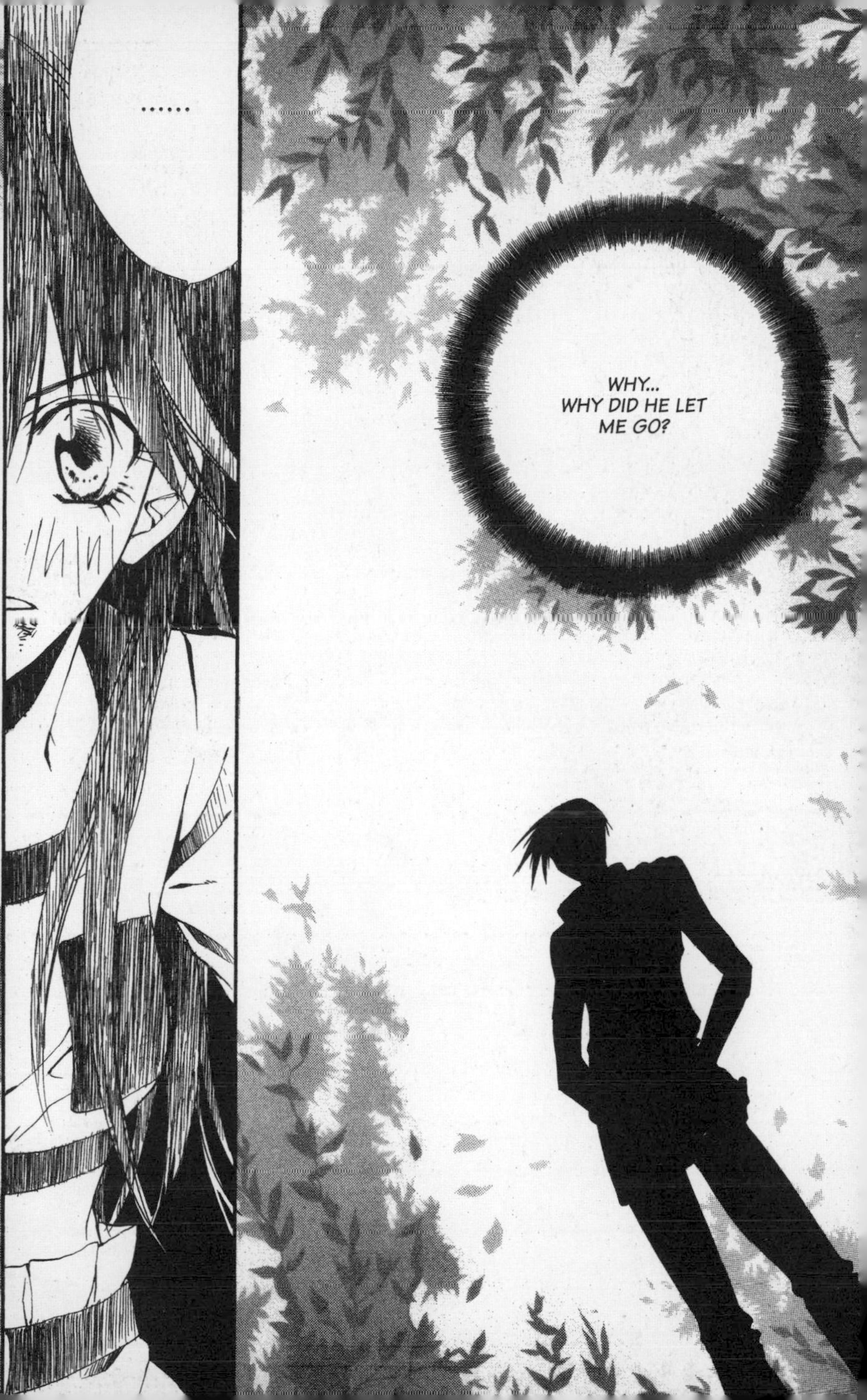
......
WHY...
WHY DID HE LET ME GO?

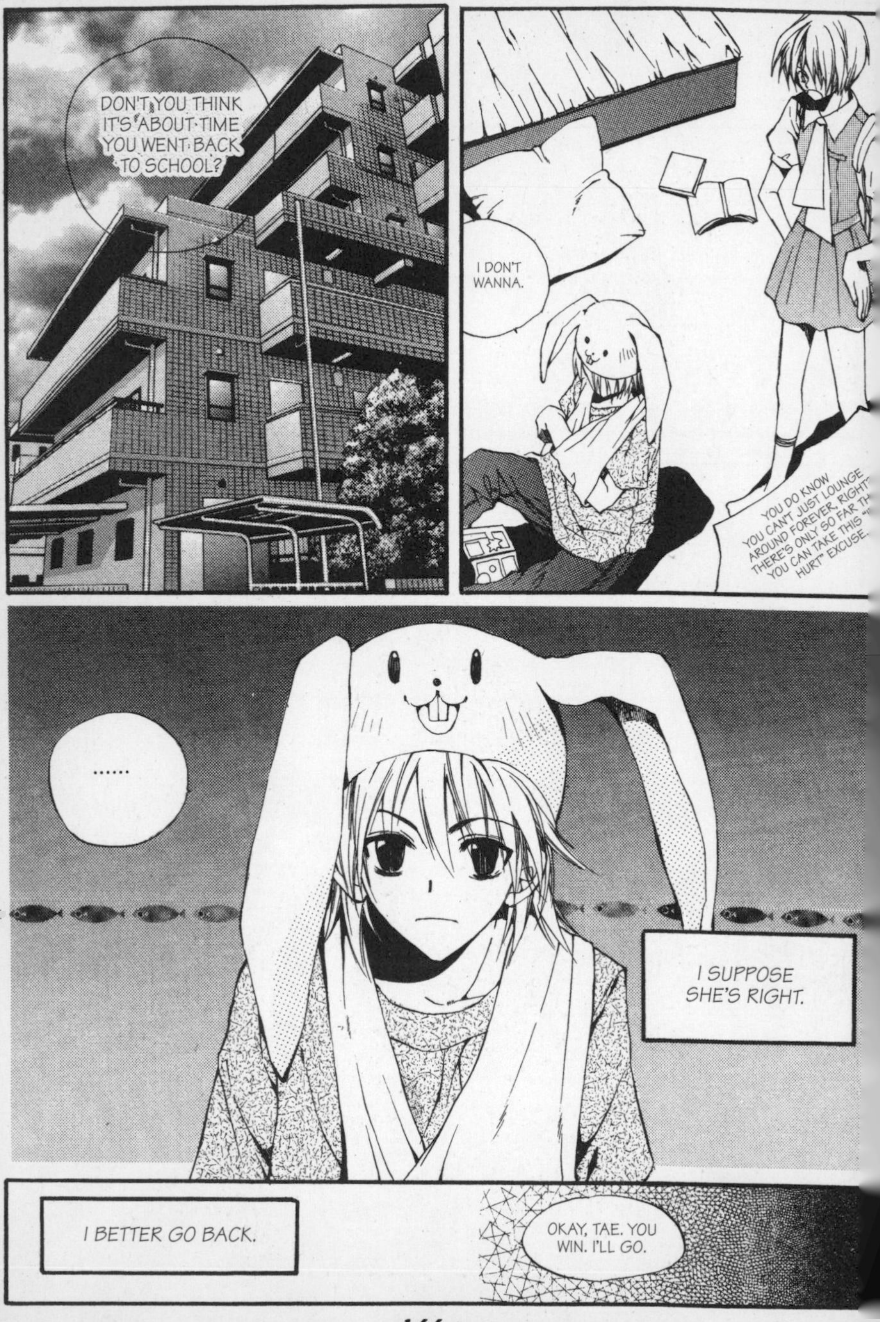
DON'T YOU THINK IT'S ABOUT TIME YOU WENT BACK TO SCHOOL?
I DON'T WANNA.
YOU DO KNOW YOU CAN'T JUST LOUNGE AROUND FOREVER, RIGHT? THERE'S ONLY SO FAR TH YOU CAN TAKE THIS " HURT" EXCUSE.
......
I SUPPOSE SHE'S RIGHT.
I BETTER GO BACK.
OKAY, TAE. YOU WIN. I'LL GO.

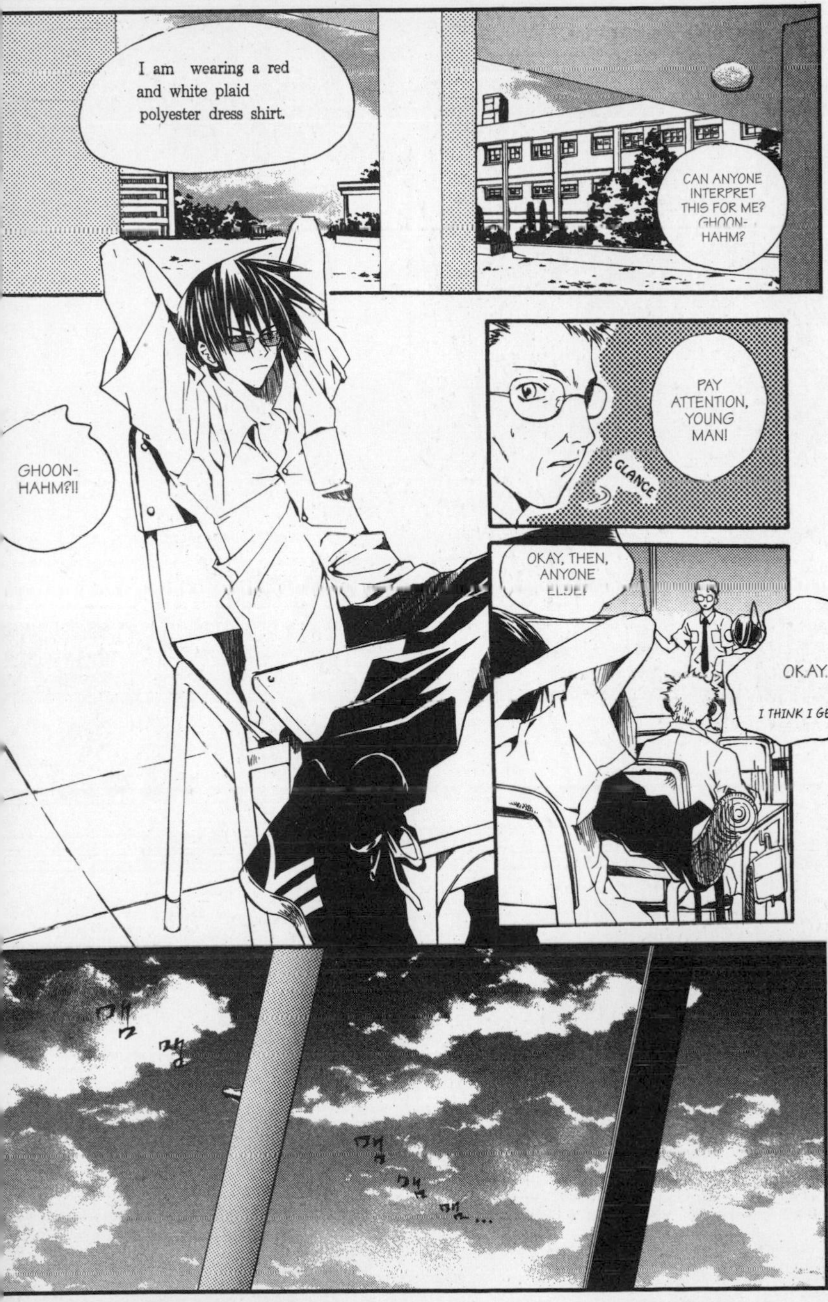
I am wearing a red and white plaid polyester dress shirt.
CAN ANYONE INTERPRET THIS FOR ME? GHOON-HAHM?
GHOON-HAHM?!!
PAY ATTENTION, YOUNG MAN!
GLANCE
OKAY, THEN, ANYONE ELSE?
OKAY.
I THINK I GET IT.

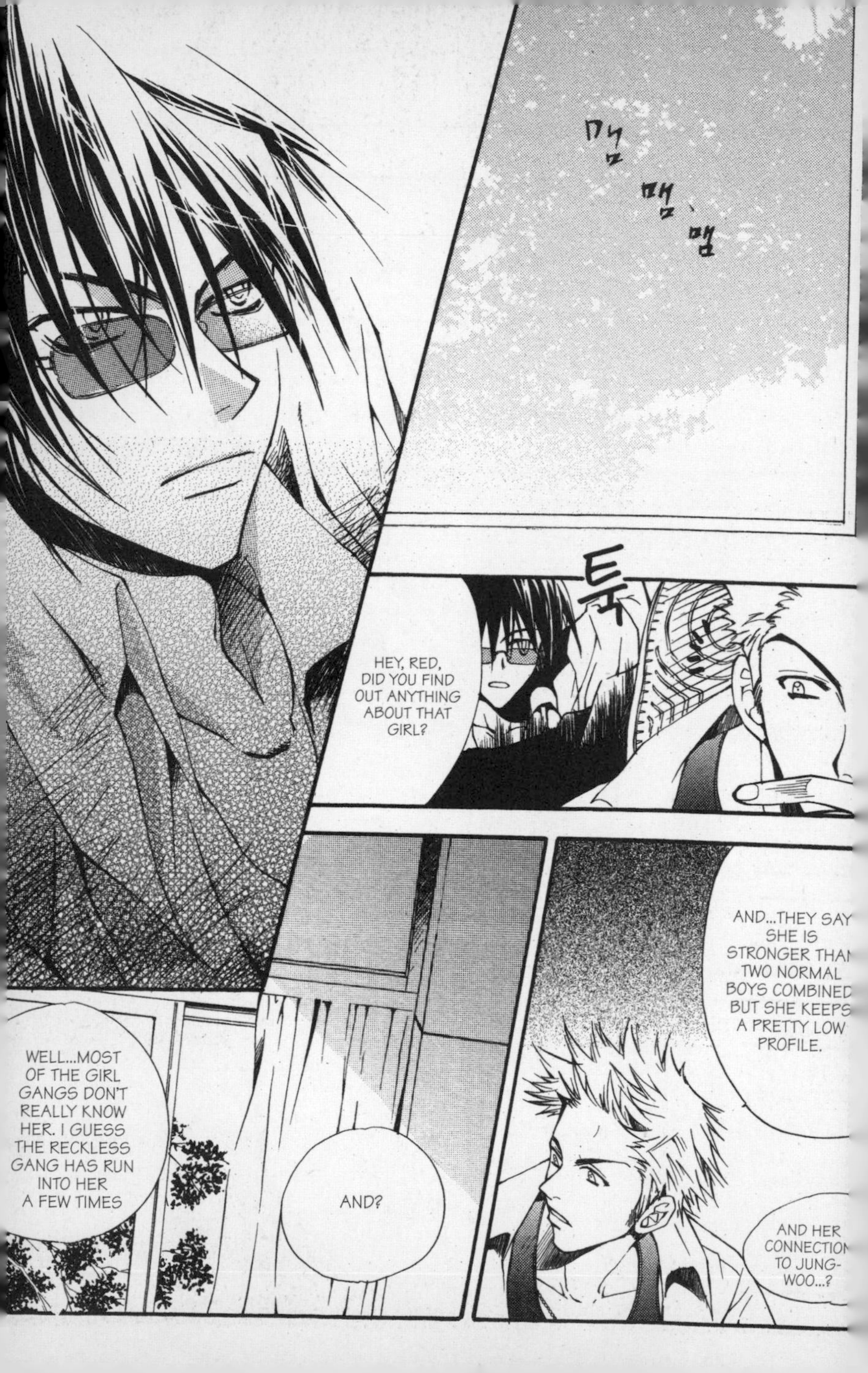
맴
맴、
맴
툭
HEY, RED, DID YOU FIND OUT ANYTHING ABOUT THAT GIRL?
WELL...MOST OF THE GIRL GANGS DON'T REALLY KNOW HER. I GUESS THE RECKLESS GANG HAS RUN INTO HER A FEW TIMES
AND?
AND...THEY SAY SHE IS STRONGER THAN TWO NORMAL BOYS COMBINED BUT SHE KEEPS A PRETTY LOW PROFILE.
AND HER CONNECTION TO JUNG-WOO...?

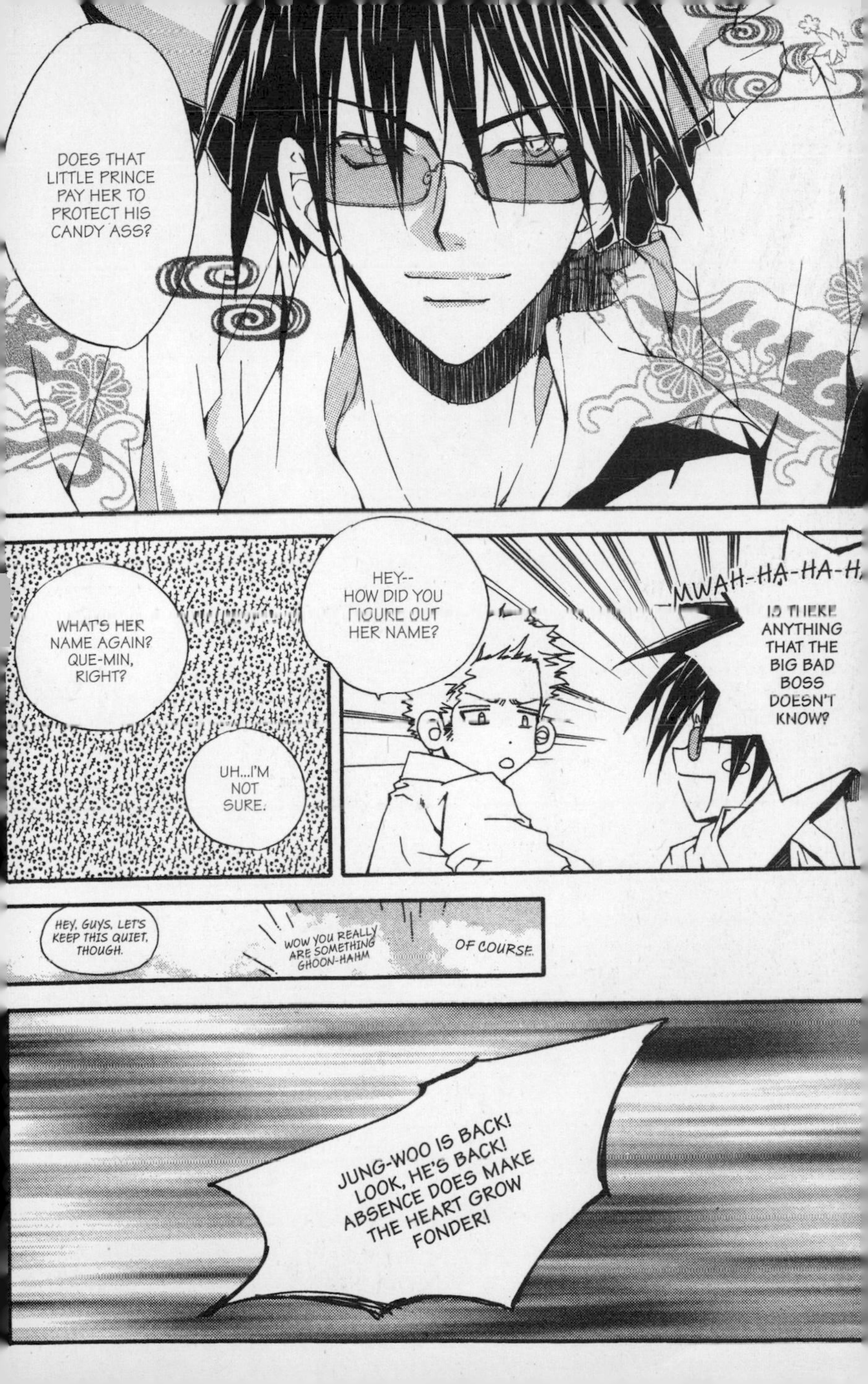
DOES THAT LITTLE PRINCE PAY HER TO PROTECT HIS CANDY ASS?
WHAT'S HER NAME AGAIN? QUE-MIN, RIGHT?
UH...I'M NOT SURE.
HEY-- HOW DID YOU FIGURE OUT HER NAME?
MWAH-HA-HA-HA
IS THERE ANYTHING THAT THE BIG BAD BOSS DOESN'T KNOW?
HEY, GUYS, LET'S KEEP THIS QUIET, THOUGH.
WOW YOU REALLY ARE SOMETHING GHOON-HAHM
OF COURSE.
JUNG-WOO IS BACK! LOOK, HE'S BACK! ABSENCE DOES MAKE THE HEART GROW FONDER!

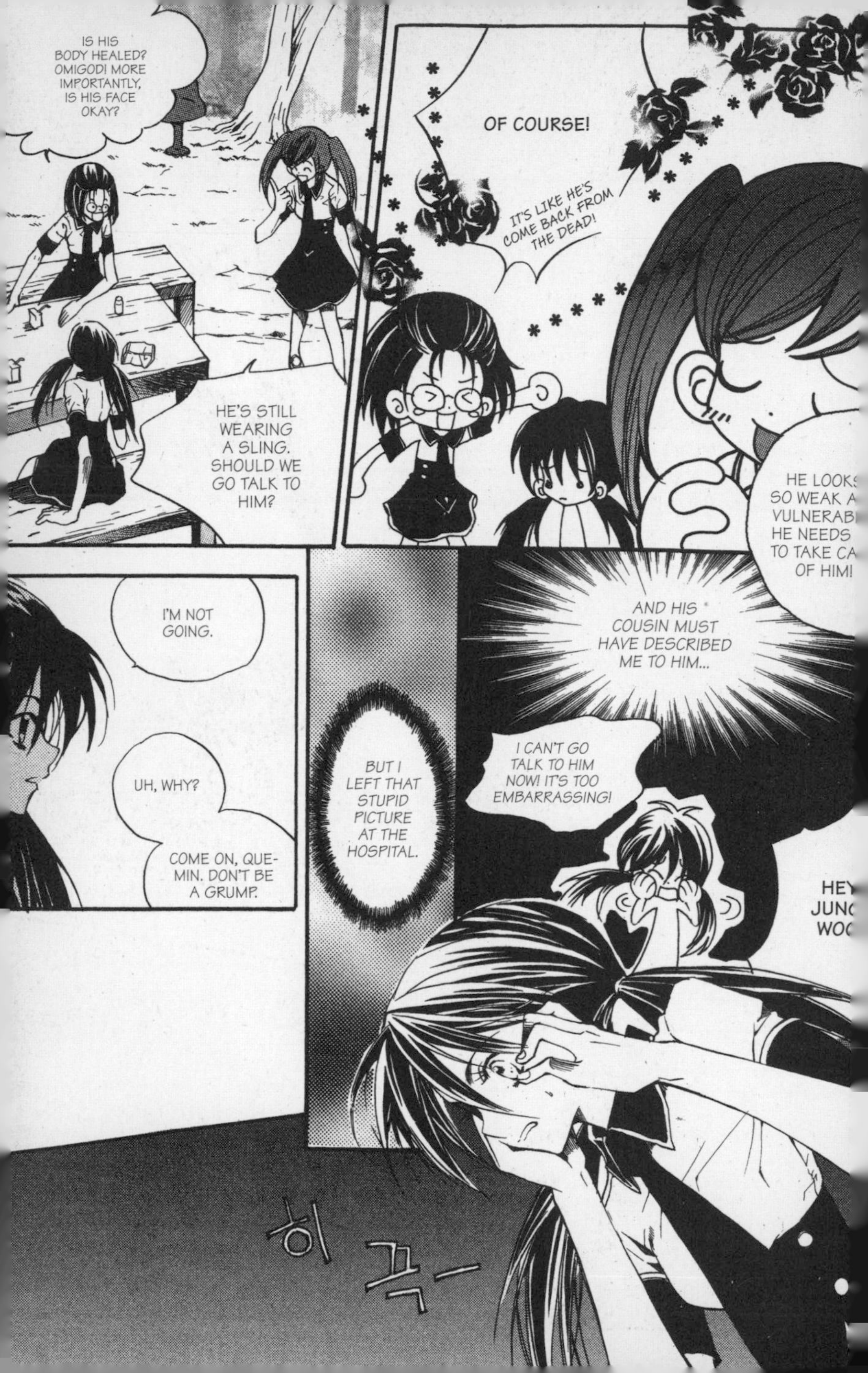

IS HIS BODY HEALED? OMIGOD! MORE IMPORTANTLY, IS HIS FACE OKAY?
HE'S STILL WEARING A SLING. SHOULD WE GO TALK TO HIM?
OF COURSE!
IT'S LIKE HE'S COME BACK FROM THE DEAD!
HE LOOKS SO WEAK A VULNERAB HE NEEDS TO TAKE CA OF HIM!
I'M NOT GOING.
UH, WHY?
COME ON, QUE-MIN. DON'T BE A GRUMP.
BUT I LEFT THAT STUPID PICTURE AT THE HOSPITAL.
AND HIS COUSIN MUST HAVE DESCRIBED ME TO HIM...
I CAN'T GO TALK TO HIM NOW! IT'S TOO EMBARRASSING!
HEY JUNG WOO
히 끅—

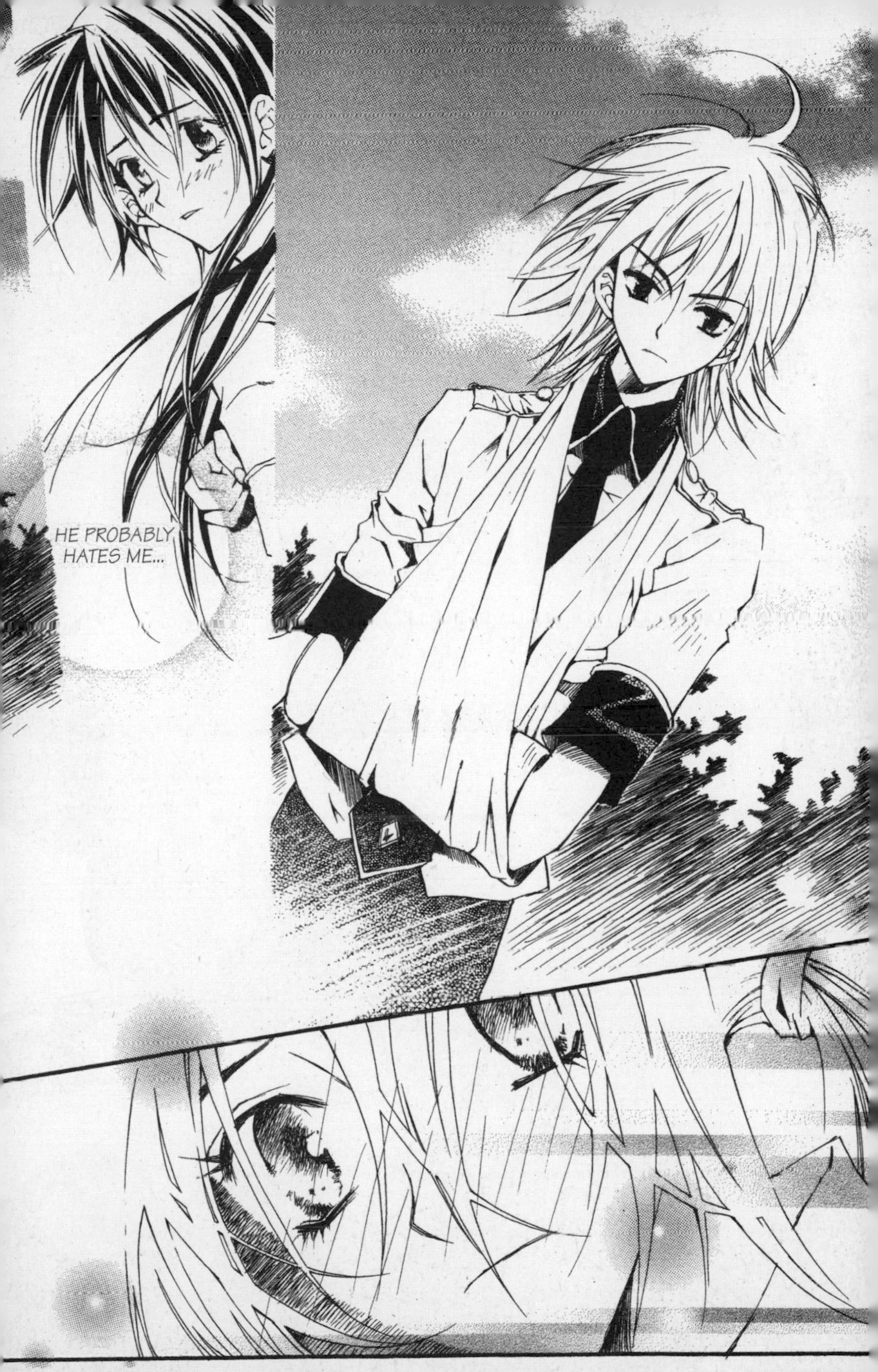
HE PROBABLY HATES ME...

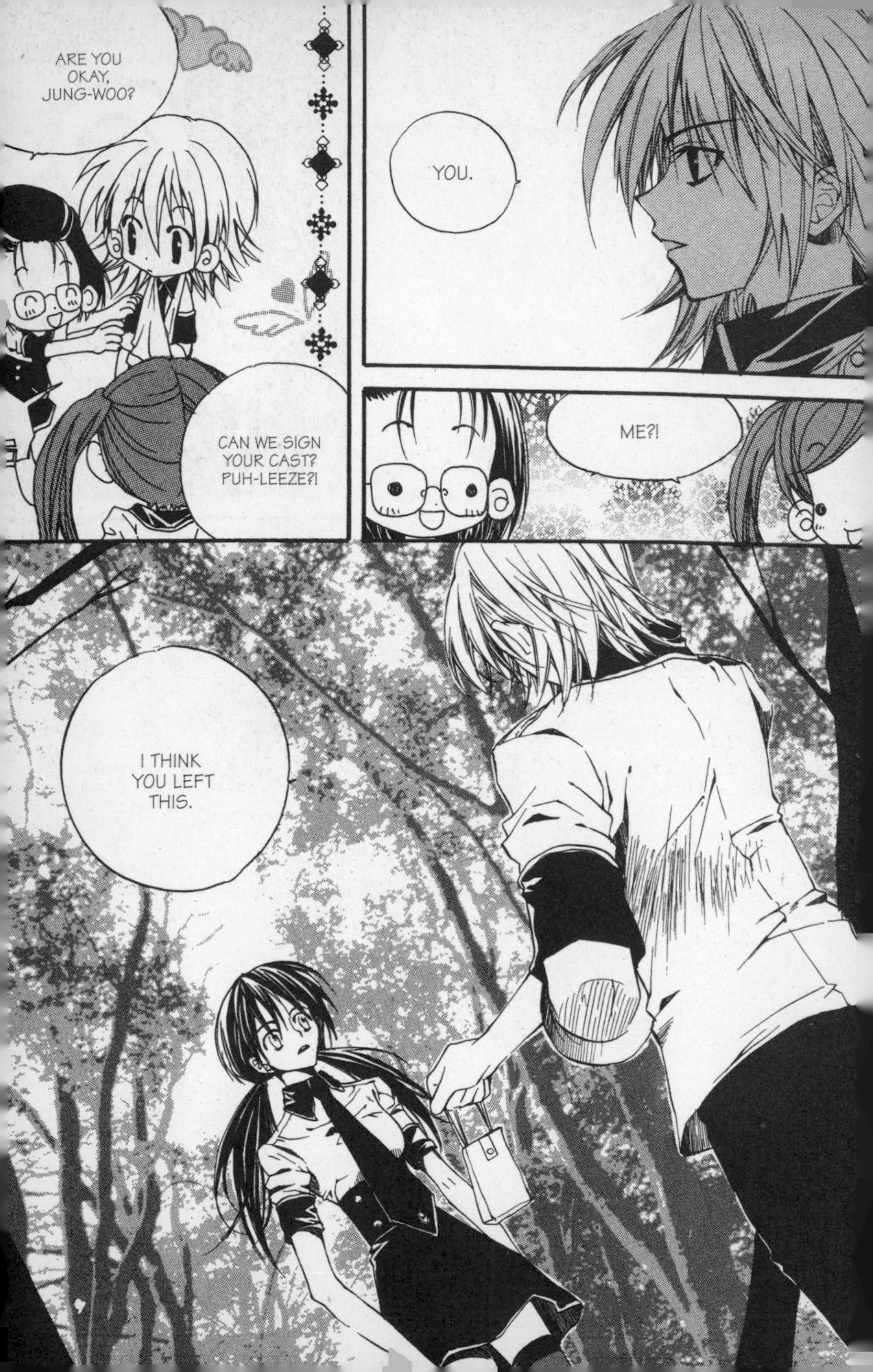
ARE YOU OKAY, JUNG-WOO?
CAN WE SIGN YOUR CAST? PUH-LEEZE?!
YOU.
ME?!
I THINK YOU LEFT THIS.

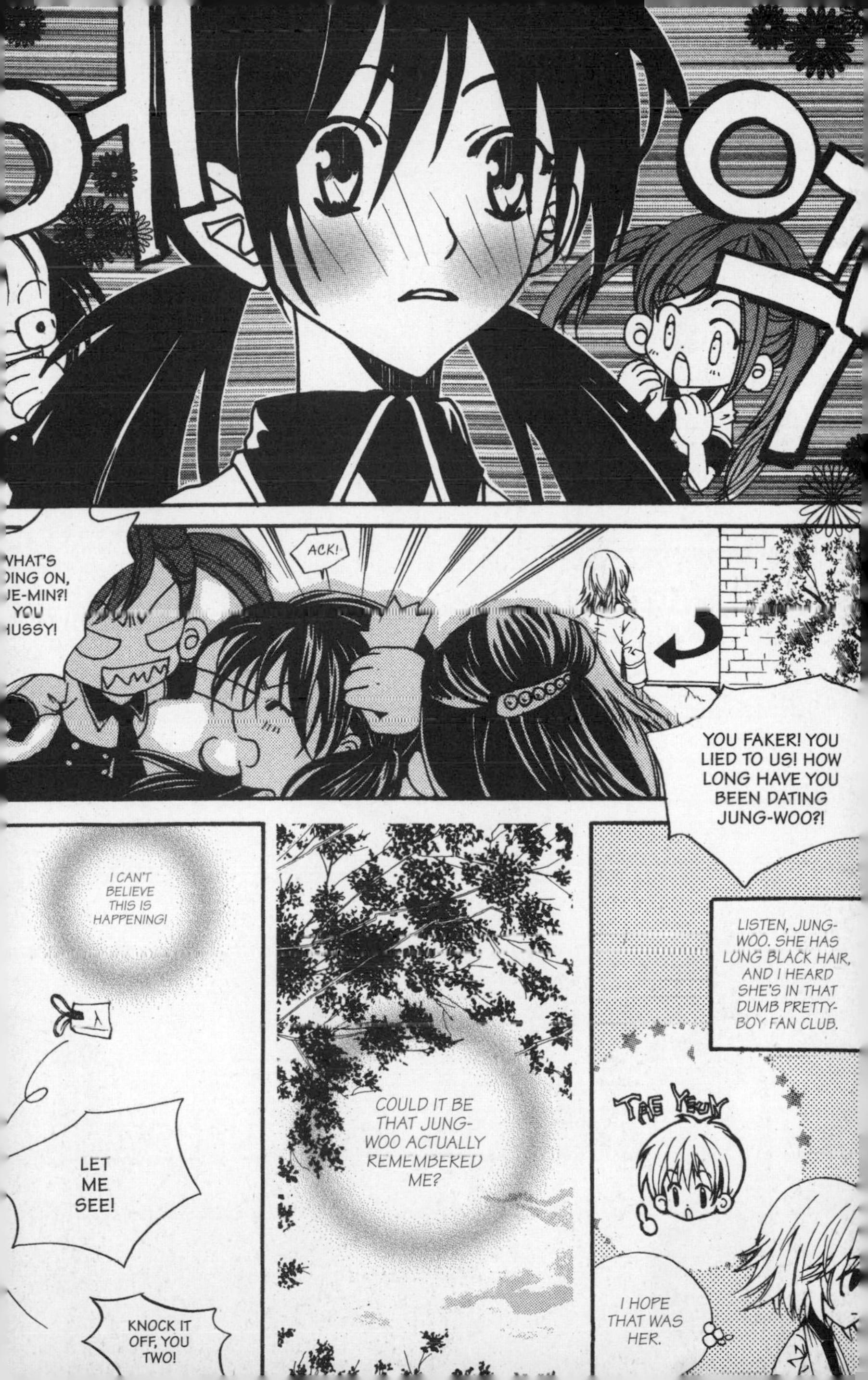

HAT'S OING ON, E-MIN?! YOU USSY!
ACK!
YOU FAKER! YOU LIED TO US! HOW LONG HAVE YOU BEEN DATING JUNG-WOO?!
I CAN'T BELIEVE THIS IS HAPPENING!
LET ME SEE!
KNOCK IT OFF, YOU TWO!
COULD IT BE THAT JUNG-WOO ACTUALLY REMEMBERED ME?
LISTEN, JUNG-WOO. SHE HAS LONG BLACK HAIR, AND I HEARD SHE'S IN THAT DUMB PRETTY-BOY FAN CLUB.
TAE YEON
I HOPE THAT WAS HER.

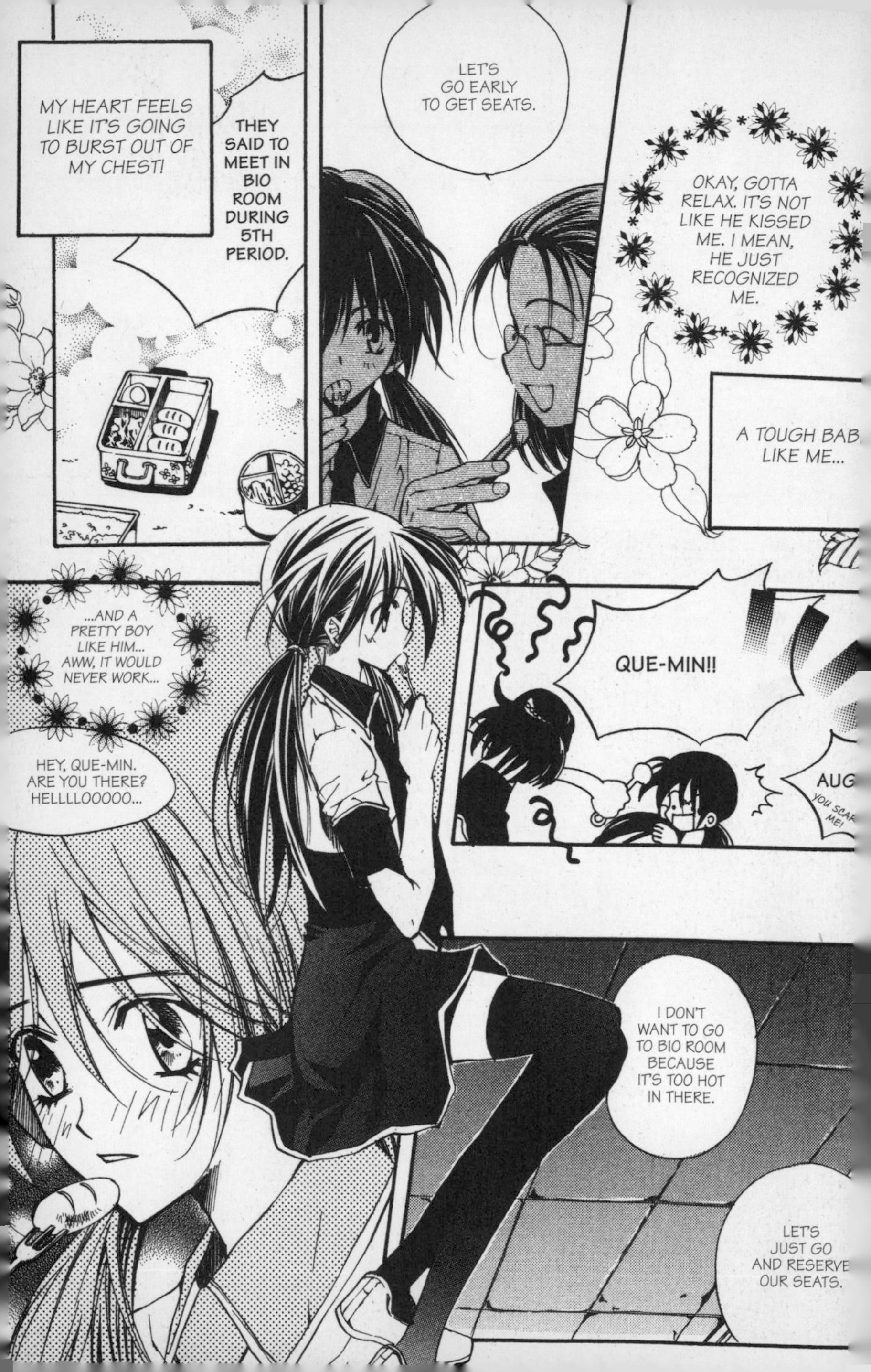
MY HEART FEELS LIKE IT'S GOING TO BURST OUT OF MY CHEST!
THEY SAID TO MEET IN BIO ROOM DURING 5TH PERIOD.
LET'S GO EARLY TO GET SEATS.
OKAY, GOTTA RELAX. IT'S NOT LIKE HE KISSED ME. I MEAN, HE JUST RECOGNIZED ME.
A TOUGH BAB LIKE ME...
...AND A PRETTY BOY LIKE HIM... AWW, IT WOULD NEVER WORK...
HEY, QUE-MIN. ARE YOU THERE? HELLLLOOOOO...
QUE-MIN!!
AUG
YOU SCAR ME!
I DON'T WANT TO GO TO BIO ROOM BECAUSE IT'S TOO HOT IN THERE.
LET'S JUST GO AND RESERVE OUR SEATS.

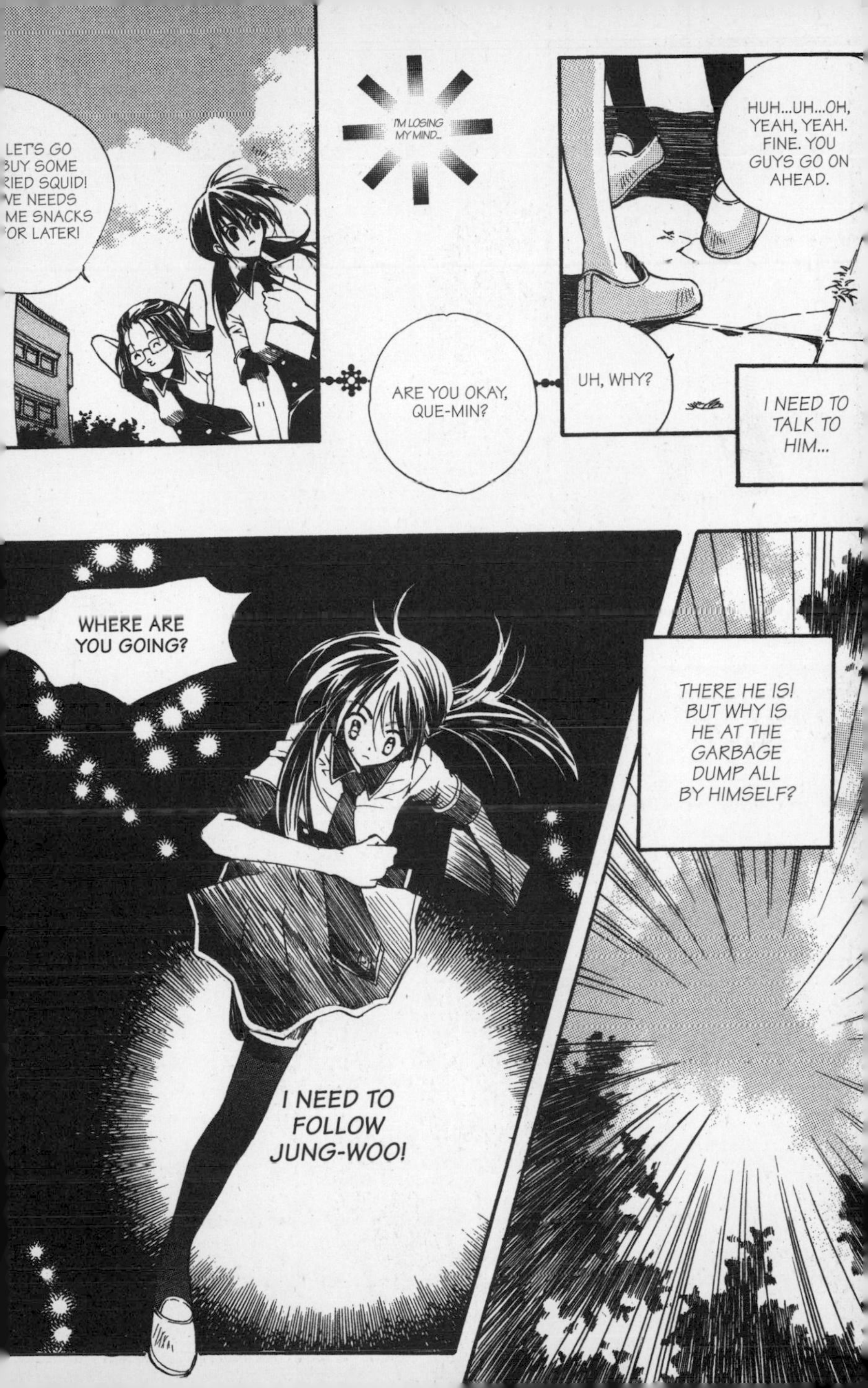
LET'S GO
UY SOME
RIED SQUID!
VE NEEDS
ME SNACKS
OR LATER!
I'M LOSING MY MIND...
ARE YOU OKAY, QUE-MIN?
HUH...UH...OH, YEAH, YEAH. FINE. YOU GUYS GO ON AHEAD.
UH, WHY?
I NEED TO TALK TO HIM...
WHERE ARE YOU GOING?
I NEED TO FOLLOW JUNG-WOO!
THERE HE IS! BUT WHY IS HE AT THE GARBAGE DUMP ALL BY HIMSELF?

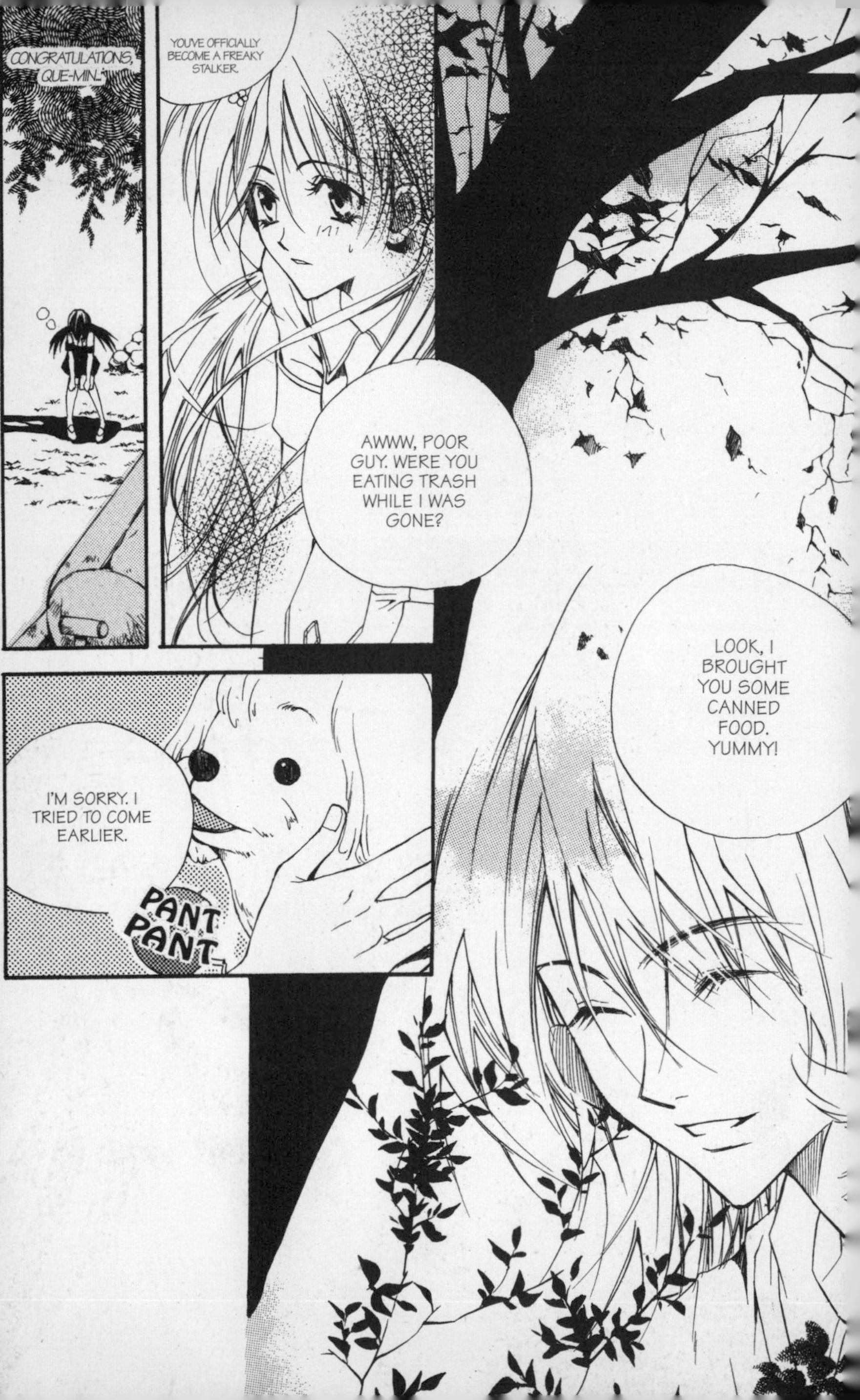
CONGRATULATIONS, QUE-MIN...
YOU'VE OFFICIALLY BECOME A FREAKY STALKER.
AWWW, POOR GUY. WERE YOU EATING TRASH WHILE I WAS GONE?
I'M SORRY. I TRIED TO COME EARLIER.
PANT PANT
LOOK, I BROUGHT YOU SOME CANNED FOOD. YUMMY!

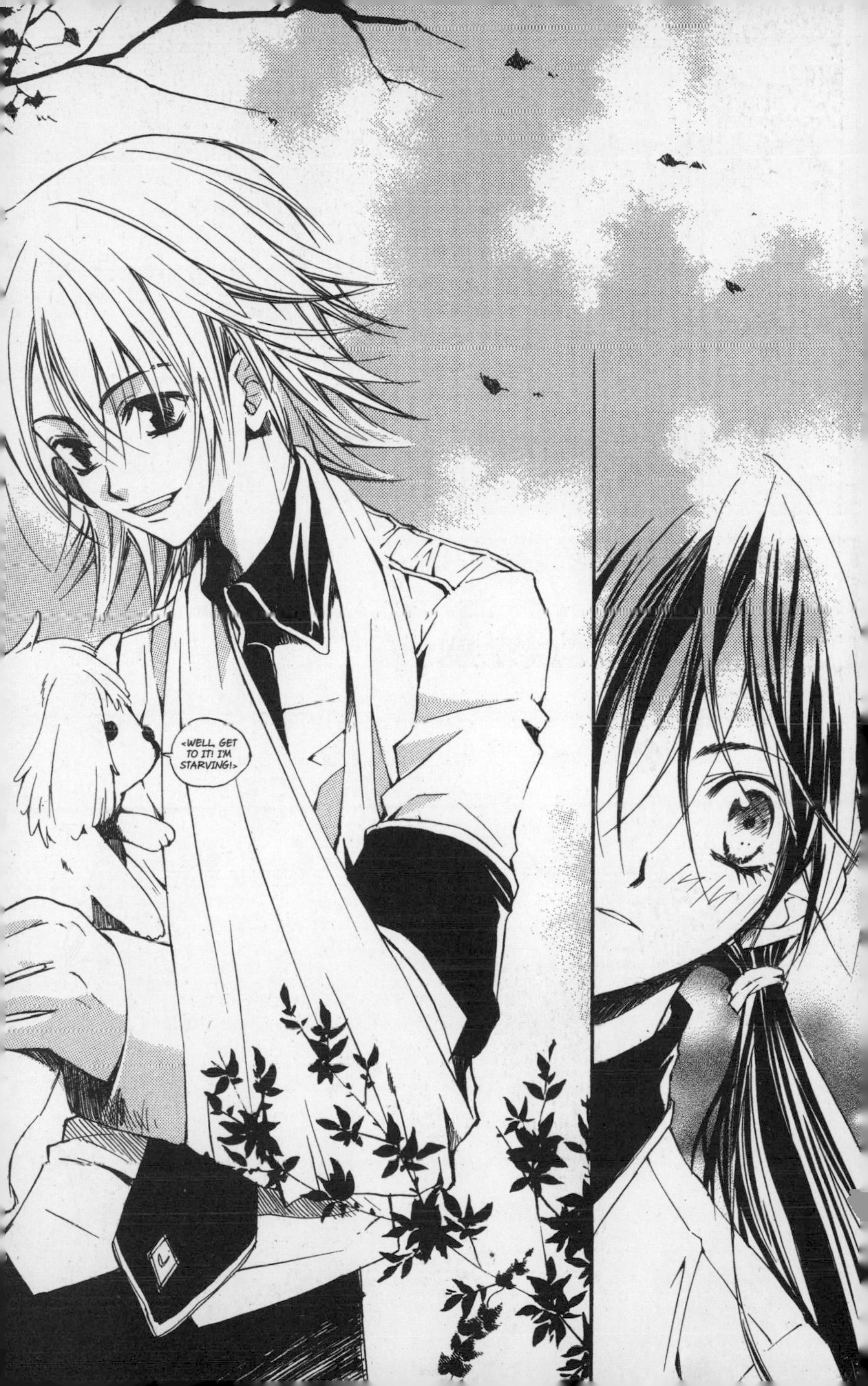
<WELL, GET TO IT! I'M STARVING!>

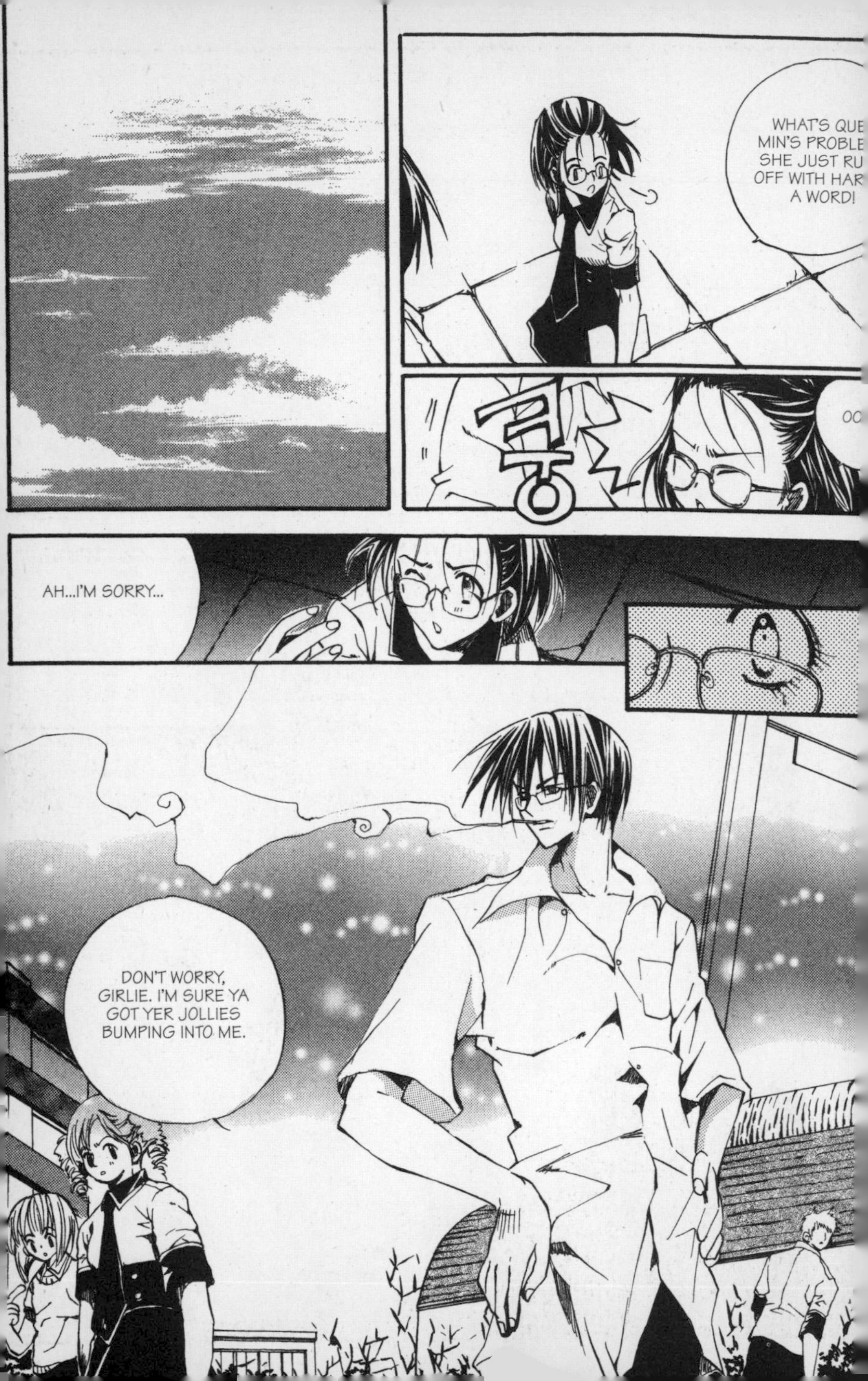
WHAT'S QUE MIN'S PROBLE SHE JUST RU OFF WITH HAR A WORD!
OO
AH...I'M SORRY...
DON'T WORRY, GIRLIE. I'M SURE YA GOT YER JOLLIES BUMPING INTO ME.

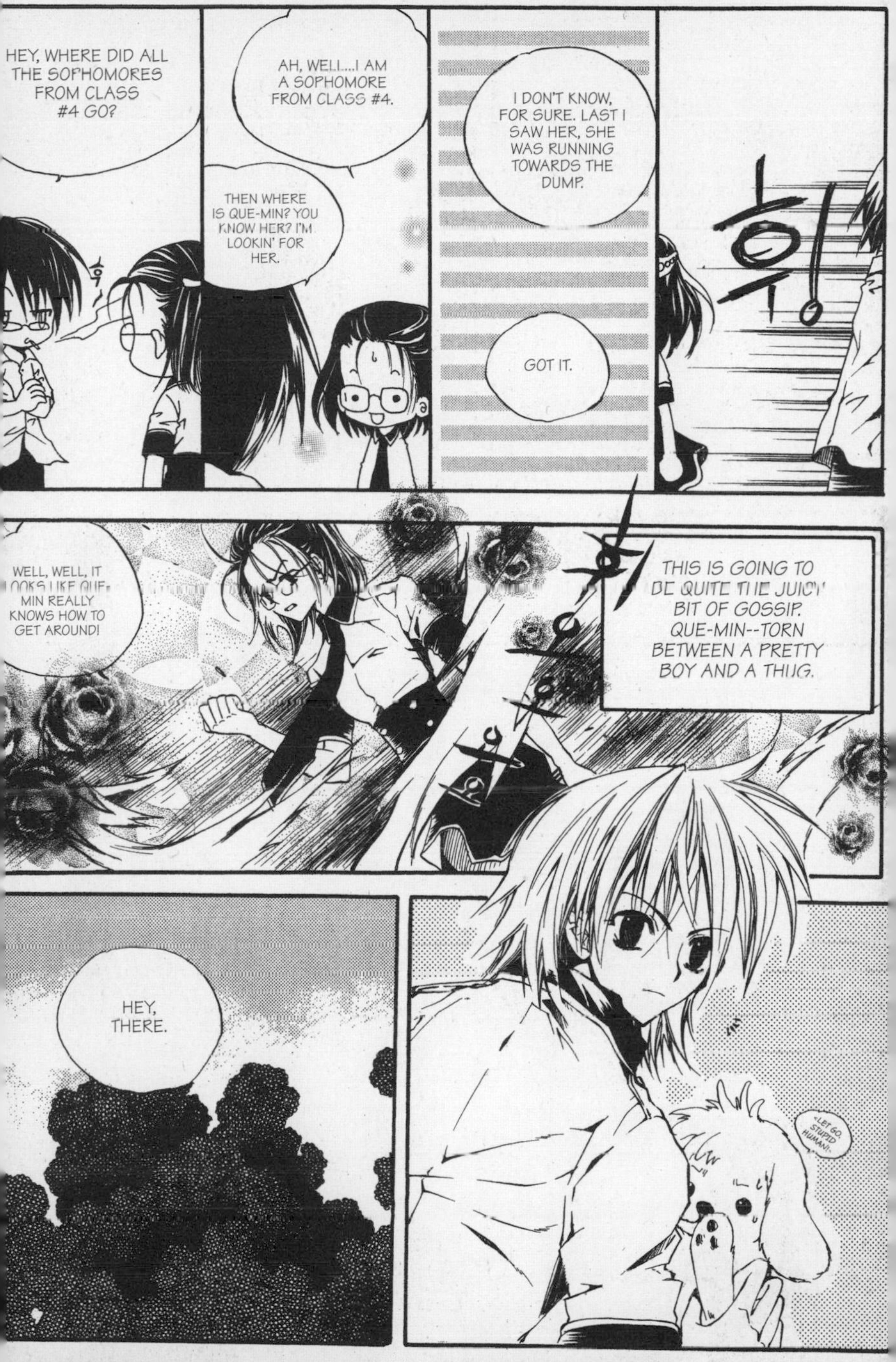
HEY, WHERE DID ALL THE SOPHOMORES FROM CLASS #4 GO?
AH, WELL...I AM A SOPHOMORE FROM CLASS #4.
THEN WHERE IS QUE-MIN? YOU KNOW HER? I'M LOOKIN' FOR HER.
I DON'T KNOW, FOR SURE. LAST I SAW HER, SHE WAS RUNNING TOWARDS THE DUMP.
GOT IT.
WELL, WELL, IT LOOKS LIKE QUE-MIN REALLY KNOWS HOW TO GET AROUND!
THIS IS GOING TO BE QUITE THE JUICY BIT OF GOSSIP. QUE-MIN--TORN BETWEEN A PRETTY BOY AND A THUG.
HEY, THERE.
<LET GO, STUPID HUMAN!>

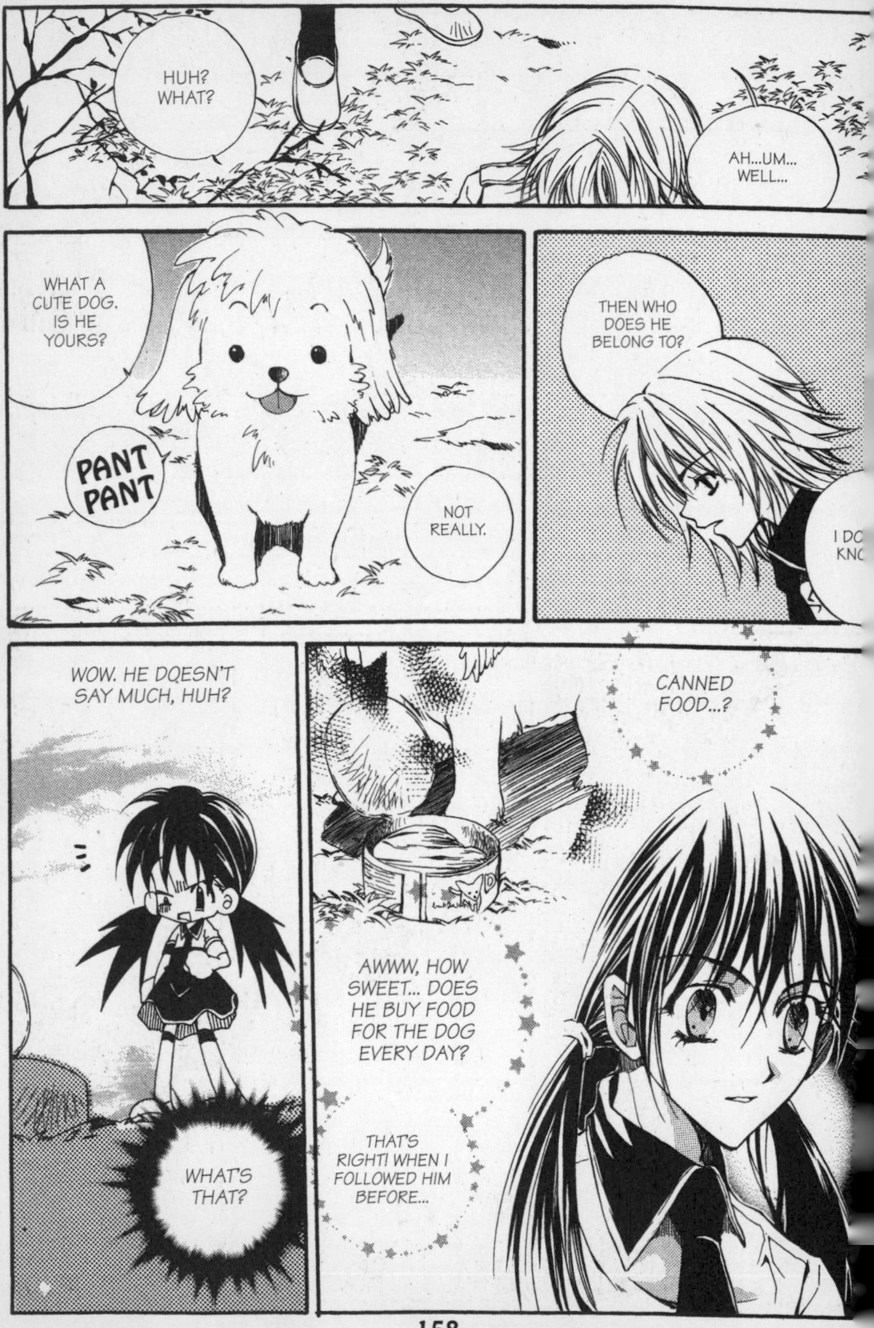
HUH? WHAT?
AH...UM... WELL...
WHAT A CUTE DOG. IS HE YOURS?
PANT PANT
NOT REALLY.
THEN WHO DOES HE BELONG TO?
WOW. HE DOESN'T SAY MUCH, HUH?
WHAT'S THAT?
CANNED FOOD...?
AWWW, HOW SWEET... DOES HE BUY FOOD FOR THE DOG EVERY DAY?
THAT'S RIGHT! WHEN I FOLLOWED HIM BEFORE...

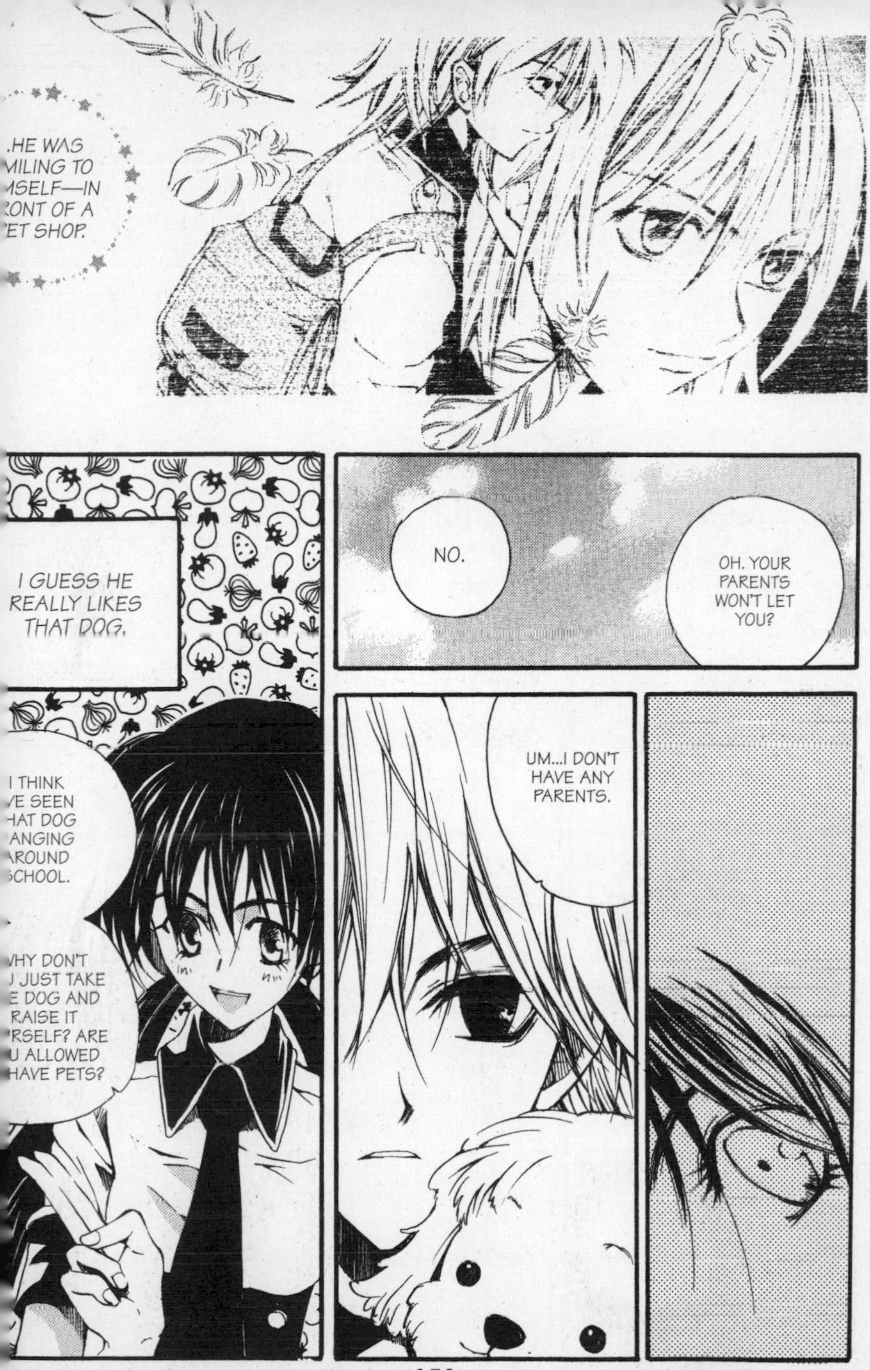
.HE WAS
MILING TO
MSELF—IN
RONT OF A
ET SHOP.
I GUESS HE REALLY LIKES THAT DOG.
I THINK
VE SEEN
HAT DOG
ANGING
AROUND
SCHOOL.
WHY DON'T
U JUST TAKE
E DOG AND
RAISE IT
RSELF? ARE
U ALLOWED
HAVE PETS?
NO.
OH. YOUR PARENTS WON'T LET YOU?
UM...I DON'T HAVE ANY PARENTS.

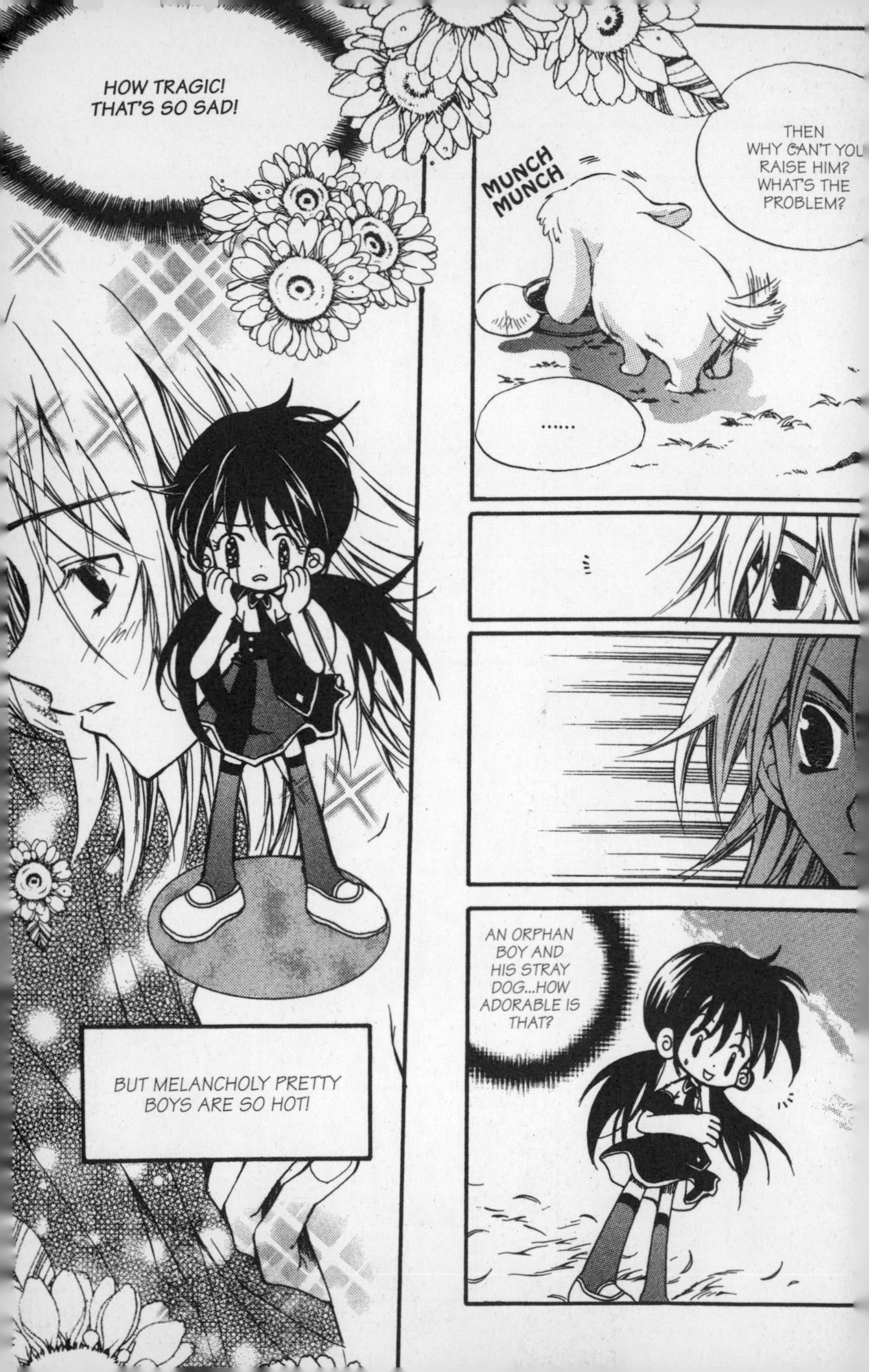
HOW TRAGIC! THAT'S SO SAD!
BUT MELANCHOLY PRETTY BOYS ARE SO HOT!
MUNCH MUNCH
THEN WHY CAN'T YOU RAISE HIM? WHAT'S THE PROBLEM?
......
AN ORPHAN BOY AND HIS STRAY DOG...HOW ADORABLE IS THAT?

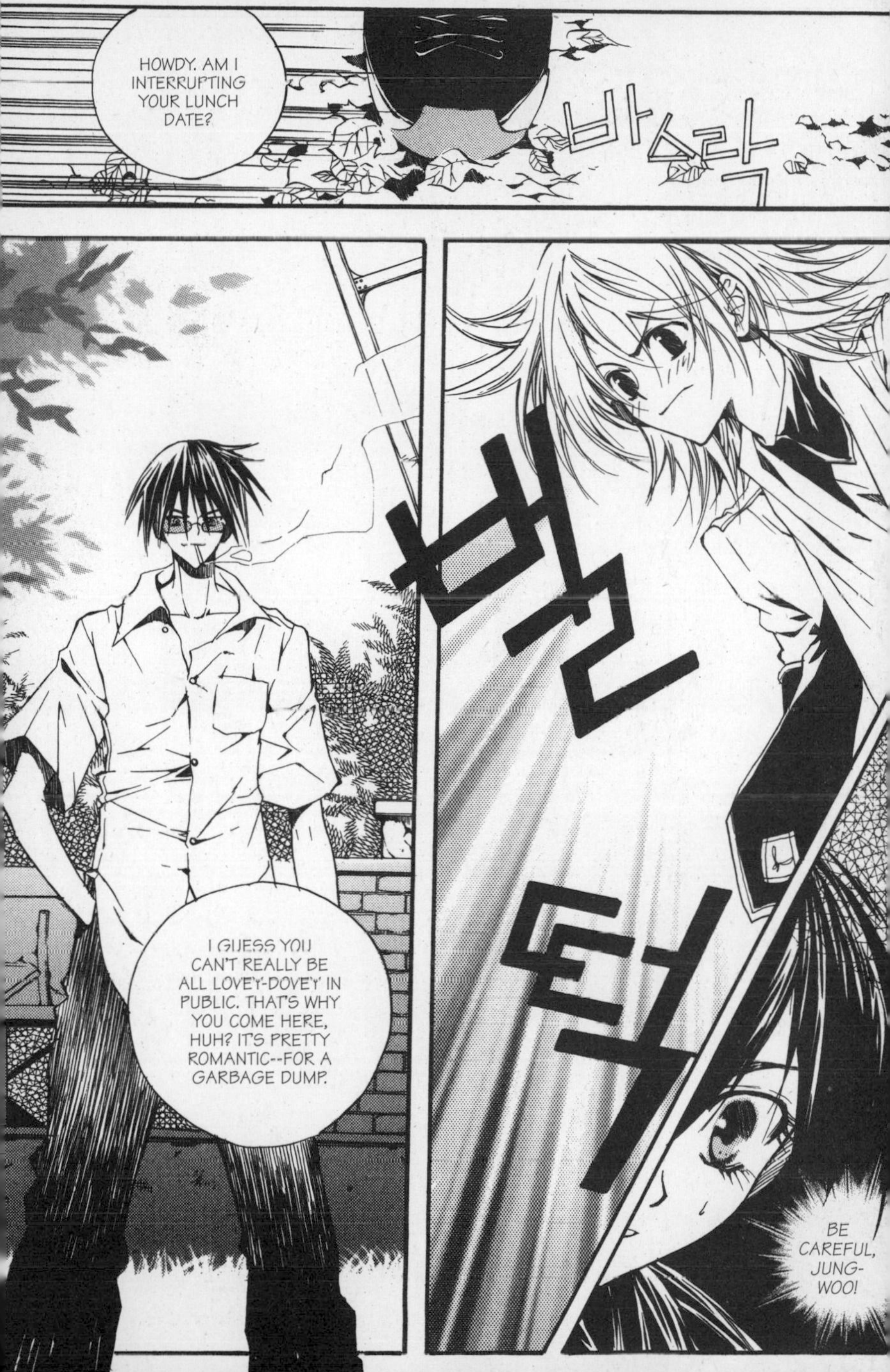
HOWDY. AM I INTERRUPTING YOUR LUNCH DATE?
바스락
I GUESS YOU CAN'T REALLY BE ALL LOVEY-DOVEY IN PUBLIC. THAT'S WHY YOU COME HERE, HUH? IT'S PRETTY ROMANTIC--FOR A GARBAGE DUMP.
BE CAREFUL, JUNG-WOO!

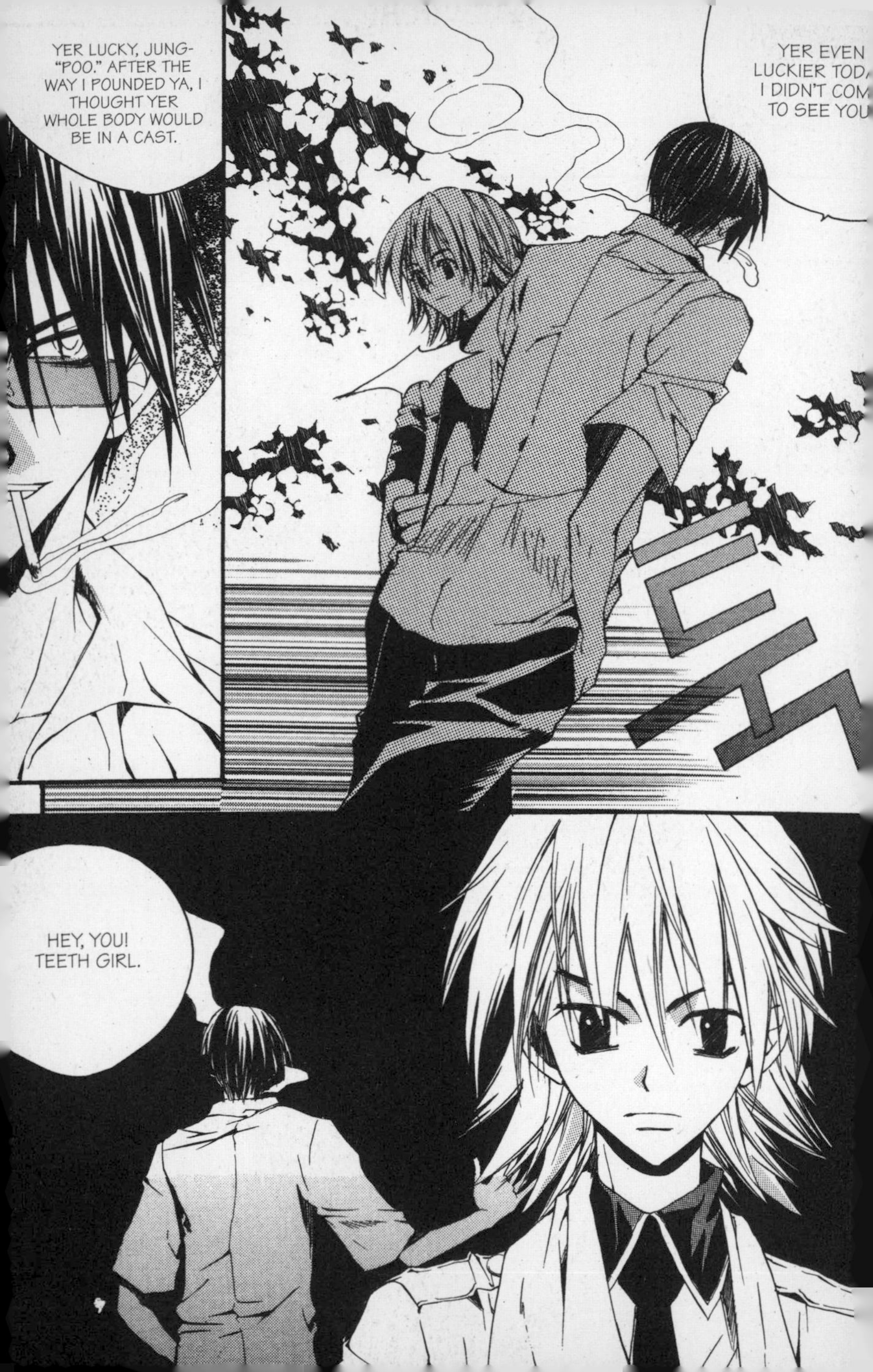
YER LUCKY, JUNG-"POO." AFTER THE WAY I POUNDED YA, I THOUGHT YER WHOLE BODY WOULD BE IN A CAST.
YER EVEN LUCKIER TODA I DIDN'T COM TO SEE YOU
HEY, YOU! TEETH GIRL.

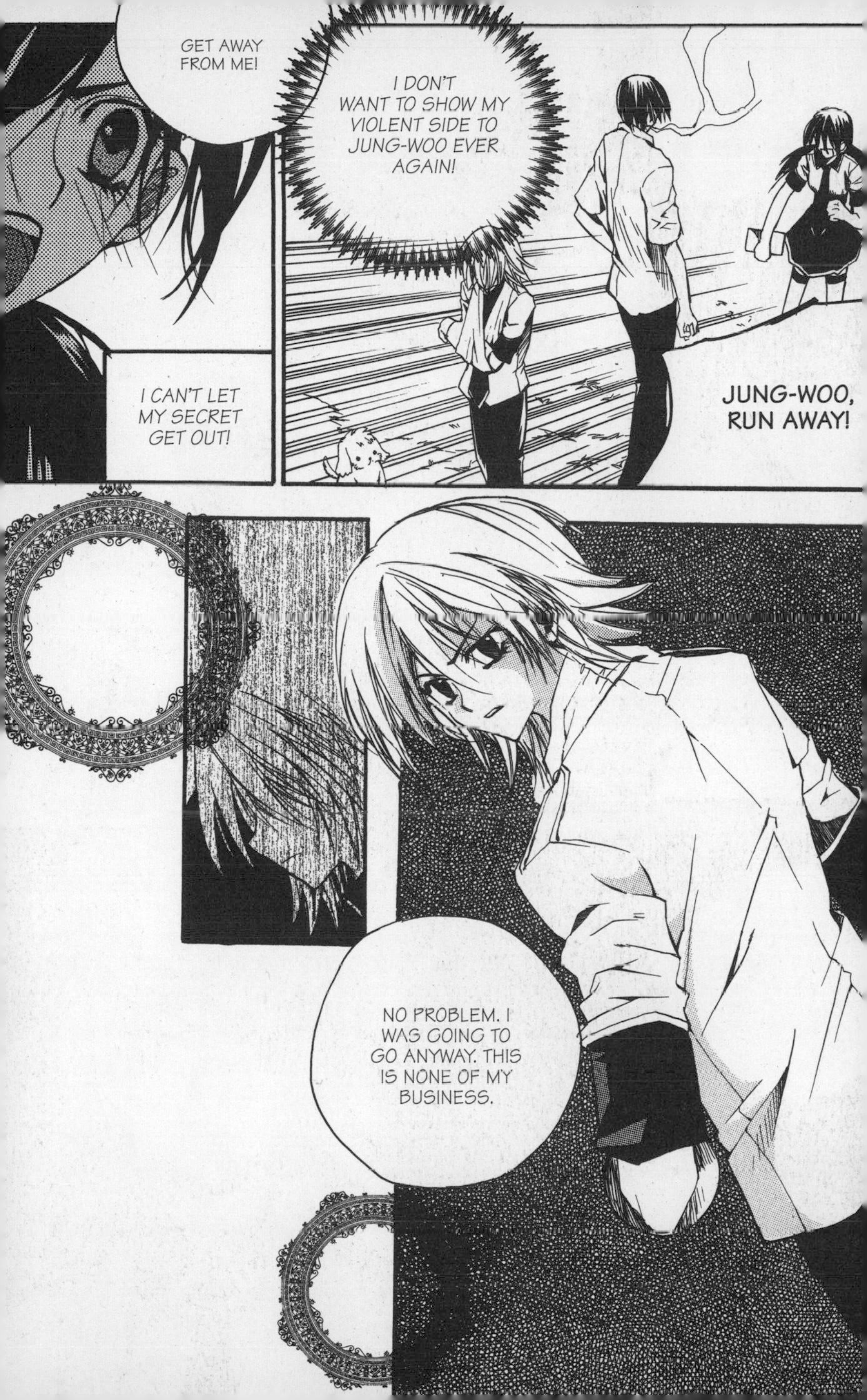
GET AWAY FROM ME!
I CAN'T LET MY SECRET GET OUT!
I DON'T WANT TO SHOW MY VIOLENT SIDE TO JUNG-WOO EVER AGAIN!
JUNG-WOO, RUN AWAY!
NO PROBLEM. I WAS GOING TO GO ANYWAY. THIS IS NONE OF MY BUSINESS.

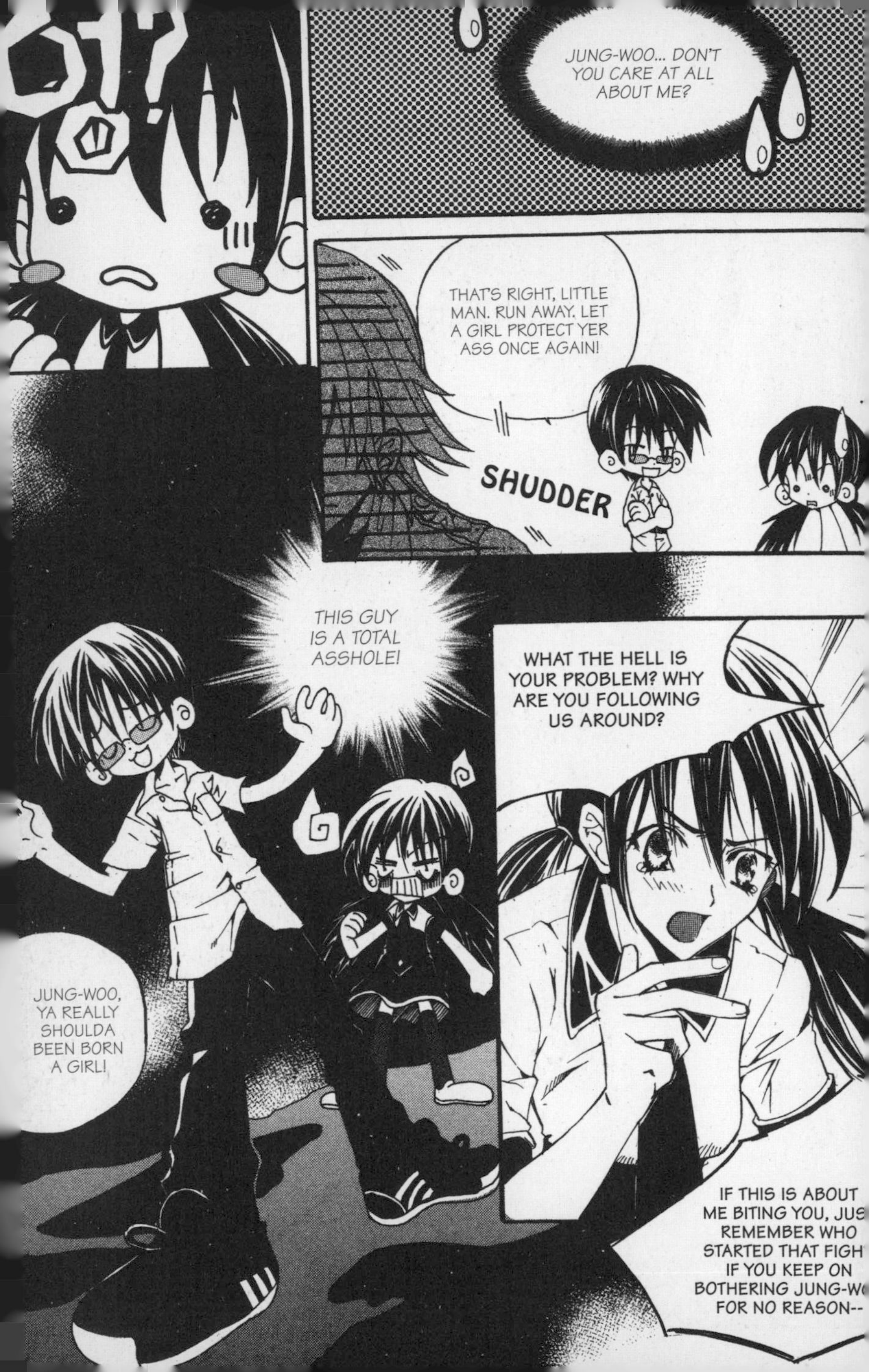
JUNG-WOO... DON'T YOU CARE AT ALL ABOUT ME?
THAT'S RIGHT, LITTLE MAN. RUN AWAY. LET A GIRL PROTECT YER ASS ONCE AGAIN!
SHUDDER
THIS GUY IS A TOTAL ASSHOLE!
JUNG-WOO, YA REALLY SHOULDA BEEN BORN A GIRL!
WHAT THE HELL IS YOUR PROBLEM? WHY ARE YOU FOLLOWING US AROUND?
IF THIS IS ABOUT ME BITING YOU, JUS REMEMBER WHO STARTED THAT FIGH IF YOU KEEP ON BOTHERING JUNG-W FOR NO REASON--

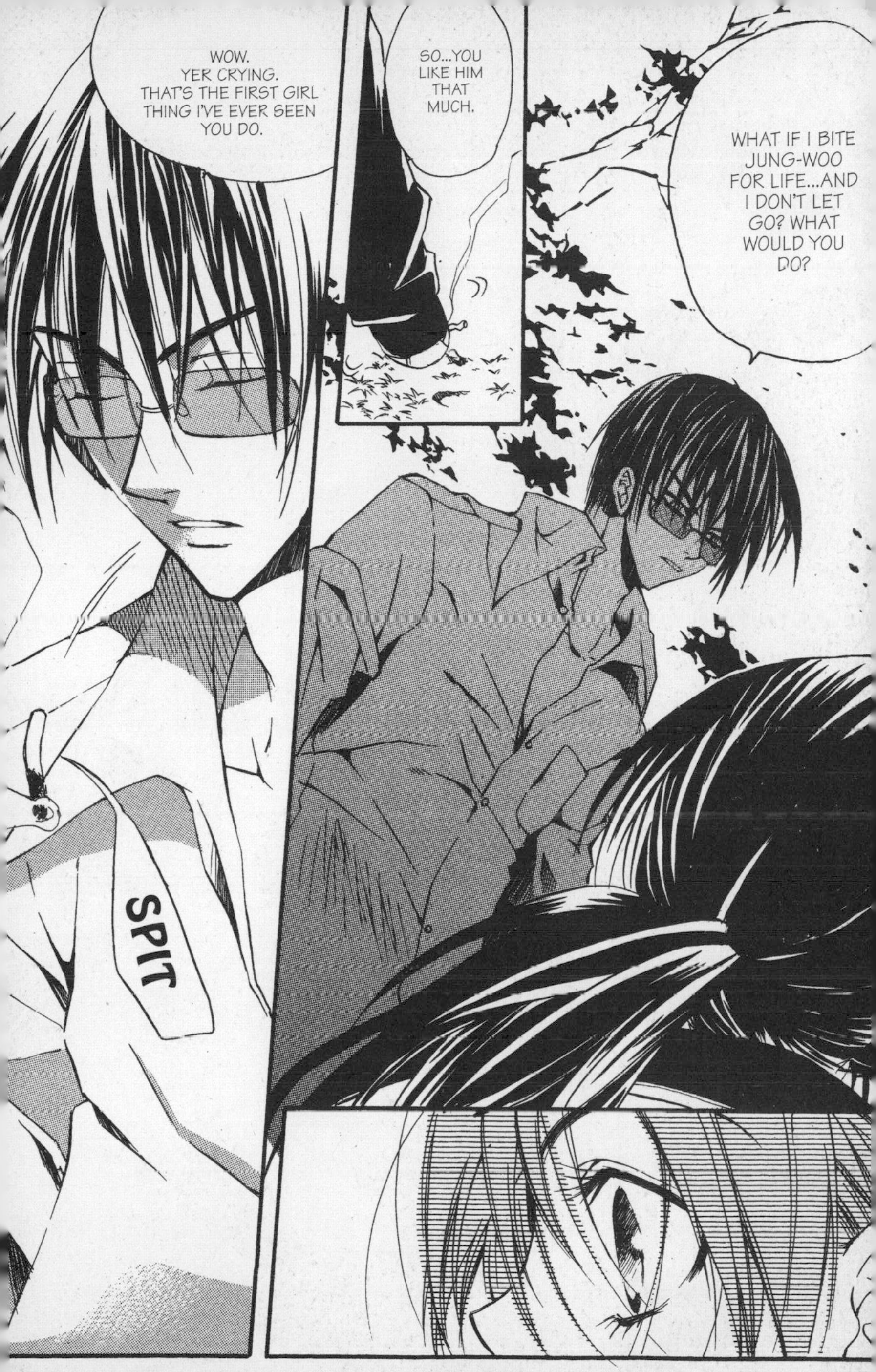
WOW. YER CRYING. THAT'S THE FIRST GIRL THING I'VE EVER SEEN YOU DO.
SPIT
SO...YOU LIKE HIM THAT MUCH.
WHAT IF I BITE JUNG-WOO FOR LIFE...AND I DON'T LET GO? WHAT WOULD YOU DO?

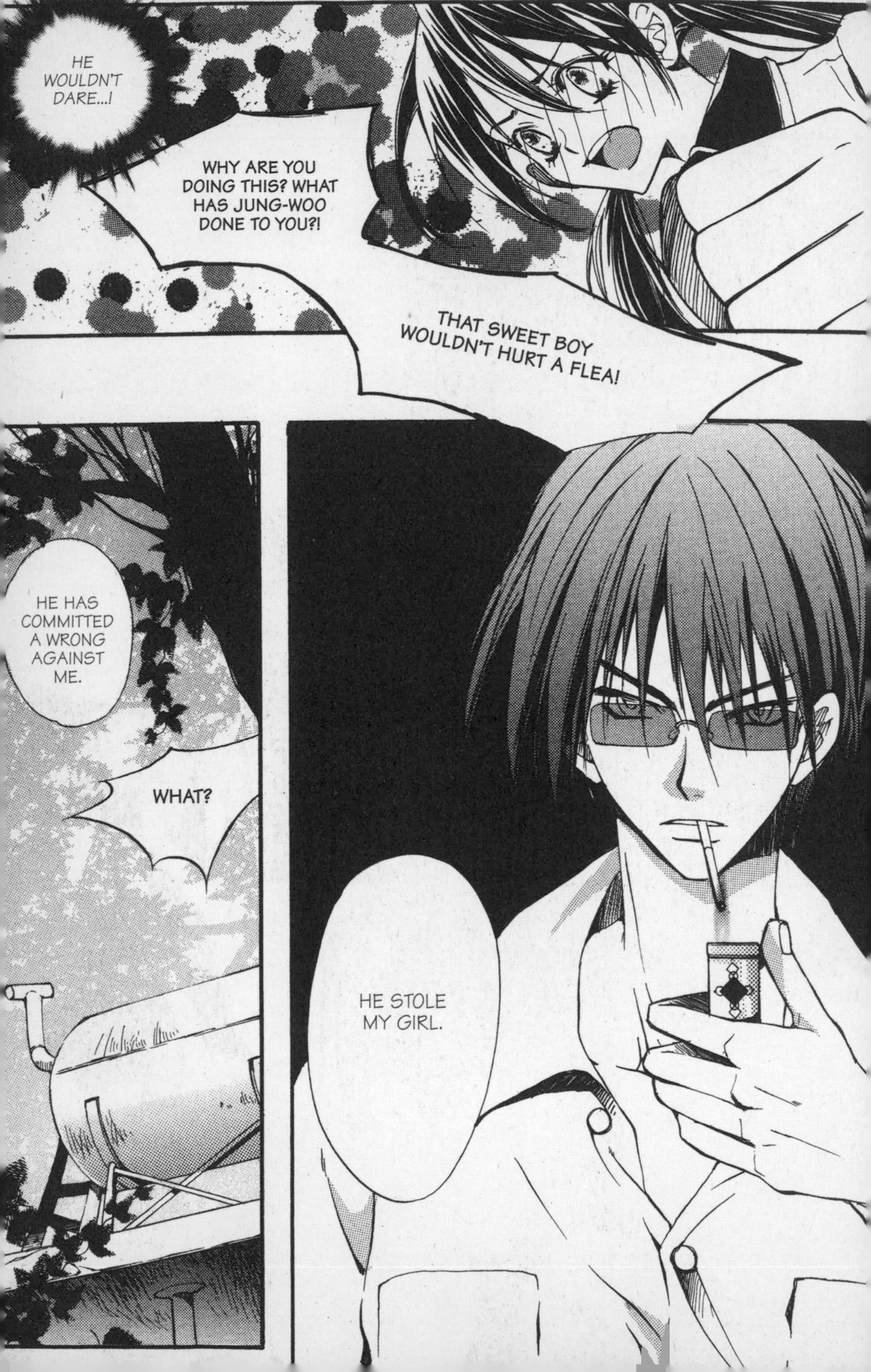
HE WOULDN'T DARE...!
WHY ARE YOU DOING THIS? WHAT HAS JUNG-WOO DONE TO YOU?!
THAT SWEET BOY WOULDN'T HURT A FLEA!
HE HAS COMMITTED A WRONG AGAINST ME.
WHAT?
HE STOLE MY GIRL.

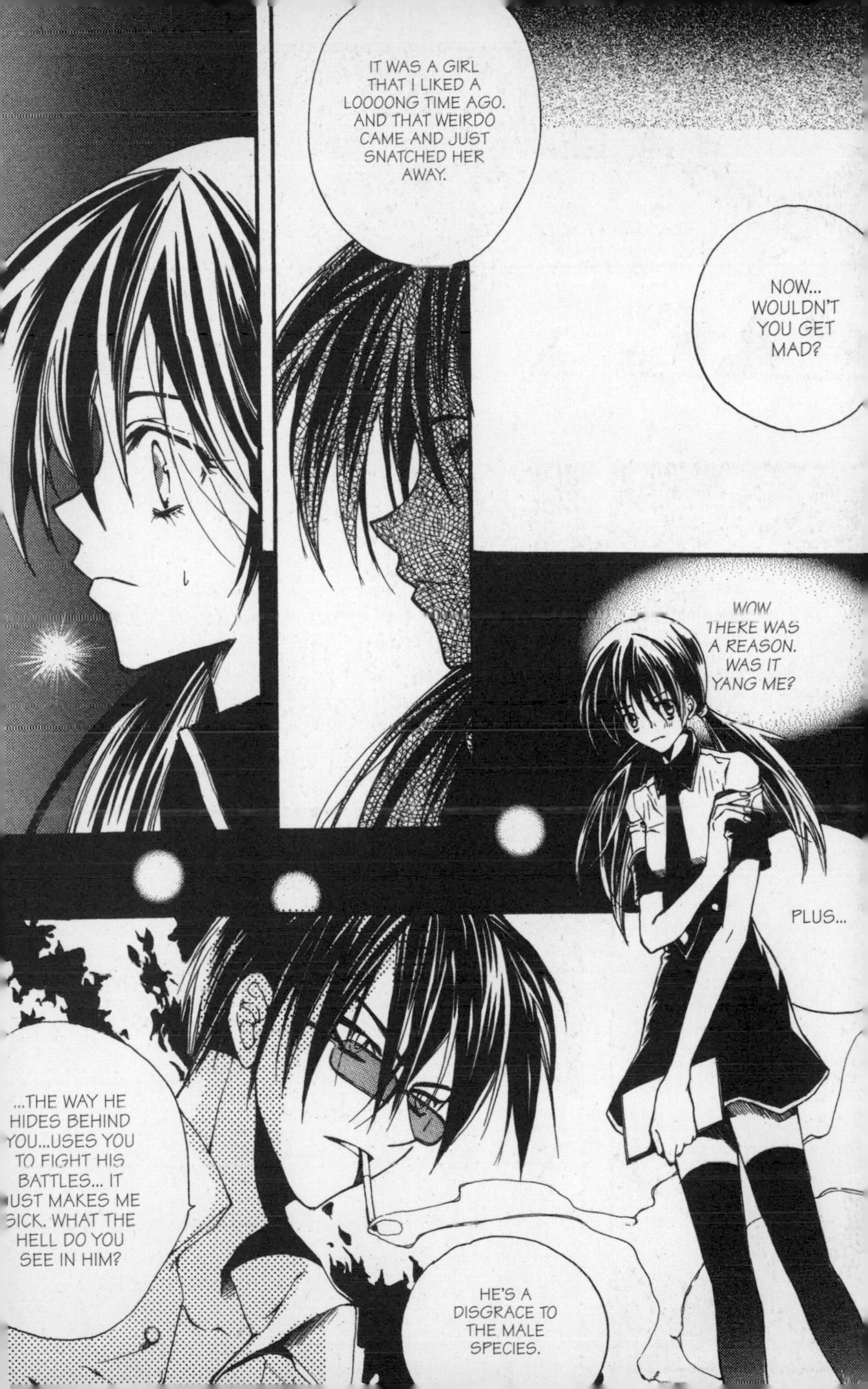
IT WAS A GIRL THAT I LIKED A LOOOONG TIME AGO. AND THAT WEIRDO CAME AND JUST SNATCHED HER AWAY.
NOW... WOULDN'T YOU GET MAD?
WOW THERE WAS A REASON. WAS IT YANG ME?
PLUS...
...THE WAY HE HIDES BEHIND YOU...USES YOU TO FIGHT HIS BATTLES... IT JUST MAKES ME SICK. WHAT THE HELL DO YOU SEE IN HIM?
HE'S A DISGRACE TO THE MALE SPECIES.

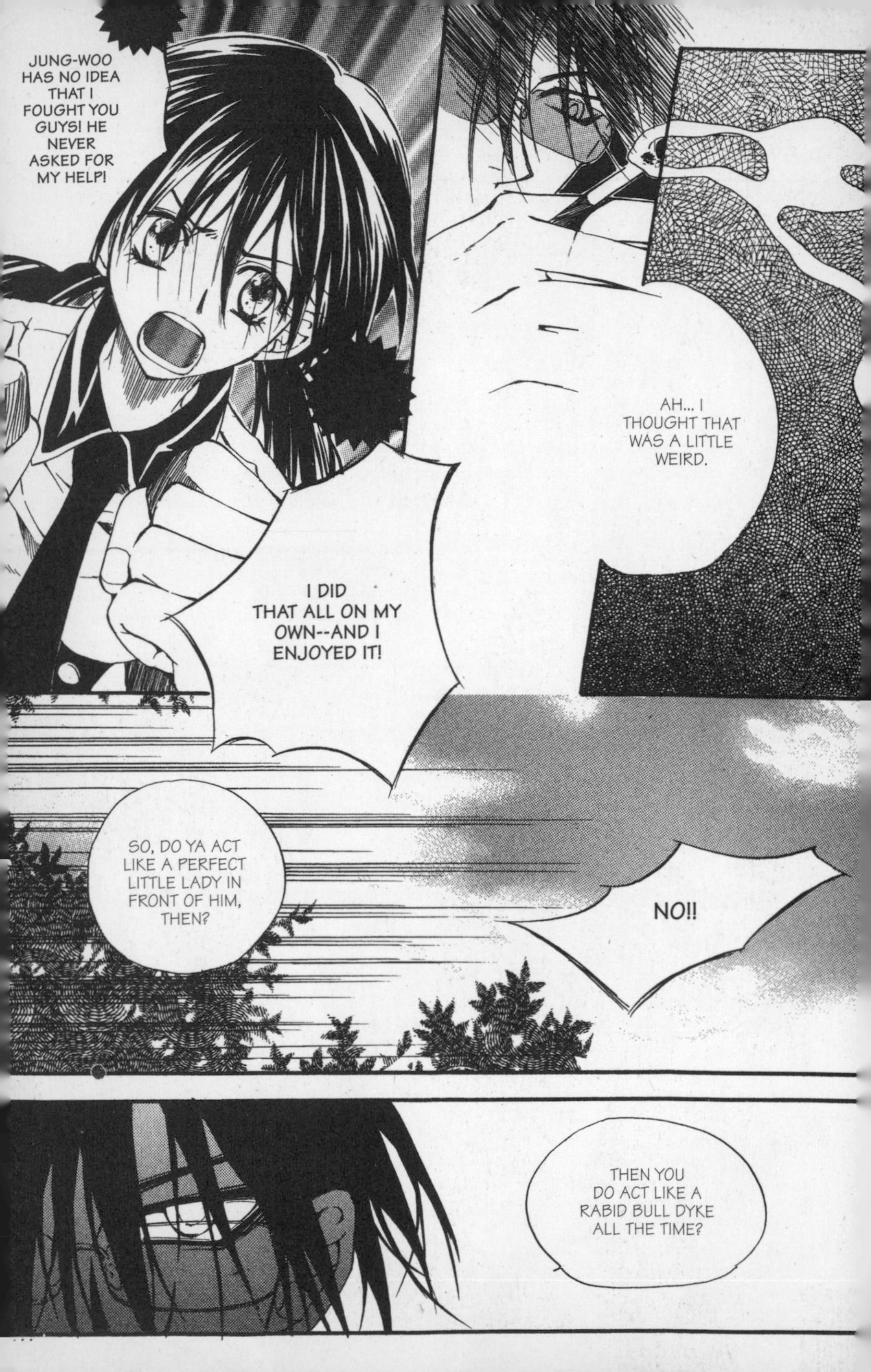
JUNG-WOO HAS NO IDEA THAT I FOUGHT YOU GUYS! HE NEVER ASKED FOR MY HELP!
AH... I THOUGHT THAT WAS A LITTLE WEIRD.
I DID THAT ALL ON MY OWN--AND I ENJOYED IT!
SO, DO YA ACT LIKE A PERFECT LITTLE LADY IN FRONT OF HIM, THEN?
NO!!
THEN YOU DO ACT LIKE A RABID BULL DYKE ALL THE TIME?

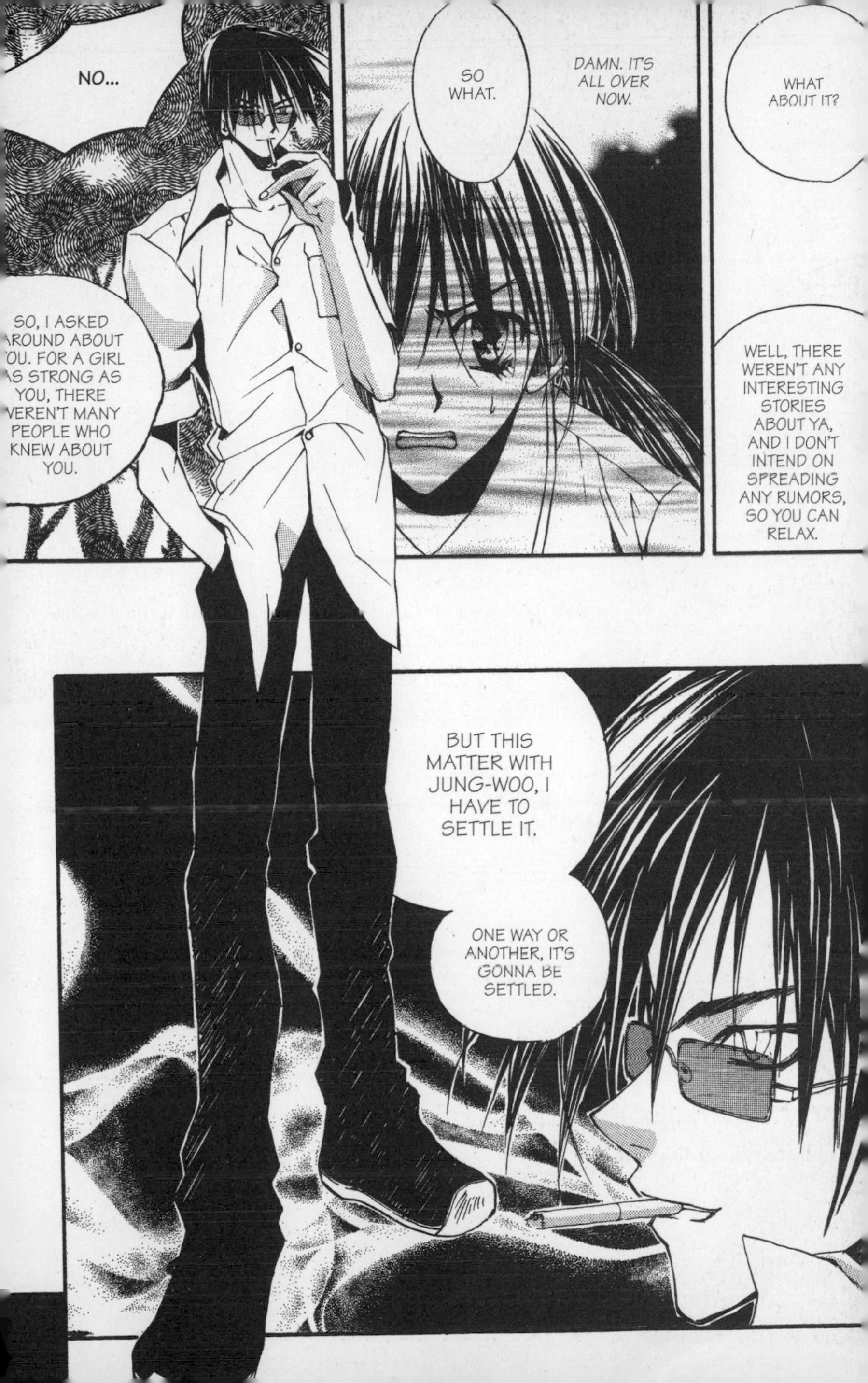
NO...
SO, I ASKED AROUND ABOUT YOU. FOR A GIRL AS STRONG AS YOU, THERE WEREN'T MANY PEOPLE WHO KNEW ABOUT YOU.
SO WHAT.
DAMN. IT'S ALL OVER NOW.
WHAT ABOUT IT?
WELL, THERE WEREN'T ANY INTERESTING STORIES ABOUT YA, AND I DON'T INTEND ON SPREADING ANY RUMORS, SO YOU CAN RELAX.
BUT THIS MATTER WITH JUNG-WOO, I HAVE TO SETTLE IT.
ONE WAY OR ANOTHER, IT'S GONNA BE SETTLED.

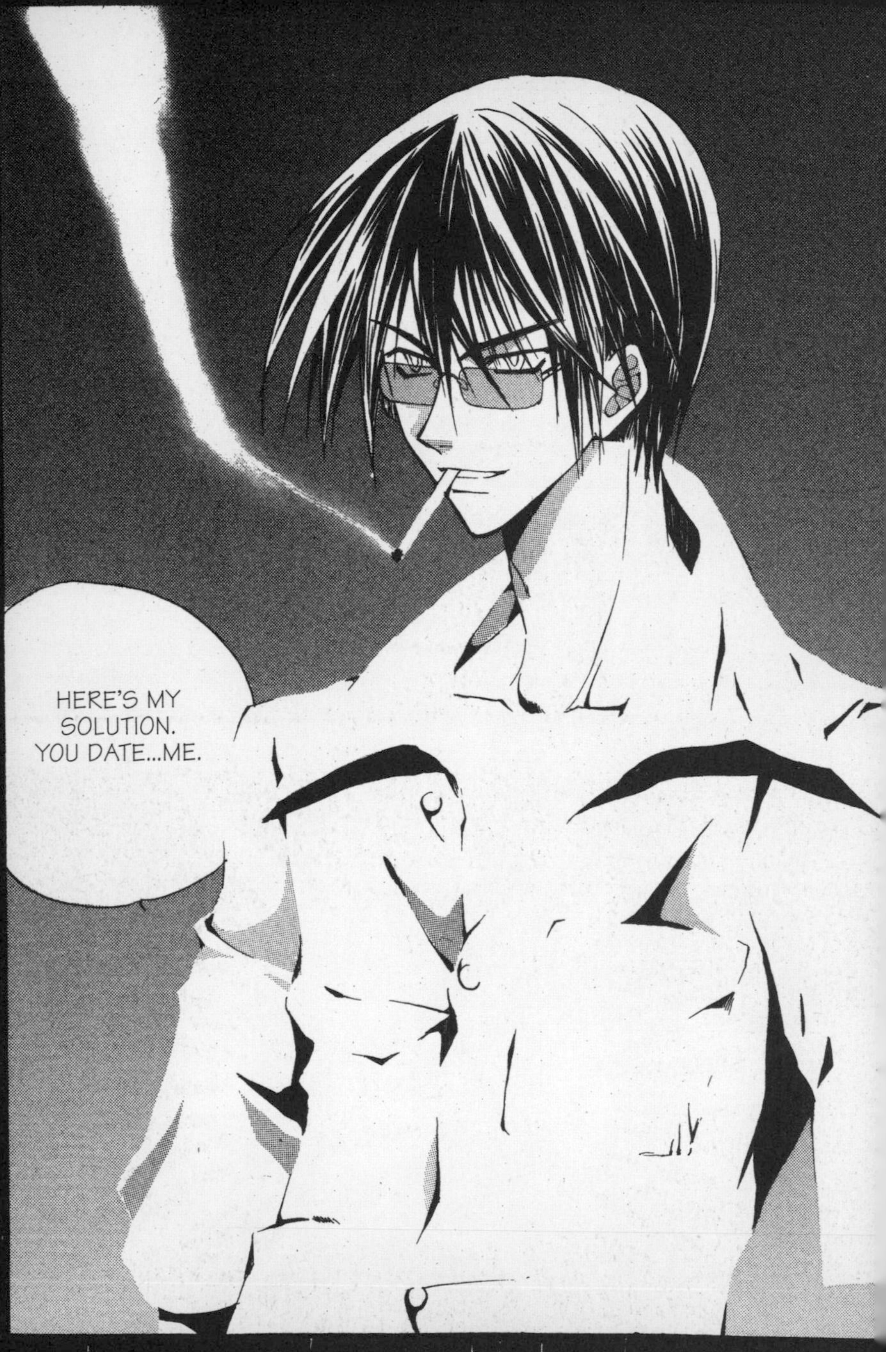
HERE'S MY SOLUTION. YOU DATE...ME.

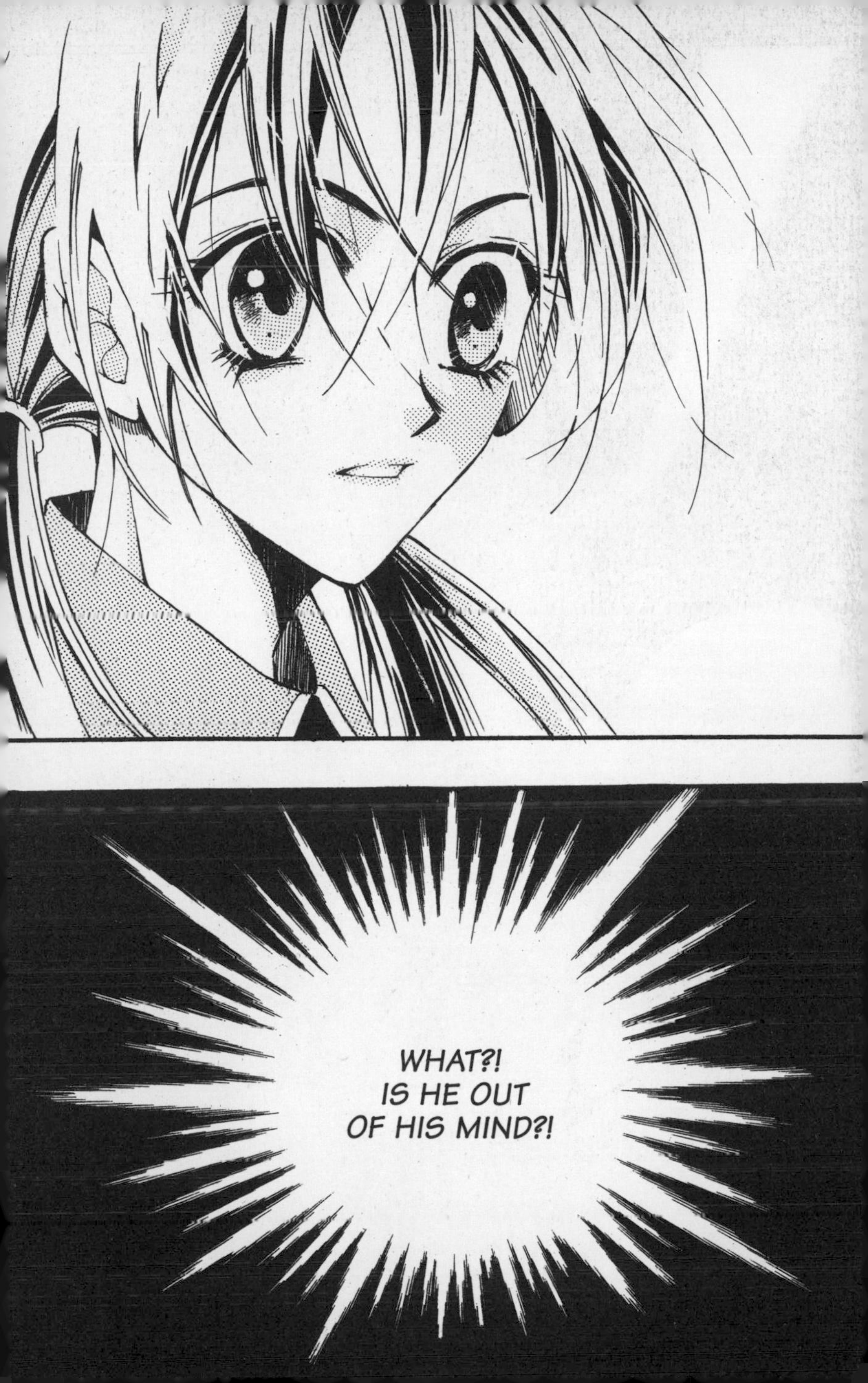
WHAT?! IS HE OUT OF HIS MIND?!

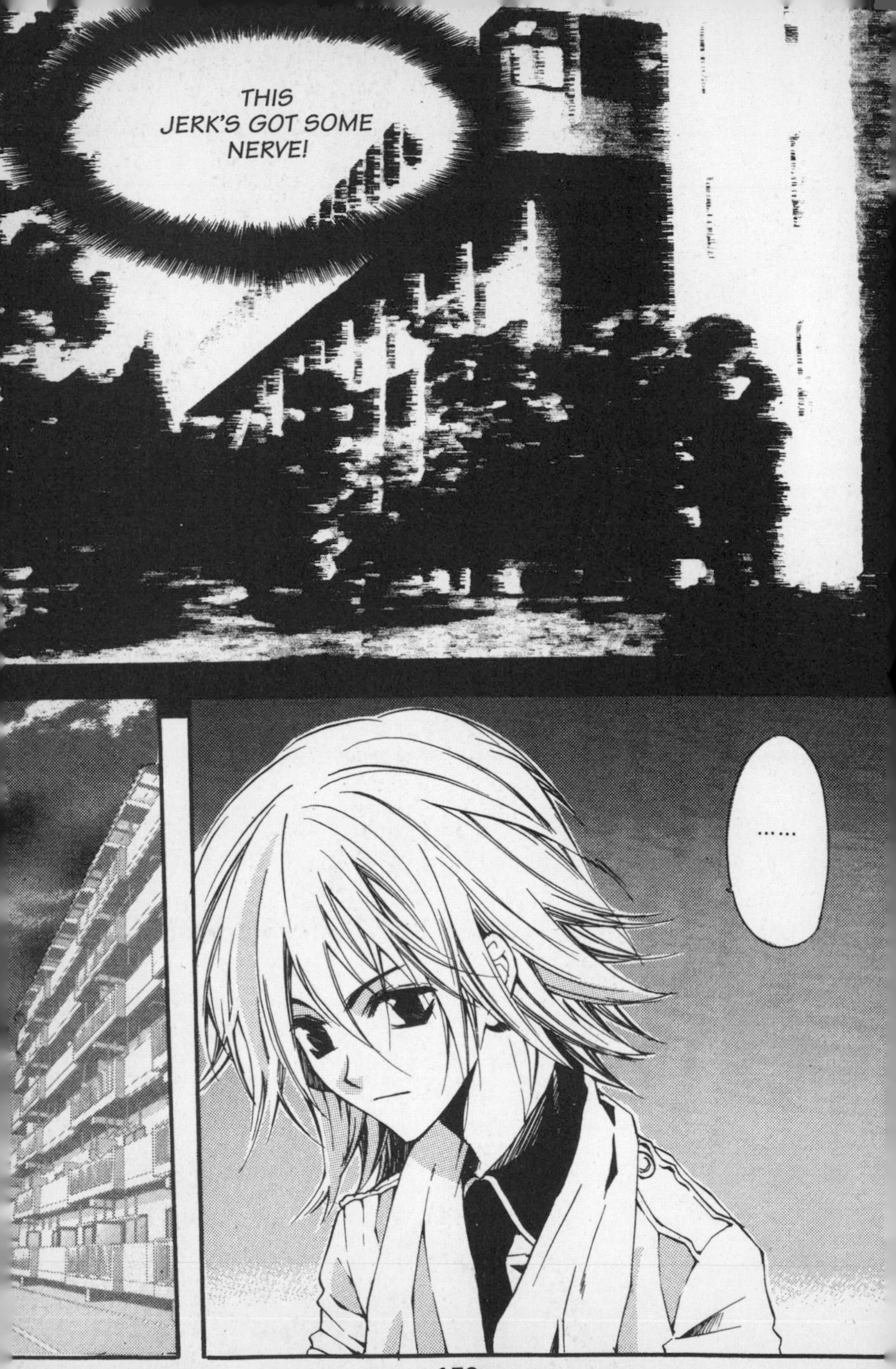
THIS JERK'S GOT SOME NERVE!
......

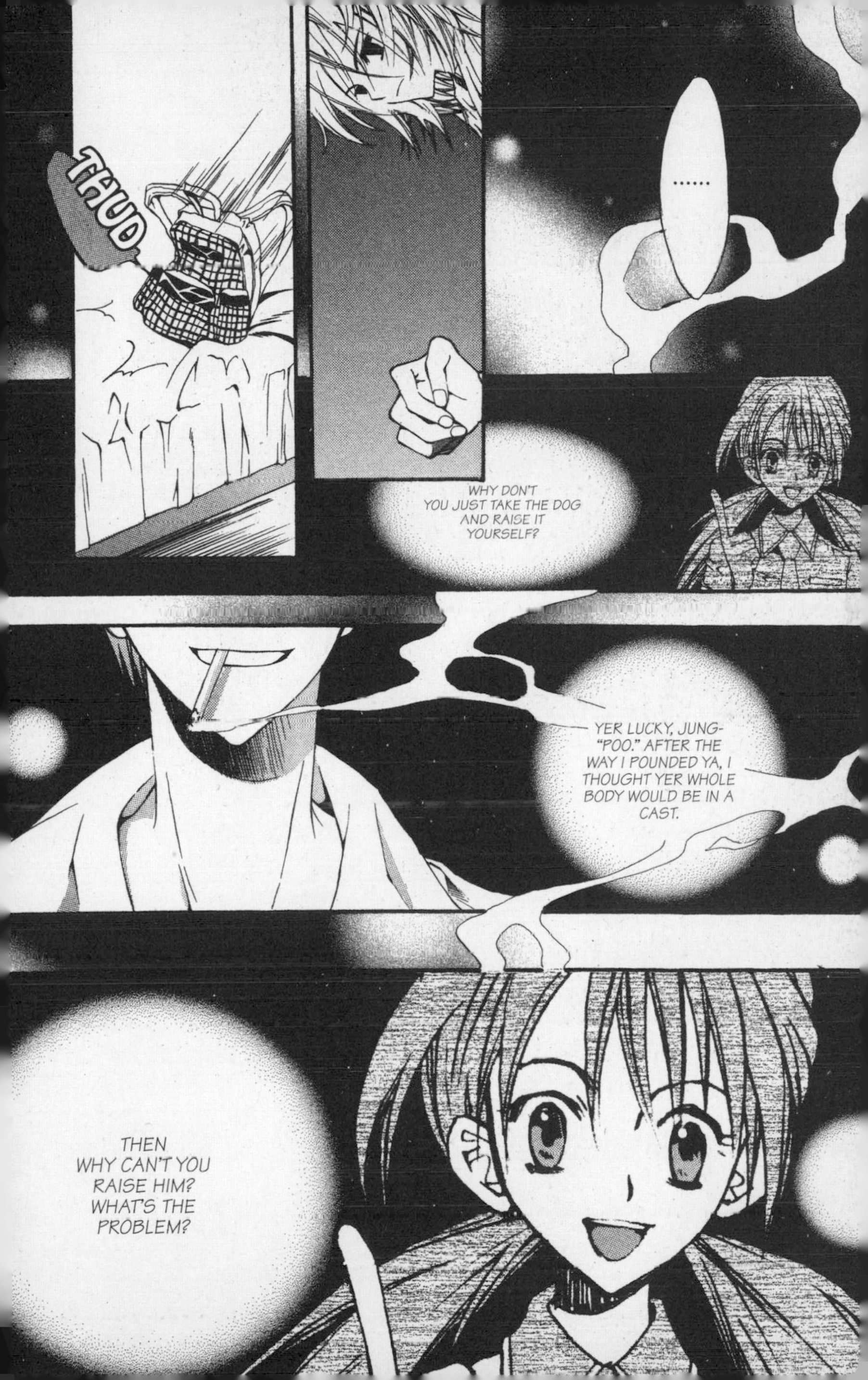
THUD
......
WHY DON'T YOU JUST TAKE THE DOG AND RAISE IT YOURSELF?
YER LUCKY, JUNG-"POO." AFTER THE WAY I POUNDED YA, I THOUGHT YER WHOLE BODY WOULD BE IN A CAST.
THEN WHY CAN'T YOU RAISE HIM? WHAT'S THE PROBLEM?

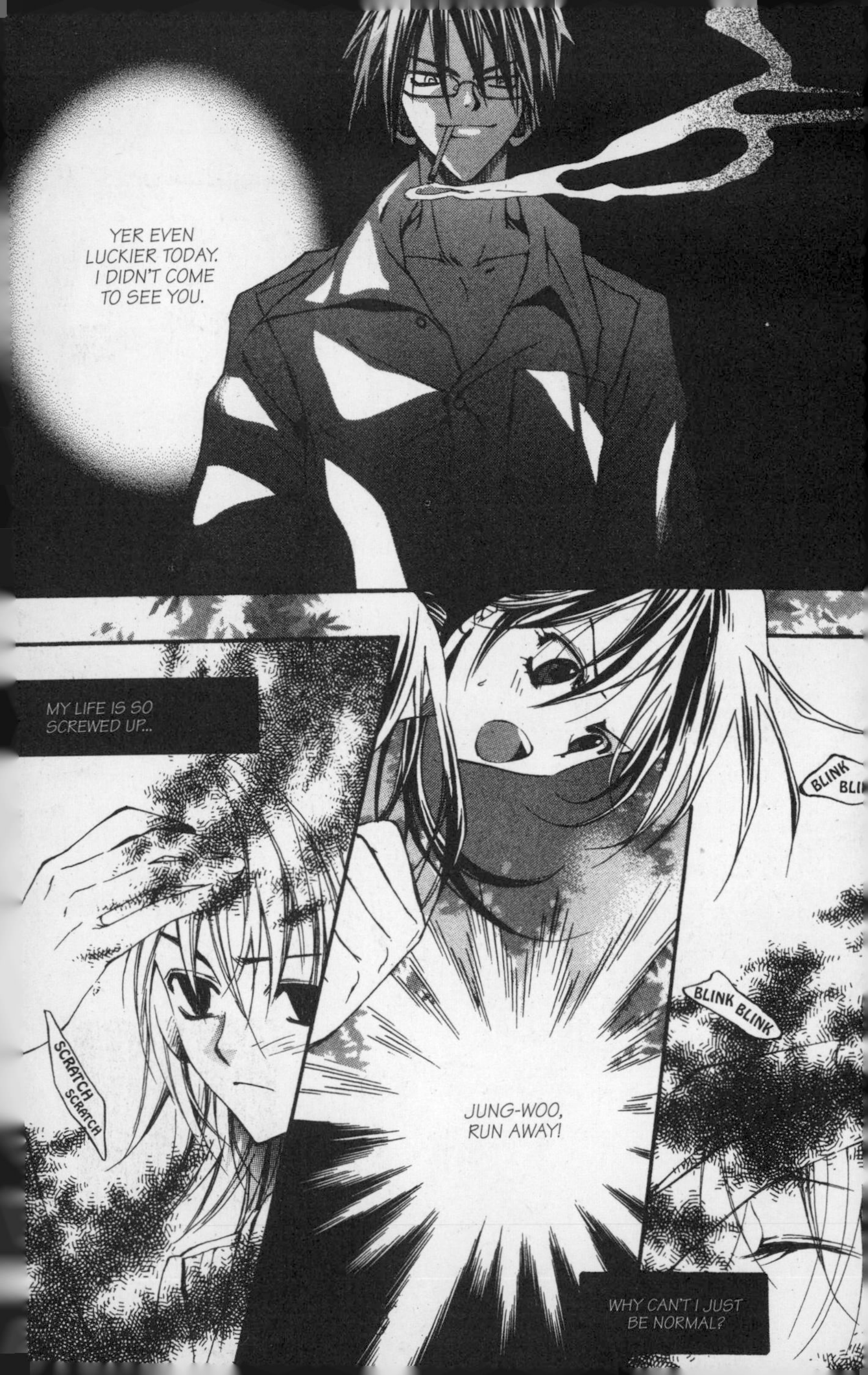
YER EVEN LUCKIER TODAY. I DIDN'T COME TO SEE YOU.
MY LIFE IS SO SCREWED UP...
SCRATCH SCRATCH
BLINK BLI
BLINK BLINK
JUNG-WOO, RUN AWAY!
WHY CAN'T I JUST BE NORMAL?

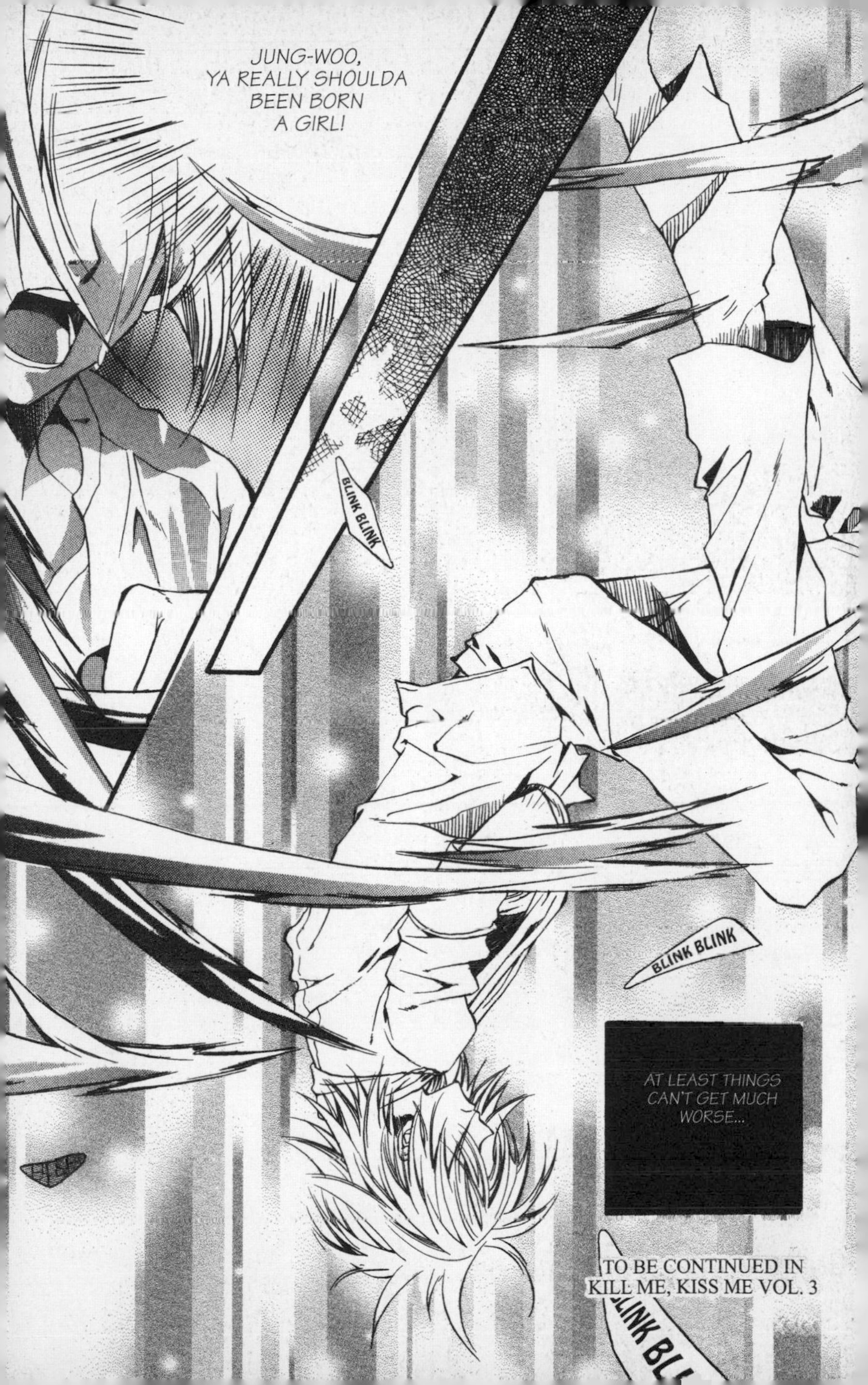
JUNG-WOO, YA REALLY SHOULDA BEEN BORN A GIRL!
BLINK BLINK
BLINK BLINK
AT LEAST THINGS CAN'T GET MUCH WORSE...
TO BE CONTINUED IN KILL ME, KISS ME VOL. 3

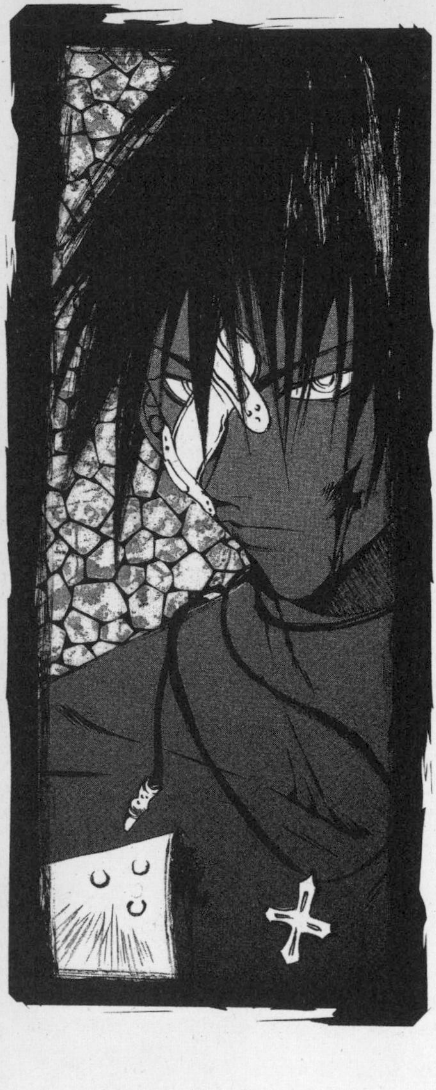

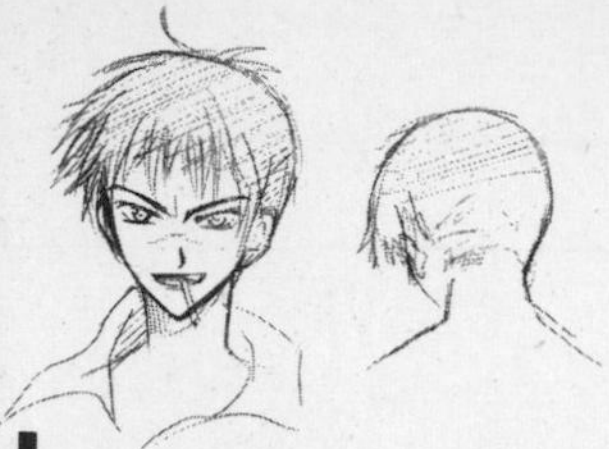

GHOON-HAHM CHE PROFILE

BORN: DECEMBER 20TH
BLOOD TYPE: O

HIS MOOD CHANGES FROM DAY TO DAY.

I DON'T HAVE A FAVORITE SINGER. THERE ARE A FEW SONGS THAT I LI THERE ARE A TON OF SINGERS THAT I CAN'T STAND, AND THERE ARE MAN SONGS THAT I HATE.

CONSERVATIVE KOREAN MALE

ONCE YOU GET TO KNOW HIM, HE'S PRETTY EASY TO HANDLE. HE IS PROUD OF BEING THE BOSS OF THE YI WON GANG, BUT HIS LACKEYS OFTEN QUESTION HIS AUTHORITY.

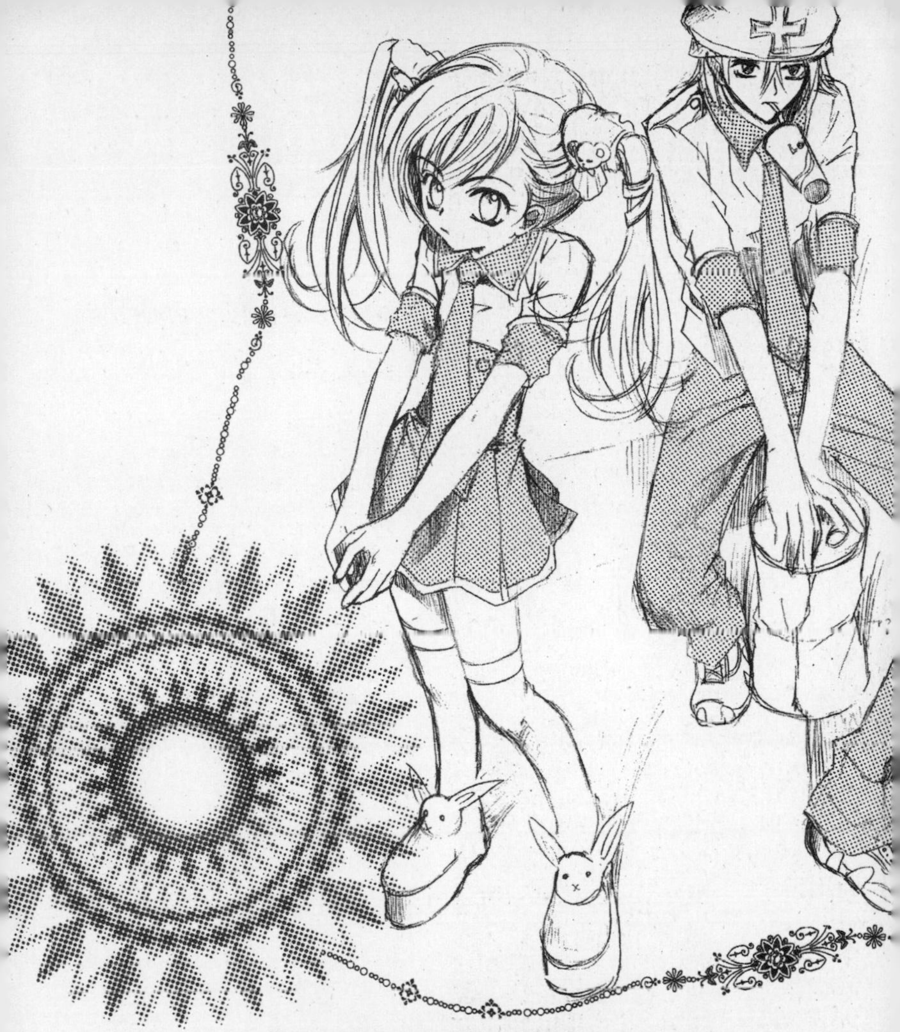

PURE WATER HIGH'S SPRING / SUMMER UNIFORMS

OVERALL, THEY HAVE BLACK & LIGHT GRAY TONES.
THE PRINCIPAL OF THIS SCHOOL IS LIBERAL, SO MODIFICATIONS ARE POSSIBLE.
MANY GIRLS MODIFY THEIR SKIRTS INTO MINIS...
STUDENTS HAVE FREEDOM OF CHOICE WITH THEIR STOCKINGS AND SHOES.
THE NECKTIES ARE WIDER THAN USUAL, AND THEY BEAR THE MARK OF PURE WATER HIGH.
THE BOYS' UNIFORMS HAVE LONGER SLEEVES THAN THE GIRLS'.
IN THE SUMMER, THE BOYS WISH THE SLEEVES WERE SHORTER, AS THE UNIFORMS CAN GET TOO HOT.
THAT'S IT!

Bonus Feature!

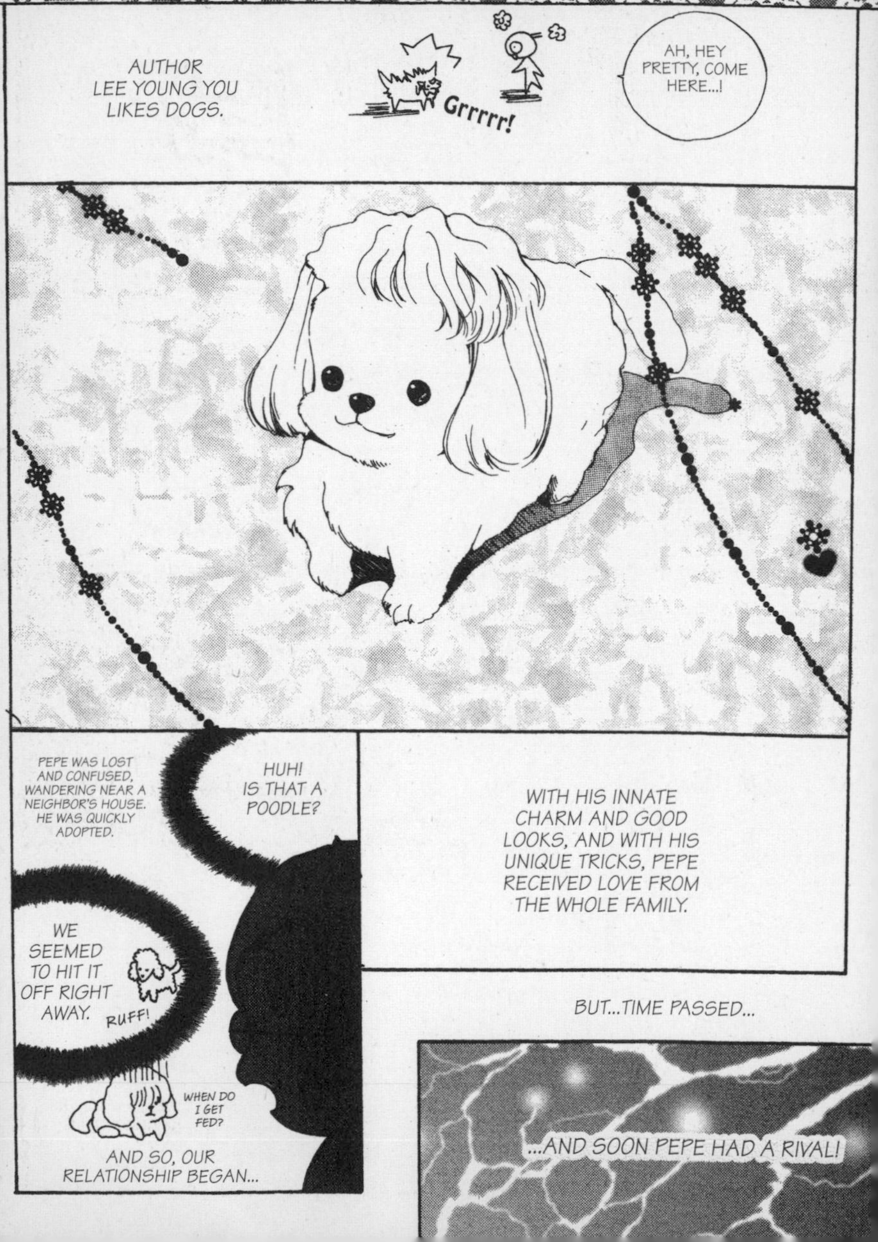

AUTHOR LEE YOUNG YOU LIKES DOGS.
Grrrrr!
AH, HEY PRETTY, COME HERE...!
PEPE WAS LOST AND CONFUSED, WANDERING NEAR A NEIGHBOR'S HOUSE. HE WAS QUICKLY ADOPTED.
HUH! IS THAT A POODLE?
WE SEEMED TO HIT IT OFF RIGHT AWAY.
RUFF!
WHEN DO I GET FED?
AND SO, OUR RELATIONSHIP BEGAN...
WITH HIS INNATE CHARM AND GOOD LOOKS, AND WITH HIS UNIQUE TRICKS, PEPE RECEIVED LOVE FROM THE WHOLE FAMILY.
BUT...TIME PASSED...
...AND SOON PEPE HAD A RIVAL!

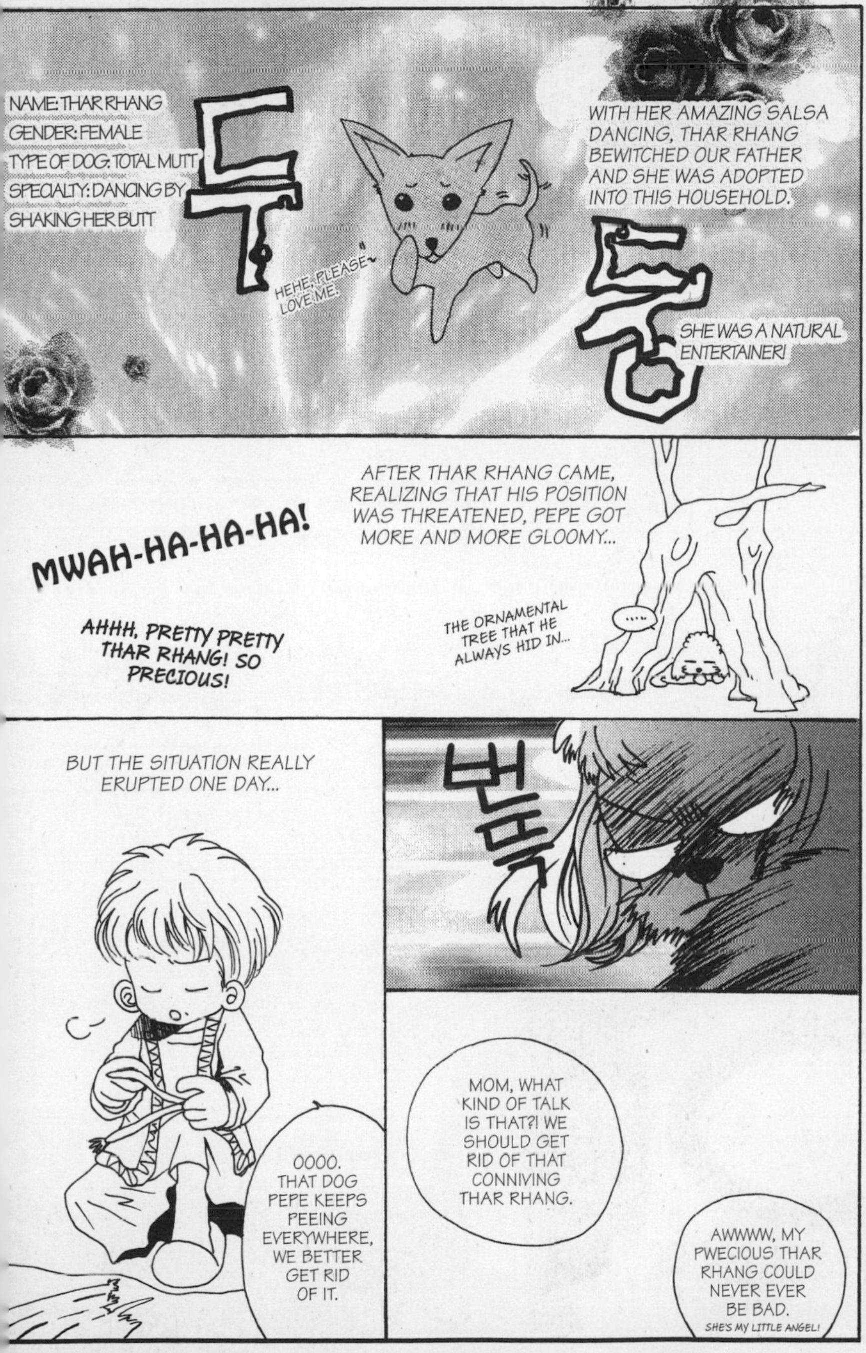
NAME: THAR RHANG
GENDER: FEMALE
TYPE OF DOG: TOTAL MUTT
SPECIALTY: DANCING BY SHAKING HER BUTT
HEHE, PLEASE LOVE ME.
WITH HER AMAZING SALSA DANCING, THAR RHANG BEWITCHED OUR FATHER AND SHE WAS ADOPTED INTO THIS HOUSEHOLD.
SHE WAS A NATURAL ENTERTAINER!
MWAH-HA-HA-HA!
AHHH, PRETTY PRETTY THAR RHANG! SO PRECIOUS!
AFTER THAR RHANG CAME, REALIZING THAT HIS POSITION WAS THREATENED, PEPE GOT MORE AND MORE GLOOMY...
THE ORNAMENTAL TREE THAT HE ALWAYS HID IN...
....
BUT THE SITUATION REALLY ERUPTED ONE DAY...
OOOO. THAT DOG PEPE KEEPS PEEING EVERYWHERE, WE BETTER GET RID OF IT.
MOM, WHAT KIND OF TALK IS THAT?! WE SHOULD GET RID OF THAT CONNIVING THAR RHANG.
AWWWW, MY PWECIOUS THAR RHANG COULD NEVER EVER BE BAD.
SHE'S MY LITTLE ANGEL!

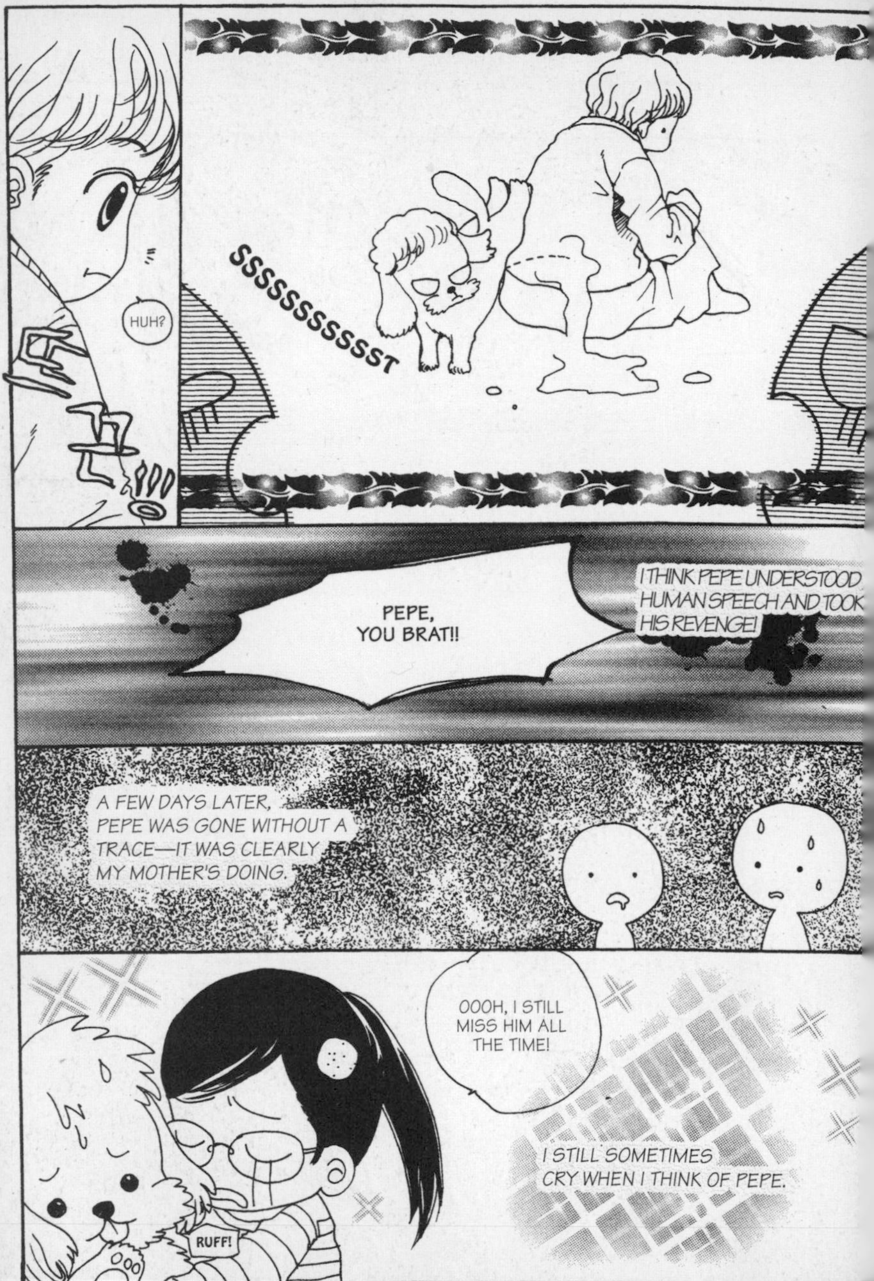
HUH?
SSSSSSSSSSST
PEPE, YOU BRAT!!
I THINK PEPE UNDERSTOOD HUMAN SPEECH AND TOOK HIS REVENGE!
A FEW DAYS LATER, PEPE WAS GONE WITHOUT A TRACE—IT WAS CLEARLY MY MOTHER'S DOING.
OOOH, I STILL MISS HIM ALL THE TIME!
RUFF!
I STILL SOMETIMES CRY WHEN I THINK OF PEPE.

HUGGING...TOO...HARD...

The En

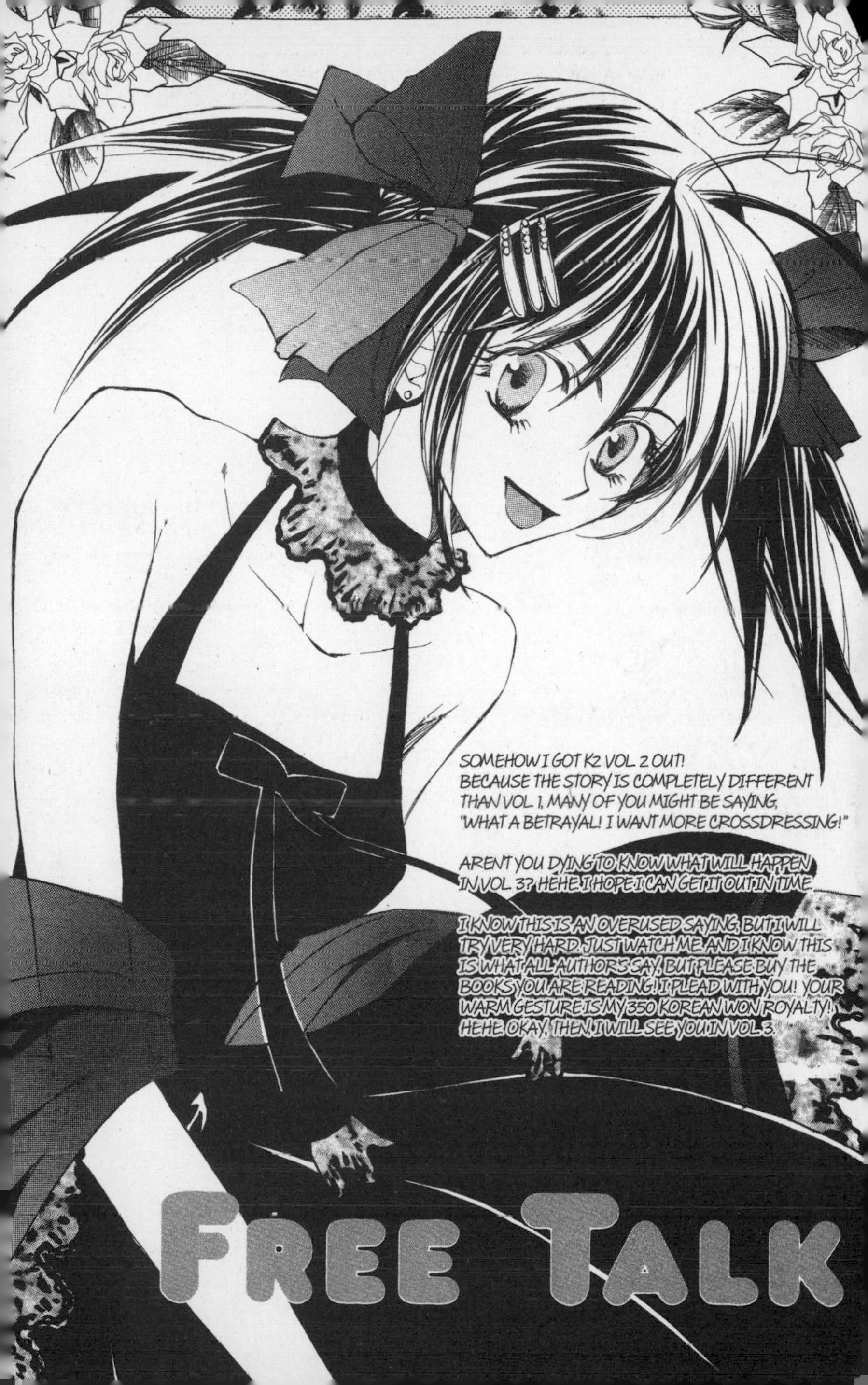
SOMEHOW I GOT K2 VOL. 2 OUT!
BECAUSE THE STORY IS COMPLETELY DIFFERENT THAN VOL 1, MANY OF YOU MIGHT BE SAYING, "WHAT A BETRAYAL! I WANT MORE CROSSDRESSING!"
AREN'T YOU DYING TO KNOW WHAT WILL HAPPEN IN VOL. 3? HEHE. I HOPE I CAN GET IT OUT IN TIME.
I KNOW THIS IS AN OVERUSED SAYING, BUT I WILL TRY VERY HARD. JUST WATCH ME. AND I KNOW THIS IS WHAT ALL AUTHOR'S SAY, BUT PLEASE BUY THE BOOKS YOU ARE READING! I PLEAD WITH YOU! YOUR WARM GESTURE IS MY 350 KOREAN WON ROYALTY! HEHE. OKAY, THEN, I WILL SEE YOU IN VOL. 3.
FREE TALK

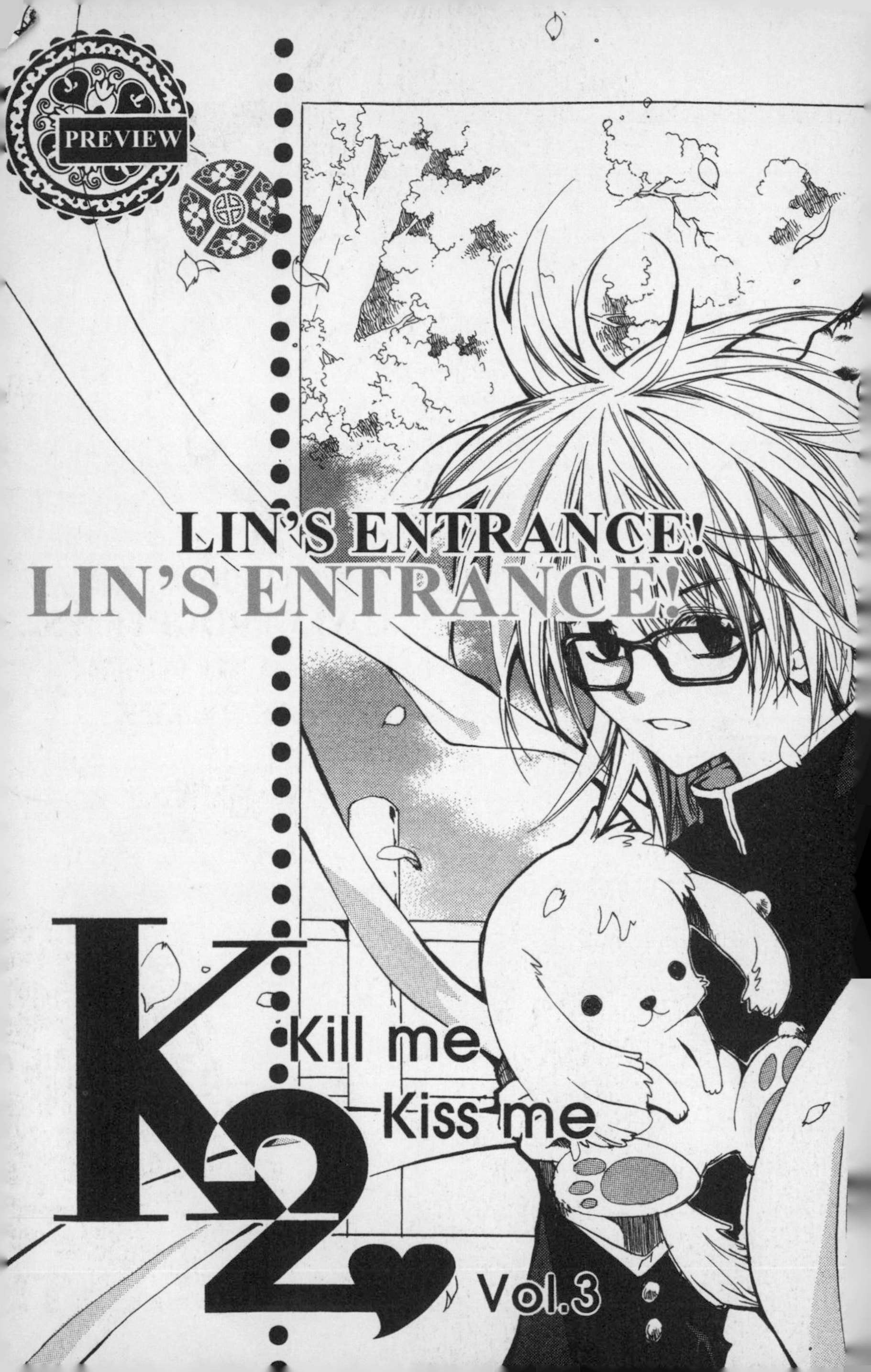
PREVIEW
LIN'S ENTRANCE!
LIN'S ENTRANCE!
K2
Kill me
Kiss me
Vol.3

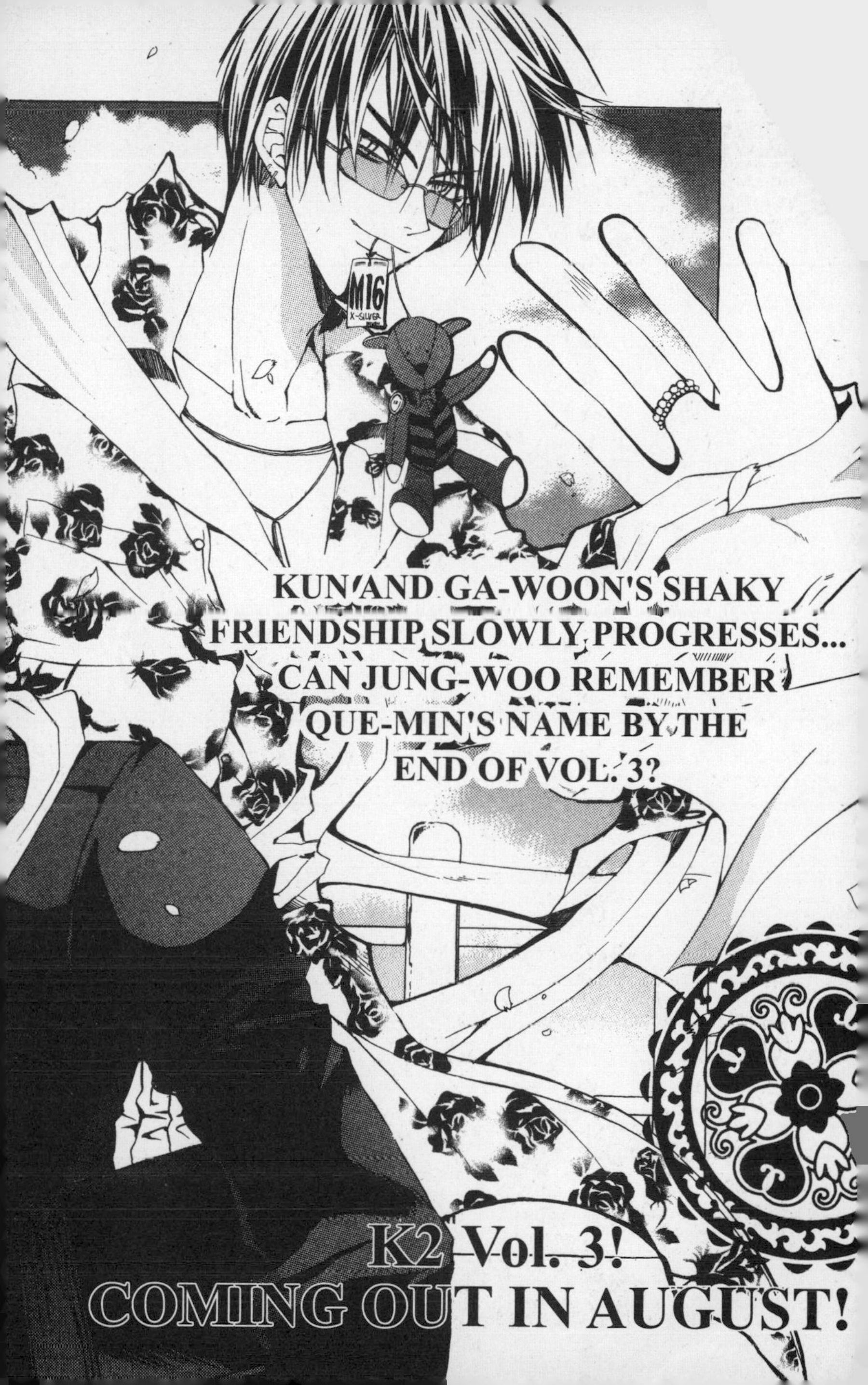
M16
X-SILVER
KUN AND GA-WOON'S SHAKY FRIENDSHIP SLOWLY PROGRESSES... CAN JUNG-WOO REMEMBER QUE-MIN'S NAME BY THE END OF VOL. 3?
K2 Vol. 3!
COMING OUT IN AUGUST!

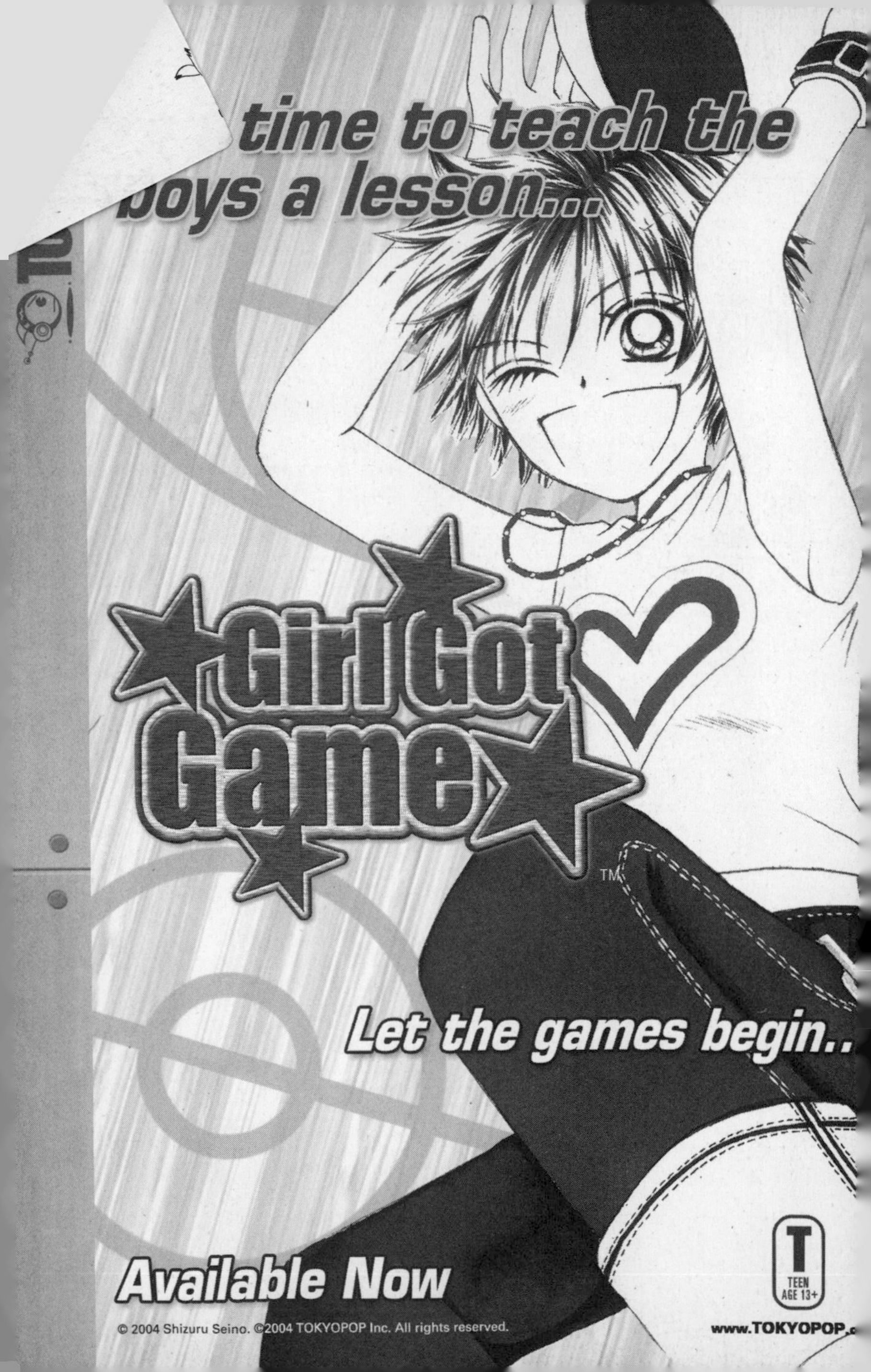
time to teach the
boys a lesson...
Girl Got Game™
Let the games begin...
Available Now
T TEEN AGE 13+
© 2004 Shizuru Seino. ©2004 TOKYOPOP Inc. All rights reserved.
www.TOKYOPOP.c

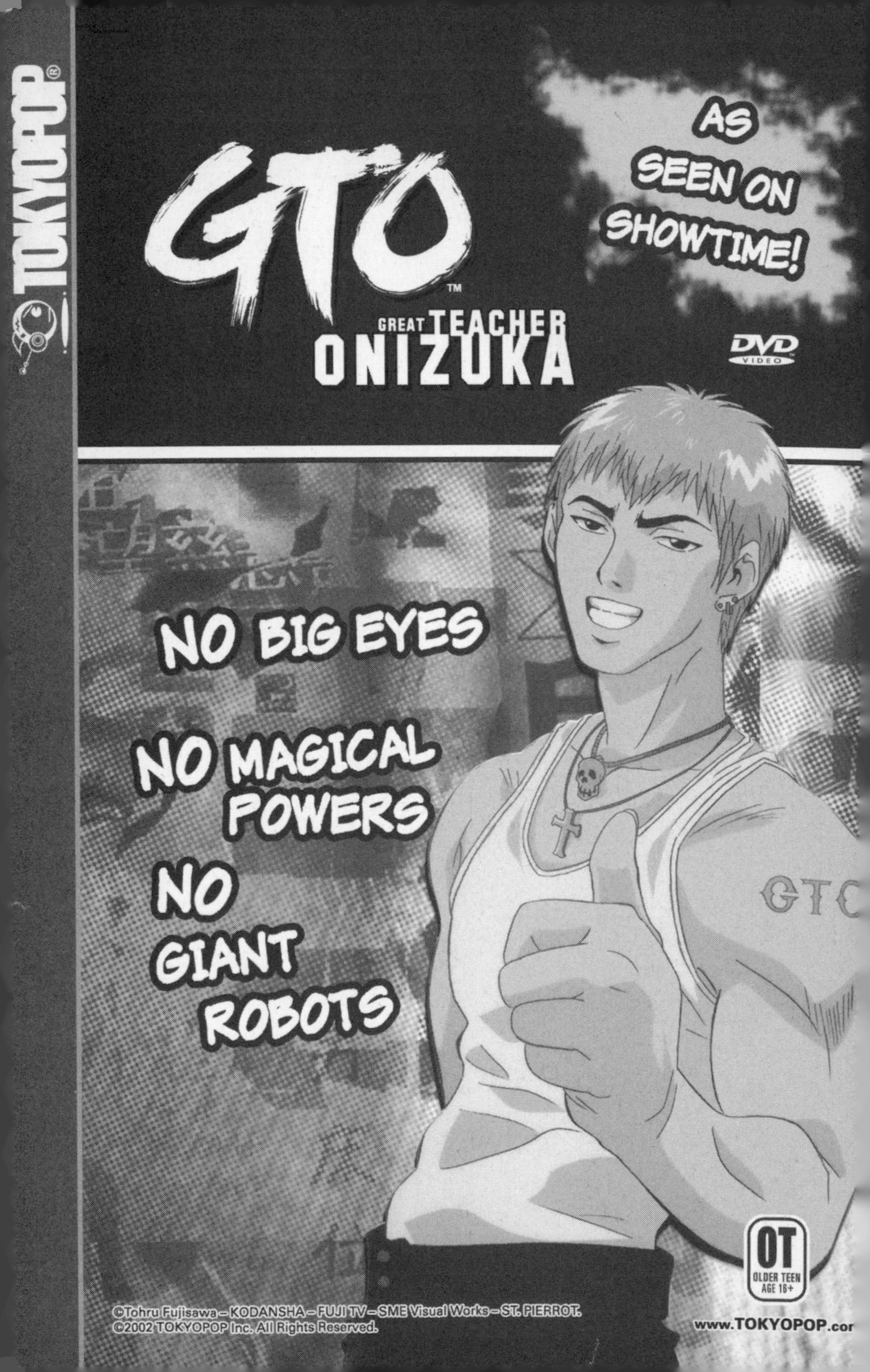
TOKYOPOP
GTO™
GREAT TEACHER ONIZUKA
AS SEEN ON SHOWTIME!
DVD VIDEO
NO BIG EYES
NO MAGICAL POWERS
NO GIANT ROBOTS
GTO
OT OLDER TEEN AGE 16+
©Tohru Fujisawa – KODANSHA – FUJI TV – SME Visual Works – ST. PIERROT.
©2002 TOKYOPOP Inc. All Rights Reserved.
www.TOKYOPOP.com

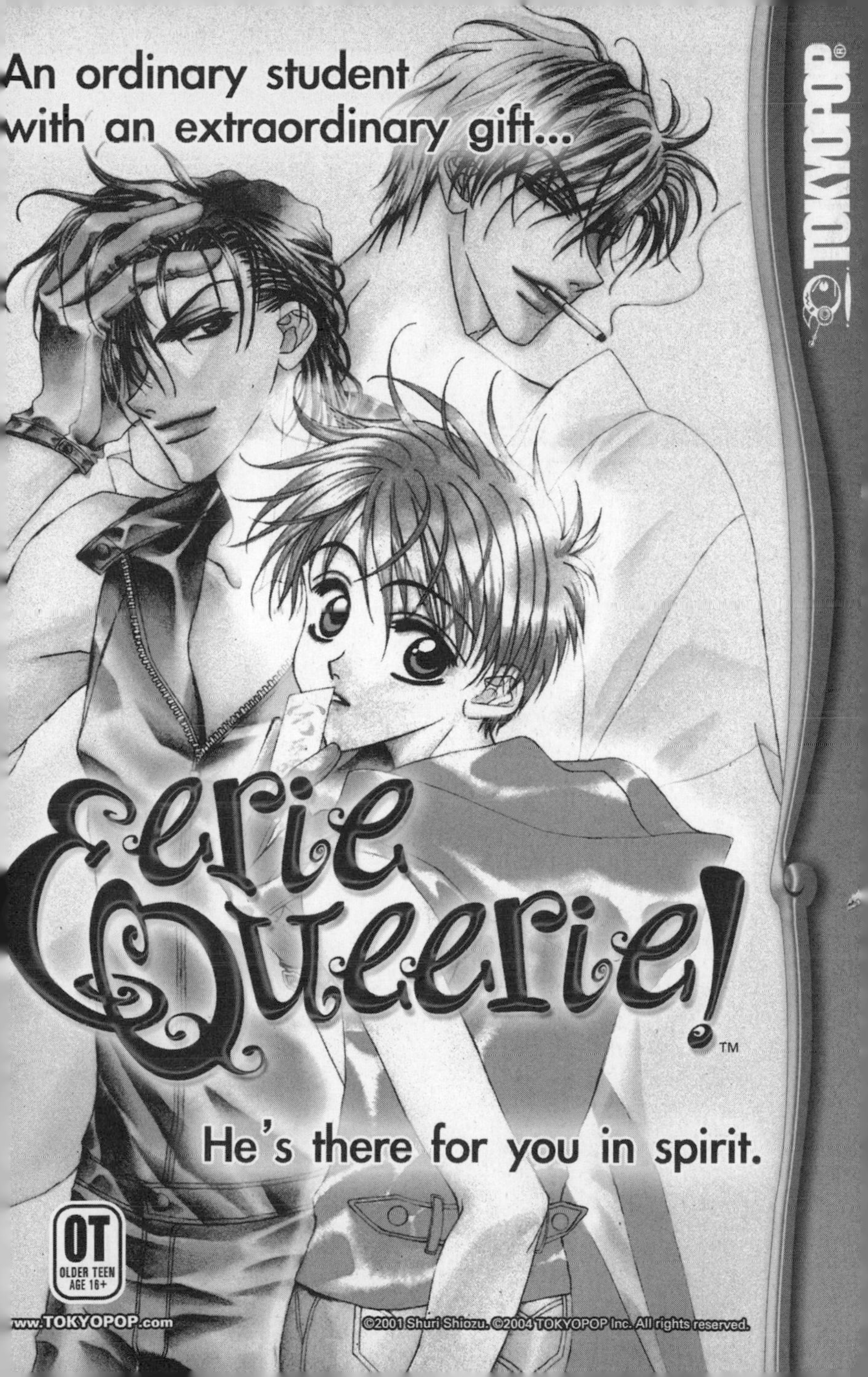

An ordinary student
with an extraordinary gift...
TOKYOPOP
Eerie Queerie!™
He's there for you in spirit.
OT
OLDER TEEN
AGE 16+
www.TOKYOPOP.com
©2001 Shuri Shiozu. ©2004 TOKYOPOP Inc. All rights reserved.

PEACH

Miwa Ueda Illustrations

While
Supplies
Last

This **Limited Edition Art Book** is a must-have for all Peach Girl fans!

www.TOKYOPOP.c

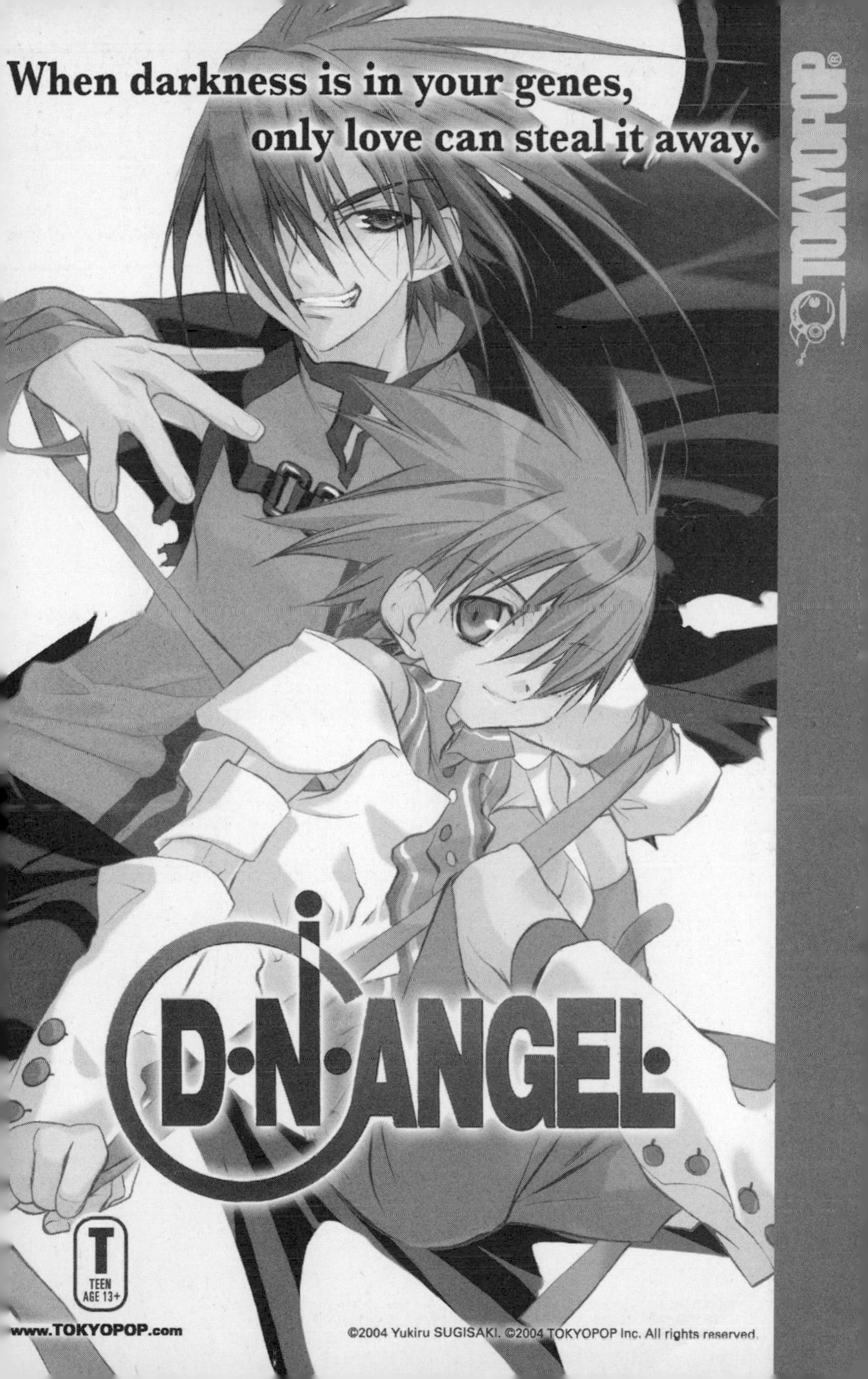
When darkness is in your genes,
only love can steal it away.
TOKYOPOP
D•N•ANGEL
T
TEEN
AGE 13+
www.TOKYOPOP.com
©2004 Yukiru SUGISAKI. ©2004 TOKYOPOP Inc. All rights reserved.

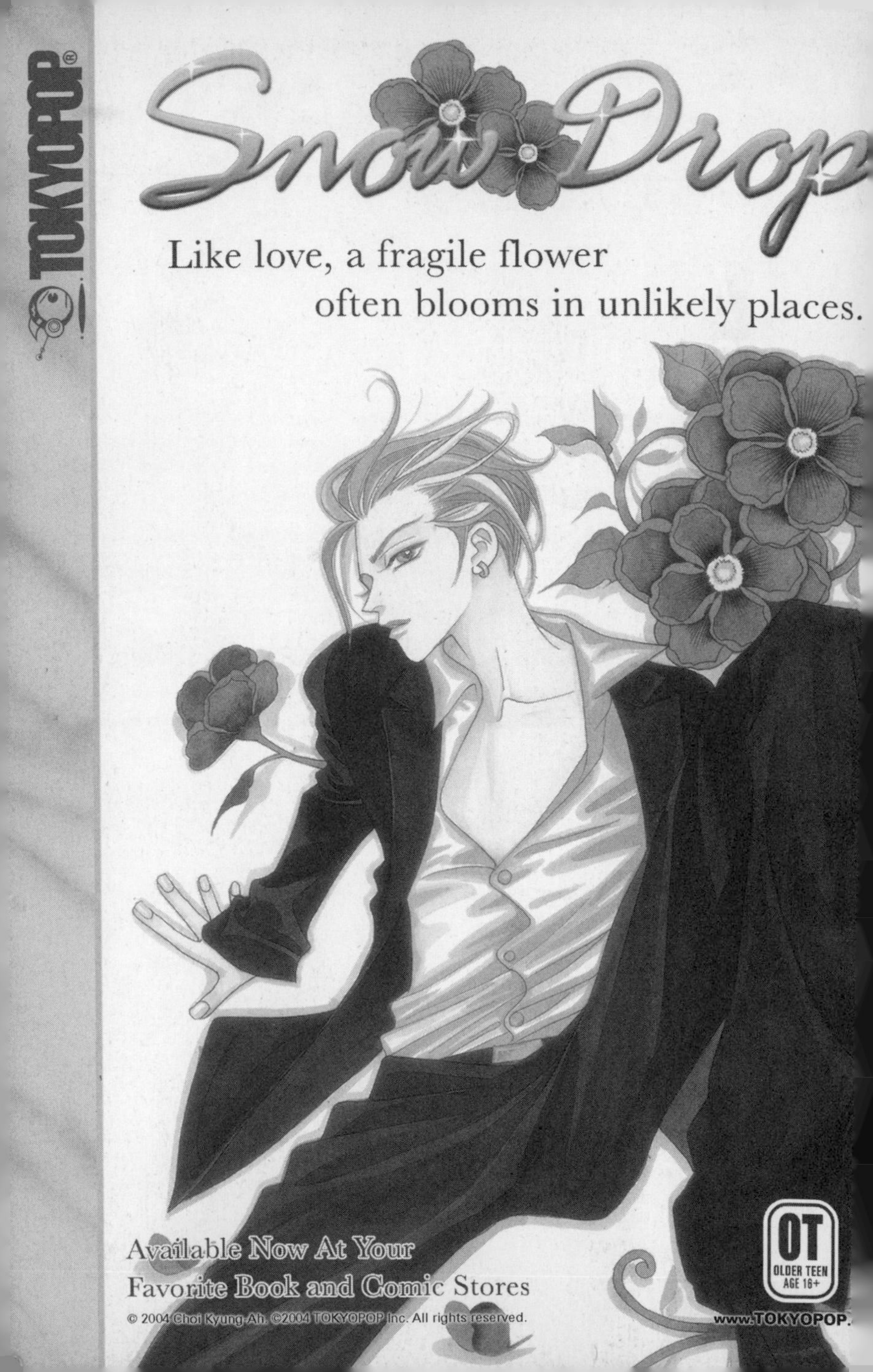
TOKYOPOP®
Snow Drop
Like love, a fragile flower
often blooms in unlikely places.
Available Now At Your
Favorite Book and Comic Stores
© 2004 Choi Kyung-Ah. ©2004 TOKYOPOP Inc. All rights reserved.
OT
OLDER TEEN
AGE 16+
www.TOKYOPOP.

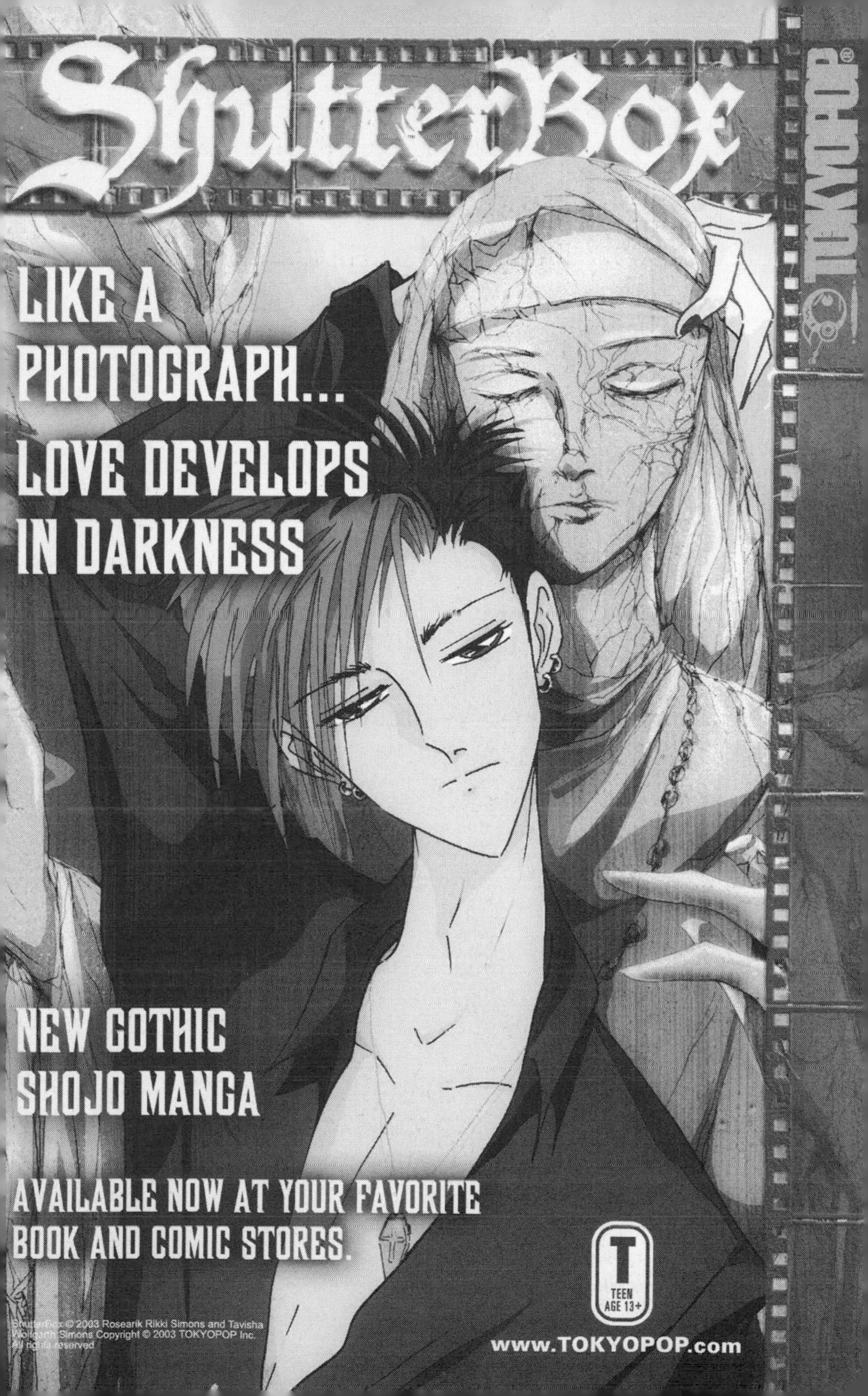
ShutterBox
TOKYOPOP
LIKE A PHOTOGRAPH...
LOVE DEVELOPS IN DARKNESS
NEW GOTHIC SHOJO MANGA
AVAILABLE NOW AT YOUR FAVORITE BOOK AND COMIC STORES.
T TEEN AGE 13+
ShutterBox © 2003 Rosearik Rikki Simons and Tavisha Wolfgarth-Simons Copyright © 2003 TOKYOPOP Inc. All rights reserved
www.TOKYOPOP.com